Anthology of
Québec Women's Plays
in English Translation
Volume III (1997-2009)

Anthology of
Québec Women's Plays
in English Translation
Volume III (1997–2009)

Catch a Tiger
Earthbound
When Books Come Tumbling Down
Public Disorder
Chinese Portrait of an Imposter
Rock, Paper, Jackknife...
Jouliks
My Mother Dog
Gisèle's Wedding Dress
The Sound of Cracking Bones

Edited by Louise H. Forsyth
Professor emerita, University of Saskatchewan

Playwrights Canada Press
Toronto • Canada

Anthology of Québec Women's Plays in English Translation, Volume III, (1997–2009)
© Copyright 2010 Louise H. Forsyth
Introduction © Copyright 2010 Louise H. Forsyth

PLAYWRIGHTS CANADA PRESS
The Canadian Drama Publisher
215 Spadina Ave., Suite 230, Toronto, ON Canada M5T 2C7
phone 416.703.0013   fax 416.408.3402
orders@playwrightscanada.com • www.playwrightscanada.com

No part of this book, covered by the copyright herein, may be reproduced or used in any form or by any means—graphic, electronic, or mechanical—without the prior written permission of the publisher, except for excerpts in a review, or by a licence from Access Copyright, 1 Yonge St., Suite 800, Toronto, ON Canada M5E 1E5   phone 416.868.1620

For professional or amateur production rights, please contact Playwrights Canada Press at the address above.

The publisher acknowledges the financial support of the Canadian taxpayers and the Government of Canada through the National Translation Program for Book Publishing for our translation activities, the Government of Canada Book Publishing Industry Development Program, the Canada Council for the Arts, the Ontario Arts Council, and the Ontario Media Development Corporation.

Cover image: *Vivanina* by Francine Simonin (2009) Acrylic on canvas.
Courtesy of Francine Simonin and Galerie Lacerte.
Typesetting/Cover design: JLArt

Library and Archives Canada Cataloguing in Publication

Anthology of Québec women's plays in English translation / edited by Louise H. Forsyth. -- 1st ed.
Vol. 2 has 1st edition note.
Includes bibliographical references.
Contents: v. 1. 1966-1986 -- v. 2. 1987-2003 -- v. 3. 1997-2009.
ISBN-10: 0-88754-868-7 (v. 1).--ISBN-13: 978-0-88754-719-5 (v. 2).--
ISBN-13: 978-0-88754-785-0 (v. 3)

1. Canadian drama (French)--Québec (Province)--Translations into English.
2. Canadian drama (French)--Women authors--Translations into English.
3. Canadian drama (French)--20th century--Translations into English.
I. Forsyth, Louise

PS8315.5.Q8A58 2006   C842'.540809287   C2006-906066-5

First Edition: May 2010
Printed and bound in Canada by Gauvin Press, Gatineau.

Permissions and Copyright Notices

L'histoire sordide de Conrad B. © 1995 Nathalie Boisvert
translation *Catch a Tiger* © 2002 Bobby Theodore
with permission of the author

Violette sur la terre © 2002 by Leméac Éditeur, Montréal
All rights reserved
First published in French as *Violette sur la terre* by Leméac Éditeur, Montréal
translation *Earthbound* © 2009 John Murrell

La bibliothèque de Constance © 2002 Marie-Ève Gagnon
translation *When Books Come Tumbling Down* © 2009 Louise H. Forsyth
with permission of the author

Désordre public © 2006 Evelyne de la Chenelière
translation *Public Disorder* © 2010 Morwyn Brebner
with permission of the author

Portrait chinois d'une imposteure © 2003 Dominick Parenteau-Lebeuf
translation *Chinese Portrait of an Imposter* © 2009 Crystal Beliveau
with permission of Lansman Éditeur

Roche, papier, couteau… © 2004 Marilyn Perreault
translation *Rock, Paper, Jackknife…* © 2010 Nadine Desrochers
with permission of Lansman Éditeur

Jouliks © 2005 Marie-Christine Lê-Huu
translation *Jouliks* © 2009 Crystal Beliveau
with permission of Lansman Éditeur

Ma mère chien © 2005 Louise Bombardier
translation *My Mother Dog* © 2009 Leanna Brodie
with permission of the author

La robe de mariée de Gisèle Schmidt © 2004 Julie Vincent
translation *Gisèle's Wedding Dress* © 2009 Maureen Labonté
with permission of Éditions de la Pleine Lune

Le bruit des os qui craquent © 2009 Suzanne Lebeau
translation *The Sound of Cracking Bones* © 2010 Julia Duchesne and John Van Burek
with permission of the author

"Where Have All the Flowers Gone"
by Pete Seeger
© copyright 1961 (renewed) by Sanga Music Inc.
All rights reserved. Used by permission.

A.S. Kline's translation of Arthur Rimbaud's
"Une saison en enfer," as quoted on P. 379 of *My Mother Dog*,
is used with permission and may be read in its entirety at
www.poetryintranslation.com

Writing a Québec Theatre Corpus into Existence

This third volume of the Anthology of Québec Women's Plays in English Translation *is dedicated with humility and admiration to all the playwrights of Québec who have created since the middle of the twentieth century a large, beautiful, and original dramatic corpus au féminin. Through their vision, talent, and determination, these wonderful writers have paid their own homage to the women who came before them and who had the guts to create and act for theatre, even when the forces of darkness were pressuring them to remain silent. Now, there are several playwrights who have created a major oeuvre; their careers are exemplary; they are models and inspiration for the many younger playwrights who have the courage, like them, to choose to be theatre artists.*

Each of these playwrights has her own unique way of seeing, being, writing, and acting. Together, their voices speak poetry; their plays dare to do bold and astonishing, sometimes outrageous, things.
Their brilliant commitment to a career that is difficult offers precious, fresh perspectives on human affairs. Their work is transforming dramaturgy, theatricality, performativity, scenography, and society itself.

Acknowledgements

My thanks are extended to the ten playwrights whose works are included in this volume and who so generously gave their permission for this publication in English. These wonderful women responded without fail to every request for clarification of a detail or verification of a document, even when their busy lives were tied up with new productions, activities in their own companies, travel, or otherwise creating, working, and making their important contributions to theatre in this country. They have been a dream to work with.

My thanks are also extended to the amazingly gifted translators of these ten plays. Their virtuosic writing inspires awe. As many have said, theatre translation is, in reality, a process of new play creation. I know how these translators grappled with inspired playfulness as they made decisions about each word, the rhythm and flow of each line, in order to be sure the script was comprehensible in its nuances and performable on an anglophone stage for English-speaking audiences. Their recreation of the poetry, wordplay, and subtle associations that flow through the original texts is nothing short of brilliant. Their willingness to expose drafts of their translations to the trials of dramatic readings and so to accept the most frank of criticism from theatre practitioners has enhanced that much more the quality of their work.

I want to extend my gratitude for the beauty and rich significance of Marcelle Ferron's and Francine Simonin's artworks that grace the covers of the three volumes of the anthology. As the first thing that strikes readers, these paintings provide immediate and compelling invitations to open the books and so be drawn into universes oriented by feminine sensitivity, ideas, and imaginative panoramas.

I acknowledge with most sincere gratitude the support and assistance that Daniel Gauthier, former responsable du centre de documentation of the Centre des auteurs dramatiques (CEAD), and Carole Lavoie, also of the centre de documentation, have given me at every turn over several years. I could not have done the research nor handled many practical matters without them, their knowledge, and the seemingly inexhaustible sources of documentary information available in CEAD files and on its website.

My appreciation goes to Annie Gibson (publisher), Blake Sproule (editor), and Angela Rebeiro (former publisher) at Playwrights Canada Press for having believed in my research and for having provided the professional support and advice that made it possible to bring this exciting project to completion. The three volumes of the anthology start with the moment when women first began writing for theatre in Québec in significant numbers and follow the path of new plays right up to the present time. Such a compilation of at least some of the major dramaturgical works in the corpus of playwriting by Québec women has never before been done, in either French or English.

My final acknowledgement is to a hazy, ether-based support network. When I began my own education and scholarly career, I wrote my essays and took my notes using a pen and a manual typewriter. No one had even yet dreamed of photocopiers, scanners, cellphones, or personal computers. What a change! The research I have done in compiling these plays and information about them and their authors, storage of the information, communication with members of a vast community of theatre scholars and critics, and transferral of files between playwrights and translators, Playwrights Canada Press and me have entailed electronic use of libraries, websites, search engines, emails, and my own small laptop. All this would have been much more difficult without the technologies that have transformed in such a dizzyingly short time the means we use to seek, compile, develop, and communicate knowledge. I am grateful for them. And now I am grateful that there will be a book with covers and pages to hold in our hands.

Table of Contents

Introduction	iii
Catch a Tiger (L'histoire sordide de Conrad B.) by Nathalie Boisvert, translated by Bobby Theodore	1
Earthbound (Violette sur la terre) by Carole Fréchette, translated by John Murrell	47
When Books Come Tumbling Down (La bibliothèque de Constance) by Marie-Ève Gagnon, translated by Louise H. Forsyth	97
Public Disorder (Désordre public) by Evelyne de la Chenelière, translated by Morwyn Brebner	159
Chinese Portrait of an Imposter (Portrait chinois d'une imposteure) by Dominick Parenteau-Lebeuf, translated by Crystal Beliveau	207
Rock, Paper, Jackknife… (Roche, papier, couteau…) by Marilyn Perreault, translated by Nadine Desrochers	271
Jouliks (Jouliks) by Marie-Christine Lê-Huu, translated by Crystal Beliveau	317
My Mother Dog (Ma mère chien) by Louise Bombardier, translated by Leanna Brodie	361
Gisèle's Wedding Dress (La robe de mariée de Gisèle Schmidt) by Julie Vincent, translated by Maureen Labonté	411
The Sound of Cracking Bones (Le bruit des os qui craquent) by Suzanne Lebeau, translated by Julia Duchesne and John Van Burek	453
Bibliography	499
About the Translators	507
About the Editor	510

Introduction

> Theatre, a collective art, is the ideal place to invent new social structures.
> —Pol Pelletier, *Joy*

> But most of all, I would say, here's a *writer*, and I think of all writers as voices in the wilderness, people who are daring to stand up and try to name the very peculiar angst or joy of this decade, this century, this place.
> —Linda Gaboriau in Beauchamp & Knowles

The ten plays in this third volume of the *Anthology of Québec Women's Plays in English Translation* provide a glimpse of the stunning imagination, probing observation, thematic richness, and theatrical diversity at work in new plays written by Québec women in recent years. The plays are in the process of revealing dazzling diversification and maturation in the dramaturgical corpus—now embracing several generations—since the 1950s and 1960s, when only a few bold and gifted women were starting to give serious consideration to a writing, performing, and directing career. I selected the plays for this volume and requested the playwrights' permission to publish translations of them because I am thrilled by their beauty, relevance, and potential for theatrical and social renewal. The plays are major works. Their authors have played significant roles, not only as gifted writers, but also as actors on stage or in radio, cinema, and television, members of companies dedicated to collective creation, *metteures en scène*, founders and directors of new-play theatre companies, teachers and members of professional theatre associations.

The 1960s, 1970s, and 1980s were turbulent years in Québec, during which political systems, socio-cultural norms, established institutions, hegemonic discourse, and dominant ideologies came under radical fire from popular movements subsequently known as the Quiet Revolution and the Sexual Revolution. Anti-colonial struggles in France's former colonies and the civil rights movement in the United States had a significant impact in Québec. The influence of these collective demands for freedom from arbitrary authority, injustice, and oppression, along with the waves of counterculture that were sweeping across the popular culture and media landscape, can be clearly felt in the exciting renewal of theatre of Québec, which had its start around mid-century. Québec women began to organize and move en masse so as to put an end to their particularly onerous condition of inferiority. A conservative estimate of the number of plays written by Québec women playwrights since the mid-twentieth century suggests that the corpus now contains well over two hundred texts written, published, and performed in Montréal, Québec City, Ottawa, and elsewhere, in France and Belgium, translated into English and many other languages, and performed on a broad international landscape.

The plays in the three volumes of this anthology give to readers, theatre people looking for challenging scripts, critics, and scholars interested in filling some of the gaps in historical knowledge about playwriting and theatrical activity by women an opportunity to hear passionate voices from the past and the present, magically giving dramatic form to human experiences, observations, ideas, and fantasies, as seen through women's eyes and lived in women's bodies and spirits. The twenty-eight plays take us through forty-four years of great and emerging authors writing for theatre, as well as through those particularly incendiary decades of the 1970s and 1980s when women worked together in the production of an amazing number of no-holds-barred feminist collective creations and the organization of spectacles, festivals, and encounters. Many theatre people—women and men—working in the 1970s and 1980s expressed stridently and vigorously the view that it is impossible to change social structures lending themselves to injustice, abuse, and tired aesthetic conventions "without changing languages, values, institutions, conventions, ways of seeing and doing. Bold experimentation became a necessary and integral component of theatre practice in most venues. The experimentation in theatrical approach and language and the innovation in theme and characterization undertaken by women playwrights was and has remained energetic and multi-faceted, even when the period of militant feminism had more or less come to an end.

Whither Feminism in an Individualistic Age?

Feminist theatre practitioners and critics of the 1970s and 1980s did disdainful and angry analyses of theatre's status quo. They criticized in particular the tyranny of prevailing character types for women (sweet, young innocent, domineering or oppressed mother, some variation on the prostitute—never subjectively motivated action figures pursuing with determination the object of their own desire), the verbal and body languages deriving from this typology and taught so aggressively in theatre schools, scenographic ramifications of these patriarchal conventions, the place of passivity assigned structurally to female characters in dramatic action, the social myths and archetypes underlying the typology. Some of these practitioners were of the view that theatrical traditions had been sufficiently corrupted by sexist ideologies that they had to be rejected in their entirety. They believed that these traditions were so ingrained in acting and directing techniques, and that they worked so effectively to render women's lived realities and potential for expression invisible and silent that not only could they not be remedied, but they were effectively serving to perpetuate gender-based injustices throughout the social fabric.

Feminist plays and collective creations made frequent use of monologues and other spectacular strategies of ostension, using the stage to affirm the legitimacy of women's voices, speaking publicly about themselves and their issues, and to show the realities of women's sexed bodies. They spoke out and, in telling their own stories while angrily rejecting the voices of authority frequently heard coming from offstage, they brought themselves into the limelight, into reality. This fresh synthesis of fiction and autobiography, theatricality and performativity, dialogic action and narrativity produced a major and lasting transformation of theatre practices and social structures.

Despite the urgency expressed by some feminists for the total rejection of theatrical conventions, assumptions, practices and institutions, such a radical move did not in fact occur in Québec theatre. Nevertheless, feminist theatre made a significant difference. As a result, women were increasingly visible in positions throughout the theatre community, even in positions of high artistic and administrative authority, and women playwrights were publishing and having their fine works performed in growing numbers. Still, the numbers of women organizing collectively for change in the theatre establishment and in the content of what was seen on stage dropped rapidly—as was dramatized by Pol Pelletier in *Joy*, the initial play of the amazing trilogy she produced in the 1990s.

It seems that the feminist agenda for those wishing to make a career in theatre had been pushed to the side by 1990, or at least, that those holding feminist views had become more careful and discrete. An example of the sidelining of feminist issues since that time is that, while there is now much greater frankness and openness about female sexuality and women's erotic energy on Québec stages, there is virtually no representation of any manifestation of sexual orientation in women other than heterosexual, even though lesbian characters were far from rare in the 1970s and 1980s. This silence and the ideological factors that might be underlying it was mentioned recently by one of today's leading playwrights, Evelyne de la Chenelière: "I'm not sure, even if homosexuality is very much celebrated in the history of theatre, that people would be comfortable with a lesbian woman" (cited by Gervais).[1]

Conversations with female playwrights indicate clearly that writers, actors, and directors of all generations remain aware of their debt to those who came before, even if they are no longer giving top priority to their objectives. These playwrights are also aware that many feminist objectives are still to be achieved and that gender matters in the reception and evaluation of the work they do. Invisibility and marginalization remain serious problems. Without denying the urgency of continuing to work for greater equity and respect for their work, they nevertheless assert the legitimacy of turning their artist's attention to subjects and issues other than those that are specifically feminist: issues of personal and social justice in dysfunctional families, failure of communication, solitude, situations of unemployment and poverty, war and population displacement. Their works dramatizing universal human problems and interrogating both established epistemological and ontological assumptions and hegemonic discourse, such as abuse of power, loss of identity and place, dissolution of the boundaries among appearances, fictions and reality, death, and the nature of creativity, theatricality, imagination, and fantasy, are richly original. Their perspective on the many forms of violence and oppression of which the human species is capable is dazzling. De la Chenelière has good reason to assert that a woman's very act of writing—taking herself seriously as an artist, visionary, and thinker—is still today a powerful feminist act, that is to say an act that is making a significant difference, whether or not she speaks explicitly as a feminist:

> To be a woman and to write is a feminist act; even if it isn't the driving force for themes in our fiction, this simple gesture brings with it women's right to occupy this space. It is our role as artists and creative women to refuse to be intimidated by a perception and to go as far as our own particular words will take us. Making art is an individual act (cited by Gervais).[2]

Another major playwright of the younger generation, Fanny Britt, agrees with De la Chenelière that the essence of making art is having the courage to boldly step out as an individual as one takes one's own unique vision and voice as far as they can go. Women's right to exercise such freedom and to be heard doing so has not always been recognized. Both Britt and De la Chenelière are aware of the rich corpus of women's original plays that already exists in Québec. The terrain was earlier opened wide through feminist action; it now offers many diverse possibilities to explore what it means to be human, as seen through women's eyes and experienced in women's bodies and minds. As Britt says, a rich and varied corpus already exists:

> The [gendered] difference is always there; we're not out of it yet. But that strip of sand is bigger now [...] The challenge is not to show [men] we can do it. Nowadays, as artists, we hold in our hands all we need to be able to do everything we want to do. The challenge is to be as good as the other women (cited by Gervais).[3]

Expansion in the Past Two Decades of This Already Rich and Varied Corpus

The plays in the second volume of this anthology offer a retrospective glance at playwriting by women in previous decades and a prospective glance at new departures already underway. Pol Pelletier's *Joy* was a powerful although poignantly nostalgic reminder of the time when feminist theatre flourished in Québec, a reminder as well of Pelletier's amazing and visionary theoretical and pedagogical work in transforming acting, the training of actors, and theatre itself. The other plays in Volume II offer complexly human characters, caught through all their contradictions in a wide variety of personal and social situations. Like all dramatic characters, they are in search of their own sense of self, their place in relation to others and the world, truth, memory, and reconciliation with the violence of present and past events, power, knowledge, and words that facilitate communication. These plays give form and meaning to the hazy and inchoate matter from which one builds as meaningful and coherent a life as one can.

Abla Farhoud's *Game of Patience*, which figures in Volume II and was first performed in 1994, is an extraordinary work of art dramatizing the terrible situation of a woman, just arrived in Montréal from the Middle East, whose daughter was gunned down in the streets of a city racked by civil war. The woman and her cousin, born in the same country but a long-time resident and well-established francophone writer in Québec, are in search of words that will allow them to communicate, bring understanding of and reconciliation with the fact of war and the devastation of the daughter's death and the mother's exile. This play can be seen to serve as a kind of prototype for most of the major elements in characterization, theme, verbal and non-verbal languages, and theatrical experimentation found in plays by Québec women over the past two decades:

i. Characters
   1. Motherhood, mothering, stereotypes of the role of mother
   2. Children and adolescents as lucid subjects and agents, witnesses, and victims

ii. Themes
   1. Mother-child relations
   2. Violence and cruelty, manifesting itself in arbitrary authority, oppression, and abuse of power
   3. The never-quite-satisfactory nature of communicative bonds in intimate, domestic, and social relations
   4. The inadequacy, biases, prejudices, and distortions of received knowledge, represented by books and authoritative voices
   5. Exile and the condition of being an outsider
   6. Creative processes, using words, movement, images, music, fantasies, stories, and actions to perceive experience in a fresh light and produce new identities and realities

iii. Theatricality and Performativity[4]
   1. Theatrical and performative experimentation that complements innovative characterization, themes, and dramatic action
   2. Open-ended processes encouraging constantly renewed erotic and spiritual energy
   3. Structures of fragmentation and disintegration reflecting characters' distress and/or quest for coherence, illumination, and reason to hope

In the first play of this anthology, *The Savage Season* (1966), Anne Hébert opened the door wide on the vast and often contradictory problematics of the theme and practice of motherhood, as determined by powerful social institutions and transcendent forces. A striking dimension of almost all of Hébert's female characters is their sensuality, their erotic power, their spiritual, physical, and social being as sexed and gendered humans with powerful desires of their own. Too often, stereotypes of mothers, as conveyed by stories, myths, and traditions through the centuries, have occulted or otherwise rendered shameful the inescapable association of femininity, maternity, and sexuality. Lori Saint-Martin has studied this cultural phenomenon in *Le Nom de la mère: Mères, filles et écriture dans la littérature québécoise au féminin*, where she shows that creatively bringing such debilitating stereotypes out for public view has been salient in all literary genres *au féminin*. Revealing the dangerously narrow and illusory basis on which these stereotypes depend has been a major determinant for writers in their exposition of what it means to speak out or to write as women.

Almost all the plays in this anthology contribute fragments of a vast, complex, and troubling portrait of motherhood, addressing its warts as practised, celebrating the love it sometimes nurtures, revealing the hatred it frequently produces simultaneously with powerful emotional attachment, casting light on the sources of the abuse of power that are so often a part of mothers' roles, and exploring the affective range that constitutes mother-child relations: longing, guilt, joy, fear, nurturance, hatred, and anxiety. Volume III begins with the implacably domineering matriarch of *Catch a Tiger*. The dramatic action of this play develops as the effect of her relentless control of her adult son becomes increasingly clear to him, the woman he might have loved had his mother not stifled his ability to love, and the audience. Dramatic insight into some of the many positive and negative aspects of mothering and its place in women's sense of identity, their relations with others, and the vitality of their inner resources, allowing them to fulfill their entire adult potential, figure centrally in Volume III in *When Books Come Tumbling Down*, *My Mother Dog*, and *Jouliks* and is important thematically in *Chinese Portrait of an Imposter*.

Samira in Farhoud's *Game of Patience*, the dead adolescent shot in the streets of the war-torn city, plays a central role in the play's action and provides a young person's perspective on the devastation perpetuated by the implacable mechanisms of prevailing institutions and ideologies. She is very much present throughout the hall and across the stage, even though she is diegetically in a time and place other than those occupied by her mother and aunt, by whom she is unseen. She is a victim of war and the cruelty, apathy, and stupidity humans are so capable of. She also provides testimony in material ways to events and commentary on them. As a filmmaker determined to face the danger in the streets in order to show what was happening there, her views resonate with the conviction of her mother and aunt that, if one is to say "No" to wanton violence, one must speak out and use imaginative means through creative processes in order to get enough psychic, emotional, and aesthetic distance to see behind appearances and gain deeper understanding of human affairs. The child figures in *Rock, Paper, Jackknife…*, *Jouliks*, and *The Sound of Cracking Bones* have similar theatrical and thematic functions as witnesses, innocent victims, and subjectively involved agents. The playwrights have invented in each case innovative narrative and theatrical devices that allow the voices or the silences of the children to be heard in situations where, in reality, children would probably not be heard or, in any case, heeded. These expressive devices involve use of objects, non-verbal languages, and various technologies, reading by an adult character of words written by the child, doubling up the roles of child characters and having them move between levels in the fictional diegeses so that they alternate between involvement in the action and a detached narrative space where they contemplate and describe it. Marie-Ève Gagnon also uses child characters and innovative narrative techniques in *When Books Come Tumbling Down* to evoke a dramatically fresh perspective on the complexities of women's place in today's world. The reported anguish of the child who never appears on stage and the appearance through flashbacks of the main character and her best friend (who plays the role of narrator throughout the play) when they were on the troubling brink of puberty provide the motivation for this play's dramatic action and thematic development.

A similar use of an innocent character, observing the suffering of the other characters and presumed to understand it, is Violet in *Earthbound*. In this case, she is not a child. However, her silently detached perspective on the characters' situation, which incites them to tell their stories, is central to the audience's interpretive process. In the end we learn that Violet is a victim, like the child narrators, of the same cruel forces faced by those who were seeking her sympathy and advice.

Using a similar theatrical device in order to provide contiguously more than one ambiguous perspective on the dramatic situation, Bombardier disrupted the chronological order and progression in the scene structure of *My Mother Dog*, thus allowing events to go back and forth among several moments in the past and present, while the daughter's memories, thoughts, and violently conflicting emotions, probably all going on at the same time in her mind through the tense night of the mother's death, alternate among scenes of "Reality," "Dream," and "Truncated Reality."

The impact of the extreme violence and cruelty that all of these characters encounter in one form or another is enhanced by the disingenuous and detached perspective offered by innocent words, that is to say, the disproportion between an irremediable reality and the powerlessness one feels in contemplating it, trying to understand it, or living through it. This recognition of the futility of language and gesture furthers the theme of never-quite-satisfactory communication and highlights the experience of solitude that almost everyone knows, even, and perhaps particularly, with those they feel closest to. Individuals in these plays are alone in their aloneness, self-doubt, vision of the present and the future, self-delusion, fear, hunger for answers, and despair. Many of them have lost their place of belonging. They may not be in exile in the same geographical and political way as Farhoud's Mariam (*Game of Patience*), Emma Haché's Frauke (*Intimacy*), Perrault's children on the brink of suicide (*Rock, Paper, Jackknife...*) and Lebeau's child soldiers running for their lives. Yet—as Emmanuelle Roy's Anath seeks to reclaim the First Nations heritage and the mother she never knew (*Shards*); as Geneviève Billette's Kalr plots grotesquely to possess for himself the discourse of power as exercised in the business world (*Crime Against Humanity*); as Conrad B. moves back and forth among the constraints of his mother's kitchen, the locked garage where his G.I. Joe dolls keep him company, the warehouse where he moves boxes around, and Lynda's apartment where he discovers himself incapable of adult intimacy (*Catch a Tiger*); as each of the characters move through the dark in search of the warmth and understanding they erroneously attribute to Violet (*Eathbound*); as Constance seeks to rebuild her sense of self and of her family's solidity following the landslide of her books, the disappearance of her daughter, and the reappearance of troubling events from the past (*When Books Come Tumbling Down*); as Max seeks to get his acting career back on course, to restore relations with friends and former lovers, and to put in place a balanced sense of self (*Public Disorder*); as Candice de LaFontaine-Rotonde resists prevailing aesthetic and cultural norms and seeks to set her own artist's voice free (*Chinese Portrait of an Imposter*); as the children who arrived in the shipping container hoping to find a place they belong in a land where they do not speak the language or understand the customs, thereby reflecting the isolation and despair of children in northern communities (*Rock, Paper, Jackknife…*); as the daughter claws her way through the violently conflicting emotions she feels as her mother lays dying (*My Mother Dog*); as Vera tries to reconcile her sense of herself as an autonomous individual, caring mother, and passionate lover with the destructive heritage her own ideologically conditioned mother passed on to her and as the Little One, "on eggshells," listens to the "sound of our house shattering, blowing away in the wind" (*Jouliks*, Scene 13); as the echoes of dreams of love and sexual fulfillment pass with the increasingly tattered wedding dress from one body to the next (*Gisèle's Wedding Dress*); and as Elikia and Joseph run desperately for nights toward freedom and out of the violent clutches of the rebel army (*The Sound of Cracking Bones*)—they are each, irrevocably, on their own path with their own inadequate resources, sharing or disagreeing with others, never quite feeling understood or even safe. They are all outsiders.

Evelyne de la Chenelière's *Public Disorder* is a particularly original dramatic representation of the problematics of communication, in that it reverses expectations when it creates a character who hears the words of others' thoughts and feelings and is unable to turn them off. The words emanating from others are so invasive that they stifle his own thoughts and feelings completely. The play explores the idea that a satisfying sense of identity and meaningful relations with others depends upon an incessantly changing and tenuous balance between honest self-awareness and genuine sympathy for others. Individual lives in the real world may be similar to the work of actors who, by definition, are simultaneously seen as themselves and someone else. The point of departure for *Public Disorder* and the incessant process of change through which the script moved from one performance to the next and from one version to the next throw into relief the message that a life lived with meaning and value is a life lived in a balance between egotism and altruism, between inner quiet and constantly renewed creative acts. There is no standing still and there is no absolutely reliable and permanently open medium of communication as long as life continues.

The condition of individuals as outsiders and never finally settled in either their sense of self and security or in their relation with others may not always be a bad thing, since desire, imagination, creativity, and fantasy are born from fragmentation and incompleteness. Like Gisèle Schmidt, whom Julie Vincent described as "inconsolably lonely" and to whom she attributed the frequently expressed regret of never having known a great love: "I would have given my entire career to have lived one great love" (*Gisèle's Wedding Dress*, Shift 1), artists and vibrantly alive individuals are inveterate seekers. It is likely that had Gisèle lived that fully satisfying experience of "one great love," she would not have become the extraordinary actor she was: the artist who *channels dreams*. The capacity to live one's life as an endless quest depends, of course, upon the good fortune of finding oneself in circumstances that continue to offer fresh paths and that are without insurmountable oppression and violence.

Parenteau-Lebeuf's *Chinese Portrait of an Imposter* is an imaginative and ludic exploration of creative processes and resistance to representational systems and factors in the socio-cultural environment that inhibit the freedom of untrammelled creativity, causing artists, particularly women artists, to feel like imposters and so to self-censor. Interestingly, Parenteau-Lebeuf makes innovative use of the aesthetic resources available to her—makeup, masks, characters, dialogue, images, gestures, and theatricality itself through a play within a play and a television show—in analysing imaginatively through a kind of fanciful mirror-talk what is actually going on in her experiences of theatre. *Chinese Portrait of an Imposter* stresses the vital importance of artistic creation and of the need to speak out, to write, to give form to truths, desire, imagination, and fantasy, however fragile they might seem. The central importance of speech, writing, and imaginatively creative processes is similarly dramatized, thematically and structurally, in Françoise Loranger's *Playing Double*, Marie Savard's *Mine Sincerely*, the collective *Clash of Symbols*, Jovette Marchessault's *The Edge of Earth is Too Near*, Violette Leduc, Lise Vaillancourt's *Marie-Antoine, Opus One*, Michèle Magny's *Marina, the Blush of Life*, Pelletier's *Joy*, Farhoud's *Game of Patience*, Billette's *Crime Against Humanity*, Roy's *Shards*, Gagnon's *When Books Come Tumbling Down*, Perreault's *Rock, Paper, Jackknife...*, and Lê-Huu's *Jouliks*. In Lebeau's *The Sound of Cracking Bones*, the young Elikia seizes the little time she has before her dreadfully cruel and untimely death to write her story in her notebook. Elikia's narrative allows the nurse Angelina to read Elikia's and Joseph's tragic story into the official record, even though the obtuse members of the commission before which she testifies have lost the capacity to hear and understand its meaning and significance.

As Gisèle Schmidt has said, the artist channels dreams. The books of all the specialists found on Constance's bookshelves might be full of expert knowledge, but the beauty of a show featuring Gisèle Schmidt, a script like Chekhov's *Three Sisters*, a song by Pete Seeger asking "Where Have All The Flowers Gone?" or one by Jean-Baptiste Clément recalling "Le Temps des cerises" produces deeper understanding and a different kind of knowledge than any carefully reasoned statement. Women's sense of identity, their perceptions of reality, and the atrocious truth of human suffering that continues unchecked today have remained hidden for too long because not enough people are speaking out, discovering a strong basis for both a sense of self and compassion, giving expression to their dreams of a world without violence and injustice.

Reading Theatre, Doing Theatre, Translating Theatre

As I come to these final paragraphs of the final volume of this twenty-eight play anthology, I feel the desire to share a few thoughts about reading and translating theatre, the creative process of interpreting theatre texts, and why I undertook this project of bringing together at least a few of the hundreds of plays in Québec's dramaturgical corpus produced over the past half-century by women artists. My primary motivation has been, quite simply, my desire to share my admiration and appreciation for the beauty and originality of these works with as many English-speaking readers, theatre artists, scholars, and students as possible. I am convinced that simply reading and enjoying them, inventing in one's own head a possible *mise en scène* for them, is richly rewarding. They have all been professionally produced at least once. And they all proffer unlimited opportunities for theatrical and performative experimentation in directing, design, interpretation, and analysis. Along with their individual theatrical qualities, they form together—along with the many fine plays I was unable to include in these three volumes—a relatively unrecognized dramatic literature corpus that deserves to be integrated into the collective memory of Québec and Canadian theatre and culture.

With regard to the oversight that many of these prize-winning, internationally known and performed plays and playwrights have had to endure at the hands and in the actions and evaluations of theatre practitioners, critics, and scholars, Josette Féral has drawn attention to the paradoxical fact that, even though they have all appeared on the theatre horizon in the form of major productions, they have rarely been seen to have much effect there—they came into view for one run, and then they were gone, known and yet forgotten:

> Appearances to the contrary, contemporary theatre written and produced by women has received little attention over the years, and studies on the subject are far from numerous. It's not that theatre practice by women is invisible on the landscape, but it has been slipping onto it without causing waves.[5]

The absence of recognition of the originality, interest, and importance of theatre written and produced by women has unfortunately impoverished the corpus of Québec and Canadian theatre as normally constructed, depriving it of a major component that has the potential to make a difference theatrically, socially, and culturally. These plays are works of art that belong to us all. It is my hope that this anthology will serve at least in some small way to cast greater light on them and, indeed, to cause some waves in the overarching patriarchal narratives of theatre criticism and historiography. Since making theatre is always risky and can never overlook the practical reality that a production (whether on stage or published) must enjoy a knowledgeable reception from a public with the necessary interpretive competence and having a willingness to see the show as interesting and relevant within its horizon of expectations (even and particularly if the show forces the interrogation and expansion of this horizon), it is also my hope that making the plays in these three volumes available to English-speaking audiences will serve to incite artistic directors, audience members, and educators to recognize that this corpus matters to them and the knowledge they have of themselves as individuals and as members of a cultural community.

It is commonly assumed that the passage of a theatre text from the written page to the stage is quite direct and uncomplicated, depending almost entirely upon the professional competence of directors, actors, and designers. It is also commonly assumed that the passage through translation of a theatre text written in one language to another language is simply a matter of finding equivalent dialects and spoken language levels. It is my belief that these simplistic assumptions can produce a conservative theatre establishment convinced that its standards for beauty and excellence are unproblematic, without examination or interrogation.

These assumptions regarding the ways in which theatre functions fail to take into account the central place of interpretations at every stage of creation, production, reception, and translation processes, such interpretations always being partial, multiple, and divergent, and quite often manipulative and biased. The infinitely expansive place of interpretive processes in theatrical creation is at the heart of its magic, power, and endless vitality. It is also at the heart of its tendency to resist too much change—once certain interpretations have established their hegemonic positions, the curtain comes down on departures in other directions.

Play texts, unlike novels or poems, are written, usually workshopped, given dramatic readings, published, and produced on stage. At each moment their components are evaluated by dramaturges, directors, actors, and others for their performability, relevance, and compatibility in a particular socio-cultural and historical context. The first performance is a milestone in their realization, but not the end of their development and evolution. After the curtain falls on any performance, written texts of the original script and other documents remain to be read by an interested public, scholars, and students, interpreted as dramatic literature or lending themselves to new stage productions that may be quite different from the first performance.

In the same way that play texts themselves depend upon endless interpretation for their realization and the renewal of their creative vitality (from particular perspectives, in specific social contexts calling upon available conventions and technologies, and from written languages on the page, through connotations and stage directions, to the multiple semiotic systems at play on theatre stages), translations involve interpretive processes requiring knowledge of and sensitivity to many different kinds of languages (verbal, non-verbal, visual, musical, kinesic, technological). Translators are not invisible transmitters of a completed text, needing nothing more than competence in two languages. Susan Bassnett was one of the first theorists to recognize that translating theatre is like wending one's way through a labyrinth. Translators, like the actors mentioned by Gisèle Schmidt, are *channellers of dreams*. As Linda Gaboriau stated, they are saying to all who will hear that the translated piece is the creation of a *writer*. Translators—like all those whose work appears in this anthology—have, therefore, positioned themselves as creative subjects engaging with the daunting challenges of the text as an original, artistic work. They are interpreters exercising their own imagination and involvement in the aesthetic and ethical issues raised by the texts, and they are professionals whose knowledge and experience of theatre in the source culture and of the cultural and theatrical context of the target audience (always different from that of the original audience) keeps them informed of the barriers, boundaries, and opportunities in which the translated text must activate appropriate conventions, stir sympathetic interpretations, and find active reception from directors, actors, teachers, scholars, students, and both the reading and theatre-going public.

Cognizant of the sometimes harsh realities that can threaten the very survival of theatre companies, theatre translators must frequently ask themselves, colleagues, artistic directors, and publishers whether the goal is to produce monuments and masterpieces for comfortable and complacent audiences or to run the risk of challenging these audiences and new ones who have not yet discovered for themselves the joy of interpreting new, innovative theatre. Like new plays that usually evolve over a period of time, playwrights revising them as they see them on stage in certain interpretations or as they are remounted for new audiences, translations of new plays change, undergo revisions as they too are seen on stage or as they are interpreted with new socio-cultural and linguistic contexts in mind. The creative process involved in playwriting and theatre translation is never-ending, and therefore very exciting in the opportunities it offers to rethink and re-experience our presence in the world, alone and with others.

Who can say whether the plays represented by the translations in this anthology will survive and slowly morph into monuments? Or whether they will be forgotten and replaced by others? The only certainty that readers, scholars, actors, directors, and critics can have is that the plays represent the voices of some of today's most thoughtful writers and that there is great aesthetic pleasure and profound understanding in responding through interpretation to the creative vitality of their works, thereby seeing ourselves and the world around us through the magnificently magical lens they offer, however disturbing we might find the spectacle.

It will please me to learn that the body of fine works by women playwrights contained in this anthology will be read, performed, and enjoyed and that it has enhanced in some small way our collective ability to be attentive to innovative women's writing. It will also please me to learn that it has generated dialogue, discussion, interrogation, and action around the gendered dynamics still prevailing in theatre and theatre publics.

Notes

1. "Je ne suis pas sûre que, même si l'homosexualité est très célébrée dans l'histoire du théâtre, on serait à l'aise avec une femme lesbienne." (translated by LHF)

2. "Être femme et écrire est un acte féministe; même si ce n'est pas le moteur des thèmes dans notre fiction, ce simple geste porte le droit de la femme à prendre cet espace-là. Notre rôle d'artiste, de femme de création, c'est de ne pas nous laisser intimider par une perception et d'aller au bout de notre parole individuelle. La création est un acte individuel." (translated by LHF)

3. "La différence est toujours là; on n'a pas fini d'être là-dedans. Mais aujourd'hui, le carré de sable est plus grand. [...] Il ne s'agit pas de montrer [aux hommes] qu'on est capable. Mais à notre époque, comme artistes, on a tout entre les mains pour faire ce qu'on veut. Il nous faut être à la hauteur des autres femmes." (translated by LHF)

4. A commitment to experimentation continues to preoccupy women doing theatre in Québec. All the playwrights in this volume have collaborated in some way—as dramaturges, actors, directors—with experimental companies in Québec and abroad, frequently working in multimedia or extending their creative work to puppets or musical theatre. Evelyne de la Chenelière's collaboration with the Nouveau Théâtre Expérimental is one example of this among many. They have also participated in the Festival de Théâtre des Amériques. Several (Fréchette, Parenteau-Lebeuf, Perreault, Vincent, Lebeau) have founded or co-founded their own theatre companies dedicated to theatre research and experimentation in new play production. Espace Go places the date of its founding at 1979, thereby identifying itself as a continuation of the Théâtre Expérimental des Femmes. Brigitte Haentjens, who founded Sibyllines in 1997, is particularly admired for the rigour, quality, and bold innovation of her directing. Sibyllines is a company whose priority is uncompromising artistry and celebration of erotic and psychic energy. Haentjens's work projects a particularly unique and powerful light on many facets of the feminine, while frequently allowing audiences to hear the voices of women authors and offering challenging acting opportunities. Her 2006 production of Louise Dupré's *Tout comme elle*, which included fifty women actors, is an example of her bold and unconventional approach to theatre production.

5. "En dépit des apparences, le théâtre contemporain écrit ou monté par les femmes a reçu peu d'attention au cours des années, et les études n'abondent pas sur le sujet. Non que la pratique théâtrale des femmes soit invisible dans le paysage, mais elle s'y glisse désormais sans y faire des vagues" (*Mise en scène et jeu de l'acteur. Entretiens Tome III. Voix de femmes*, 17). (translated by LHF)

Works Mentioned

Bassnett, Susan. "Ways through the Labyrinth. Strategies and Methods for Translating Theatre Texts." *The Manipulation of Literature. Studies in Literary Translation* (1985). Ed. Theo Hermans. London: Croom Holm. 87–102.

Eichhorn, Kate & Heather Milne, eds. *Prismatic Publics. Innovative Canadian Women's Poetry and Poetics* (2009). Toronto: Coach House Books.

Farhoud, Abla. *Jeux de patience* (1997). Montréal: VLB Éditeur. *Game of Patience* in *Plays by Women, Book Two. International Anthology* (1994). Tr. Jill Mac Dougall. New York: Ubu Repertory Theater. 37–84. Also in *Anthology of Québec Women's Plays in English Translation, Volume II (1987–2003)* (2008). Ed. Louise H. Forsyth. Toronto: Playwrights Canada Press. 173–218.

Féral, Josette. *Mise en scène et jeu de l'acteur. Entretiens Tome III. Voix de femmes* (2007). Montréal: Québec/Amérique.

Forsyth, Louise H., ed. *Anthology of Québec Women's Plays in English Translation, Volume I (1966–1986)* (2006). Toronto: Playwrights Canada Press.

———. *Anthology of Québec Women's Plays in English Translation, Volume II (1987–2003)* (2008). Toronto: Playwrights Canada Press.

Gaboriau, Linda. "A Servant of Two Masters: An Interview with Linda Gaboriau. Interview by Hélène Beauchamp and Ric Knowles." *Canadian Theatre Review* 102 (Spring 2000). 41–47. Special issue on theatre and translation edited by Beauchamp and Knowles.

Gervais, Lisa-Marie. "Les Fées ont encore soif." *Le Devoir* (18 January 2010). www.ledevoir.com/culture/theatre/281209/les-fees-ont-encore-soif (accessed 18 January 2010).

Pelletier, Pol. *Joie* (1995). Montréal: Éditions du Remue-ménage. *Joy* in *Anthology of Québec Women's Plays in English Translation, Volume II (1987–2003)* (2008). Tr. Linda Gaboriau. Ed. Louise H. Forsyth. Toronto: Playwrights Canada Press. 107–71.

Saint-Martin, Lori. *Le Nom de la mère: Mères, filles et écriture dans la littérature québécoise au feminine* (1999). Québec: Éditions Nota bene.

Smart, Patricia. *Écrire dans la maison du père. L'émergence du féminin dans la tradition littéraire du Québec* (1988). Montréal: Québec/Amérique.

Catch a Tiger
(L'histoire sordide de Conrad B.)

by Nathalie Boisvert

translated by Bobby Theodore

Introduction to
Catch a Tiger (L'histoire sordide de Conrad B.)[1]

Catch a Tiger is a dark play exploring one dimension of the dangerous yet all-too-common nexus of destructive human relations that produce domestic violence. The disturbing dramatic impact of its relentless drive to a tragic conclusion is alleviated only by the humour and unexpectedly rich innuendo Boisvert's language produces through the sprightly and laconic dialogue among her characters. The words they exchange are a poetic transformation of the most banal conversation in ordinary daily rituals. They show all that can be packed into one short, curt remark or command when people with intimate bonds share years of unspoken conflict or desperation. Despite the surprisingly humorous effect such communicative shorthand can produce, the darkness of *Catch a Tiger* grows increasingly intense as mechanisms of control over the Other intensify their vice-like grip and as the young man caught in that grip struggles to understand himself and make known to Mother, his tormentor, his urgent psychic need for self-respect, freedom, and physical and emotional gratification. With regard to the sex of the child whose freedom to develop the full potential of his life has not been respected, Boisvert has said that the character could as well have been a young woman.

Catch a Tiger is a one-act play in thirty-five short, snappy scenes, with four characters playing out a few weeks of their lives in several different locations: various places in a modest home, a factory, an apartment, and a zoo. As the French title indicates, it is the sordid story of a thirty-three-year-old man, Conrad B., who has been so controlled and dominated by Mother that he enjoys absolutely no independence, no ability to make decisions on his own, no capacity for pleasure, no friends, nor even feelings that could lead to romance and sexual intimacy, and no psychic space that would provide the distance needed to chart his own life course. Without his recognizing it at first, the pressures generated by powerfully real but unacknowledged feelings, repressed desires, displaced fantasies, and futile dreams have been building implacably inside him to an unbearable intensity. In the beginning of the play he shows he has been ineffectually releasing some of these pressures using strategies of silence, quietly snide comments, and passive aggression. He nevertheless has been maintaining a facade of compliance with the unwavering and deadly boring rituals and ideological positions of Mother.

Conrad B. has been letting off steam every evening when he is alone in the garage, assuming a masculinist persona, putting on the costume of a mechanic, and imitating the controlling, sadistic, and demeaning methods he has learned through painful daily personal experience at Mother's hands. Thus, he ludicrously exercises the same cruel and violent control over his collection of G.I. Joe dolls. As a grown man Conrad B.'s imaginary plays of power, combined with his actual powerless situation, are pathetic. His encounters with Lynda at his warehouse job make it impossible for him to avoid the evidence that the life he is leading has a terrible potential for producing unhappiness, guilt, self-delusion, fear, and psychic paralysis, for sapping the ability to undertake independent action and build sound affective bonds with others. Mother, whose motivation may be seen as incestuous, has completely eclipsed Conrad B.'s sense of self as a sexed human being. The choice he faces as the dramatic tension increases is either to assume his freedom and agency, get in touch with his own feelings and desires, enter into relations of love and friendship with others, or else explode under seething pressure into devastating violence against himself and others. In the intensity of his rage, Conrad B. feels himself to be a vicious tiger caught in a hellish cage. This metaphor, captured in the English title, conveys the desperation of Conrad B.'s solitude, his sense of entrapment, his will to destroy, and his longing for death: "I want to go back to my workshop and wait for the smell of the garage to fill me up and make me explode" (Scene XXXIII).

Catch a Tiger begins with a one-line Prologue in which Mother makes an *apocalyptic appearance* to announce to the audience that, although there is no evidence she has religious faith, "life is a battle and our reward is in heaven." This harsh announcement sets the tone of the play, where Mother and Conrad B. are locked in a duel that cannot fail to lead to disaster. Mother, who sees the world in black and white, has already made all the moral decisions she deems necessary. She has positioned herself to learn nothing more. Her sterile path is clear.

The problematics of motherhood, mothering, children's relations with mothers, mothers' relations with children continue to preoccupy many of today's artists, writers, scholars, and social workers. As I have discussed in the Introduction, this theme has had particular resonance in Québec for decades because of the way hegemonic ideologies traditionally positioned women as mothers. Boisvert's *Catch a Tiger* adds a new chapter to the representation of this heritage in that it does not go into the socio-cultural history of the devastating impact of the imposition of the maternal role on all women nor of mothers' abuse of power in Québec society. Nor does she provide us with many facts about the characters' past that might offer some kind of hook for the understanding of their sad relations. A mysterious haze surrounds Conrad B.'s childhood, since Mother offers different versions of the identity of his father and her own background. She makes enough brief suggestions, however, about her own sad past, the violent abuse she endured at the hands of her alcoholic husband, her lost beauty, her frustrated desires for education and career to produce at least a trace of sympathy in audiences for her. Yet one feels little understanding for the snap negative judgments she makes of others, her obsession with others' transgressions that confirm her conviction that life is a battle and that she bears a heavy burden of suffering, and the implacable, unrelenting power she exercises over the only person she could ever control: her son.

Catch a Tiger is, therefore, not a realistic study of a social phenomenon nor a psychological study of characters' motivation. It is a tragic tale where the will to power crushes all of life's erotic and spiritual power. In the finest of French classical theatre tradition, it is the dramatization of a moment of crisis when the opposing forces represented by the characters—both externally in society and within the main character—must be resolved, whether positively or catastrophically. It is a dramatic representation of the dynamics of power where each brief scene and each brief speech, wonderfully and magically suggestive of the force that drives them, represents an implacable step toward the ultimate confrontation. The mechanism and inescapable conflict are already in place before the play begins. The only change that occurs as events unfold derives from the growing awareness of the main character, Conrad B., who, increasingly, is able to see clearly what is happening in his life and yet is unable to assume the power available to him and so change the course of events.

Scene I is a cameo scene by which the distorted relations between Mother and Conrad B. are shown. The scene takes place in the kitchen, where Mother reveals her strategy of incessantly infantilizing her son by displaying her preoccupation with the need for her child to wash his hands and elbows well before dinner, mind his manners, be happy, eat up all his meal and enjoy the special dessert she has made for him, work hard and well, and agree without question to all she says (to the point of automatically parroting her words). Mother and Conrad B. have constructed their lives by weaving into their most intimate fabric, through the tangles of love and hate they feel for each other, the elements of codependence upon which each chooses to rely without reflection. Audiences would have no difficulty grasping immediately the anomalous quality of this relationship, since Conrad B. is a good-looking and seemingly healthy adult. The actor playing the role of Conrad B. would have the daunting task of projecting a character with the virtual potential—physically, mentally, and emotionally—of a fully functioning adult, yet whose inner child has been so nurtured by Mother that it has distorted his perception of reality, eclipsed adult feelings, and cut off the power to the mechanisms for normal adult male responses to events around him.

Conrad B. fantasizes about being a man of action and speed. He dresses like a mechanic when he is in the garage, the space of his fantasies with his G.I. Joes. There is the suggestion that he sees himself as a G.I. Joe or a speed-devouring race-car driver. Knowing his fantasies, Mother gives him a car for his thirty-fourth birthday. Ironically and cruelly, she knows that the car—which seems to be the vehicle of Conrad B.'s dreams—does not run.

Lynda serves as the catalyst, bringing the conflict between Conrad B. and Mother out into the open, obliging him to see what he has never before dared to look at, and precipitating the final catastrophe. A new fellow worker at the factory where Conrad B. works stacking boxes, the charming Lynda is introduced in the third scene. She is a friendly young woman who likes having a job so she can buy herself things she thinks are nice, like a new chrome kitchen set and a VCR. She likes to smoke, drink, go out with her friends, shop, have sex, and enjoy herself. The director of the play and the actor playing the role of Lynda would have discretion in deciding whether she is a compassionate and relatively mature person whose world view offers a genuine alternative to Conrad B. in the alienation for which Mother is responsible, or whether Lynda is a superficial young woman whose casual lifestyle offers no real passage to a meaningful life. However her character is interpreted, it is her initiatives to incite

Conrad B. to withdraw from Mother's sphere of influence, to discover sensual pleasures, to get in touch with his own sexual drive, to become part of the social fabric of the community, and to discover for himself the meaning of the word *freedom* (Scene XVII) that precipitate the ultimate crisis.

The play does not end, however, with a bang but with a whimper. The last of the G.I. Joes is burned, as Conrad B. recognizes in his solitude that he has been playing out his life in a cage. His awareness extends to Mother and Lynda as well, both of whom he sees in cages. It remains unclear whether the unhealthy fabric of their lives has finally been shredded or whether all will go up in flames.

Notes

[1] The typescript of *L'histoire sordide de Conrad B.* is available from the Centre des auteurs dramatiques (CEAD) in Montréal. A dramatic reading of the play was organized by CEAD on December 6, 1995.

About Nathalie Boisvert

Nathalie Boisvert holds a bachelor's degree in acting and a master's degree in drama (1993) from the Université du Québec à Montréal. During her studies she wrote and directed her first play, *Murmures de guerre* (1993). In 1997, her first professionally performed play, *L'histoire sordide de Conrad B.*, was presented at the Festival de Spa in Belgium. This play received an award when it was reprised in Brussels in 1999. It was translated into English in 2003 by Bobby Theodore during a residency at the Banff Centre for the Arts. A dramatic reading of the play was held in Paris and in Amiens by the Compagnie À Vol d'oiseau. In 1999 Boisvert's play *L'été des martiens* was published by Éditions Lansman and produced simultaneously in Québec City by Théâtre Niveau Parking and in Montauban, France by La Comédie de la Mandoune. In 2000, the production was taken on tour in several cultural centres and was then performed in Belgium at Brussels's Théâtre de Poche and Charleroi's Centre culturel. Translated into English by Bobby Theodore, *L'été des martiens* was performed in 2002 by Theatre Direct in Toronto. In 2006 the play was produced simultaneously at the Landstheatre in Düsseldorf and at the Grips in Berlin in a German translation by Frank Heibert.

Nathalie Boisvert has written several other full-length and short plays and has participated in the collectives 4 X 4 and 38. In 2006, her play *Vie et mort d'un village*, prize winner of the Journées de Lyon, was published by Éditions Comp'Act and given a dramatic reading by the Centre des auteurs dramatiques (CEAD) in Montréal during the Semaine de la dramaturgie and in Lyons. It was also read in Paris in 2007 at Théâtre du Rond Point. Boisvert received in 2007 the Prix Gratien-Gélinas, an award established to encourage a new generation of playwrights, for her play *Buffet chinois*. It was produced at Espace Go in Montréal in May 2010. Also in 2010, her only comedy, *Sauver Fabrice*, was presented at the Arts Station, a theatre in Mont-Saint-Hilaire, Québec, her hometown. This play was the opening dramatic reading the same year at CEAD's Semaine de la dramaturgie. In 2008, she translated Anton Dudley's play *Substitution* and wrote *Labyrinthe*, a play for adolescent audiences first performed in 2009 by Montréal's Youtheatre. This play, dramatizing the search for identity, represents the modern city as a metaphor for the world where it is difficult not to get lost.

Published Works by Nathalie Boisvert

L'été des martiens (1999). Carnières, Belgium: Lansman Éditeur.

Vie et mort d'un village (2006). Lyon: Éditions Comp'Act.

L'histoire sordide de Conrad B. was first produced in August 1997 by Théâtre IKS at the Britannique for the Festival de Spa in Spa, Belgium, with the following company:

Conrad   Jean-Charles Hauterat
Mother   Béatrice Didier
Lynda   Anne Huckert

Directed by Cyril Bacqué

...

The play was also produced at Le Botanique de Bruxelles in 1999 and won the "best production" award at the Festival de théâtre en compagnie.

Characters

Conrad
Mother
Lynda
Rita

CATCH A TIGER

Prologue

An apocalyptic appearance of CONRAD's mother.

MOTHER   *(to the audience)* Life is a battle and our reward is in heaven.

Scene I

In the kitchen.

MOTHER   Conrad, did you wash your hands?

CONRAD   Yes, Mom.

MOTHER   Show me. How many times do I have to tell you! When you wash your hands, you have to use a brush. Always. Nails, Conrad. Look at them. They're filthy.

CONRAD   Sorry.

MOTHER   It's okay *this* time. Go ahead, you can start. Conrad?

CONRAD   Yes.

MOTHER   Elbows.

CONRAD   Yes.

MOTHER   Mind your manners, dear.

CONRAD   I'll try.

Pause.

MOTHER   Sometimes I try to imagine you with a wife, children, a house, you know, in a… normal life. But I can't. Funny, isn't it? Anyway, we're happy together. Right, Conrad?

CONRAD   Yes, Mom.

Pause.

MOTHER   I made you something special for dessert.

CONRAD   What?

MOTHER   Black cherry pie. You want a slice?

CONRAD   Yes please.

MOTHER   You have to finish your meat, though. A working man needs his strength.

CONRAD's mother feeds him. He lets her.

That's good.

MOTHER goes to get the dessert.

It's a special recipe: no fat, no sugar, and no flour. So you'll stay slim. You have such a nice figure. Lucky I'm here to look out for your health. What would you do without me.

She clears the table and pours some tea.

So, how was work today?

CONRAD The boss wasn't there.

MOTHER My goodness, was he sick?

CONRAD They said he wasn't.

MOTHER Maybe he's burned out like Uncle Roger. Rita says he doesn't do anything. He gets up at noon, drinks beer, and goes back to bed. He doesn't even wash anymore.

Beat.

Conrad, be careful. Burnout can happen to anyone. They say it's the sickness of the century. With overtime… you never know.

CONRAD You never know.

Scene II

In the garage. CONRAD undresses facing a large, cracked mirror. He puts on coveralls. He takes a cork and burns it. Once it's blackened, he blows on it, waits a while, and then blackens his face. He puts a baseball cap on his head. He looks at himself, happy with what he sees. CONRAD repeats this ritual every time he enters the garage.

He searches through a box, takes out two G.I. Joes and sets them on a work table. He also has a box with a new toy model (a race car) and a tube of glue.

CONRAD *(to his G.I. Joes)* All right. I'm going to tell you about glue. You always always always always have to remember it's poison. It's there in big letters on the tube. There's even a picture… one with a skull with an "X" on top of it. You understand? Good. Sometimes there are exceptions, like when you're gluing paper or cardboard. They're fragile. It takes a lot of patience. I know. But that kind of glue isn't dangerous. You can get it on your fingers. But you have to rub very hard to get it off… sometimes it's like skin. *(He laughs.)* Sorry. A model gluer has to stay cool. Cool. Okay…. How to open a tube of glue safely! You have to read the instructions. Always. Make sure you have a dictionary, in case you don't understand all the words. *(reading)* "Push and unscrew." *(He tries but can't do it.)* Dammit! As if we're going to poison ourselves…. Okay! Once you take the tube out, you have to make a hole with a pin. Don't forget, never ever squeeze the tube or you'll get glue in your eye. Nice way to wind up in the hospital.

Pause.

Now that you understand… right, guys… let's keep going. Always always read the instructions. *(reading)* "Magic Glue required. One tube is enough." It better be. For those of you just starting out in the model-building business, two is acceptable, but not for me. I'm thirty-three years old.

Pause.

Thirty-three thirty-three thirty-three. It's not a nice number. Too many Rs. Rrrr. Rrrrrrrrat. Rat. Rrrridiculous! Rrrrabble. Rrrrrock. Rotten. Roger. Rrrrat. Rat. Rare…. Rrrair. Air… air, there's not enough air in here. I have to buy a fan. I'll talk to Mom about it tomorrow.

Scene III

Break time at the factory.

LYNDA   So, what's your name?

CONRAD   Conrad Boucher.

LYNDA   Hi, my name's Lynda. I've only been working here a week. People aren't too friendly. It's like they don't like their jobs. It's okay here, I guess. A bit hard on the back, but the boss doesn't seem too mean. And at least we get paid. What do you do here?

CONRAD   I stack boxes in the warehouse.

LYNDA   You like it?

CONRAD   I don't know what else there is.

LYNDA   So, you worked here long?

CONRAD   Seventeen years.

LYNDA   Wow…

LYNDA lights a cigarette.

You smoke?

CONRAD   No thanks. My mother says it causes cancer.

LYNDA   Oh, yeah? Well, lately they're saying that about all sorts of stuff. You open your mouth to eat or breathe and… you're signing your death warrant. They want us to stop living. But I say, you got to die of something.

Pause.

Hey! You hear about the girl who got her finger caught in the machine this morning?

CONRAD   Yes, I saw her get into the ambulance.

LYNDA   Was she all right?

CONRAD   I don't know… she wasn't talking. She was white and her lips were blue. The boss had her finger in a plastic bag.

LYNDA   Gross.

CONRAD   It's no big deal, it happens all the time.

LYNDA   Why?

Silence.

Why?

CONRAD   *(whispering)* Some of them sleep on the job. We all end up doing it, sooner or later. You'll see, it'll happen to you.

LYNDA smokes. Pause. Sound of an ambulance siren from far off.

LYNDA   Well then… almost quitting time, huh?

CONRAD   Yes.

LYNDA   What are you doing tonight?

CONRAD   Nothing.

LYNDA   Do you live alone?

CONRAD   No.

LYNDA   Oh, you're married?

CONRAD   No.

LYNDA   Shacked up?

CONRAD   No, I live with my mother.

LYNDA   Oh, yeah? Is she sick?

CONRAD   I don't know, maybe.

She smokes. He looks at the ground. A bell rings, signalling the end of the break.

Scene IV

The kitchen. MOTHER serves dinner. The telephone rings.

MOTHER   Hello? Oh, hi, Rita! What a nice surprise! How are you, dear…? Always good, you know me… Conrad? Not much…. Work. Yeah, that's right, still the same place. So, when are you coming by for a visit? Conrad will be so happy to see you, right Conrad? Conrad, I'm talking to you.

CONRAD   Yes, Mom.

MOTHER   We could play cards, it's been a while. How's Roger? Still depressed? My goodness, what we have to suffer through, huh Rita…. This isn't a life, it's hell… hell… we'll have earned our place in heaven…. Yes…. Yes…. Like me with Conrad…. But what can I do, he's helpless in the kitchen…. And besides, the child is so innocent…. If I wasn't here…. Yeah… yeah… what can I do, I have no choice…

CONRAD starts eating.

Conrad! Wait for me. Really, where are your manners? Oh, nothing, we're about to eat. Yeah, sometimes I wonder if I was really the one who brought him up…. He's like a wild animal. He's never been too social. What about yours? Oh with him it's girls. My goodness…. Lucky for me my Conrad isn't like that, huh Conrad? Conrad, I'm talking to you, are you deaf?

CONRAD   What?

MOTHER   You're not interested in girls, are you?

CONRAD   No no.

MOTHER   Anyway…. So, what else is new? Roger wants to sell his car? Why's that? Oh, he lost his licence… oh well. How much? A thousand… yeah… I'll think it over. Anyway, I've got to go, I'm getting hungry. See you next week, dear. That's right… that's right… okay, bye. Go ahead, Conrad.

Blackout.

The garage. The ritual. CONRAD sets three G.I. Joes on the edge of the table.

CONRAD   When you build a model, I mean when you decide that… uh… I mean when you start, there is one important detail you never forget. Guess. You don't know, huh…. Well too bad for you. You're out! *(He sticks a G.I. Joe to the wall with a strip of tape. He grabs another G.I. Joe.)* What about you? I'm asking you a question! There's one thing you never forget when you start a model. What is it? Idiot! You never know anything. *(He puts him in the garbage and grabs a third one.)* Your turn. What's the answer? I'm talking to you. *(He throws him with all his might.)* No one ever knows anything around here. I'm sick and tired of you. You're not trying hard enough. From now on make an effort. Okay. I'll explain it to you then. *(He picks up the three G.I. Joes and sets them on the table once again.)* Sometimes people spy on you. So keep your pieces in perfect order. All laid out. From left to right, top to bottom. You can even map them out, with a number under each piece.

Like this. Then, if someone goes into your workshop and touches anything, you'll know. You'll always know.

Scene V

Break time at the factory.

CONRAD   I was wondering where you were.

LYNDA   I screwed up. They had to stop production because of me. The boss wasn't happy.

CONRAD   It happens.

LYNDA   Conrad, are they going to fire me?

CONRAD   I don't think so.

LYNDA   I hope not, 'cause I just bought a new kitchen table and chairs. Now I have to pay for it all.

LYNDA looks at CONRAD while she smokes.

CONRAD   What?

LYNDA   Why don't you come over for lunch? I live right next door.

CONRAD   I can't do that.

LYNDA   Come on, I have some leftovers that'll go bad. I can show you my new table and chairs. You'll be the first one to see it all.

CONRAD   I can't. I have my lunch.

LYNDA   You'll eat it tomorrow. Come on, Conrad.

CONRAD   No. I can't.

LYNDA   Come on! What are you afraid of?

CONRAD   Nothing. I'm not afraid of anything.

LYNDA   Well, you're coming then.

Later at LYNDA's.

Yeah, so this is it. As you can tell, I'm not rich but at least there's some colour. *(She shows him her kitchen table and chairs.)* I bought it last week. I wanted to get it in yellow but then I said sky blue'll go great with the white cupboards and dirt won't show. You like it, Conrad?

CONRAD   Oh it's nice. It's really nice.

LYNDA   Well, sit there. I'll heat up our lunch. *(She puts two bowls in the microwave.)* You don't talk much. I barely know anything about you.

CONRAD   I'm boring.

LYNDA But there's gotta be something you really like. Isn't there?

CONRAD Models.

LYNDA Huh?

CONRAD Toy models.

LYNDA Oh! That's nice. Is that what you do in your spare time?

CONRAD Yes. I go in the garage and build models: planes, cars, and spaceships. I even built a miniature house. It had everything—furniture, carpets, paintings… everything.

LYNDA So, you're good with your hands then?

CONRAD Yes, I'm not bad. Once when I was twelve, I won a model-building contest. My mother was proud of me. I was so happy I almost cried.

>   *Pause.*

LYNDA Well… that's nice. What was the prize?

CONRAD Three hundred models. I made them all.

>   *Pause.*

LYNDA But… besides all that, Conrad, do you do other stuff?

CONRAD No.

LYNDA You don't… you know, go out sometimes… I don't know, to bars or out to eat with friends.

CONRAD I don't have friends.

LYNDA Not even one? A buddy… that you see sometimes?

CONRAD No.

LYNDA Oh. That's too bad. I have friends. Not that many, but I really like them. We have a lot of fun sometimes. Once, we drank so much I fell on my ass. I was so embarrassed.

CONRAD I bet.

LYNDA But don't think I drink like that all the time. It's not like I'm an alcoholic or anything, but I think it's good to let loose now and then. Don't you, Conrad?

CONRAD Sure.

LYNDA Sometime, if you feel like it, maybe we can go for a drink somewhere. What do you say?

CONRAD I don't know. I've never drank lots of beers at the same time. My mother has though. She told me.

LYNDA Oh? Well, then I guess she can't be too sick.

CONRAD   It's been a while. Now she just drinks at Christmas.

LYNDA   Christmas! Hey, it's coming soon. I can't wait.

CONRAD   I hate it.

LYNDA   Why? What do you do for Christmas?

CONRAD   My mother and my aunt Rita play cards. I sit and watch them. At midnight we open presents. Then I go to bed.

LYNDA   Poor you! That's no way to live. Why don't you move out?

CONRAD   I don't know.

Scene VI

The kitchen. It is quarter past five.

MOTHER   My goodness, Conrad, do you know what time it is? We eat at five o'clock, you know that. Where have you been?

CONRAD   Sorry, I was daydreaming and missed my stop.

MOTHER   Conrad! You've never done that before! What's the matter? Are you sick? Tired? Maybe I should make an appointment with Dr. Martin, you haven't been for six months.

CONRAD   I'm fine, I swear. I'm just tired.

MOTHER   I'm worried about you. Are you hungry?

CONRAD   What are we having?

MOTHER   Meatloaf.

CONRAD   Oh.

MOTHER   Conrad, I know you don't like it, but you have to eat red meat regularly. Anemia, Conrad.

She serves him. He takes two bites and pushes his plate away.

CONRAD   I'm full.

MOTHER   Conrad, don't make Mommy angry.

He eats.

Good. That's more like it. How was your day?

CONRAD   Good.

MOTHER   Anything new?

CONRAD   No. Oh, yeah. A new girl just started. She's really nice. Her name's Lynda.

MOTHER Oh? How old is she?

CONRAD I don't know, I didn't ask her.

MOTHER Is she middle-aged, or what you might call a spring chicken?

CONRAD Something in between, I guess.

MOTHER A woman in her thirties?

CONRAD Yeah, around there.

MOTHER Be careful, Conrad. They're the most dangerous.

CONRAD Come on, Mom, don't worry. I'm not interested in girls, you know that.

MOTHER I hope so. How about a little piece of cake?

CONRAD No thanks.

MOTHER Really, Conrad, I'm worried about you.

She clears the table.

CONRAD Mom, may I be excused?

MOTHER No.

She serves him tea. She turns on the TV. It's a quiz show. She watches the screen and CONRAD watches her.

Blackout.

Scene VII

The garage. The ritual. He gets a G.I. Joe and a Barbie as well as a box containing a miniature table and two chairs. He speaks for both dolls.

BARBIE Mommy made you ground beef, good ground beef she bought on special at the grocery store, extra lean meat with the Styrofoam packaging all runny with blood. Blood, Conrad: it's good for you.

G.I. JOE I feel sick.

BARBIE There's iron in it, you have to eat meat every day of your life when you're a man.

G.I. JOE I feel sick.

BARBIE You'll lose your hair if you don't eat.

G.I. JOE I don't give a shit.

BARBIE What did you just say?

G.I. JOE I don't give a shit.

BARBIE   I spend all day racking my brains so we can eat a proper meal. It's meat, Conrad.

G.I. JOE   The other day on TV there was a show about butchers, and they showed what ground beef looks like under a microscope.

BARBIE   So?

G.I. JOE   It's full of worms.

BARBIE   Oh, you're so innocent, dear. You shouldn't believe everything they say on TV.

G.I. JOE   You're one to talk!

BARBIE   You better change your tone with me, young man.

G.I. JOE   You make me sick. I can't stand looking at you anymore. I'm getting the hell out of here. You can rot like an old tomato in the fridge.

BARBIE   Now you're going to get it!

CONRAD makes the dolls wrestle. G.I. Joe is winning and CONRAD ties the Barbie to a pipe.

CONRAD   I'm the one in charge.

CONRAD lights a fire in a garbage can and puts it under the Barbie. The smoke alarm goes off.

Fuck.

Blackout.

Scene VIII

Night. MOTHER slowly moves toward the door to CONRAD's room. She opens the door. She sits on the bed and looks at her son.

CONRAD   What are you doing?

MOTHER   You know, Conrad, I was a very beautiful woman.

CONRAD   Yeah?

MOTHER   I used to be more than just your mother.

CONRAD   I know, Mom.

MOTHER   And I have a name. Did you know that?

CONRAD   It's Martha, isn't it? Right?

MOTHER   Yes. Martha Josiane. I dropped the Josiane because it sounded too special. All the girls at the convent laughed at me. They called me "the star."

Back then I had long blond hair. They were all jealous, so my mother cut it off. I cried the whole night.

Pause.

You know what, Conrad? Once I was twenty years old and had dreams.

CONRAD   Like what?

MOTHER   Oh, stupid stuff. I wanted to be a doctor... to heal people when they were sick. I think I would've been good at it, don't you?

CONRAD   Of course. Why didn't you do it?

MOTHER   I got married, got pregnant, and forgot all about it.

CONRAD   Mom, who's my father?

MOTHER   He was a regular guy. A worker. Sometimes he drank too much... so did I back then. Alcohol, Conrad. That's why you're here. Maybe that's why you're such a good boy. Sometimes I wonder if you're even normal.

CONRAD   Where's my father now?

MOTHER   I don't know, Conrad, I really don't know.

She exits.

Scene IX

The garage. The ritual.

CONRAD   Hello, boys! Thanks for coming out in such large numbers for this special class. Today, we're going to tackle one of the most important aspects of the profession: driving. First step: always buckle your seat belt. These days, there's lots of lunatics out there, even on the highways. If one of them runs into you and you forgot to buckle up, your body will squash up against the windshield and, boys, it won't be pretty. We seem solid, but bone, flesh, and skin are like chalk; it all breaks and makes a big mess. So please, let's keep it clean. Once your seat belt is buckled, it's time to start the engine. Be very careful because the engine can be a problem. It can overheat, catch on fire, and the fumes can drive you nuts, burn your brain cells, and after that, hello—goodbye. When the engine's running, that's when real life begins. Everything starts to disappear and nothing matters anymore except speed. And people'll be walking in the street and you won't give a damn. You've got to keep going, keep going, and if someone gets hit, screw them, they shouldn't have been in your way in the first place. Put the pedal to the metal, till nothing else is moving, until there's nothing nothing nothing, no more cars, no people, no city, no mountain, no house, no road, no nothing, nothing but you and speed, and you and you alone sitting in your car with the radio at full blast covering up the screams of the people you left behind. Nothing.

MOTHER *(off)* Conrad, it's midnight, time for bed.

Blackout.

Scene X

Break time at the factory.

LYNDA Conrad, I have something important to tell you.

CONRAD What?

LYNDA Well, I said to myself, Lynda, stop fooling around, you need a change... so I decided to buy myself a VCR.

CONRAD That's great.

LYNDA Isn't it? To celebrate, I decided to invite you over to watch a movie. You can't say no. You're not allowed.

CONRAD Oh... well... thanks. I'd like to but—

LYNDA But what... your mother?

CONRAD No, no, I'll fix things so I can make it.

Scene XI

The kitchen at CONRAD's house. MOTHER is alone, sitting at the table, not moving. There are two plates that are untouched. She's watching a late-night talk show.

Meanwhile, at LYNDA's house.

LYNDA Well, I think that's everything. I have some pop. Do you want some?

CONRAD No thanks.

LYNDA Would you like a beer instead?

CONRAD I don't drink.

LYNDA Okay. *(She opens a beer for herself.)* I rented a movie. I hope you haven't seen it. It's called *A Star Is Born*. With Barbra Streisand, you know, the actress with the big nose. She's an amazing singer. I think it's a love story. You like those, I hope.

CONRAD Sure.

LYNDA Love.... Anyway. What about you, Conrad, uh, a good-looking guy like you, you must've had a lot of girlfriends?

CONRAD No. Never.

LYNDA   Come off it, you're kidding me. Conrad! That's impossible. Not even a little fling?

CONRAD   It happened just once.

LYNDA   Oh, yeah? Was it long ago?

CONRAD   I was around twenty-five years old.

LYNDA   Yeah… and?

CONRAD   It was the girl from across the street. She wanted to get in bed with me. I said yes. Then she started licking me all over my face. It was disgusting. I kept pushing her away but she wouldn't stop. I had to hit her so she'd leave me alone.

LYNDA   Then what happened?

CONRAD   Well, she went home crying, and I stayed in the bathtub for a half-hour.

LYNDA   You mean you never touched a woman in your life, except that one time?

CONRAD   That's right.

Long pause.

LYNDA   Well! I guess I'll start the tape.

Music from the film A Star is Born. *LYNDA starts the popcorn machine. CONRAD stares at the screen blankly.*

Scene XII

CONRAD's bedroom, night. MOTHER enters the room. She watches him sleep.

MOTHER   Conrad! Conrad, wake up!

CONRAD   Yeah?

MOTHER   Now that you're old enough it's time for you to know the truth. Your father was a race-car driver. I never told you but he died in an accident.

CONRAD   When? What are you talking about?

MOTHER   Right before you were born. I was eight months pregnant. All the TV cameras caught every last detail of his death. At the start he was winning. It was his first time in an international race. There were Chinese, American, and French drivers. Everyone was sure he was going to win.

CONRAD   Stop it, Mom. You're not making any sense.

MOTHER   At the start, your father was in the lead; he was the fastest. Then, I don't know what happened. He accelerated and must've blacked out.

CONRAD   Go to bed.

MOTHER His car started skidding. The crowd screamed. Then his car flipped and caught on fire. In two minutes there was nothing left, just a blackened body. Your father burned to death. Like a war hero.

CONRAD Mom, stop bothering me with your stories.

MOTHER One day you're going to die too, Conrad.

Scene XIII

In the kitchen.

MOTHER Hello, dear. Come on in, no use standing out there freezing.

RITA Hello, Martha. Jesus! It's cold as hell.

MOTHER Please watch your language.

RITA Still a saint, aren't you? Well you're not going to change now. Anyway. Well if it isn't the handsome Conrad.

CONRAD Hello, Auntie.

RITA Don't you have a kiss for your godmother? Never mind. If the mountain won't come…

She kisses him passionately on the mouth. He wipes it off.

MOTHER Would you like a coffee?

RITA Sure. You wouldn't happen to have a little cognac to go with it?

MOTHER There's no alcohol here except for the holidays and you know it.

RITA Conrad, would you bring me my purse?

CONRAD Yes, Auntie.

RITA takes a flask of brandy out of her bag and pours a generous slug into her coffee.

RITA Well now I'm ready to start playing. Up to thirteen?

MOTHER Okay.

They play.

So? How's Roger?

RITA Not good at all. Honestly, I don't know what to do with him anymore. He spends the entire day sitting there staring at nothing, and when I try talking to him, he doesn't even answer. Sometimes I think he's lost his tongue.

MOTHER My goodness, Rita, that's awful. Have you tried taking him to the doctor?

RITA Sure I have. I ask him to go every day.

MOTHER   And?

RITA   He doesn't answer.

MOTHER   Well... is he drinking?

RITA   One after the other. I'm telling you, I spend more money on beer than on groceries. I even had to cut back on bingo.

MOTHER   How awful.

RITA   You're telling me. Bingo is my only night out. I barely go anywhere now. Tonight's the first time in a month I've set foot out the door.

MOTHER   If I were you, Rita, I'd get rid of him.

RITA   I think the problem will take care of itself.

MOTHER   How so?

RITA   When he does open his mouth, you know what he says? He wanders around the house screaming "I want to die!" And he smashes whatever he can get his hands on. He even broke my blue vase.

MOTHER   Not the one Mom gave you for your wedding?

RITA   That's the one.

MOTHER   Poor Rita, I don't know what to say.

RITA   Don't say anything and play. Oh, and pass me my purse, why don't you.

Brandy.

MOTHER   Conrad, make yourself useful and heat up our coffee.

CONRAD   Okay.

RITA   And what about you, anything new?

MOTHER   Same old. I keep house and take care of my son. It's boring. But what can I do? At my age, no boss'll want me. All I know how to do is cook and clean.

RITA   Yes, but... I don't know, you should go out. I don't know... go shopping.

MOTHER   You know, Rita, we've got everything we need, but with Conrad's small salary, we barely make ends meet.

RITA   Don't you have a little something tucked away?

MOTHER   No.

RITA   Martha... you told me last Christmas. You have money stashed away somewhere.

MOTHER   Oh that... I can't touch that. I like knowing that if something happens, at least we're not out on the street. And besides, that's money from my late husband.

RITA So what?

MOTHER There's a curse on that money. Something bad will happen to Conrad if I touch it.

RITA What are you talking about? Your husband is dead. He can't hurt you anymore. You should be making the most of it.

MOTHER I guess you're right. It's your turn.

Scene XIV

Early morning. CONRAD's room.

MOTHER Do you know what the date is today, Conrad?

CONRAD November second.

MOTHER And what's special about today?

CONRAD It's All Souls' Day. The Day of the Dead. My thirty-fourth birthday.

MOTHER Mom has a wonderful surprise for her baby boy. Look out the window.

CONRAD What is it? I can't see anything.

MOTHER Tomorrow, you're going to renew your licence.

CONRAD Not the yellow car with a black top? The one parked in front?

MOTHER Look. Here are the keys.

CONRAD You bought me a car? A real one, that moves and makes noise and you can get into?

MOTHER Just for you. But you'll have to be very careful. You know, darling, this represents my entire life savings. Don't do anything crazy, okay! Especially since you haven't driven since your lessons. Be careful, Conrad!

CONRAD Can I go see it right now?

MOTHER Go on, you maniac! After, I'm going to make your favourite breakfast.

CONRAD Thank you.

> *CONRAD looks at the car parked in the street for a long time. He runs his fingers over it and goes into the garage. He performs his usual ritual and lays a multitude of G.I. Joes on the edge of the table.*

Guys, I have brought you here today because our situation has changed. We have received high-tech equipment straight from abroad. This means you'll have to adapt. You'll have to take lessons, and if you can't keep up, too bad. That's life. These are important changes. Now we can start expanding. Expanding. This means we can move out onto the highway. I've spoken to you about that before, but I never thought it could happen... uh... for real. Real. Real real real

real. The idea is to drive as fast as you can and not let yourself get hypnotized by the white line. That's hard at night, 'cause that's all you see. That damned white line gets in your head and makes you crazy. That's all you see. Everything else is melted, warped by speed… you never know, one day we might reach the speed of light. Maybe then we'll disintegrate. Hey guys, maybe I'll take Lynda out for a drive. Where could we go? New York, Paris, Las Vegas, Québec, Chicoutimi, Granby. There's so many places I don't know where to go. Anyway, we'll drive as far as we can, until we're broke. We can tie Mom to the roof like a hunting trophy. *(He laughs.)*

MOTHER *(off)* Conrad, come and eat, I made you pancakes.

Scene XV

Break time at the factory.

LYNDA Hi, Conrad. *(pause)* What's going on? You're smiling like you won a million bucks this morning.

CONRAD I got a car.

LYNDA You bought a car?

CONRAD My mother gave me one for my birthday.

LYNDA Wow, that's great. Now you can get out of town.

Beat.

CONRAD You want to go for a ride?

LYNDA Sure. But not right now.

CONRAD Why not?

LYNDA I want you to come by my place tonight.

CONRAD Yeah, uh… my mother doesn't like it when I go out.

LYNDA Come on, Conrad. Try and get away, okay? I have a surprise for you.

The bell rings, indicating the end of the break. Blackout.

Scene XVI

Early evening. CONRAD goes up to his car. He walks around it, looks at it, and touches the body gently. He goes to the door, opens it, and stands there, frozen, staring at the empty seat. He takes out his keys, shakes them, slams the door, and leaves.

Scene XVII

LYNDA's house. The door is open. A bedroom with soft lighting. LYNDA, dressed in a negligee, is sitting on the bed. CONRAD rings the bell.

LYNDA   Come on in, Conrad!

CONRAD enters.

Hi, Conrad… I was waiting for you.

CONRAD   Lynda? What are you dressed like that for?

LYNDA   Uh… well, this was my surprise. Don't you think it's pretty? *(long pause)* Geez, what's wrong? Are you mad?

CONRAD   No, no, nothing's wrong.

LYNDA   You can sit on the bed.

CONRAD   I think I'll sit on the floor. It's better for your back.

LYNDA   Whatever you want.

Pause.

CONRAD   Do you dress like that a lot?

LYNDA   I did it special for you. Do you like it?

CONRAD   Oh, it's real nice. But… aren't you cold?

LYNDA   No!

CONRAD   I'm always cold. I always wear my long johns. You can catch a cold just stepping out the door. It's better not to take any chances, like my mother says.

LYNDA   Not her again!

CONRAD   She's always worrying about me. She thinks I'm going to break.

Pause.

LYNDA   You're something special. A kind of dinosaur.

CONRAD   I know what you mean.

LYNDA   Hey, are you sure you don't want to sit on the bed?

CONRAD   No. Yes! I'm sure.

LYNDA gets up, puts on her bathrobe and Phentex slippers.

LYNDA   Is this better?

CONRAD   Okay, I'll sit next to you.

LYNDA   Conrad?

CONRAD   Yes?

LYNDA   Are you okay now?

CONRAD   Sure. I'm really comfortable.

LYNDA   Do you want a beer?

CONRAD   No thank you.

LYNDA   Do you want to watch a movie? I got a video.

CONRAD   No, no, that's okay.

Long pause.

LYNDA   Okay. Listen, Conrad, I invited you here tonight because I want you to open your eyes.

CONRAD   My eyes are open.

LYNDA   Conrad?

CONRAD   Yes.

LYNDA   Why do you still live with you mother?

CONRAD   I have no choice.

LYNDA   What do you mean?

CONRAD   I don't know. That's just the way it is.

LYNDA   Why?

CONRAD   How would I know?

LYNDA   Sometimes I wonder if you're alive.

CONRAD   I'm still breathing.

LYNDA   If that's living, I'd rather be dead.

CONRAD   What else do you want me to do?

LYNDA   Be a little happy maybe?

CONRAD   You're asking a lot of questions.

LYNDA   Okay, okay... I'll stop.

Very long pause. He exits.

   (after him) Conrad!

CONRAD   What?

LYNDA   When you get home, look up the word "freedom" in the dictionary.

Scene XVIII

The garage. The ritual. A dictionary is on the table. CONRAD undresses his G.I. Joes and he ties them together two by two. He hangs them from a pipe on the ceiling. He hits them so they swing wildly.

CONRAD Freedom. Freedom freedom. Power. Power to move. Power to choose. Choose. Free. Destroy. Burn. Burn. Destroy. Forced. Tied up. Forced. Controlled. Rocks around your neck. Rocks going through windows.

MOTHER *(knocking on the door)* Conrad!

CONRAD Hold back. Desire. Desire. Want. Want something.

MOTHER Conrad, are you deaf? Open the door, that's an order.

CONRAD Want something tied up in jail burn destroy.

MOTHER Conrad, Mommy is getting angry.

CONRAD Freedom.

MOTHER If you don't open up, I'm selling the car.

CONRAD Freedom.

MOTHER *(screaming and banging on the door with her fists)* Conrad!

Scene XIX

A living room with furniture covered in plastic. CONRAD, MOTHER, and RITA are sitting.

MOTHER I'm so happy to see you, Rita.

RITA Me too, dear. Me too.

MOTHER Conrad, why don't you go and get the hors d'oeuvres from the kitchen.

He goes and gets a tray from the kitchen. After offering some to his mother and his aunt, he sits down.

It's been a long time since we've seen the sun, huh, Rita?

RITA That's for sure. If you ask me, I think it's shy. It's been hiding since the end of August. I'd be surprised if it came out any time soon. In the farmer's almanac, they're predicting the worst winter since '61.

MOTHER The year Conrad was born. I suffered so much.

RITA It really hurts.

MOTHER And no one can take the pain for us.

RITA That's right. They used forceps on Conrad, didn't they?

MOTHER   Yes, dear. After I pushed two days for nothing, the doctor gave up and yanked him out.

RITA   You wanted to stay in there, huh, Conrad? You were all warm and happy and you weren't coming out.

MOTHER   Your aunt Rita is talking to you. Answer, don't be rude.

CONRAD   I don't know. I don't remember.

MOTHER   The doctor was afraid he didn't get enough oxygen.

RITA   That's right, wasn't he supposed to be retarded?

MOTHER   Well, looks like he isn't.

RITA   Looks like. Conrad, are you retarded?

The women laugh.

MOTHER   He is a bit, sometimes. Especially since I bought him his car. There's no doubt about it, he's getting obsessed.

RITA   Do you go cruising around in it, Conrad? You getting more action since you got your car?

MOTHER   Don't start, dear. He hasn't even tried it. He's scared. It's been at least ten years since he drove last.

RITA   Oh yeah? Well well well. So, Conrad… you're chicken.

CONRAD   Mind your own business.

MOTHER   What? What did you just say?

CONRAD   Mind your own business.

MOTHER   That's not how I brought you up. Go to you room. I don't want to see your face until dinner.

CONRAD exits.

RITA   My goodness, what got into him?

MOTHER   I have no idea, Rita, but let me tell you, he's not going to get away with it. He better change his attitude or else.

Scene XX

At LYNDA's.

LYNDA   Well, look who's here. Hey, what's wrong?

CONRAD collapses into a chair.

Do you want a beer?

CONRAD   Yeah.

LYNDA Here. You don't look so hot.

CONRAD Lynda, I feel like throwing myself to the bottom of the St. Lawrence.

LYNDA Conrad… what's wrong? Did you have a fight with your mother?

CONRAD No no.

LYNDA Then why are you saying that?

CONRAD I feel like smashing everything.

LYNDA Conrad, calm down. Talk to me. Why do you feel so crappy?

CONRAD My mother… my mother was playing cards with my aunt Rita and they were talking and then they started saying stupid fucking shit. I hate them.

LYNDA Conrad, you just have to get out of there. It's normal that you can't stand your parents when you're thirty. I left way before that. And if you don't have anywhere to go, you can stay here, there's room on the couch.

CONRAD I can't.

LYNDA But you can't stay there until you retire. Get off your ass and get the hell out of there. I'll help you.

CONRAD It's no use. I'm dead. Give me another beer.

LYNDA You're not dead. You're just fed up.

CONRAD I feel empty, I feel so empty. Please, Lynda, give me a beer.

LYNDA Okay, okay. But Conrad, you have to cheer up. Don't let yourself get like this. I'm sure you can find a way to be happy. I don't know. Isn't there something you'd really like to do?

CONRAD No.

LYNDA Come on, just try.

CONRAD chugs his beer.

CONRAD I'd like to be a race-car champion, then I'd be on TV and everyone would applaud and…

LYNDA And everyone would love you. That's what you need… a little bit of love.

CONRAD Don't ever say that word in front of me.

LYNDA Why? Why not?

Pause.

CONRAD Because it makes me feel like killing.

Pause. LYNDA gets up and puts on some music.

LYNDA Come on. Let's dance. Words hurt too much.

They dance. Lights go down slowly.

Interlude

MOTHER Alcohol turns man into a beast and often leads to his death.

Scene XXI

Late at night. CONRAD enters his room staggering. His mother, in her nightclothes, is sitting on the bed.

MOTHER Where were you?

CONRAD Work.

MOTHER Liar.

CONRAD I swear.

MOTHER Liar. You were at Lynda's. I know it. And you were drinking. Tell Mommy the truth, ungrateful child.

CONRAD I have nothing to say. I have absolutely nothing to say.

His mother grabs him by the hair and smashes him against the wall. He laughs.

MOTHER Goddamned hypocrite. Treating your mother like this after all I've done for you. You lied to me. To me. You go out with women without telling me, and worse, you go out with women who have no class. You think I'm so stupid I won't notice. You're a worthless bastard just like your father. You'd like it if I died, huh, then you could be up to your tricks all day long. Well I have no intention of dying. I'll bury you, as God as my witness.

She exits and locks the door.

CONRAD Mom, open the door.

MOTHER You'll leave your room when I say you can.

Scene XXII

The next day. CONRAD's room. MOTHER slides a plate under the door.

MOTHER You're going to eat. It's the only thing that matters now. Eating three meals a day. Health, Conrad.

CONRAD waits until his mother has gone. He looks at the plate and spits on it. He waits. Later, he tries to dismantle the lock, unsuccessfully. The sun sets and it gets darker and darker. CONRAD lies down.

Scene XXIII

LYNDA knocks on the door to CONRAD's apartment. MOTHER goes to open it.

MOTHER   Go away, we don't want anything.

LYNDA   I don't want to sell you anything. I'm Lynda, a friend of Conrad's from work.

MOTHER   Oh, it's you.

LYNDA   What's wrong with him, is he sick?

MOTHER   Yes, that's right.

LYNDA   Can I come in? I'd like to see him. I brought him a little present.

MOTHER   He's not here. He's in the hospital. I'll take the present and give it to him for you.

LYNDA   I'd like to give it to him myself. Which hospital is he at?

MOTHER   It doesn't matter. He's coming back tonight.

LYNDA   Oh yeah? What time?

MOTHER   I don't know.

LYNDA   Fine. I guess he'll be back at work soon.

MOTHER   Who knows.

LYNDA   Is it serious?

MOTHER   They say it's in his head.

LYNDA   You sure it's not in yours?

MOTHER   You've got some nerve! Mind your own business!

LYNDA tries to force her way in. MOTHER slams the door on her fingers and locks it.

LYNDA   Ow!

MOTHER   Get out of here or I'm calling the police.

LYNDA   You old bag!

She leaves.

Scene XXIV

CONRAD's room.

CONRAD's sitting on the floor. There are fifteen untouched plates on the floor.

CONRAD   I hear the snow falling. *(He laughs.)* There's not enough for them to use the snow blower yet. Maybe tomorrow? I can wait for a long time. Until Christmas… Christmas… I have to kiss my mom and Aunt Rita. Yuck! Aunt Rita smells like cheap perfume. And Mom… she always smells like ground beef. She makes me sick. What am I going to do? I don't want to be here anymore. It stinks.

    CONRAD hits his head against the wall. He hears voices.

MOTHER   Thirty years of sacrifice, Conrad. Thirty years.

LYNDA   Get off your ass and leave, that's all.

MOTHER   Worthless. Just like your horrible father.

RITA   You were happy in there. You didn't want to come out.

MOTHER   Your father was a race-car driver. He was burned alive like a war hero.

LYNDA   Come on, Conrad, come on, come on, come on.

MOTHER   Conrad, finish what's on your plate.

RITA   Your husband's dead, he can't hurt you anymore.

MOTHER   I suffered so much.

LYNDA   You never had sex?

RITA   When he was little he had the devil in him. A real terror.

MOTHER   Conrad, don't be rude.

LYNDA   You never had sex?

MOTHER   Finish what's on your plate.

RITA   Don't you have a kiss for your aunt Rita?

LYNDA   Say yes, Conrad, say yes.

MOTHER   A sin of the flesh before marriage, a sin.

RITA   They had to yank him out…. Forceps…

MOTHER   He didn't get enough oxygen. No wonder he's a little retarded.

LYNDA   Conrad! Conrad!

RITA   You getting more action since you got your car?

MOTHER   Nails, Conrad. Conrad, finish your food. Hands, Conrad.

LYNDA, MOTHER, RITA   Conrad, are you retarded?

CONRAD   *(screaming)* I'm in charge!

    He collapses. The door opens slowly. MOTHER enters.

MOTHER My goodness! *(She checks to see if he's breathing.)* My baby... my big baby... if only you knew how much I love you.

She strokes his hair. He regains consciousness.

CONRAD What do you want?

MOTHER I'm letting you out. It's over. You can come out.

CONRAD Oh.

MOTHER There's just one thing.

CONRAD What?

MOTHER I don't want you to see Lynda ever again.

CONRAD Okay.

MOTHER Come with Mommy to the kitchen and I'll make you something to eat. Then you'll clean your room.

CONRAD Okay.

Scene XXV

Night. CONRAD looks at his car. He takes out his keys and sits in it. Blackout.

Scene XXVI

The garage. The ritual. He goes and sits at his work table.

CONRAD Is anyone here? Guys? Come here! Stop hiding like a bunch of idiots! It's me! I'm back! *(CONRAD opens a box containing a model and starts to cut out the pieces. Then he gets a G.I. Joe and sets him on the table.)* You make it, okay? I can't. I'm sick of doing it. *(pause)* Come on! You do it! *(pause)* What's the matter? Oh, you don't remember. You don't know how. You think you're too dumb. You didn't go to school long enough. *(Pause. He hits his fist on the table.)* You little shits! Now you're going to get it! *(He gets a little model house.)* Thirty years of sacrifice, huh! Here! *(He destroys it.)* Where did you all go, you bastards? *(He empties a box full of G.I. Joes on the floor.)* Bunch of pussies. I'm going to teach you a lesson. *(He gets an axe and chops them to bits. Suddenly, one of them attracts his attention.)* You. You. I don't know where you came from but... oh yeah... you showed up on my tenth birthday. You're special... a real army guy. A general. Fred... always stronger than the others. Always won all the fights. You always talked louder than the others. Once, you even jumped in the pool to save another soldier. I remember, I almost drowned when I saved you. I forgot I didn't know how to swim. *(pause)* I don't know how to swim.

Scene XXVII

At the factory.

LYNDA Conrad. Conrad? Hey, dummy, I'm talking to you! Are you deaf?

CONRAD Leave me alone, I'm not allowed to talk to you.

LYNDA What do you mean?

CONRAD Go away and stop asking me questions.

LYNDA Oh no. No way. Conrad, I know you weren't sick. Your mother did something. I'm right, aren't I?

CONRAD Yes.

LYNDA Your mother found out you came over to my place and she locked you up, right?

CONRAD Yeah.

LYNDA And now, she doesn't want you to see me anymore or talk to me or anything? That it?

CONRAD Yeah.

LYNDA Look, I'm not going to play this game. I mean, your mother hasn't hired spies to watch you, has she?

CONRAD Maybe. You never know.

LYNDA Okay, now stop it and come sit down. That's an order.

CONRAD goes and sits next to LYNDA. He looks at the floor. Pause.

Sorry. I didn't want to be mean.

CONRAD That's okay.

LYNDA I went to your house when you were sick.

CONRAD I didn't know.

LYNDA I really think your mother's crazy.

CONRAD Yeah, so?

LYNDA Well, I just wanted to say that if you ever want to come to my place until you find something, it's okay.

CONRAD Okay.

Bell rings—end of the break.

Scene XXVIII

In the kitchen.

MOTHER   Hello, dear.

CONRAD   Hello.

MOTHER   Sit down. We're eating shepherd's pie tonight. Isn't that nice?

CONRAD   Yeah.

MOTHER   You know, Conrad, it'll be Christmas soon.

CONRAD   Yeah.

MOTHER   Did you have a nice day? You seem strange.

CONRAD   Yeah? Oh.

MOTHER   Of course it's hard to start working again after you've been sick. Do you feel better now, Conrad?

CONRAD   Yes. I feel better.

MOTHER   Good. Then why aren't you eating!

CONRAD   Mom…

MOTHER   Oh, of course… I know what you want.

She sits next to him and feeds him.

It's much easier this way.

MOTHER gets up and goes to wash the plates.

You can go play in the garage if you want. Mommy gives you permission.

CONRAD   Thank you.

The garage. The ritual.

CONRAD puts the only G.I. Joe that's left (Fred) on the edge of the table.

Fred. Fred. What are we going to do tonight? All the others are dead. There's just you and me. I don't think I have any models left. I made them all. I thought maybe, if Mom goes to bed early, maybe I could show you my car. I could show you how to start the engine. You know, Fred, I have a car now. But I've never touched it. I have the keys. *(He shakes the key ring.)* That noise, Fred, that noise… I've been waiting to hear it for years. It's like music. Come with me, buddy. We're going to see the highway.

He goes up to his car. He unlocks the door and gets in front of the wheel. He hangs Fred from the mirror. He tries to start the car. It doesn't start.

What the hell. Fucking piece-of-shit car.

    MOTHER comes out of the house.

MOTHER   Conrad! It's too late to go driving. Come inside this instant.

CONRAD   It doesn't even work.

MOTHER   That car works all right, you just don't know how to drive anymore. Come on in. It's time for bed, dear.

CONRAD   You're nothing but a big fat liar. You made me think it was a real car, but it's just a toy.

MOTHER   Now that's enough, Conrad. Go to bed. You have work tomorrow.

CONRAD   No.

MOTHER   Now don't make Mommy lock you up again, Conrad. Come with me.

CONRAD   No.

MOTHER   Okay, well, then I'm going to have to punish you.

CONRAD   Go ahead and try.

    MOTHER goes back inside the house.

Scene XXIX

    CONRAD's room. Night. CONRAD is sleeping. His mother comes in and sits on his bed.

CONRAD   What are you doing?

MOTHER   I'm watching you sleep.

CONRAD   Why?

MOTHER   It's an old habit. I listen to you breathe. I've done it since you were small. I was afraid you'd die in your sleep. The Creviers's baby died like that. And you were the only person I really had, well… I don't sleep much anyway.

CONRAD   'Cause you're not tired enough?

MOTHER   Oh that's not it. I think about all sorts of things. Sometimes, I get so mad…

CONRAD   At me?

MOTHER   Of course not.

CONRAD   Then why?

MOTHER   Oh it's nothing. I'm mad at life. It's so boring. Sometimes I can't stand it. I'd like to erase everything. Take a big sponge and wipe the board clean. In school, the nuns always asked me to clean the board. I liked doing it. I felt like

I was starting from scratch. The lesson was over, the nun's voice wasn't echoing in the classroom anymore, and the boring hour we just spent no longer existed. Sometimes the marks stayed on the board, especially when they wrote with coloured chalk. They made a strange code like... hieroglyphics... that's it. You know that Egyptian writing?

CONRAD Yeah.

MOTHER Anyway. Sleep, Conrad. You have to work tomorrow.

She exits.

Scene XXX

The next day. Kitchen.

MOTHER You know, Conrad, I've been thinking. I think it's time you and me got out of the apartment. I've decided we're going to eat at St-Hubert Bar-B-Q tonight. What's the matter? Aren't you happy? Don't you like St-Hubert?

CONRAD No no, that's not it. I'm just tired. You go.

MOTHER I'm not going to leave you here alone. You don't want to go out? Fine. We'll stay home where it's warm. You and me. We'll whip up something quick for dinner.

MOTHER takes out various canned goods that she opens and pours into a large bowl. She mixes everything and places the bowl in front of CONRAD. Then she turns both the radio and the TV on at full volume.

(*yelling*) Bon appétit!

CONRAD gets up very slowly. He turns off the TV and the radio, then he goes to his room. He comes back after a few moments with some things in a plastic bag.

What are you doing, Conrad?

CONRAD I'm leaving.

MOTHER Where to?

CONRAD Somewhere else.

MOTHER You're not going anywhere. Is that clear?

CONRAD Let me by.

MOTHER No.

CONRAD pushes her and leaves the room.

CONRAD I'm stronger than you. It's useless to try and lock me up.

MOTHER Conrad, you can't. Go back to your room immediately, that's an order.

CONRAD I'm leaving, Mom.

MOTHER You're abandoning me! At my age! After all the years I spent slaving over you!

CONRAD Yes.

MOTHER Conrad, if you do this I'll kill myself.

CONRAD You're already dead.

MOTHER Go ahead. Get out of here. You're worthless, just like your father. You'll start drinking and they'll find you choked to death on your own vomit in an alley. That's all your father was, Conrad. A loser, a man, beaten by life, who drank and smacked me around just to let off steam. Your father was nothing but a wimp, less than half a man. And you're going to wind up just like him. A frozen corpse that no one notices. It took a week before they found him, you understand? That's life, Conrad. As goddamned sad and shitty as that.

CONRAD disappears into the garage.

Don't go don't go don't go…

He comes out with an axe and goes toward the car.

Conrad! What are you doing! Don't do anything stupid, you'll end up in jail. Conrad!

CONRAD starts to hit the car with the axe.

Stop that right now, Conrad. That's an order.

CONRAD Here's the dash, Mom. Watch out, it's sharp. Catch.

MOTHER You can't. It's my car.

CONRAD A gift is a gift. It's too late. Here. *(He throws a piece of tire at her.)* You can sell the tires.

MOTHER You crazy bastard, you're going to get it. Thirty years! Thirty years of my life for this.

CONRAD Here, take your car! Here! The muffler, the gas tank, the windshield, the velour back seat! They'll all go really nice in the living room with the other furniture. You can put plastic on it all to keep it clean.

MOTHER You're going to pay for this.

CONRAD throws the air freshener at his mother.

CONRAD Give this to Aunt Rita. It'll cover up her perfume.

MOTHER Conrad! Come back here this instant! Don't leave me alone. Conrad!

Scene XXXI

CONRAD knocks on LYNDA's door. She's not there. He knocks again, then he sits in the hallway. He waits. We hear LYNDA coming up the stairs singing. She's a bit tipsy.

LYNDA   Who's there?

CONRAD   It's me.

LYNDA   Me who?

CONRAD   Conrad.

LYNDA   What are you doing lying on the floor!

CONRAD   I came to your house. I didn't know where else to go.

LYNDA   Your mother kicked you out?

CONRAD   I left.

LYNDA   Oh yeah? I can't believe it. You finally made up your mind? Hey, that's great. Come in, come on, we're going to celebrate. I think I have a half a bottle of gin left…

Scene XXXII

The next day, at the kitchen table.

LYNDA   I can't believe it… you've only been here a day and I've started looking at new clothes. Now that we'll be sharing the expenses, we'll finally be able to dress the way we want, huh, Conrad?

CONRAD   That's true.

LYNDA   If you want, tomorrow is payday. We could go shopping together, it'll be so much fun. You could look for stuff, too. I think there's a sale on for men now. Then, when we go out, we'll look nice. Of course, we can't dress up for work. It's dirty and people might get jealous. *(pause)* What time is it?

CONRAD   Five past seven.

LYNDA   I'm so excited you're here I almost forgot about my show. You coming, Conrad?

CONRAD   No no, uh, I'd rather stay here.

LYNDA   You don't know what you're missing.

She goes into the living room. We hear the sound of a TV quiz show.

CONRAD is sitting in the kitchen. He pokes at the food on his plate. He picks the plate up, empties it into the garbage, and goes back and sits down. He looks around. We hear LYNDA cheering on the

> *contestants in the living room. CONRAD gets Fred and puts him on the table. He looks in the living room from time to time to make sure LYNDA isn't going to come in.*

CONRAD   Look at us, huh, Fred? You hear me? People are out in the alley. There's snow, but there's still some pavement…. Girls are playing elastics. They're happy. They have no idea what's waiting for them. I wanted to play elastics too. But boys didn't play that. We played jungle. We all hid in the ravine and some of us were hunters and others were animals. I climbed trees and growled like a wild animal. When they caught you, which never took long, you had to run away as fast as possible and hide in the rink. I always got beat up by Serge. One time, he caught me and he started punching me in the face. I got so mad I bit him until he bled. I wouldn't let go, he had to beg me. I was really a tiger. I liked the taste of his blood in my mouth. He cried like a baby. Now he's in jail. He robbed a corner store and got caught. That's the way it is, Fred. You always get caught.

> *LYNDA appears in the doorway.*

LYNDA   You want to come for a walk, Conrad?

Scene XXXIII

> *The next evening. CONRAD and LYNDA are in bed.*

LYNDA   Conrad?

CONRAD   Yes?

LYNDA   Would you get me a glass of water?

CONRAD   Yes.

LYNDA   What are we doing tomorrow?

CONRAD   I don't know.

LYNDA   We have to do something.

CONRAD   Why?

LYNDA   It's Saturday.

CONRAD   I never do anything on Saturday. Or Sunday.

LYNDA   Well that's going to change. You'll learn.

CONRAD   Sure.

LYNDA   Maybe we could go to the country? I haven't been for a while. How about it, Conrad?

CONRAD   What'll we do there?

LYNDA   I don't know. We'll find something, someplace to go. *(pause)* Say yes, Conrad!

CONRAD   Yes.

LYNDA   This is so great. We can wear our new clothes. Aren't you happy?

CONRAD   Yeah…. What you made me buy is really nice, but I don't feel comfortable like that. I feel like a mannequin in a window…

LYNDA   You'll see, Conrad, I'll teach you how to have taste in clothes…. It'll feel weird at first, but pretty soon, you'll like dressing in style.

CONRAD   You think?

LYNDA   Promise. Well, goodnight. Don't dream too much, you know how it wakes me up.

CONRAD   Don't worry. I'll be quiet.

> *LYNDA falls asleep. CONRAD gets up and goes to the kitchen table. He puts Fred on the edge of the table.*

I want to go back to my workshop and wait for the smell of the garage to fill me up and make me explode.

Scene XXXIV

At the Granby zoo.

LYNDA   Look how funny they are, Conrad. I'm going to give them some peanuts.

CONRAD   Careful, Lynda, maybe monkeys bite.

LYNDA   No way! They're used to it. Come here, you, come here. Ow! Oh well, you were right. He bit me.

CONRAD   Is it bleeding? Show me. It's nothing, Lynda, he just scratched you.

LYNDA   You're not getting any more peanuts, you bastard!

CONRAD   Don't yell at him. He doesn't understand.

LYNDA   You dirty little monkey! Here! You want some peanuts?! *(She throws them at its head.)*

CONRAD   Calm down, the security guards will throw us out if you keep acting like that.

LYNDA   Don't you tell me how to behave.

CONRAD   That's not what I'm saying. I just don't want any problems.

LYNDA   Problems, problems… you're the problem.

CONRAD   What do you mean? I didn't do anything.

LYNDA Exactly, you never do anything.

CONRAD What do want me to do?

LYNDA Get off your ass instead of talking to yourself in the middle of the night.

CONRAD runs away.

Conrad! I'm sorry! I didn't mean it. I didn't mean it, Conrad!

They wander apart and both get lost in the zoo.

CONRAD ends up facing a couple of tigers in their cage, protected by a fence. He climbs the fence. He goes over to the tigers very slowly, until he is touching the cage.

CONRAD You know. You know how things work.

He slips his hand in between the bars to pet their fur.

Scene XXXV

CONRAD, his arm in a sling, sitting up in bed. LYNDA gets ready for bed.

LYNDA Conrad Boucher, I can't take you anywhere. What were you thinking? Going to pet the tigers…. Sometimes, I wonder if there's anybody home. Why did you do that?

CONRAD I wanted to stay with them.

LYNDA You want to eat raw meat and stay locked in a cage? That's so dumb. Anyway. I have to sleep.

CONRAD Goodnight.

CONRAD gets up. He paces around the apartment, turns on the TV, turns it off, opens the fridge, opens a beer.

Yuck!

He pours the beer into the sink. He goes to get Fred.

You never saw a tiger have you, Fred? That's an animal I like. They don't let anyone get to them. When tourists try to take their pictures, they roar and try to bite them and scratch them through the bars. *(He laughs.)* Look at this, Fred! They almost ripped my arm off when I tried to pet them. They're beautiful even if they're mean and their fur is all matted with blood. Even with the bits of flesh stuck in their teeth. Hey, when I went near the cage, there was a tiger who looked at me and talked to me. He said I should go visit him one night and open his cage. Then, he'd give me a big hug and we'd go into town and we'd bust everything up. After that, when the sun came up, he'd slit my throat with his scissor teeth while I stuck a knife in his neck. We'd die in a pool of blue blood (tigers have blue blood, he told me) and I'd be so messed up no one would be able to recognize me, that's how ugly I'd be. I'd really like to be ugly. Then, no one would bother me anymore and I could just hide in my hole. But I don't have a hole anymore. I can't hide. I'm like a turtle on its back. I can't turn over. Shit, shit, shit. How can I turn over? The sun's coming up, I don't want to see the light. Fred! Help me! Tell me what to do!

Long pause. CONRAD gets a jerry can full of gas and douses Fred.

Fred, Mom, Lynda, then me. A bunch of tigers in a cage out of breath from going round and round. Sun's coming up, I don't want to see the light. Fred, Mom, Lynda, then me. Fred, you first. You were always the strongest…

He sets Fred on fire. Blackout.

The end.

Earthbound
(Violette sur la terre)

by Carole Fréchette

translated by John Murrell

Introduction to
Earthbound (Violette sur la terre)

Earthbound by Carole Fréchette is a compelling dramatization of the search for meaning in life and a place in society when everything seems to be lost, even one's sense of being alive. The radical loss for four of the characters in the play was caused by the closing of the mine, the main employer, in their northern community. Fréchette's play explores the impact of this devastating event, which has now had enough time to worm its way into the psyche of individuals and throughout the community, on the sense of self and of place, the ability to care and to love, the possibility of hope, the kind of desperation that produces violence, the fracturing of social bonds, and the silences that accompany alienation. Although the characters are all in the dark, they cannot avoid the fact that they are at a critical moment in their lives when they must make choices. They are asking themselves how they can recognize the right choices for themselves: are there words to express what they are going through? can renewed relationships with others offer the promise of happiness in the future? should they stay or should they go? is there any way, short of blowing everything up, to address and resolve at least some of the injustices of which they are victims? Their frank and quiet courage in addressing these difficult questions, none of which can have definitive answers, is a spectacular celebration of the resilience of the human spirit in people who wish nothing more than to live lives of dignity and compassion. This courage is apparent despite the conflictual situations that beset them as they move ahead with their lives.

Violette sur la terre was commissioned in 1999 by theatre companies in three mining communities in Canada and France (Sudbury, Ontario; Rouyn-Noranda, Québec; Roubaix, France). Fréchette visited all three communities, meeting several women and men in them. Despite this real point of departure and the relevance of the dramatic action for the people living in these real places, the play is not a realistic representation of the lives of those Fréchette met. These lives are magically transformed into the theatrical representation of universal themes—solitude, loss, silence, inability to communicate, pain, yearning for love, doubt, inextinguishable rage, violence, compassion, hope. The characters confront the particular manifestation of these themes in their own existence and realize that they have choices they must make and that they, singly and collectively, control their own destiny.

Earthbound has no divisions into acts or scenes. The events of the play take place over a hot summer of an otherwise unspecified year in a landscape that has the appearance of a wasteland—"there"—initially so dark that neither the characters nor the audience know with certainty where "there" is. Like the narrow, personal horizons of the characters when the play opens, the set's horizons cannot be seen. It is "pitch black." The featureless landscape feels initially like an environment of dread where all the characters feel the urge to burst into tears or as though, as Violet says and repeats: "you've got this lake inside you and it's overflowing." The first light seen in this darkness is the tiny flame of a lighter. The play moves somewhat toward greater illumination, but never departs from the connection with the dark depths of the old mine on which the characters play out their stories. They know each other and they meet in fleeting encounters in this mysterious place, but they distrust and avoid each other, do not initially count on each other for support, and do not come together for a conversation until the final sequence, when they seek shelter from the approaching downpour in the still dangerous mine shaft.

The first character to appear is Paul, who is haunted by the memory of having been buried during a mine cave-in. He expresses the inexplicably urgent call he felt to come to this dark place, and he speaks of the song going around in his head, Pete Seeger's "Where Have All the Flowers Gone?" The haunting lyrics of this song, like Jean-Baptiste Clément's "Le Temps des cerises," which Fréchette chose for the original in French—both are simultaneously love songs and protest songs—introduce into the fabric of *Earthbound* the conflict that runs throughout human affairs between beauty, love, and a life lived with meaning and the chaos caused by war, injustice, exploitation, and violence. "Where Have All the Flowers Gone?" weaves its way throughout *Earthbound*, and two of its stanzas are finally sung in unison by four of the characters. Early in the play, Paul hears the echo of the song's second verse: "Where have all the young girls gone,/Long time passing," but is unable to find the remaining words of the song. His search for the words in the song resonates with the characters' search for meaning, purpose, and love in their difficult lives: "What comes next?"

The unresolvable absurdity of the human condition, in the sense of Samuel Beckett's theatre of the absurd, and the power of the human spirit in its refusal to be defeated by this absurdity, even if such resistance seems futile and insignificant, is highlighted by Fréchette at several moments, as, for example, in this exchange between the violently cynical Steve and the gently optimistic Paul:

> **STEVE** Great. You sang. What now? What did it change?
> **PAUL** Nothing, Steve. Nothing changed. But we sang.

Paul is the first to sense an unfamiliar human presence in the darkness on stage: "I heard a noise. Like somebody breathing. Real close by." Paul is followed into the dark stage space by, progressively, Steve, who's "got a knife twisting around inside [his] head," Marie, who compulsively follows Steve, her husband, and Judith, who relives the intense pain and pleasure of orgasm and wonders if that's all there is. The presence of whom Paul becomes progressively aware is that of the ephemeral Violet, with her "funny little hat," met earlier by Steve, who explains to her the constant outrage he feels because of widespread injustice, hypocrisy, and apathy that have caused him to turn into a mad man: "As if I'm the crazy one, as if there isn't enough ugliness on earth to make anybody permanently mad. It's the calm ones who give me a laugh, the ones who refuse to look at... at the aberrations of the earth." As a man of action and very few words, Steve stops to reflect on the big word *aberrations*, in which he feels he has captured all the "ugliness on earth" in a nutshell. In doing so, he draws attention to one of the play's major themes: the importance of words to give meaning and make communication possible. It could happen that aberrations will be corrected if they are named and discursively recorded. This emphasis on the search for words, for the right words that speak truth and are powerful enough to illuminate the meaning of one's own life and bring people together, places language at the heart of what it means to be human and to dream of a brighter future.

As the characters interact with the enigmatic and taciturn Violet, they share their yearnings, personal secrets, and fears with her in ways they cannot talk about with anyone else, not even those with whom they are most intimate. They perceive her as having experienced the same frustrations they have known and as being the key to their release from unhappiness. In their eyes, she is the reflection of all they have been and long to be, the only person who understands them and knows what they should do, who is in a position to assist them to move on. She is the aura of beauty and love that has vanished from their lives. They project their will to understand their own longings and actions and their visions for a way out of their impasse onto her. They treat her like a friend and bring her gifts, hoping she will use and share them and also that she will agree to accompany them in their personal quest. This fantasy is quite contrary to her own representation of herself. She never makes any claims to have transcendent symbolic status. However, the fantasy itself proves too performative for the other characters. Thus, in addition to being a fascinating focal point for the ambiguity, thematics, and dramatic conflict in *Earthbound*, Violet functions as an exutory, by means of whom the other characters are moved to articulate and contemplate their pain and powerlessness and also to explore the choices available to them.

Like the millions of people caught in Haiti's devastating earthquake in early 2010, Paul tells Violet he feels as though his life has caved in and he has joined the living dead. He longs for reassurance that he actually exists:

> Do you ever feel like, maybe, you've disappeared? I mean, when it gets so dark that you can't see anything, and maybe the world's disappeared and you have too? A thousand feet below the surface of the earth, there's suddenly a cave-in, and a ton of rock falls on top of you, and all at once there's no floor, there's no ceiling—you've got no arms, no legs, no face, just a bit of brain with a song stuck inside it [...] there's no more minutes, no more seconds, no more need to scream, to cry, or to be afraid—just this feeling that you don't exist, that you're just one more rock among all the other rocks, way down deep there.

Paul longs for the nearness of a woman who would reach out and touch him and so restore his lost vitality. Marie, who desired fruitlessly to have children, is "always dreaming of getting away but never going," while Judith, not knowing who she really is and doubting that the social myths surrounding sex, marriage, and motherhood will bring their promised dreams ("Sure, but what if...?"), seeks both authentic affection and an inexplicable beyond she can only glimpse occasionally. She knows that the life well lived is made from choices, but what if you choose poorly? Are you, as so many of us are forced to ask ourselves in mid-life, permanently stuck: "How many lives can you live? [...] If you've made bad choices, can you choose over again? Or is it... terminal?"

Despite the characters' delusions about her, Violet makes no claim to being the paragon they see in her, nor to having made good choices in her life. She repeats on several occasions, enigmatically: "I have made a mistake." Her notebook, filled presumably with a record of all her experiences, shows that she has scratched them all out, leaving only the same statement: "I have made a mistake. Sorry." Judith describes Violet as "a woman who writes her story, her thoughts, her love, all the little details of her life, then scratches it out, line after line." At one final moment, Violet offers an explanation for her uncompromising position of isolation and refusal to join the human parade. Her explanation draws attention to the dark, physical place of the abandoned mine and sees in it a metaphor for the dark psychic place produced by human stupidity and the human condition:

> I scratched it all out because... it was not right [...] My words, my tunes, are all wrong, like an out-of-tune violin. A violin that you want to smash on a rock—break into a thousand pieces [...] If I say "I had the words, millions of words in my head, on my lips, in my notebooks, to explain the world, but they slipped away and got lost"—that sounds wrong [...] If I say "I have looked at the dead fields, the slag heaps, the abandoned mine deep inside me, the plants which will never again sprout inside my head, inside my heart"—it sounds wrong [...] I've lost my words, my tunes in the right key, I am lost, I am all alone...

While the characters' difficult material situation is not ameliorated in the end, their perception of it and their belief in their own shared ability to bring about change has been transformed by their courage, honesty, lucidity, tenacity, and recognition of each other. It is only in their resilience and awareness that real hope lies. Along with the "ugliness, hypocrisy, and dishonesty" that has obsessed Steve from the start, Marie sees "beauty, goodness, courage, and walking away." After five months of neither touching each other nor talking to each other, she and Steve are speaking directly again. Like Marie, Paul has come to hope, using the image of sunlight: "There's a square of sunlight on the wooden floor—and it makes you want to go on living. Even though you're lying there with your bones aching and your mind full of darkness—it makes you want to go on living." Nevertheless, great uncertainty remains, and as Judith's enigmatic answer shows, none of them has yet found the precise question underlying their search for meaning and proper choices: "I said to myself, 'If it's in Violet's slice, then the answer is "No." If it's in my slice, then the answer is "Yes" [...] If nobody gets it, then it's "Maybe."'"

As mortal beings we all have unspoken longings so powerful they could disrupt the course of our life. These longings catch us in the middle of our thoughts and conversations; they surge forth at the sight of an image, object, or person; they wake us up in the night, making sleep impossible, forcing us to get up, probably without knowing where we need to go. These longings have links with our sense of self and purpose in life, our physical being, our relations with others, the love and affection we need and receive, our memories, our place in the world, and the feeling that the work we do is contributing to our own well-being while making a difference, however small, in the world. Although such longings can never be entirely and definitively gratified, they provide the motivation and psychic energy that give our lives coherence and meaning. They bring hope when we seem to get one step closer to them as we travel along life's path.

But sometimes events occur that can only be seen as terrible setbacks in the direction our longings have been carrying us. Such events are particularly terrible when they are created by forces beyond our control. The longings to which we have been responding as we construct the meaning of our lives—which we have felt without necessarily giving words to them even for ourselves—suddenly become urgent needs at such moments, demanding realization in the very situations where their objectives seem most out of reach. The trauma of the immediate problem must be dealt with, while at the same time the present crisis may well risk bringing all other needs, desires, and losses crashing in to demand attention and resolution, as they do theatrically in *Earthbound*.

About Carole Fréchette

Award-winning playwright Carole Fréchette was born in Montréal and is a graduate in acting of the École Nationale du Théâtre/National Theatre School. She was a founding member of the Théâtre des Cuisines between 1973 and 1980 and participated in three of its shows. During these years she was active throughout Québec theatre: teaching, organizing festivals, working as a critic. She was president of Québec's Centre des auteurs dramatiques between 1994 and 1999. Still based in Montréal, she has been a force in Québec theatre for over thirty years.

Her plays, translated into eighteen languages, have been staged all over the world, from Montréal to Reykjavik, and Paris to Tokyo, and many have been heard and seen on radio and television in France. Fréchette is also the author of novels for adolescents, translated in several languages. She translated Colleen Wagner's *The Monument*, produced in Montréal in 2001. She won the 1995 Governor General's Literary Award for Drama for her play *Les quatre morts de Marie* and the 1998 Chalmers Canadian Play Award for John Murrell's English version of that play, *The Four Lives of Marie*. She also was shortlisted for the Governor General's Literary Award for *La peau d'Élisa* in 1998, for *Les sept jours de Simon Labrosse* in 1999, for *Jean et Béatrice* in 2002, and for *Serial killer et autres pièces courtes* in 2008.

Fréchette was the 2002 winner of the Siminovitch Prize, the most prestigious award in Canadian theatre. The same year the Société des auteurs et compositeurs dramatiques in Avignon, France, awarded her the Prix de la Francophonie in recognition of her renown throughout the francophone world. She received the Prix Sony Labou Tansi des lycéens in 2004 for *Le collier d'Hélène*. She was one of the five finalists in 2009 for Le Grand Prix de littérature dramatique in France for *La petite pièce en haut de l'escalier*. Two of her plays have been shortlisted for the Dora Mavor Moore Award.

Published Works by Carole Fréchette

Baby Blues (1989). Montréal: Éditions les Herbes Rouges.

La peau d'Élisa (1998). Montréal & Arles: Éditions Leméac/Actes Sud-Papiers. *Elisa's Skin. Carole Fréchette: Three Plays* (2002). Tr. John Murrell. Toronto: Playwrights Canada Press.

Les quatre morts de Marie (1995). Montréal: Les Hebres rouges. *The Four Lives of Marie. Carole Fréchette: Three Plays* (2002). Tr. John Murrell. Toronto: Playwrights Canada Press.

Les sept jours de Simon Labrosse (1999). Montréal & Arles: Éditions Leméac/Actes-Sud Papiers. *Seven Days in the Life of Simon Labrosse. Carole Fréchette: Three Plays* (2002). Tr. John Murrell. Toronto: Playwrights Canada Press.

Le collier d'Hélène (2002). Carnières, Belgium: Éditions Lansman. *Helen's Necklace. Carole Fréchette: Two Plays* (2007). Tr. John Murrell. Toronto: Playwrights Canada Press.

Jean et Béatrice (2002). Montréal & Arles: Éditions Leméac/Actes-Sud Papiers. *John and Beatrice. Carole Fréchette: Two Plays* (2007). Tr. John Murrell. Toronto: Playwrights Canada Press.

Violette sur la terre (2002). Montréal & Arles: Éditions Leméac/Actes-Sud Papiers.

Route 1. Fragments d'humanité (2004). Carnières, Belgium: Éditions Lansman.

La pose (2007). *La Famille*. Paris: Éditions de L'avant-scène–La Comédie Française.

La petite pièce en haut de l'escalier (2008). Montréal & Paris: Éditions Leméac/Actes-Sud Papiers. Tr. John Murrell (unpublished).

Sérial killer et autres pièces courtes (2008). Montréal & Arles: Éditions Leméac/Actes-Sud Papiers.

Violette sur la terre was first produced in Sudbury at Théâtre du Nouvel-Ontario on January 24, 2002 and in Douai, France, at the Hippodrome on March 12, 2002, with the following company:

Étienne	Pierre Drolet
Judith	Miriam Cusson
Marie-Jeanne	Micheline Marin
Paul	Marc Thibaudeau
Violette	Geneviève Couture

Directed by Vincent Goethals

Playwright's Introduction

In the summer of 1999, Théâtre du Nouvel-Ontario (in Sudbury, Ontario, Canada), Théâtre du Tandem (in Rouyn-Noranda, Québec), and Théâtre en Scène (in Roubaix, France) asked me to write a play inspired by the world of miners and mining. At first, I was astonished by their proposal. I was not familiar with the mining profession, nor with the northern mining lands where these theatres are located. Eventually, I accepted in the spirit of adventure, on the condition that I could explore these worlds, so distant and unknown, freely and without assumptions. A few months later, I paid brief visits to each of the three regions, and talked with people who had lived, and who still pursue, lives related to mining. I observed, listened, and soaked up the atmosphere of these places. I met around thirty men and women of various ages who spoke to me about their lives with a generosity that touched my heart. Although their true stories are not a part of my play—and were never intended to be—their tenacity, their vitality, their courage, and their humanity constitute the raw material of *Violette sur la terre*. Their stories are the rock from which I have attempted to extract precious minerals. I am grateful to them for sharing the rich fragments of their lives.

Linda and Melvin Labine, Denis Mainville, Patricia Whitehead, Carole Rhéaume, and Joseph-Arthur Pharand from Sudbury; Jacques Bertrand, Fernand Ouellette, Françoise Hébert, Jacques Beattie, Réal Boissonneault, Pierre Gaulin, Carole Desrosiers, and Katherine Zamanchuk from Rouyn-Noranda; Gérald Harvey and his entire family from Larder Lake; Henri and Christiane Wosniak, Fernand and Irène Chopin, Serge and Catherine Lestienne, Colette Rigault, Cédric, and Agata Romano from Loos-en-Gohelle—this play is for you.

—Carole Fréchette

Translator's Note

In Carole Fréchette's original text, Paul and the others do not sing Pete Seeger's poignant ballad "Where Have All The Flowers Gone?" Rather, they sing "Le Temps des cerises," a popular French song of the nineteenth century (words by Jean-Baptiste Clément, music by Antoine Renard). Originally written as a love song, it soon became closely associated with the leftist movement in France, and was sung by the insurgents on the barricades during the struggle to establish and maintain the Paris Commune of 1871.

Carole and I discussed leaving the song in French, even in this version, because of the difficulty of finding an English-language equivalent, which is sufficiently well-known and which somehow signifies both romance and revolution. But Carole was convinced that all resonance would be lost on an English audience, who would have no knowledge of the piece or its historical background; and also that English-speaking actors would find singing it in French unmanageable.

Ultimately, I suggested the Seeger song, and we agreed, although its context and sound are quite different, that it is the most suitable substitute. It's probably a good idea, however, for anyone producing the play in English to check out the original French music and lyrics, which are available at several sites online.

—John Murrell

Characters

Paul
Steve
Marie
Judith
Violet

EARTHBOUND

PAUL   It was nearly dark. Must have been around 8:30. I felt hot. I jumped into my car. It's strange to feel heat like that, at the beginning of June. It's crazy—so hot, before it's even summer. Then it freezes in July. Maybe I was getting sick. I just know I don't like feeling hot. I don't know what to do with myself. It just got to be too much. I paced all around the house. Then I walked out and let the door slam behind me. Once upon a time, I would've been more careful. I would've closed it carefully, so I didn't upset Suzanne. But now—I just don't give a damn—I let it slam. I jumped into my car. I drove toward town. I was thinking: "Right about now, Johnny will be going over to Romeo's Bar. And Benny, too—especially if his wife's holding one of her union meetings." His wife's always calling meetings at night. We like to tease him about that. "Better watch out, Benny. You never know what kind of union your wife has in mind!" But he's not bothered. You can say whatever you like to Benny, and he never gets mad. I don't know how he does it. Meanwhile, I'm also thinking about all the beers they'll be having—and about how Romeo says the same stupid thing every time I walk in: "Hey, Paul, you better get yourself another woman—looks like you slept in your clothes again." I can picture the giant TV at the end of the bar—and Johnny, moping around as usual—somebody cracks a joke every once in a while—but mostly it's quiet…. All of a sudden, I turn off sharply—just like that, on impulse. And it's only after I've turned off the highway that I figure out where I'm headed. It's been a long time—eight or ten months. Maybe more. Years ago, I used to go there all the time. Some nights, I'd stay out there for hours on end, looking around. Even though there's not much to look at. Once or twice, I even cried. I think I cried. I got choked up and my nose ran, just like when I was a kid. But that was a long time ago. Then, that particular night— I don't know why—I went back there. Maybe just to get some fresh air. And then I realized there was a song running through my mind. The same song that…. The brain's a funny thing. I was trying to remember the second verse. I heard a noise. Like somebody breathing. Real close by. But I couldn't see anything. It was pitch black. I reached for my lighter.

STEVE   I got there around 5:15–5:20. Normally, it only takes me twenty-five minutes or so. But then I bumped into Albert Brizinski, pacing up and down outside his house. I tried to avoid him by going through the alley behind the grocery store, but he saw me and headed me off. I was trapped. He started to tell me about his herniated disc. He says, "So there I am, pacing up and down, from one end of the kitchen to the other, when I thought, 'I might as well be doing this outside, where I can get a little air.' Especially since it's so hot. Doesn't make sense for it to be this hot this early in the year! What's going on, Steve? You think it's because of the ozone layer?" I said, "Listen, Albert—" But then he launched into Jacqueline's stomach problems. "She's had every test they can give her, but they can't find anything wrong. She's going crazy because her sister Theresa died of liver cancer two years ago, and it started out almost the same way." I said, "Listen, Albert—" But he just went back to his hernia, describing the pain, like a knife in his back, somebody twisting the knife slowly between his vertebrae: "I cry like a baby," he said, "I want to scream!" Meanwhile, I'm thinking, "Yeah, well, I've got a knife twisting around inside my head, Albert." Then he tells me about his cousin Jim's operation, and how they fused three of his vertebrae, and now he's free from pain, but stiff as a board. I said, "Listen, Albert, I've got no time." If you let Albert Brizinski go on, he'll still be talking illnesses the next morning—his hernia, his acid reflux, his cousin's migraines, his brother-in-law's cancer. I said, "Listen, Albert, I'm in a hurry, tell me some other time." I walked on ahead. He shouted, "How come you're in such a hurry? At five o'clock in the morning?" I said nothing. He shouted, "Where are you off to?" But I just kept walking. It's none of his business where I'm going or why or how early. It's not about him. I finally got there around 5:15. I went straight to my hiding place and took out my stuff. Talking to myself. When I'm in a funny mood, I always talk to myself. Marie says I mutter all the time, even in my sleep, like an old car with engine trouble. I was looking through my stuff. All of a sudden, I felt something, like warm breath on my back. On my neck. Something warm. I turned around.

PAUL lights his lighter in the darkness.

PAUL Anybody here?

Silence.

Is anybody here?

Silence. PAUL looks around. He sings to himself:

"Where have all the young girls gone,
Long time passing,
Where have all the young girls gone,
Long time ago…?"

Silence.

"Where have all the young girls gone…?"

Silence.

What comes next? After "Where have all the young girls gone"? Do you know?

MARIE I heard him get up and get dressed in the next room. It was still dark out. As usual, I didn't budge. I heard him pacing up and down in the kitchen, opening the fridge, muttering to himself. I was thinking, "That's right! There's no more orange juice, I forgot to buy any." He muttered something and shut the fridge. Then he went out. As usual, I looked at the time: 4:42. I thought, "Hey, he's getting away late this morning." And then—I don't know why—instead of turning over and going back to sleep, I jumped out of bed. I threw on my dress and some sandals, didn't even wash, didn't even comb my hair, and ran out of the house. He hadn't got far, just to the corner. So I slowed down. He turned to the right. I slowed down some more. I turned to the right. He stopped at Albert Brizinski's. To talk. Even from a distance, I could see he was getting impatient. He was tense all over. He stopped for seven or eight minutes at least. I hid behind Maurice Lambert's truck. My heart was pounding. I was sweating. It was getting hot. Already real hot, at that hour. That's not normal. Annette and me almost got into a fight over it the other day. She said, "It's just like Egypt." So I had to say, "This is nothing like Egypt. Obviously you've never been there." I shouldn't have said anything—it just popped out. So she said, "You've never been there either, Marie. Not to Egypt, not to Morocco, not even to Honolulu." It's true I've never been to Egypt, but I know it's not like it is here. They've got real heat down there, and palm trees all along the major thoroughfares. That's real heat. People die from it. And the light is just blinding, and there's not a drop of water. And besides—I don't know—everything's a bright colour and they've got sand and pyramids, which have been there for millions of years. She said, "You piss me off, Marie," and she hung up. I was thinking, "I'd better call her up, later today, and explain…" I got lost in my thoughts—so I didn't see him take off again. Then I took off after him, fast as I could. Then—when he turned to the left, just before Raymond's Garage—I knew where he was going. I was thinking, "What's got into you, Marie? What are you turning into? A woman who chases after her husband." But I kept going. I couldn't stop. He walked fast, leaning forward. Like a man on his way to an important meeting. I stayed as far behind as possible, so he wouldn't hear me. But I don't think he would have anyway. He was completely lost in what he was doing. Probably muttering all the way. Once he got there, I saw him take some stuff out of a ditch. I couldn't see what it was. Then he got real still for a few seconds. His back was turned. I crept up as close as I could. I heard him. He said, "Go away. Get away from here."

PAUL holds his lighter up in the darkness.

PAUL   "Where have all the young girls gone…?" Is anybody here?

Silence.

Answer me. *(He turns the light in all directions.)* Here's what I propose. I'm going to turn off my lighter. And sing. And, if you know what comes next, please chime in.

"Where have all the young girls gone,
Long time passing,
Where have all the young girls gone,
Long time ago…?"

Silence.

"Where have all the young girls gone…?"

Silence.

JUDITH He said, "I want you, baby," without taking his eyes off the road, "I want you now." It's a game we play sometimes. Like we're in a movie. Like he's a vagrant from Texas and I'm the pretty girl he picked up on the side of the road. "I want you, baby." It's stupid, but it always shakes me up when he says that. He put the pedal to the metal. Must've been about—I don't know—1:30 in the morning. Maybe later. I said, "Where are we going?" He said, "Into the desert, baby." He drove and drove and then he stopped on the side of the road. He got out, rummaged around in the trunk and took out an old blanket, then he came around and opened my door. He took me by the hand and said, "Come on." I said, "Here? You're crazy! There's nothing here. No grass, no trees to hide behind." He said, "Welcome to the desert, baby." He held my face in his hands, my cheeks, my chin held tight in his hands, and he started to kiss me gently, on the forehead, the nose, the mouth. When he does that, something melts inside me. Like my muscles, my bones, my insides, everything melts, like I am becoming—I don't know… a lake, or the sea, and he's a fish prowling the ocean floor. He stretched out on top of me. I looked at the stars. A sky full of them. "I want you, baby." He took off my shirt, kissed my breasts, my shoulders, my belly. Then it all started to go much faster. That's how it is with Eric. At first, he's so gentle, he looks at me, he touches me everywhere, and then he becomes a madman. He tears off my clothes, he tears his own off, fast, fast, like he's on fire, like—I don't know… like his life depends on it—then he's inside me with one stroke. Sometimes I say, "Look out, Eric, you're going to tear my dress—look out, that hurts," but he doesn't seem to hear. He's inside me with one stroke. I yell. With pain or pleasure—I'm not sure. I told him, "Stop. Stop for a minute. Look at me." I'm always saying that, "Look at me. Slow down." And sometimes he does. He stops for ten or fifteen seconds. I can feel him inside me. It's so strange. Something inside me, something alive, like a little animal. I said, "Stop, look at me," but he didn't stop. His eyes shut tight, he lifted his head, he rose and he fell, he breathed and I breathed, and then, between our breaths, suddenly, I heard something. I whispered, "Listen, Eric." But he continued to rise and fall, his eyes shut tight. The sound got closer. I said, "Listen, Eric, I think maybe…" He kept rising and falling. I said, "Listen, Eric, somebody's crying!" He grabbed my hips. He fell into me and rose out of me, digging his fingers into my hips. He breathed and I breathed, and something else cried and cried, big sobs which came from the belly, rising, falling, and then Eric got tense all over, stretched tight as a rope, then he shouted out, like he always does, then he smothered his shout, and I cried out, "Eric, Eric, Eric, there's someone here who's…." And he fell onto me like a stone, and I opened my eyes and saw the stars again. But I didn't hear anything. Not a sound, except for Eric breathing against my ear while he slept. I thought, "Maybe it was me crying." I felt my face. It wasn't wet.

PAUL "Where have all the young girls gone…?"

In the darkness, a faint VOICE repeats, almost inaudibly:

VOICE "Where have all the young girls gone...?"

PAUL immediately lights his lighter.

PAUL Where are you? Answer me.

Silence.

"Where have all the young girls gone...?"

Silence.

MARIE He said, "Get away from here." For five months I hadn't heard the sound of his voice. It seemed so strange.

JUDITH Eric woke up. He whispered, "Isn't it great, to be alone together in the desert?" "Yeah, it's great, Eric." "I love you, baby."

• • •

STEVE is speaking to an unseen person. MARIE watches from a distance.

STEVE Get away from here. Stop looking at me. What do you want? You're spying on me, is that it? You want to know what I'm up to, so you can go tell Albert Brizinski, who will tell Jacqueline, who will tell Annette Bellemare, who will tell everybody else in town. You'll tell them, "I saw Steve Gauvin down by the old mine this morning. He was digging around in a ditch. Like he was mad at the world." Then somebody will say, "Steve Gauvin is permanently mad at the world." And everybody will laugh. As if I'm the crazy one, as if there isn't enough ugliness on earth to make anybody permanently mad. It's the calm ones who give me a laugh, the ones who refuse to look at... at the aberrations of the earth. *(silence)* "Aberration"—Marie uses that word all the time. Meaning stuff that doesn't make sense. *(silence)* Why don't you say something? It pisses me off when people don't talk. They just sit there, looking at you, looking down on you, pretending to listen, but really they're judging you. They find you irritating, unclear, not articulate enough. "Articulate"—I learned that word from André—Marie's brother. When he was company foreman, I tried to tell him why the regulations had to be changed, and he'd always say, "You've got to be more articulate about your thoughts, Steve." So one day I grabbed him by the throat and said, "Okay, is this clear enough? Is this articulate enough for you? Shall I get a little more specific...?" What's wrong? Did I scare you? Don't be scared. *(silence)* Don't shake like that. You want... you want a drink of water? I don't know how fresh it is. It's been buried here for the past week. I haven't touched it. *(silence)* Careful! You're getting it on your shirt. You're going to get soaked. *(silence)*

• • •

MARIE He said, "Get away." Afterward—I'm not sure—I moved further off, so he wouldn't see me. And then, after a while, he moved closer to her. Offered her something. A bottle, I think. He offered so carefully… almost tenderly. Then he moved back toward the ditch. I panicked. I lay down on my belly and crawled to the edge of the field. Then I ran all the way home, couldn't breathe, I got undressed and crawled into bed, and then I started to cry. All alone in the bedroom, I started to cry.

...

The beam of a flashlight penetrates the darkness.

PAUL Anybody here? *(He looks around with the flashlight.)* Now I remember what comes next. Listen. *(He trains the flashlight on a small notebook that he carries, and sings.)*

"Where have all the young girls gone?
Gone to young men every one,
When will they ever learn?
When will they ever learn?"

(silence) I've got all the words right here. I wrote them in my notebook. A long time ago. Right after I…. After my…. I just couldn't stay at home anymore, locked up inside my own head. I went into town, to Gardner's, and bought a notebook. I said, "It's for business." I don't know… I felt like I had to explain. When I got home, I didn't open it right away. I wasn't sure what to do. Then, one morning, I made up my mind. I took out a pen and I wrote: "I bought a notebook with a green cover, white pages, and blue lines." The next day, I wrote: "My house is grey with red around the windows, and a black roof. I am inside my house and I can't breathe." *(silence)* Ever since then I… I write from time to time. It's nothing… I mean, it's not… it's just a notebook, that's all. But sometimes it comes in handy, for remembering something. Like the words to a song. *(silence)* I kept thinking about it, all day long. About bringing you the words. I said to myself, "Maybe she's tired too, trying to remember the words. It's irritating when you can't remember something." *(silence)* Don't you find that irritating?

He searches the darkness with his flashlight. A face appears in its halo of light. There is something on its head. A hat. The flashlight beam descends gently. A woman's body.

Yesterday, you sang. I know I didn't just dream that. Say something now. Just one word. So I can hear your voice. I've been thinking all day about your voice. Say something.

VOICE *(a whisper from the darkness)* Aberration.

PAUL What?

VOICE Aberration.

PAUL "Aberration"?

The beam of light is extinguished.

. . .

Later. PAUL is gone. A brighter ray of light appears.

JUDITH   Ouch! What's…? A ditch. I nearly fell into a ditch. I…. Ouch! I twisted my ankle. I…. That hurts. Ridiculous. Judith, you're ridiculous. Stumbling around in an abandoned field at three o'clock in the morning, looking for somebody who might be crying. You're ridiculous. Ouch! There's nobody around—that's obvious. Ouch! Ouch!

She sits and plants the flashlight beside her. She rubs her ankle. A soft noise. JUDITH jumps up.

What's that? Is somebody here? Where are you? *(She shines her flashlight around.)* Was that you crying, the other night? I knew I heard you. Eric says I imagine things, but I knew—I'm not crazy. I came out here especially, to look for you. I lied to Eric so he'd let me use his car. I told him I was going to sleep over at Eve's place, which is fifteen clicks from here. I just made it up. He thought I was going to meet some guy. He made me swear that there's nobody else. So I swore. Besides, it's true, there's no other guy in my life. But still… I lied. Can you hear me? I know you're there. *(silence)* Why were you crying? *(silence)* For two days I've been asking myself, "Why does a woman cry like that, in the middle of the night? What happened to her? She lost her husband, or her child—or her boyfriend ran away? Or maybe because of something that didn't happen. A trip she never got to take, a man she never got to love, a child she never got to have. Maybe she just feels so alone, doesn't understand anything anymore, doesn't know what to do with her life. Or maybe it's just a question of her water level. What I mean is… she's full of water, she feels it moving around inside and she tries to contain it, she digs trenches to manage it, but sometimes, no matter what, it overflows, and everybody keeps asking why, 'Why are you crying?'" And you don't know how to answer. *(silence)* Why were you crying? You've got this lake inside you and it's overflowing. Is that it?

Silence. Then a VOICE murmurs:

VOICE   "Where have all the young girls gone,
Long time passing,
Where have all the young girls gone,
Long time ago…?"

JUDITH   You like to sing? I know that song. Somebody at school used to sing it all the time. It always made me want to cry. I don't know why.

. . .

Another day.

PAUL   What's your name? *(silence)* You don't want to tell me? Is it a secret? *(silence)* Here's what I propose. I'll say some names. If I say yours, you let me know. Okay?

The WOMAN looks at him and says nothing.

Louise. Sylvia. Mary. Diane. Monique. Estelle. Carol. Janet. *(silence)* Okay.... Nicole. Bernadette. Charlotte. Francine. Lisa. Andrea. Lucy. Suzanne.... No, not Suzanne. You're not a Suzanne, I'm sure of that. I... I once lived with a Suzanne... *(silence)* Okay.... Elizabeth. Judith. Joanne. Okay.... Margaret. Rosa. Violet—

The WOMAN raises her hand.

Violet? Is that it? That's a nice name, Violet. It suits you. Now we can be less formal. My name's Paul. Why don't you say something?

VIOLET   Why does a woman cry like that, in the middle of the night?

PAUL   Are you crying, Violet? Why are you crying? What's making you so sad?

• • •

In the wee hours. The WOMAN sits motionless. More visible now. Her clothes are dirty and faded: trousers and walking shoes, which are too large for her—and a strange little hat that is at odds with the rest of her apparel.

STEVE   You're still here? I thought for sure you'd be gone. In fact, I asked myself if you were ever really here. I don't know why you came, and I don't need to know. But I need to... I've got to do this. I've got to get on with it. You can watch me if you want to, but don't spread the word about what I'm up to all over town.

Silence. He picks up a shovel and begins digging a shallow ditch.

You've had it with the world—haven't you? That's why you're out here, all alone? You've had it with all the ugliness, just like me. Ugliness, injustice, dishonesty, hypocrisy. *(silence)* At first, you think you can tough it out. You think that's what everybody else is doing, too. But then you understand that the rest of them are really okay with things—they're ready to accept any compromise, to believe any lies. *(silence)* I'm telling you, if they stopped lying, the whole thing would fall apart. If people said what they're really thinking—to their husbands, to their wives, to their bosses, to their families, to their friends—there'd be nothing holding us together anymore. Marie says we've got to hold things together, and if it takes a few lies to hold things together, what's the big deal? But I can't accept that. What about you? Can you accept that? Right now, for example, wouldn't you like to scream at me? But you hold back, because it's just not done. It's just not done—to be rude to your guests, to let the door slam, to shout at your boss, to tell your wife you don't want her anymore because.... It's just not done! Stop looking at me like that! Answer me!

VIOLET   You... you've got this lake inside you and it's overflowing, is that it?

STEVE A lake. I don't have any lake. Marie says I'm filling up with molten lava. And she's right. For once she's right. *(silence)* Okay, I've got to do this. I've got to get on with it.

> *He rummages in his hiding place and takes out a scrap of cardboard. He writes on it. Then he groans and rubs out what's he written.*

That's not it. I know what I want to say but I can't find the words. Shit. So, once again, they'll all say I'm not articulate enough.

> *He tosses the cardboard into the ditch he's been digging, covers it with dirt, and plants a stick on top—a stick with a red scrap of fabric tied around it, like a flag.*

• • •

> *Dusk. MARIE comes in, carrying a small package. She stops at a distance from VIOLET.*

MARIE What did he say to you? Did he explain why he's been coming out here, every morning for the past two weeks? What's he up to? I know all about his craziness. I've seen him, screaming at the others "Don't go back down there!" I've seen him throwing cans of paint all over the walls, I've seen him start fires, break windows, camping out for three solid days in front of the mine manager's house. But I thought he was done with all that. Since the mine closed, I thought he was settling down. What's he up to now? Do you know? *(silence)* Did he say anything about me? "Marie." Did he tell you it's been five months since he spoke one word to me? Did he tell you I'm the one who stopped talking to him, because he finally pushed things too far? Five months without a word, not even at supper, not even to say "Don't forget to buy milk" or "Don't slam the door." Just little notes left on the kitchen table. Did he tell you about that? No. I'm sure he didn't. *(silence)* He didn't talk to you about me. Right? *(silence)* First time I saw him, I thought, "You'd have to dynamite that guy, to bring him down." He was so straight, so solid. "But I can change him—gradually," I told myself. And, for twenty-four years, I tried to. He hasn't shifted an inch. He's planted in the earth, he's rooted in these rocks. *(silence)* Did he smile at you? Did he speak to you sweetly? He can be so sweet when he wants to be. He's got a beautiful smile. But when he gets worked up, it's awful. The first few times, it really tore me up. *(silence)* I… I brought you these. Chocolate-chip cookies. I thought, "When you've been travelling, it's nice to have a little something sweet." Everybody likes chocolate-chip cookies. Here you go.

> *She puts the cookies down near the WOMAN and notices the little flag left by STEVE.*

Did you plant that flag? How come? *(silence)* You came from up north, right? I was thinking about it. I said to myself, "She must've come from up north. Otherwise, why would she pass through here?" When you run away, you run away to the south, naturally. You run away to the warmth, the light, to where it's pretty, to the sea. That's where you're going, right? You're running away. I can understand that. Sometimes it's the only thing to do. When your life is an aberration.

VIOLET   Aberration.

MARIE   Yes. "Aberration." Meaning stuff—

VIOLET   Stuff that doesn't make sense.

MARIE   Exactly. Stuff that doesn't make sense. Like not speaking to your husband for five solid months, like spending fifty-one years in a place you hate, like always dreaming of getting away but never going, like loving somebody who's destroying you.

VIOLET   Aberration.

MARIE   Don't stay here. There's nothing here. Just rock and slag. You've already done the hard part. You made a decision. You left your husband, your family, your friends, you left a little note on the kitchen table, you didn't slam the door. So, get on with it. Steve says you can't start your life over. He says you are what you are and that's all there is. "Besides, it's no better anywhere else, it's the same everywhere, the same ugliness—"

VIOLET   Ugliness, injustice, dishonesty, hypocrisy.

MARIE   Exactly. But I say it is possible. What's to prevent us from selling the house and the car? What's to prevent us from laughing while we throw clothes into a suitcase, from just grabbing each other and loving each other, like we used to? Answer me!

VIOLET   You have this lake inside you and it's overflowing, is that it?

MARIE   A lake? I don't know. I don't know what I have. Maybe more like a handful of sand—or like a sudden draft in a shut-up room.

VIOLET   Are you crying?

MARIE   I'm not crying. Feel. Only one thing makes me cry. The babies I never had. The two that died coming out of my womb and all the others that are still inside my head.

VIOLET   What's making you so sad?

MARIE   I don't know... I.... My life's making me so sad. *(silence)* I need to ask you.... Was it hard to go away? Did you have trouble making up your mind? Did you leave in the morning, or in the afternoon, or at night? How did it feel, to watch your house disappearing in the distance? To travel alone, to eat alone, to sleep alone? Were you afraid? Were you sad? Were you sometimes sorry? What do you miss the most? The smell of your kitchen, your husband's quirks, his shirttail hanging out, his footsteps, his shouting, his silence? *(silence)* What did you say when you walked out? Did you find some way to explain? You probably found the right words. The right couple of words. Tell me. *(silence)* Please.

VIOLET   I have made a mistake.

MARIE   That's what you said?

VIOLET   I have made a mistake.

Silence.

MARIE   Can I ask you…? Don't tell him, okay? That I came here. That I followed him. Don't tell. *(silence)* Are you going to eat those cookies?

• • •

Toward the end of the day.

PAUL   I brought you some coffee, Violet. Coffee's always good when you've been travelling. You've come a long way on foot, haven't you? I can tell that by your shoes.

He takes a Thermos and two cups from his bag, pours coffee, and offers it to her. VIOLET takes a small package from her bag and offers it to PAUL.

What's that? Cookies? For me? That's so nice. Did you bring them all the way from…. Did you bring them with you? Did you make them yourself? *(silence)* Do you ever feel like, maybe, you've disappeared? I mean, when it gets so dark that you can't see anything, and maybe the world's disappeared and you have too? A thousand feet below the surface of the earth, there's suddenly a cave-in, and a ton of rock falls on top of you, and all at once there's no floor, there's no ceiling—you've got no arms, no legs, no face, just a bit of brain with a song stuck inside it, not even a whole song, just the first part, the part about where all the young girls have gone, which keeps playing over and over like a broken record—there's no more minutes, no more seconds, no more need to scream, to cry, or to be afraid—just this feeling that you don't exist, that you're just one more rock among all the other rocks, way down deep there. Did you ever feel like that, Violet? *(silence)* Did you ever have a cave-in in your life? You thought it was all solid, but you must have done a crappy inspection, because one day somebody says to you, "I don't love you anymore" and slams the door and your little house caves in. You can sing inside your head for as long as you like, but nobody comes to rescue you, and you think you're going to die, but you don't die. Has that ever happened to you? *(silence)* Why don't you say something?

• • •

Later.

JUDITH   Are you there? Is somebody with you? I thought I heard someone. *(silence)* I brought you this.

She gives her a blanket.

It's not cold, but you still have to cover up at night. *(silence)* I… I want to show you something.

> *She extends a photo.*

That's Eric and me at Amelia's wedding last month. They had a photographer strolling among the guests. We'd had quite a bit to drink. We didn't even know when he snapped it. Everybody says it's a good picture of us—he's touching my cheek and I'm smiling. I had it enlarged last week and I…. Take a good look. *(silence)* What do you see? See Eric's hand on my cheek, see how I'm leaning to one side. Would you say my face is welcoming his touch or rejecting it? Look at Eric's eyes. What do you see in those eyes, besides the fact that he's been mixing beer with wine? And look at my eyes. Doesn't it seem like I'm looking past him, like I'm staring at something or someone behind him? What am I staring at? Do you know? *(silence)* Everybody says it's a great photo. But I…. What am I staring at like that? Say something.

VIOLET   This feeling…

JUDITH   What feeling?

VIOLET   This feeling that you don't exist. That you're just one more rock among all the other rocks, way down deep there.

JUDITH   You have that feeling too. It's strange, isn't it, not to know who you really are? *(silence)* I was at the drugstore this morning. I bought a test. It says it's real easy to use. If the colour changes, then it's "Yes." I haven't tried it yet. It's in my bag. I keep taking it out and looking at it. Exploring it with my fingertips. *(silence)* I came to tell you about it. And to ask…. But I know I ask too many questions. I'll shut up. *(silence)* Would you like to brush my hair? When my mother used to brush my hair, I always felt my thoughts getting clearer.

> *She takes a brush from her bag and extends it to VIOLET. VIOLET brushes her hair.*

I'm scared. Hold my hand, please.

> *VIOLET holds JUDITH's hand. Silence.*

Are you scared sometimes? Scared to leave, scared to stay, scared to choose? How many lives can you live? What do you think? If you've made bad choices, can you choose over again? Or is it… terminal? I know, I know: too many questions.

• • •

> *A little time has passed. A simple shelter has been set up with the blanket. Four or five small flags are now planted in the earth. It is dark. VIOLET cannot be seen; just a shadow behind the hanging blanket.*

PAUL   You… you built yourself a tent. The sun is pretty harsh nowadays. It's really strange, heat like this. You staked out your territory. Are you moving in?

The shadow moves behind the blanket.

Stay there, okay? I... I want to read you something and I.... It's better if I'm not looking at you. Good. I'm reading. Okay? *(He takes out his notebook and reads.)* "Last night I dreamed about her. It was the day of my accident. My body was buried in the rocks, but my face was free. All of a sudden, I felt something on my lips. It was cool. Like a cheek. But it was the curve of a breast—all at once I realized—the part where the skin is softest and most beautiful. I opened my eyes wide, but I saw nothing. My heart was pounding and I shook all over and my cock was hard as a rock. And then I thought, 'I don't want them to search for me, I want to stay here for all eternity, with her on my lips,' and then I felt—"

A VOICE comes from behind the blanket, not VIOLET's voice.

JUDITH   Stop.

PAUL   What...?

JUDITH steps out.

What's... what are you doing here?

JUDITH   What are you doing here?

PAUL   I... I'm here to see a friend...

JUDITH   The woman with the funny little hat?

PAUL   You know Violet?

JUDITH   Her name's Violet?

PAUL   Did she go away? I didn't think she'd go away. Not without warning me.

JUDITH   I don't think she's gone. Her bag is still here.

PAUL   Oh good.

Pause.

JUDITH   I told her I was coming back tonight with some pictures.

PAUL   Pictures?

JUDITH   Yes. Of me, when I was little.

PAUL   Okay.

Uneasy pause.

JUDITH   You were in an accident?

PAUL   Accident? Oh yeah... a long time ago.

JUDITH   What happened?

PAUL   A cave-in. Somebody did a crappy inspection. A ton of rock fell on top of me.

JUDITH   How long were you down there?

PAUL   Four hours.

JUDITH   My dad had an accident too. But he was killed immediately. At least, that's what they told me. I was four years old. Everybody said, "He had no time to suffer." But who knows? Nobody knows what he was thinking, what he felt.

PAUL   How did it happen?

JUDITH   I don't know. Probably a cave-in. *(silence)* Was it her you dreamed about?

PAUL   Who?

JUDITH   Violet.

PAUL   Yes.

JUDITH   How did you know it was her? You didn't see her. She didn't speak.

PAUL   I know.

> *Silence.*

JUDITH   Your accident—was that the worst thing that ever happened to you?

PAUL   Why do you ask?

JUDITH   I don't know. Was it?

PAUL   None of your business.

JUDITH   Sorry.

> *Silence.*

PAUL   She hasn't gone away. I'm sure she hasn't gone away. She would've warned me.

JUDITH   She left her bag. *(She picks it up.)*

PAUL   Yeah, she left her bag.

JUDITH   Maybe we should look. There might be something in here that would…

PAUL   Would what?

JUDITH   I don't know…. Maybe she left a note.

PAUL   In her bag?

> *Pause. JUDITH makes up her mind and opens the bag carefully. PAUL comes closer. JUDITH takes out a small notebook.*

JUDITH   There's no note. But there's this.

PAUL   What is it?

JUDITH   A litte notebook.

PAUL   None of our business.

    JUDITH reads in the notebook.

JUDITH   That's strange.

PAUL   What?

JUDITH   Everything's scratched out.

PAUL   Scratched out?

JUDITH   Everything she wrote is scratched out with a dark pencil. Can't read it.

PAUL   Put it back in the bag. None of our business.

JUDITH   Hold on! At the very end, there's one sentence that's not scratched out. Just one.

PAUL   Really? What's… what does it say?

JUDITH   "I have made a mistake."

PAUL   That's all?

JUDITH   Yes. That's all.

    Silence.

PAUL   What mistake?

JUDITH   Her destination, maybe. She meant to go somewhere else, but she ended up here.

PAUL   Where did she want to go?

JUDITH   I don't know. Maybe somewhere nicer, greener, shadier.

PAUL   No, that's not it. I'm sure. This is where she meant to come. She came here for…

JUDITH   For what?

    Pause.

PAUL   I… I don't know. And anyway, she's not gone.

JUDITH   You're right. Why would she build a shelter, why would she plant these flags, if she was planning to go?

PAUL   She hasn't gone. I know she hasn't.

    • • •

    Morning. VIOLET is sitting under her shelter.

STEVE   It's holding up well, isn't it? What I built for you. Of course, there's no wind right now, but that won't last. It's just not normal, this heat. *(silence)*

Listen. You can't stay here. I built this for you because I didn't want you to have to sleep out in the open. But it was just temporary. Until you were strong enough. But you can't stay. This is my place. I've been coming here for years. This is where I.... You understand what I'm saying? Answer me.

VIOLET I have made a mistake. Sorry.

STEVE Why do you say that? You haven't made a mistake. You didn't know that I come out here every morning.

VIOLET Sorry.

STEVE You don't have to say that. There's no reason to be sorry. Everybody's always saying "I'm sorry." That's ridiculous. *(silence)* But, in a couple of days, you'll have to go because... because the weather's going to change.

VIOLET I have made a mistake.

STEVE Stop saying that! It's not your fault that the world doesn't make sense. It's not—

A VOICE is heard from the distance, then PAUL comes in.

PAUL Violet? You're back? *(He sees STEVE.)*

STEVE Go away.

PAUL *(to VIOLET)* I knew you weren't gone.

STEVE Get out of here.

PAUL *(to STEVE)* I don't take orders from you.

STEVE You know who I am?

PAUL You're Steve Gauvin, the best dynamiter around. With the biggest head. I once saw you give the mine manager hell. It took three guys to pull you off him.

STEVE I never saw you before.

PAUL That's because I never jumped in front of the camera to shout "Goddamn bastard!" at the minister when he visited the mine. I never got featured on the six o'clock news.

STEVE That's because you like to have somebody else do your fighting, while you sit back and reap the benefits.

PAUL Well, I never led eight hundred men out on strike, when it was a lost cause from the get-go, and I was never on the front page of the newspaper because they thought I blew up the old warehouse... I guess that's why you've never seen me.

STEVE Get out of here.

PAUL I came to talk to Violet. I'm going to talk to Violet.

STEVE There's no "Violet" here.

PAUL   I brought you some oranges, Violet. I knew you hadn't gone away.

STEVE   You think you know me? What do you know? What somebody else told you. The bosses, the foremen, the minister's flunkies.

PAUL   *(to VIOLET)* I couldn't sleep last night. I told myself, "She hasn't gone, she's just strolling around, exploring the neighbourhood. She'll be back."

STEVE   The warehouse wasn't me. I already proved that.

PAUL   *(to VIOLET)* I couldn't start the day without knowing. I had to stop by here before going to work. You're back. I'm so happy.

STEVE   Listen up! You've got no business here. This is my place! I've been coming out here for a couple of weeks.

PAUL   This land still belongs to the company, and the company doesn't belong to you. *(to VIOLET)* I wrote in my notebook all night long, Violet.

STEVE   Get out!

PAUL   Leave me alone.

STEVE   I'm telling you to get out! *(He grabs PAUL.)*

PAUL   I came to talk to Violet. I'm going to talk to Violet.

STEVE   Who's Violet?

VIOLET   I have made a mistake. Sorry. *(She stands and gets ready to leave.)*

PAUL   No! Don't go. You don't have to go. We'll leave you in peace. We're going. Right, Steve Gauvin? We're going now.

> *He looks at STEVE. Pause.*

STEVE   That's right. We're going.

> *Pause.*

PAUL   *(to VIOLET)* I'll come back later, okay?

STEVE   *(to VIOLET)* Don't forget. In a couple of days…

PAUL   In a couple of days, what?

STEVE   In a couple of days—the weather's going to change.

• • •

> *Afternoon. MARIE comes in quietly. VIOLET is not there.*

> *MARIE sits under the shelter. She rummages through VIOLET's bag. VIOLET comes in. MARIE jumps up.*

MARIE   You scared me! I… I was rummaging around. I know I shouldn't have. *(silence)* There's not much in your bag. Didn't you bring any souvenirs? Not even a picture of your house or your family. Not even a key, in case you…. You just brought your hat, eh? *(silence)* I've got a hat, too. *(silence)* I bought it to go to Africa. I never went to Africa, but I did discover Steve that summer. He said, "I am a tropical country all by myself. Visit me." I melted. At first, I loved exploring his tropical landscape, but later on… *(silence)* I've been trying to decide what to do. I… I'd like to leave with you. All by myself, I'll never do it. Understand? I've never been all by myself. But with you, I think I could. I'd need you at first. Until I got used to it. I don't want to bother you. I'll adapt to your pace, your method. If you want me to talk, I'll talk. I could tell you stories about Steve, about my friends, about the babies I wanted to have. But if you want quiet, I'll shut right up. I can shut up. I promise. I just need somebody beside me. Understand?

JUDITH comes in.

JUDITH   Are you leaving?

MARIE   What…. What are you doing here?

JUDITH   Where are you going?

MARIE   You heard what we said?

JUDITH   Where are you going?

MARIE   I… I don't know. We don't know yet. Somewhere south, naturally.

JUDITH   When?

MARIE   Well… soon. Very soon.

JUDITH   Are you a friend of Violet's?

MARIE   Violet's?

JUDITH   How long have you known her?

MARIE   Not that long.

JUDITH   You don't know her, but you're going away with her.

MARIE   Don't tell anyone, okay? What you heard. Tell nobody.

JUDITH   You've got no family?

MARIE   No, I never had children. I couldn't. Have you got something to say about that?

JUDITH   No, no, I—

MARIE   Not that it's very complicated. It doesn't take any special talent. You just have to be a good growing place for a few months. Nothing to it, just plant and wait. But I'm not a good growing place. Not rich and dark enough. Too unstable. One day hot and humid, the next day desperately dry.

JUDITH   Don't talk like that. I wasn't asking for—

MARIE   I've got to leave right away. *(to VIOLET)* I'm an enthusiastic walker, Violet. Is that really your name? I've got great stamina and I never complain.

JUDITH   What about your husband?

MARIE   What about my husband?

JUDITH   Maybe it was because of him?

MARIE   No.

JUDITH   Eric says he wants lots of kids. Four, five, six! I tell him, "Don't exaggerate." He kisses me all over and laughs and says, "Of course I'm going to exaggerate!" But I—

MARIE   So what do you say to him?

JUDITH   I say, "It's not that easy, Eric," but he says, "Of course it's easy. You finish school, you get married, you move to the north, you make love all the time, you have kids, you pay down the mortgage, you've got it all, you're happy."

MARIE   "You've got it all." That's what he says?

JUDITH   And he kisses me, so I say nothing, but I think, "Sure, but what if…? What if you get bored, what if the winter's too long, if I'm sad at night? What if, all of sudden, I don't know why, I just don't want him to touch me anymore? What if I fall in love with his best buddy? That can happen. What if we start to hate each other, if I can't stand his quirks anymore, the noises he makes when he eats, the way he throws his shoes in the corner instead of putting them away, the way he oversimplifies everything?" What if… I don't know… what if I'm not a good growing place…

MARIE   Don't talk like that.

JUDITH   "What if I'm not a good lover, what if I spoil everything by asking too many questions and by having too much water inside me, rising and rising and about to overflow?" I go on and on like that, and sometimes I try to say a little something to Eric, like "I don't know if… I'm not so sure that…" But I never finish the sentence and he…

MARIE   What does he do?

JUDITH   He holds my face in his hands and he says, "I love you, Judith."

MARIE   Judith?

JUDITH   That's my name, "Judith."

MARIE   I have to go. Violet, I have to go get ready. With two of us, it's going to be easier, you'll see. Bye, Judith. You should finish your sentences—for Eric.

She goes out. JUDITH remains alone with VIOLET.

JUDITH   Are you really going away? Why did you come here? You ended up in the wrong place, is that it? Why were you crying? Why do I cry every night? Why don't I know if I love Eric? Why do I come back here every day? Why would I like for you to hold me? Why? Answer me!

She shakes VIOLET, who tries to leave.

No! Don't go. Not yet. Please. I won't ask any more questions. I promise. *(silence)* Don't go now, okay? Wait until…. I'm going to go find out. If the colour changes, then it's "Yes." Promise me you'll wait. *(silence)* Please. Promise. *(silence)* Repeat after me: I…

VIOLET   "I…"

JUDITH   I promise.

VIOLET   "I promise."

JUDITH   I promise you, Judith.

VIOLET   "I promise you, Judith."

· · ·

Daytime.

STEVE   You have to leave. Today. The weather's changing tonight. The radio said so. If you like, I'll take you into town. But you can't stay here. I mean it. I told you. I'm working up to something. Today's the day…

VIOLET doesn't move.

Listen. I planted dynamite down there in the mine shaft, all around the struts and the crossbeams. Every stick I could get my hands on—I've been saving it up, ever since they shut us down. When I push the plunger, the whole thing is going to blow. They'll hear it ten clicks from here. They'll see the flames all the way to town. They'll all come running out here. Nothing will be left of the mine. They'll prowl around in the rubble. They'll find what's left of my little flags. They'll dig around underneath. They'll find and read my inarticulate little notes. Everybody will be here. It'll be the biggest boom of my career. *(silence)* When I used to work down there, an explosion was the high point of my day. Lots of the guys were afraid of them. Not me. I'd always volunteer for the riskiest jobs. After everybody else went back up, I'd reel out the fuse, and count to ten, and push the plunger. I'd feel the earth shake. Like the explosion was inside of me. As if it was thundering and shattering windows and collapsing doorways inside of me. *(silence)* It's five years ago today that they shut the mine, walked away, and never came back. We have to mark the occasion, right? You can't just let the company leave you behind, like slag. You have to light a little fire, make a little noise. Even if it doesn't change a thing. Just to say: we remember what you did. We remember how you walked away with all the money and started over somewhere else, somewhere warmer. In the tropics that Marie's always chattering about. We know! And we don't accept the hypocrisy, the injustice—not without making something go "boom!" We don't accept the world's ugliness, and that love is so difficult, and that little kids die in pools of blood. We can't accept that—not without making a little noise! Boom! Unacceptable! Horrible! Boom! *(silence)* At 8:30 exactly, I'll push the plunger, and, if I've got the guts, Violet, I'll be standing right there in the middle of it, and my body will explode in a thousand pieces, and it will all come to a stop. At least inside my head, it will all come to a stop. And Marie will be free at last, and everybody can say, "We were right all along about that hothead." *(silence)* You don't say anything, but I know you understand. Because you're like me. With those big eyes and that funny little hat, you look so sweet, but you're like me. It goes on exploding inside your head, and you can't take it anymore.

> *Distant thunder.*

Now you've got to go. The wind's rising. The weather's changing. Please.

> *He moves to her. All of a sudden, he grabs her, hugs her tightly, and kisses her desperately. VIOLET doesn't resist.*
>
> *JUDITH comes in.*

JUDITH Violet?

> *STEVE immediately lets go of VIOLET.*

STEVE What's... what do you want?

JUDITH I came to see Violet. I didn't know... you were together...

STEVE It's not what you think.

JUDITH I brought some cake.

STEVE She's going away. Violet.

JUDITH I know, but I... I made the cake this morning. When I get nervous, baking is the one thing that settles me down. I picked out a long, complicated recipe. It took me all afternoon.

STEVE You can't stay here.

JUDITH It's a hazelnut sponge cake—

STEVE I said you can't stay here.

JUDITH When I bake a cake, my mind's a complete blank. I only think about the texture, the colour, the aroma—

STEVE Who gives a shit about your cake? I said—

JUDITH I came to share it with Violet.

STEVE Go away.

JUDITH No! You go away.

> *A gust of wind.*

STEVE Feel that? The wind's rising. Time to go.

Pause.

JUDITH *(to VIOLET)* I brought plates and forks.

STEVE She doesn't want to eat. She wants to get her stuff together and get out of here, before the weather turns really bad.

JUDITH Is that true, Violet?

STEVE She's seen all she needs to see here. Now she needs to get on with her journey.

JUDITH Is that true?

STEVE She's had enough.

JUDITH You promised me, Violet.

STEVE Promised you what?

JUDITH Remember? "I promise you, Judith."

STEVE You're Judith?

JUDITH Repeat after me…

STEVE Marie's sister was called Judith, so we decided, if it's a girl—

JUDITH "I want to stay with you, Judith. For a little while." Repeat after me: I want…

VIOLET "I want…"

JUDITH I want to stay…

VIOLET "I want to stay…"

JUDITH For a little while…

VIOLET "For a little while…"

Distant thunder.

JUDITH She wants to stay.

STEVE No, she doesn't.

JUDITH The three of us can eat together. I only brought two forks, but we'll work something out.

STEVE I don't want to eat.

JUDITH What do you do when you get nervous?

STEVE What?

JUDITH I bake cakes. What do you do when you get scared?

STEVE I… I don't know. I walk around and rub my hands… like this.

JUDITH That's all?

STEVE   I check my watch.

JUDITH   Why?

STEVE   To make the time go faster. Maybe I check it a thousand times.

JUDITH   Don't you want a slice?

STEVE   No.

JUDITH   Violet and I need to talk.

STEVE   Remember what I told you, Violet.

JUDITH   Eric called me yesterday, Violet.

STEVE   Listen up!

PAUL comes in with a bouquet of flowers.

PAUL   What are you doing? You've got cake? Is it your birthday, Violet?

STEVE   It's not her birthday.

JUDITH   Did she tell you that?

STEVE   What?

JUDITH   That it's not her birthday?

STEVE   No—but—

PAUL   I brought you flowers, Violet. What a coincidence!

STEVE   I'm telling you, it's not—

JUDITH   It could be her birthday.

PAUL   I also brought sparkling wine and two glasses.

STEVE   Violet has to go. She's got no time for your wine and cake and all your chatter.

PAUL   I wasn't talking to you.

JUDITH   You guys know each other?

PAUL   Everybody who used to work here knows Steve Gauvin, the hothead.

STEVE   Stop.

PAUL   The troublemaker, the fight starter.

STEVE   I said stop.

JUDITH   Would you like some cake?

PAUL   The one guy who's never satisfied, who always wants more.

STEVE   The one guy who stands for something, who made the company bend over, lots of times.

PAUL   Who hated the rest of us if we hestitated, if we didn't instantly back him up.

JUDITH   We could all eat together.

STEVE   Who took risks for the rest of you, who wasn't afraid to speak the truth.

PAUL   Whose truth?

STEVE   The everyday, unbearable truth. Like, "You work all your life, but you're screwed anyway, because there's no justice, there's no respect or solidarity, it's every man for himself."

PAUL   That's right, we're all screwed, and everybody's got everything wrong, except you—

STEVE   The truth. Like, "Today is not Violet's birthday, and she doesn't want flowers or cake or sparkling wine." The truth, like, "Violet's going away, and in a couple of hours she'll have forgotten all about us."

PAUL   You don't know what Violet's going to do any more than I do. You come on strong and everybody thinks you know something. But I don't. I don't think you know anything.

JUDITH   She promised.

PAUL   What did she promise?

JUDITH   To stay for a little while.

PAUL   Violet, I need to talk to you.

STEVE   She didn't promise anything. She just repeated.

PAUL   Leave me alone with her. There's something I need to tell her.

JUDITH   Me too.

PAUL   Give us fifteen minutes.

STEVE   I'm not going anywhere.

PAUL   Go away!

STEVE   I'm not moving.

PAUL   Okay. *(He moves close to VIOLET, takes out his notebook, and reads.)* "Violet, I have a house in a clearing, with three bedrooms upstairs, a kitchen painted yellow, and a balcony with southern exposure. There's also a screen door that slams really loud if you don't—" No, I shouldn't talk about the door. "Violet, I could remain underground for hours in the pitch dark while singing "Where Have All The Flowers Gone?" to myself and hoping somebody will come to rescue me—and I could remain in bed for months while waiting for my bones to mend—and I could adapt to a whole new job—but I can't—"

STEVE   That's enough.

PAUL   "I can't live alone anymore—"

STEVE   Stop.

PAUL   "I can't live the rest of my life without touching a woman. I can't."

STEVE   You can see she's not listening to you.

PAUL   I brought flowers and wine and I'd like to ask you—

STEVE   Look at her. She wants you to stop.

PAUL   Violet—come and live with me.

STEVE   Ridiculous. You don't even know her.

PAUL   It's true, we don't know each other, Violet. But you can never know everything about somebody else. You never know what's going on inside their heads and their hearts. We don't even know what's going on inside ourselves. Then one day, in the silence, you discover yourself, and you're taken completely by surprise.

STEVE   Stop!

PAUL   Leave me alone!

JUDITH   Both of you stop! Violet doesn't like it when you shout.

PAUL   I won't shout anymore, Violet. And I won't let the door slam. I promise you. And if... if you don't want to talk, at first, you can just write in your notebook.

STEVE   Sure. Or you can just leave little notes on the kitchen table.

PAUL   You don't need to give me an answer right now. Take some time, think it over. I'll stay right here. I'll wait for you.

STEVE   Go away.

JUDITH   Would you like some cake?

PAUL   Quiet! Let her think.

STEVE   It's nearly eight o'clock, Violet.

PAUL   Quiet! I'm waiting, Violet. Take your time.

Thunder. MARIE comes in, wearing a hat and carrying a bag.

MARIE   Violet?

They turn and look at her.

STEVE   Marie? You followed me. What are you up to?

MARIE   Somebody tell him: I'm going away.

STEVE   Going away? Where? With who?

MARIE   Somebody tell him: I'm going away with Violet.

PAUL   Violet's not going. She's thinking.

STEVE   You can't just go away without any reason.

MARIE   Somebody tell him: I left a little note on the kitchen table.

JUDITH   I baked a cake. It's Violet's birthday.

MARIE   Really? Happy birthday, Violet.

STEVE   It's not anybody's birthday.

MARIE   Somebody tell him: he's mistaken.

STEVE   You won't find anything different out there, Marie. Just more men who suffer. More men who are screwed but pretend that they aren't, more men who lie with every breath.

MARIE   Somebody tell him: I know all about ugliness, hypocrisy, and dishonesty. But, somebody tell him, there is also beauty, goodness, courage, and walking away.

STEVE   You think you'll find your innocence again, walking off down the road like a twenty-year-old?

PAUL   Violet, I forgot to tell you—

MARIE   Somebody tell him: I am fifty-one, my legs get tired much quicker than they used to, my bones are more brittle, and my eyes are a little cloudy, but I can still go the distance. Tell him my feet are not rooted in these rocks. I'm not just a stone statue carved out of anger and bitterness.

STEVE   Go on then. Go explore your illusions with your fingertips. Go sit beside the sea on the other side of the world and feel the emptiness inside, exactly like you felt it here. Go listen to the same old voice, telling you "You've got to move on, Marie. Don't stop here. Keep moving. Keep moving south."

PAUL   Listen, Violet. My house isn't very pretty, that's true, and the land around it isn't much good, but—

MARIE   Somebody tell him: he's confusing "illusion" with "hope."

STEVE   I'm not confused. You're the one who's all mixed up.

MARIE   If you stab your illusions to death, your hope dies too. You turn into an old man, nursing his anger.

PAUL   But my bedroom has a window that faces the east, and on sunny mornings there's a big square of sunlight on the wooden floor—

STEVE   If you spend your whole life dreaming about a different life, then you never settle anywhere, you never put down roots, and you— *(He stops himself.)*

MARIE   Say what's on your mind—on the tip of your tongue—say it.

PAUL   There's a square of sunlight on the wooden floor—and it makes you want to go on living. Even though you're lying there with your bones aching and your mind full of darkness—it makes you want to go on living.

MARIE Say what's burning inside you.

STEVE Stop it, Marie.

MARIE Say what you already said to me, five months ago: "If you think your real life is somewhere else…"

STEVE Stop.

MARIE "If you think your real life is somewhere else, if you're always dreaming about walking away, then you'll never create a life here. You don't want children, Marie. That's the truth of it. You want to be free to walk away, to live another life. A different life. That's why you let my children die in a lake of blood."

Silence.

JUDITH In a lake of blood?

STEVE I never meant to say that.

MARIE You never meant to, but you did. You told me, "That's the real truth, Marie."

STEVE And can you swear that there's no truth in it?

MARIE Somebody tell him: that's enough. I'm going away now.

STEVE I left you a little note too, Marie.

MARIE Somebody tell him: I didn't see any little note.

STEVE I hid it. But one of these days you'll find it.

JUDITH What happened to your babies? How did they die?

PAUL Violet, I don't know where you're from or what's going on inside your head—

MARIE Shall we go now, Violet? I brought the cookies.

PAUL I don't know how many men you have known, how many trains you have caught, how many places you have visited—

MARIE At first, I stuffed a big bag with photos and jewellery and postcards and mementos, but then I said to myself, "No, Violet is right, don't take anything," so I just brought the cookies.

PAUL If you want to tell me, I'll listen. Listening is something I know how to do.

MARIE Shall we go, Violet?

PAUL But, if you want to keep it to yourself, that's fine too.

MARIE Shall we go?

PAUL I also know how to wait.

JUDITH Violet, please don't leave right now.

Thunder.

STEVE It's 8:15, Violet.

JUDITH We're going to have cake, for Violet's birthday.

STEVE It's not Violet's birthday.

JUDITH I feel sure it is.

STEVE It's the birthday of the slag heap, of all those who rot away inside their good intentions, inside their plans to change, inside their illusions. Why don't we celebrate them?

MARIE Why is he saying that? Somebody ask him why he's saying that.

PAUL Violet's still here. She's chosen to stay here. That's what we're celebrating.

STEVE It makes you want to shout, doesn't it?

MARIE Shout what, Steve?

JUDITH Let's eat.

STEVE Shout: "Enough! I've had it!"

JUDITH I'm cutting the cake.

MARIE You've done nothing but shout, Steve—your whole life.

JUDITH Have a slice, Violet. You're going to love it, you'll see. Everybody loves it. It's got a subtle, delicate flavour.

MARIE And what did it get you? Is the world any less injust, are you any less unhappy?

STEVE That's not the point.

JUDITH Have a slice, Paul.

PAUL No, thanks, I… I don't want any. Neither does Violet.

JUDITH I baked it myself. It took me all afternoon.

MARIE So, what is the point?

STEVE We've had this talk a thousand times, Marie.

JUDITH Have a slice, Paul.

PAUL I just told you—

JUDITH Please.

PAUL Okay.

MARIE The truth is, you don't want to change anything. You just want to break windows and be mad at the world every day, and every night too. Something to chew on all night, while everybody else is asleep. Outrage—that's your true south—the tropical country that surrounds you and makes you feel like you're truly alive.

STEVE   You don't understand. You never did.

JUDITH   Have a slice, Steve.

MARIE   You just pretend, Steve! At first, there was a real anger flowing through your arms and your chest and lighting up your eyes. It gave you that burning, lively look—but now you just pretend.

STEVE   How can you say that? What do you know about what flows through my arms and chest and what goes on inside my head?

JUDITH   Marie, have a slice. Please.

MARIE   You're pretending, Steve! Pretending to be mad, pretending to suffer because others suffer.

STEVE   You're just chattering.

MARIE   I'm saying what I've seen for months now, for years.

STEVE   You see nothing. You just dream about walking away.

JUDITH   *(shouts)* Everybody, eat!

MARIE   That's not true!

STEVE   From the first, you wanted to walk away!

JUDITH   *(louder)* Come on, everybody! Eat!

> *Silence. Startled by JUDITH's outcry, they freeze, each of them holding a slice of cake.*

Taste it and you'll love it.

STEVE   I'm not tasting it.

JUDITH   Taste it and you'll say "This cake is delicious, Judith."

> *They begin to eat in silence. PAUL bites down on something hard.*

PAUL   What's that? *(He takes something out of his mouth.)* A ring?

JUDITH   I said to myself, "If it's in Violet's slice, then the answer is 'No.' If it's in my slice, then the answer is 'Yes.'"

MARIE   Yes what, Judith?

JUDITH   "If nobody gets it, then it's 'Maybe.'"

PAUL   You baked a ring in your cake?

JUDITH   Since you got it, I don't know what the answer is.

PAUL   Why a ring?

JUDITH   I didn't have anything else. I said to myself, "Gold is very pure, so it won't affect the flavour. And it won't melt." I know it's stupid. The answer was already there, inside me—so, no matter what game I made up, it wouldn't change anything. But I just couldn't stop myself.

MARIE   What answer, Judith?

JUDITH   I woke up this morning thinking, "If it stays hot, the answer is 'Yes,' but if the weather changes, then it's 'No.' If that guy on the bus who's so handsome smiles at me, then it's 'Yes,' but if he doesn't look at me, it's 'No.'"

MARIE   What is "No," Judith?

JUDITH   I know, it's something real, physical, and it's got nothing to do with rings or cakes or guys who smile. Either the paper changes colour or it doesn't. But I was searching for a sign.

MARIE   You're pregnant, Judith?

PAUL   Pregnant?

JUDITH   Tell me one thing, Violet. Please.

MARIE   *(to JUDITH)* What are you going to do?

JUDITH   Just tell me to accept this, and later on we'll see. Otherwise, tell me, if I have any doubts, not to go there. I know I have to pay attention to the signs. But there are so many of them.

MARIE   You're pregnant, Judith?

JUDITH   Sometimes I close my eyes and I see myself with a big belly, living with Eric in our home in the north. Other times, I see myself staying thin, all alone in the big city, surrounded by noise, and my shoulders are rising and falling. But I don't know if I'm crying or laughing. I can't tell.

STEVE   You're pregnant.

JUDITH   Violet, you tell me what I am.

PAUL   Stop it, Judith.

JUDITH   You tell me, "You're a girl who stays planted in the earth, like a tree who finds happiness in sending out new branches."

PAUL   You can't ask this of Violet.

JUDITH   Or tell me, "You're a girl who needs more. More room, more happiness, more certainties."

STEVE   Stay here, Judith. Make babies. Love Eric. There's nothing else.

MARIE   Do what you want, Judith. If you want to go, then go. If you want to dance, then dance with whoever you like.

JUDITH What am I going to be, Violet? A woman in a house crammed with kids and noise and worries—or—or a woman like you, all alone in the wilderness, with a funny little hat on her head, who cries in the middle of the night, and who says, "I have made a mistake."

PAUL Violet's not all alone.

JUDITH A woman who scratches out everything she writes in her notebook, pages and pages with black scratches across them.

STEVE What notebook? What did you scratch out?

PAUL That's none of our business.

JUDITH A woman who writes her story, her thoughts, her love, all the little details of her life, then scratches it out, line after line.

PAUL You don't know what she wrote.

JUDITH Why did you scratch it all out?

MARIE She scratched it all out because she wanted to start over. That's why. Sometimes you have to scratch out everything you did before, so that the road lies open ahead.

STEVE No. She scratched it all out because she was finished.

JUDITH Say something, Violet. Say: "I scratched it all out because…"

MARIE Leave her alone. We don't need to know why. We just need to get on with it. Are you coming, Violet?

STEVE It's nearly 8:30, Violet.

JUDITH "I scratched it all out because…"

PAUL Are you coming, Violet?

STEVE If you want to, Violet, you can stay right here, with me, surrounded by all the noise, watching the little pieces flying around in the air. I'll hold your hand if you get scared.

MARIE What noise, what little pieces flying around? Steve?

JUDITH "I scratched it all out because…"

STEVE We could shout together, if you want to. If there was nobody to shout, to burn, to chew things over at night, the world would've died out long ago.

MARIE To burn what, Steve? What are you up to? Do any of you know what he's up to?

STEVE We're going to fly around up there, in a thousand little pieces, along with what's left of the mine, what's left of hope, all the little scraps of our shattered loves. We're going to count to ten and then push the plunger.

MARIE What have you done, Steve?

PAUL You planted dynamite in the mine shaft, didn't you? You're going to blow it sky-high?

JUDITH Is that true, Steve?

STEVE We're going to blow us sky-high, and then look down, from way up there, on all the little flags—all the flags we planted in our illusions.

MARIE Flags?

> *MARIE digs underneath one of the flags planted by STEVE. She reads the message planted under the flag:*

"List of Aberrations:
Elevators out of order
Doors that slam
Abandoned mines
Men sitting at home staring at the TV
Men who have lost hope and it has lost them
The Great God Profit
Fear of authority
Fear of breakage
Empty days
My silent home
The thought that I leave no one behind
No one to inherit my eyes, my courage, my anger
No one who will go on wanting what I wanted
The feeling that I am a broken piece of furniture
A plant dying in the corner of the room
Marie breathing in the next room
Marie's look, which says that I am not enough
Not gentle enough
Not reasonable enough
Not exotic enough
Marie's body, which I don't touch anymore
Desire, which disappeared one day
You wake up and it's not there
Where did it go?
Into someone else's body?
My silent home
My noisy mind
Every day
Every night"

> *Silence. A gust of wind.*

You wrote that, Steve?

> *Silence. Uneasiness. Then VIOLET's gentle voice.*

VIOLET I scratched it all out because…

JUDITH Because why, Violet?

VIOLET I scratched it all out because… it was not right.

JUDITH What wasn't right?

STEVE The world—life—there's nothing that's right.

JUDITH Is that it, Violet?

VIOLET It wasn't right… like singing off-key.

JUDITH What are you trying to say?

VIOLET The music should come from our lips in the right order, the right notes, in the right key.

PAUL You were trying to sing?

VIOLET My words, my tunes, are all wrong, like an out-of-tune violin. A violin that you want to smash on a rock—break into a thousand little pieces.

PAUL I don't understand, Violet.

VIOLET Everything sounds wrong. Except for "I have made a mistake."

MARIE Why?

VIOLET Why? I don't know. It's come to this… and now…

JUDITH Now?

VIOLET If I say "I did—I was—I had…" I had a home, and love, and plans, but if I say "I left my home, and love, and plans, because I wanted, because I hoped for more, always more" or "because I couldn't breathe there"—it sounds all wrong. Or if I say "I had the words, millions of words in my head, on my lips, in my notebooks, to explain the world, but they slipped away and got lost"— that sounds wrong too. Or if I say "I thought, I believed, I imagined that things would turn out differently, that I would always have lots of people around me, like at a party, with singing and music and noise, and never any emptiness, never, never any emptiness"—it sounds wrong. Don't you hear that?

PAUL No, Violet.

VIOLET If I say "I didn't mean to end up here, at an abandoned mine, with an out-of-order elevator, which will never again descend deep inside the earth full of strong men ready to blow everything sky-high…." If I say "I have looked at the dead fields, the slag heaps, the abandoned mine deep inside me, the plants that will never again sprout inside my head, inside my heart"—it sounds wrong. And if I say "You have to stay, you have to go, you have to love, you have to live"—it sounds wrong. Don't you hear? And if I say "Hope, courage, faith, certainty, forward, continue, explode, love," that sounds wrong. And if I say "I've walked a long way, I found a hat on a park bench, I put it on my head to protect me from the sun, the cold, the world—to say to the world 'I know who I am, I'm a woman wearing a hat, a funny little hat on her head....'" And if I say "My name is Violet, and here I am, on earth, earthbound"—it sounds wrong. And if I say "Please help me, I've lost my words, my tunes in the right key, I am lost, I am all alone…"

Silence.

JUDITH *(whispers)* "Please help me."

MARIE What happened to you, Violet?

Pause.

VIOLET I have made a mistake, about my road, my plans, my love, my life.

JUDITH How did you make a mistake about your life?

VIOLET I didn't see it coming. I walked straight ahead, but then, all of a sudden, I had no more words to think, to name, to decide, to ask my way. I didn't know where I was. I didn't have the words. Only these: "I have made a mistake."

PAUL Everybody makes mistakes, Violet. Me too, one day deep down in the earth, I thought I had checked out the support beams, but I was mistaken. Then I thought it was all over, but, after four hours, I heard somebody shouting, "He's over here, I found him!" The most beautiful thing I ever heard—that man's voice in the pitch black.

VIOLET I have made a mistake. Sorry.

MARIE Never mind what you are, never mind what you've done, it's always possible to start again, start over. Even if you're all alone, in the middle of nowhere, in the middle of the ocean, it's still possible. It has to be possible.

JUDITH You have to do something. What will you do?

PAUL Look, Violet. We've got sparkling wine, we've got cake. We can drink, we can laugh, we can make some noise. We've even got a ring. I can kneel down in front of you and propose.

Thunder.

STEVE Time to go. Now.

JUDITH She said "Please help me."

PAUL And we can sing, too.

JUDITH Sing?

PAUL I've got a song, right here in my notebook.

JUDITH It's getting cold all of a sudden. Don't you think so?

PAUL We're going to sing. Come on, everybody. It'll warm us up.

STEVE That's ridiculous.

MARIE Look at me, Steve.

> *Thunder.*

JUDITH You're cold, Violet. Give me your hands.

PAUL We're going to sing. I've got the song, here in my notebook.

MARIE We've got to live, Steve. It's all we've got. You have to enjoy the little things, look around for beauty, lean on other people.

STEVE I don't know how. Not anymore.

MARIE Sure you do. We all know how.

PAUL *(sings)* "Where have all the flowers gone,
Long time passing,
Where have all the flowers gone…"

PAUL & JUDITH "Long time ago,
Where have all the flowers gone,
Gone to young girls every one…"

MARIE You know this song, Steve. You always said it's a song about how we have to change everything. I don't know where you got that. It's obviously a love song.

PAUL Sing, Violet.

PAUL, JUDITH, & VIOLET "When will they ever learn,
When will they ever learn?"

MARIE Sing, Steve.

STEVE It's ridiculous. They're ridiculous, singing like that.

MARIE Maybe.

> *Eventually they all sing, except STEVE, who stands apart.*

PAUL, JUDITH, VIOLET, & MARIE "Where have all the young girls gone,
Long time passing,
Where have all the young girls gone,
Long time ago?
Where have all the young girls gone,
Gone to young men, every one,
When will they ever learn?
When will they ever learn?"

> *A gust of wind. Thunder. It grows colder.*

"Where have all the young men gone,
Long time passing,
Where have all the young men gone,
Long time ago?

Where have all the young men gone,
They are all in uniform,
When will they ever learn?
When will they ever learn?"

Uneasy pause.

STEVE   Great. You sang. What now? What did it change?

PAUL   Nothing, Steve. Nothing changed. But we sang.

JUDITH   What are you going to do, Violet? What are all of us going to do?

Pause.

MARIE   You're not coming with me, Violet. I know that. And I—should I go? Would that be the courageous thing? Is that what's needed? Courage?

A gust of wind.

STEVE   You have to go now.

JUDITH   We can't just rush off. Violet hasn't given Paul an answer. Or me either.

MARIE   Violet has run out of words. That's what she said.

Pause.

PAUL   You're not coming, Violet. I know. You think it doesn't make sense. You think you need something more, in order to say "Yes." More words, more certainty. And maybe you're right. But who is coming along? Who's going to reach out and touch me for the rest of my life?

Thunder.

STEVE   You can't stay. It's going to pour down. You have to seek shelter.

MARIE   Where? There's no shelter here.

STEVE   There's the mine shaft.

MARIE   Which is full of dynamite.

STEVE   It's all we've got.

Thunder.

We have to go in. Hurry up! Violet, come and find shelter at least. Violet?

ALL THE OTHERS   Violet?

VIOLET is no longer there.

The end.

When Books Come Tumbling Down
(La bibliothèque de Constance)

by Marie-Ève Gagnon

translated by Louise H. Forsyth

Introduction to
When Books Come Tumbling Down
(La bibliothèque de Constance)

When Books Come Tumbling Down is the dramatic representation of a normal middle-class family at a moment of crisis. The three family members—parents and daughter—seem to possess everything that prevailing socio-cultural values tell us are needed to be happy and prosper: a stable relationship, good jobs, a nice home, a delightful child. Yet, as Gagnon skilfully and imaginatively shows, love has difficulty showing itself and speaking inside this home—the potential for violence lurks and even happens on two occasions—solitude, unhappiness, and self-delusion are the norm. The play's remarkable first scene reveals the gap between appearance and reality as Constance, the play's central character and a respected physician specializing in eating disorders in adolescent girls, is seen on stage gorging on food and then immediately making herself vomit. One knows immediately that something is out of joint in her life. From that starting point, Gagnon uses fantasy in the form of a ghost from Constance's past to take the audience beyond the immediate manifestation of insatiable hunger represented in the opening scene through some of the dynamics of mental illness and domestic violence, beneath the surface of sexist hegemonic discourse, and into Constance's psyche, where powerful unacknowledged conflicts have simmered for years.

When Books Come Tumbling Down is a play in twelve scenes with three characters: Constance and Antoine, a couple in their early thirties, and the Woman. The Woman is a featureless phantom figure who morphs during the final five scenes into Constance's dead childhood friend Estelle at ages twelve and sixteen. It is her insistent visitations that produce fresh but painful awareness in Constance and which may, in the end, lead to a resolution of the crisis in the home. Scenes Two and Seven dramatize the fragility and superficiality of the bonds holding the couple together and the silences on which their preservation depends. In both scenes Constance and Antoine are on stage. Yet they do not speak to each other. They deliver monologues revealing the way they see themselves and the other, their life together, the deluded assumptions they dare not talk about that their love is sound. They implicitly acknowledge that their sex life is unsatisfactory and that they do not know what love is. Both characters know there is uncontrolled erotic violence in Constance. The enigma of this violence underscores the dramatic conflict and thematic structure of *When Books Come Tumbling Down*. Antoine has always preferred until now not to understand her outbursts, just to enjoy the excitement they offer. Although Constance's bulimia suggests that the violence within her is being masochistically turned against her, she has lived with it and felt its thrill whenever it brought extreme pleasure:

> I have fantasies that don't belong to me, fantasies of violence, but that's the way I have an orgasm. I want to be taken. The images are so strong

in my head. They arouse my body, and at the same time they hurt my head.

You could say that there are things that make no sense to my thinking mind, things that are powerfully anchored in me (Scene Seven).

The single component of their lives that they have shared and that has allowed them to know genuine love—if not for each other, at least for another—has been their daughter Mathilde, whom Constance acknowledges they "decided to have [...] because there was no other possible way to express what we felt for each other. We needed to have a child" (Scene Two). Although never appearing on stage, Mathilde is a symbol throughout the play of the simple joy and meaning in life for which both Constance and Antoine yearn.

In the same way that the opening scenes of *When Books Come Tumbling Down* reveal Constance's psychic desperation and the illusion-based fragility of the couple's relationship, her professional life as a respected physician is shown to be on the verge of cracking. The ring of the telephone from colleagues whose teen patients are in need of her expertise show her avoiding participation, responding to calls testily, and assuming a callousness that conflicts with the approach she knows is appropriate when working in her field. She has kept up appearances all these years in her existence by adhering closely to the dicta of hegemonic discourse. Setting aside her own desires, she was obedient to her parents. She graduated from medical school at the top of the class; her ideas about romantic love and marriage conform to dominant norms; she has read all the right books and knows the formulas for assessing and treating patients in her field of specialization. While both she and Antoine say that they do not wish to follow the crowd and be like everyone else, she has, in fact, kept up the appearance of being the epitome of values prevailing in contemporary society. She has thus managed to be not only a model of conformity, but indeed a role model illustrating that women can be and do anything they wish, paying the price of distancing herself from her own experiences and repressing her feelings. As is dramatically shown in the opening scene by her desperation during the bulimic episode, this repression has been having serious effects for many years.

The tumbling of the books from the enormous bookshelves in Scene Three represents a radical tear in the entire epistemological and ontological fabric of the illusions Constance has maintained in her existence as an individual, a lover, a mother, and a professional. Until this moment, she has never dared doubt that "The more things you know [through education and books], the freer you are" (Scene Six). However, the authoritative words and definitive knowledge represented by the books have built a barrier between the objectively established, authoritative truth Constance claims to live by and the opposing truths insistently bubbling up inside her. As long as the books remain solidly on their shelves, they provide her with an intellectual and psychological distancing within which she can position herself and so avoid seeing clearly, knowing herself intimately, having to consider the significance of her corporeality, her sense of self, her family, and the world she lives in. The ideas and values of others have wormed their way so deeply into her mind that they have assumed almost complete control of her behaviour. Nevertheless, they have not managed to stifle the psychic processes which haunt her. Although her brain has been conditioned to think in certain ways by signs and meanings other than her own, her feelings, which have stubbornly refused to be checked and silenced, have been bringing her extreme anxiety.

The disappearance of Mathilde at the same time that the books fall from their orderly places puts Constance in a situation she has no choice but to address. Her urgent search for Mathilde, which is the immediate problem of the play's dramatic action, parallels her search for reconciliation with her unresolved past and for fresh understanding of both the way the world turns ideologically and who she is.

The shadowy body of the mysterious Woman walks around the set at the outset of the play. The power of her material presence is almost immediately reinforced by the assertive yet familiar voice with which she addresses Constance. It soon becomes clear that, like Jacob Marley of Dickens's *A Christmas Carol*, the Woman has appeared out of Constance's past to incite her to recognize the need to construct a new perspective on society and to change her ways before it is too late to prevent harm to herself and others. The Woman's familiarity strongly displeases Constance, who is terrified by all the Woman knows about her bulimia, her recent behaviour, and events in her past. The Woman knows that Constance hit Mathilde a few days ago, causing her great pain: "You emptied your daughter's eyes" (Scene Four), and it is she who effected the little girl's disappearance. Constance, who clearly had no intention of revisiting that explosive eruption acknowledges that her violence burst out when Mathilde revealed she was uncomfortable in her own skin. Constance saw this as a sign that her own tiny daughter was already on the path leading to the lack of self-esteem, discomfort with their bodies, and such disorders as bulimia to which girls and women are so prone.

The letter produced by the Woman, eerily the same letter Estelle sent Constance when they were twelve, introduces an important piece in the thematic composition of *When Books Come Tumbling Down*. Estelle's disgusted announcement in her letter that she has begun to menstruate indicates her refusal to embark on the path to womanhood, as this event in a girl's life is coded in all cultures. The letter raises the urgent question of what it means to be a woman. Is there a connection between the young Mathilde's discomfort in her body and the womanhood that inevitably awaits her?

The Woman's feminist analysis of the patriarchal systems in which we all still live is developed in the conversation she insists on having with Constance. For her, it is culture's representations of *Woman* that almost inevitably capture individual girls and women in their behavioural imperatives, depriving them of the spontaneity and authenticity that would otherwise flow from their own uncensored perceptions and experiences. These dangerous representations in cultural practice are so ubiquitous that they usually remain unnoticed, appearing normal and self-evident. They are transmitted throughout dominant social systems by the functioning of hegemonic discourse, for which the books in Constance's library are a metaphor and a vehicle, as the Woman insists:

> No! You don't think as you like. You think as you have been learning to think for two thousand years. You see the world through all these books. And in most of these books, you don't exist. As a result you accept as reality a world where your existence is less or not at all [...] Take a look! The Bible, *The Odyssey*, *Don Quixote*, and all the others that history has decided to retain [...] Tell me what you have learned about what it means to be a woman in those books. Tell me! (Scene Six)

Constance acknowledges the aberrations regarding women found in the works of those that are taken to be the world's greatest writers. She also acknowledges that the feminist movement of the 1960s and 1970s produced important changes and led to the production of great works written by women, even though these works have not been admitted to the mainstream pantheon of canonical texts. Little has changed over the past fifty years in the cultural representation of women and the ideas about them. When challenged by the Woman to know what she plans to do about the distortions based on gender that are integral to received knowledge and values in patriarchal society, Constance responds "Nothing. Because those days have come and gone. That's the past." It's "the jargon of the 1970s" (Scene Six).

Reflecting prevailing ideas in today's period, which has been called post-feminist, Constance has unthinkingly but determinedly bought into the belief that she and her daughter can be whatever they wish to be. She chooses not to look at the impact of the beauty myth imprinted everywhere by popular culture and the mass media nor at the taboos that surround women as independent thinkers or agents lucidly heeding the messages of their own sexed bodies and working out their own agenda. She thereby chooses not to see that the psychic forces driving her to bulimia and violence against her daughter are telling her that social and financial success are leading her to be dangerously untrue to herself and preventing her from feeling free to express herself and to love. Like Estelle, who said she lost her personal voice when she entered puberty, she has allowed formulaic words articulated by social leaders to determine her behaviour and has learned to use the full range of patriarchal authoritarian discourse in her professional practice. These words, expressions, and languages have formed her reality, a reality in which she is made uncomfortable in her body and is unable to escape her own anguish, guilt, and violence. Feeling herself to be somehow dirty and fat, she has suppressed her awareness of the "many things to think, to create, to build" (Scene Nine). As the flashbacks show in the final scenes of *When Books Come Tumbling Down*, the conditioning, indeed the brainwashing, of Constance began many years ago. Unlike Estelle, who knew she did not want to become *Woman*, Constance did not directly resist society's pressures. Still, she has not escaped their powerful negative impact. The play's ambiguous ending leaves some room for hope that, in place of the death chosen by Estelle, there is the possibility for Constance and Mathilde to have the courage to come alive by thinking and speaking out for themselves, by refusing society's myths about their feminine bodies, minds, and sexuality—to be truly unlike everyone else who conforms to the unjust and distorted values of today's sexist consumer society.

Marie-Ève Gagnon has created a moving feminist play for the twenty-first century. The characters come alive in their rich humanity as they confront their own contradictions and vexing misunderstandings with others. The fantasy built into the flashbacks, where a dead girl appears, and into the central role played by a ghost, who incites the major character to new departures and enunciates some of the play's ideological premises, speaks to the imagination and the latent passions of those who feel stifled by all that is apathetic and conformist in today's society. Gagnon has created in Constance a middle-class, professional woman of today: intelligent, well-educated, needing love, longing to be a good mother, and at the same time living a life of stress, guilt, doubt, and lack of self-esteem. The feminist movement of the 1960s and 1970s addressed and resolved many injustices and inequities. It produced a social climate in which all thinking and morally responsible people believe in the legitimacy of equity for all. It led to the widespread belief in this post-feminist moment that girls and women can do anything they want to do, be anything they want to be. Yet there are many signs that this laudable objective remains elusive. How does one combine mothering with satisfying emotional and sexual relationships and a serious professional career? A clear look in any direction on our public stages shows that most often women with successful careers hold their tongue when it comes to women's issues. Hegemonic patriarchal values, systems, and structures prevail largely unchallenged. And even with such respect for tenacious, lingering sexist taboos, women everywhere are still not represented equitably in positions of power. The challenges of mothering seem to be growing more and more complex, while the stubbornness of social myths surrounding women's bodies, their sexualities, and their intellectual abilities produces anguish in many quarters, often revealing itself, as in the case of Constance, in mental illness and irrational violence against oneself and others.

About Marie-Ève Gagnon

Author of twenty-five theatre texts and director of about thirty shows and dramatic readings in Québec's professional theatre, Marie-Ève Gagnon defines herself as a person passionate about life in all its mobility and about processes of creativity. *Trois sombres textes pour actrice éclairée* was first performed at Le Périscope and Espace Libre in Montréal. *Pitié pour les vieilles chiennes sales* was first performed at the Festival de Théâtre des Amériques in 1999. In 2004 *L'enfant nègre de ma tante Céline* was created under the direction of Alice Ronfard with Marina Orsini and Denis Bernard as part of the evening *Les hommes aiment-ils autant le sexe qu'ils le disent* at Espace Go. In 2007, *No Matter What* was first performed at Espace Libre. In 2009, Gagnon directed her play *Et je sais que cela doit être le paradis* at La Petite Licorne. Her play *Le doré*, written for Frédéric Zacharek and Nathalie Gascon, had a dramatic reading in October 2009 at Le Quat'Sous during the annual CEAD event Dramaturgies en dialogues. In late 2009 she directed Catherine Sénart's musical *L'amour selon Venne*. In spring 2010 she directed one of Larry Tremblay's short plays as part of the show entitled *L'Amour Trois* at Espace Libre, organized by the theatre company Omnibus.

Marie-Ève Gagnon is president of the Association québécoise des auteurs dramatiques (AQAD) and a member of the women's committee of the Union des Artistes (UDA). For her, activism in these organizations allows her to work toward the improvement of the status of artists in today's society. Meeting with young people and encouraging them at the beginning of their career as artists bring her great professional satisfaction. Gagnon has been teaching acting, playwriting, and directing for many years.

Gagnon is the author of the AQAD commissioned report *Rideau de Verre, auteures et scènes québécoises* (2009), a landmark study of the place of women playwrights in Québec theatre. Basing her findings on statistics from the past seven years, such as the fact that only 29% of the plays produced on Québec stages were written by women (even though a majority of audience members are female), Gagnon concludes that women playwrights find themselves limited and disadvantaged in their careers by an invisible but very real and tenacious glass curtain, particularly in the large institutionalized and well-funded theatres. Her study shows that equity has not yet been achieved on Québec stages, despite the commonly held belief that we are in a post-feminist age. Of particular relevance at this moment in the twenty-first century in the findings of *Rideau de Verre* is the resistance Gagnon encountered throughout the community of those with whom she spoke—both women and men—to the hypothesis that the sex of individuals influences opportunities available to them. There appears to be a widespread yet unexamined will to believe that equity of all kinds has been achieved.

Published Works by Marie-Ève Gagnon

Trois sombres textes pour actrice éclairée, suivi de *Pitié pour les vieilles chiennes sales* (1999). Montréal: Les Herbes Rouges.

Rideau de verre. Auteures et scènes québécoises. Un Portrait socio-économiques (July 2009). Association Québécoise des Auteurs dramatiques.

La bibliothèque de Constance was first produced in La Salle Jean-Claude Germain of the Théâtre d'Aujourd'hui in Montréal on March 13, 2002, with the following company:

Constance Lussier   Lyne Rodier
Antoine Melançon   Daniel Desputeau
La Femme   Priscillia Roger

Directed by Diane Dubeau
Stage design by Jean Bard
Lighting by Louise Lemieux

Characters

Constance Lussier, thirty-three years old, physician specializing in treating female
    clients with eating disorders
Antoine Melançon, thirty-five years old, husband of Constance
The Woman

Translator's Note: In all conversations between Constance and The Woman, Constance uses the formal and distancing pronoun *vous*, while The Woman uses the familiar and intimate pronoun *tu*.

Setting

The living room in the comfortable Lussier-Melançon home. Immense shelves filled with books of all kinds dominate the space.

WHEN BOOKS COME TUMBLING DOWN

Scene One

Chocolate bar and other empty food wrappers lie on the table in front of the television. The room is in disorder and dimly lit.

CONSTANCE can be heard vomiting in the wings; she vomits violently several times.

She comes on stage, out of breath and exhausted.

She sits on the floor, leaning against the bookshelves.

A WOMAN walks around. Like a shadow, like a presence so powerful that she invades us.

CONSTANCE feels something; she begins to cry softly.

THE WOMAN is no longer there.

CONSTANCE looks at her fingers, which are trembling. She is cold. She gets up and goes to get her gloves from the pocket of her coat, which is hanging near the front door.

She turns music on very, very loud, as a teenage girl would.

She leaves and goes to the kitchen. She returns with a load of food, which she places on the table in front of the television. She begins to eat more and more rapidly, and then runs to make herself vomit in the bathroom.

She returns even more exhausted, but this time she is extremely agitated.

The telephone rings; she jumps. The telephone rings. She turns the music off and answers.

CONSTANCE *(trying to breathe normally)* Hello…

Well, very well…

And how about you, Monique, things okay…?

Hm…

Yes, I understand. But I just don't think I can take her. I already have too many clients…. It's important for me to be able to treat them the way they deserve. Anyway, I don't have to explain that to you, do I…?

…Hey, wait a minute. Don't you try to lay a guilt trip on me…

Good, okay, I'll take her but only until you find something else for her. Do we have a clear understanding about this? You'll keep looking for a place somewhere else. I'll take her as a temporary outpatient. Okay…?

Yeah, you can send the file to my secretary. Thanks.

She hangs up. The doorbell rings.

CONSTANCE hesitates between putting the food away and answering the door. The doorbell rings again. She starts to gather up the food, then stops. The bell rings for a third time. She looks around for something to put on. She picks up her coat and puts it on. She goes toward the door and opens it.

THE WOMAN   Nice neighbourhood y'live in.

CONSTANCE   *(dryly and defensively, not appreciating the stranger's familiar tone)* How can I help you?

THE WOMAN   Nothin' special, but then again everything in general.

CONSTANCE   Well then, in that case you must excuse me. I don't wish to buy whatever you're selling, nor do I want to become a member of your party, and I don't believe in God. And so… *(tries to close the door)*

THE WOMAN   Were you going out?

CONSTANCE   That is none of your business.

THE WOMAN   I didn't imagine you like this, Constance. You know, I thought you'd've changed more than that. No, your body's 'most the same. So you were leaving, eh? This won't take long.

CONSTANCE   How do you know my name?

THE WOMAN   Yes, I know your name. We went to school together, to the Convent of the Marcellines. You don't remember me?

CONSTANCE   No, I'm sorry. What is your name?

THE WOMAN   I was in the same class as you. I remember you very well. You were always with Estelle Ménard. You had those red braids that you rolled up on each side like Princess Leia in *Star Wars*. That was you, wasn't it, Constance Lussier?

CONSTANCE   What is your name? You haven't told me your name.

THE WOMAN   *(coming into the room)* Wow! How many books do you have? Five hundred? Six hundred? There must be a small fortune in all of them.

CONSTANCE   I did not give you permission to come in. I do not remember you at the Marcellines.

THE WOMAN   Don't worry about that. It happens to me too, I forget faces sometimes. Don't worry, I'm not a serial killer.

CONSTANCE   Stop right there, madam. I don't want to be rude, but I must ask you to leave. If you won't even tell me your name…

THE WOMAN   You must have all the important books.

CONSTANCE   Out! That is enough! Do you want me to call the police? I did not give you permission to come in.

THE WOMAN   Well, well, aren't we touchy!

All I wanted to do was talk about you, and about Mathilde.

CONSTANCE   Do you know Mathilde?

THE WOMAN   Your daughter Mathilde isn't here?

CONSTANCE   That is certainly none of your business.

THE WOMAN   Yes, that's true, it's none of my business.

But I like her; I like your little girl; I'd like to help her.

CONSTANCE   You, who are you? How do you know my daughter? Why do you want to help her? My daughter does not need help. I forbid you to speak of my daughter.

THE WOMAN   My gosh, you're suspicious! You're right, you know, the world is rotten, isn't it? One horror after another, first greed and then scandal. How could you be expected to be anything but suspicious. It's all about survival, isn't it? It's as if everything that's beautiful has always hidden rot, like shit nicely wrapped up in tissue paper with a silk ribbon. Yes, you're absolutely right to be suspicious, but for sure not of me.

CONSTANCE   Madam, I have no wish to hear your profound thoughts about the world. This has gone on far enough. You are going to leave.

THE WOMAN   You're not capable of just talking with a woman who comes and rings at your door. You can't do it, eh? Just two people who meet each other and speak to each other. Oh, it's not idle chatter. No, it's deep conversation. But there's no need to raise your voice because the other person is listening to you with her entire being. You can't do it, eh? But I already knew you were like that. I knew you wouldn't want to listen to me. So, I'll just have do things the only way I can. I have no choice.

CONSTANCE   You are threatening me. You know that it is a crime to utter threats. I am going to lay a complaint against you.

THE WOMAN   I'm going. I've finished for the time being. But first I have a letter for you. Here, take it!

> *CONSTANCE shoves THE WOMAN out, then throws out the letter, bangs the door shut, and locks it. The doorbell rings.*

It's a letter from Estelle. Look at the handwriting.

> *She slips the letter under the door. CONSTANCE takes it.*

Look, isn't that her handwriting? Doesn't that look like her handwriting? And the drawing on the envelope. It's one of her drawings, isn't it?

CONSTANCE opens the envelope.

You're right to be suspicious. The world is rotten.

She can be heard going away, then coming back.

One last thing. If I was you, I wouldn't gulp down all that stuff to eat that's sitting on the table. You'll ruin your health making yourself vomit.

Scene Two

The same living room. CONSTANCE and ANTOINE are sitting beside each other on the couch. Each speaks as if the other was not there.

ANTOINE   I look at other women. Constance looks at other men. We've never talked about it, but the *evidence* is so *evident* that it would be ridiculous to talk about it. And then too, this has nothing to do with the way we feel. I mean the feeling that exists between us. It's a feeling that goes way beyond the reality of our lives, and our little personality weaknesses.

CONSTANCE   I love Antoine. Even if it makes me a bit uncomfortable to say it.

I love him, but not like two years ago, not like two hours ago. I don't know if I'll love him two months from now. I don't know anything about love.

ANTOINE   I find her violent. Oh, if you saw her you'd decide right away that she's like a little stuffed puppy. But I know…

CONSTANCE   Antoine and I decided to have a child because there was no other possible way to express what we felt for each other. We needed to have a child.

ANTOINE   I know there's a hidden face. That violence, I'm familiar with some of it; I'm afraid of it, but I also know it excites me. It excites me to feel a seething in her that I don't understand.

CONSTANCE   Whenever I hurt Antoine, he starts to act like a high and mighty monarch.

Everything in him is hurt, everything. Even his little toe, even the cells of his skin, even his childhood memories.

Forgiveness is always hard to obtain. And I can understand why, because when it comes right down to it he's better than me. He's better because he's more generous, less mean, more open, more human. I'm not being ironic. That's the reality.

ANTOINE   I admit that her illness…. I know it's an illness, but for me, and I'm a bit ashamed to admit it, what it is instead is something special that troubles me and at the same time attracts me. I don't want the woman I love to harm herself. I'm not crazy, nor sadistic. But the release of the inner forces that inhabit her and make her move. Ah! It's fascinating for me.

CONSTANCE   I know that his love saves me... will save me. Already, I'm a better person than I was before.

Antoine isn't a saint. It's just that he's measured. I mean, he doesn't go to extremes. Then again, maybe he does go to extremes, but he doesn't show it. In fact, I just don't know.

ANTOINE   I've learned with her. I'm still learning.

CONSTANCE   Do you have to make love wildly to make love genuinely? That's what I thought for a long time. And I told myself that I was an amazing lover and that sex could never be more than a passing thrill.

Antoine taught me otherwise. He made me understand that I knew nothing about love.

ANTOINE   We make a common front together, against her family, against mine, against all people who would like to make us fit into roles. We're a team. As well, of course, there's Mathilde.

CONSTANCE   If Antoine hadn't been here, I'd be dead. Maybe not, you never know.

ANTOINE   When I saw Mathilde for the first time, I was so afraid! I wondered if I could ever meet the needs of this little being.

Constance reassured me.

CONSTANCE   I knew he'd be a good father. I knew my daughter would be lucky enough to have one marvellous man in her life.

ANTOINE   Without Constance in my life, I wouldn't have had any important goals.

I had never lived that before, such intense closeness with another human being. I felt myself in osmosis with her.

People said to me: "Ah, lovers are beautiful. Enjoy it as long as it lasts.... Sooner or later the daily routine will take over, and you'll fall back down to reality."

So? Where's the problem? I like reality. I like routine. That has never stopped me from being happy. As if you had to live your life on a constant high, always travelling from one altered state to another. No, I like things that are certain. That doesn't make me mediocre or idiotic.

Constance lives on highs. But with me her life has become more calm. And then when Mathilde arrived, our lives changed again. We had to give her structure, create a family, the workings of a family. Not in order to be a follower like all the rest of the followers. No! Simply because a baby needs a structure.

And those who say otherwise are irresponsible people who want others to believe that their laxity is a school of thought. You have to let children be free.... Free to do what? Free to lose their lives?

Life is a series of efforts and rewards. Being free does not mean flying from one gratification to another, from one reward to another. No, all you have to do is learn to love the effort. Being free is loving to make an effort and then loving to take a break afterward.

Scene Three

At this moment, the books on the bookshelves begin to fall in a fearful crescendo. CONSTANCE protects herself as best she can. She cries out.

When all the books have fallen, CONSTANCE stands up calmly, still in shock. Then, all of a sudden, she walks out of the house.

THE WOMAN is walking among the books, picks one up, opens it, and reads.

She closes it back up, smiles, and lets it fall. She leaves.

The front door opens. ANTOINE enters, followed by CONSTANCE.

ANTOINE   There's a logical explanation. We just have to find it, that's all.

CONSTANCE   I really thought the books were going to bury me.

ANTOINE   I'm going to call the city to find out whether they're doing work in the neighbourhood, dynamiting, or something like that. I'm going to call the insurance company as well. We mustn't touch anything until an inspector has seen it.

CONSTANCE   How much time will that take? We can't live long with this. It doesn't make any sense with Mathilde…

ANTOINE   Precisely. Where is Mathilde? You were the one who was supposed to go and get her.

CONSTANCE   I'm going to call the school.

ANTOINE   Don't bother. I'll do it myself.

He makes his way through the piles of books and dials the number.

Yes, good afternoon. This is Antoine Melançon, Mathilde's father. She's in grade three. I expect that she's still in after-school care. Yes, I'll wait…

Beat.

What! She's not there? That's not possible. Have you looked everywhere? Yes, yes, please go and look…

CONSTANCE   Not there?

ANTOINE   Yes… no… no. She's not with us. Yes, we'll call the neighbour. Maybe she's there. Thank you. Yes, I'll call you back.

Scene Four

CONSTANCE is smoking a cigarette. The books have not been picked up. The telephone rings.

CONSTANCE Yes, yes. I won't have the strength to just keep on waiting. Tell me something!

I'm staying here in case she comes back. Okay. Okay.

She hangs up.

The doorbell rings. CONSTANCE rushes to the door. She opens the door and THE WOMAN is there, looking as she did the previous evening. They look at each other for a moment. And then... CONSTANCE throws herself at THE WOMAN and hits her repeatedly.

Where is my daughter? I'm going to kill you, do you understand? I'll kill you, kill you!

THE WOMAN does not reply. CONSTANCE beats her with her hands and her feet.

She's in a fit of rage. Completely exhausted, she stops. THE WOMAN gets up.

THE WOMAN Kill, that's a big word. It's a word that takes up a lot of space. A word that takes up all the space.

She staggers back and goes to sit down on the couch.

I wonder how many times the word *kill* is in all the books you have here. Have you read them all? Wow, that's what reading's all about. It's about hours spent sitting all alone, almost completely still with an inanimate object in your hands.

CONSTANCE If you want money, I'll give it to you.

How much do you want?

THE WOMAN I don't want money.

CONSTANCE What *do* you want?

THE WOMAN I've already told you. I just want to talk to you. Just talk.

CONSTANCE Where is my daughter?

THE WOMAN Mathilde is safe. I too love Mathilde.

But it's you I love the most.

Did you read Estelle's letter?

CONSTANCE Why me? What have I ever done to you?

THE WOMAN Nothing. You didn't do anything to me. The person you hurt the most is yourself, not me. Mathilde as well. You hurt Mathilde.

CONSTANCE Rot. How can you dare say that?

THE WOMAN You hit her last Saturday. You slapped her. Her cheek stayed red for the whole morning. And Mathilde couldn't stop crying. Her eyes went empty. You emptied your daughter's eyes.

CONSTANCE How can you possibly know that? How long have you been spying on me?

THE WOMAN And why did you slap her, why? I'd like you to tell me.

When I look at things from my point of view, I have the impression that Mathilde is better off with me than with a mother who beats her.

CONSTANCE I didn't intend to hit her. I had never hit her before that day. I don't have to justify myself.

THE WOMAN …Listen, you haven't understood yet that all I want is to have a little conversation with you, just two people talking.

CONSTANCE I'd like that. I'd like to understand just what it is that you're going to get out of this whole story. Have you kidnapped my daughter in order to force me to have a conversation with you? That's it? And then, when it comes right down to it, it's not really a conversation you want. Instead, it's a confession. You want me to say to you that I am a bad mother, an unworthy mother who beats her daughter?

THE WOMAN No, I don't want to accuse you of anything. All I want is for us to talk about you, about your life, about your work…

CONSTANCE *(shouting)* But why?

THE WOMAN You slapped Mathilde because she said to you that she wanted to go on a diet.

When you heard those words, you went crazy with rage, and at the same time with anguish. No, not your daughter, not your love child, not your cherished little chick barely out of diapers, who is already beginning to be uncomfortable in her little skin. Not the same story repeating itself yet again, not another girl who is going to make herself vomit, make herself get thin. Not another weak person, like you.

CONSTANCE gets up and goes toward the telephone.

Are you calling the police? Go ahead. But I'm keeping Mathilde. And I know that you won't be able to live without her. So I recommend to you that you come and sit down, here, beside me. We're going to talk like two old friends. Oh, I'm not saying to you that this will be entirely painless, but it will go quickly. And then, after, Mathilde will come back. Your life will start again, not completely as before, but it'll start. You decide.

After a certain moment of hesitation, CONSTANCE comes and sits down very slowly.

Good.

I would like you to read Estelle's letter.

CONSTANCE Why?

THE WOMAN Because I want to hear it.

CONSTANCE I don't know where I put it.

THE WOMAN It's under the book in front of you.

> *CONSTANCE leans over and picks up the letter, which is in fact under the book. She opens it and begins to read, totally upset.*

CONSTANCE My dear Countess,

Ever since I had that red stain that soiled my pants and that humiliated me in front of everybody, ever since I became that disgusting thing, the universe has turned upside down.

…

I don't want to alarm you unnecessarily, dear Countess, but watch out. This could happen to you soon. And I've been told that this disorder is incurable.

Signed, the saddened Archduchess of Mirepoix.

THE WOMAN Good. What was she trying to say exactly? Was she traumatized by starting to menstruate? Poor little thing!

CONSTANCE You stole this from me. I have no idea how you managed to get into our house, dig around in my room, then in my papers…

THE WOMAN No, I didn't steal it. It was Estelle who gave it to me.

CONSTANCE That can't be. Estelle gave me this letter when we were twelve years old. It can't be that she gave it to you.

THE WOMAN Why can't it be?

> *Beat. CONSTANCE, frozen, does not answer.*

I was one of Estelle's friends too. Didn't Estelle ever talk to you about me?

Didn't Estelle tell you everything? Does that hurt you? Well, no, I'm sorry, but you weren't the only one in her life. She had other friends.

CONSTANCE That can't be.

THE WOMAN On the contrary. It can be. Wake up!

You spent so much time studying that you lost bits of it.

Of course. You wanted to be a doctor. You had to study.

And there you are. You are a doctor. Doctor Constance Lussier.

> *Beat. CONSTANCE looks at her watch.*

Why are you watching the time? Are you thinking that your husband is going to arrive and that he'll be bringing the police with him? Is that it?

CONSTANCE   On top of everything, must I share with you the slightest thought that crosses my mind? Because if you want, I can give you a list of all the nice things I'm thinking about you.

THE WOMAN   Are you still wanting to smack me? Go ahead.

CONSTANCE does not move.

Fine. So then, you're a doctor.

CONSTANCE   Yes.

THE WOMAN   But you're not an ordinary doctor. Your clients are little teen girls who have quit eating so they look like the models they see in magazines. Little spoiled girls looking for trouble.

CONSTANCE   This is not really a conversation. That's provocation.

THE WOMAN   It's the same old story of the shoemaker who has no shoes. You look after the others, but you…. You spend your life going on diets, and then on your little food binges, don't you? That's what you were doing when I came. I heard you vomiting. Tell me, Constance, do you think you're fat?

CONSTANCE laughs nervously, a despairing laugh, an end-of-the-world laugh.

Yep, you have good reason to laugh because all that is so futile, so meaningless to find yourself fat, while there are thousands of people who suffer real sufferings, there are thousands of people dying of hunger, they've never had a choice.

Beat.

But when you see yourself in a mirror, do you think you're fat? Are you fit to be seen? People don't like that, looking at "fat people." What could you say to them, to those people, about yourself? What do you think best defines you, Constance? Answer! Is it being a fat woman?

CONSTANCE   I'm a human being.

THE WOMAN   Yes, a human being. Whoa! That's something to be a human being. It's not nothing. A soul inhabiting a body.

She moves very close to her.

A warm body, trembling, sweating, living.

Do you often think about the body of your daughter? The little body of the baby that you held against yourself for hours because she was colicky. The marvellous pink flesh that you kiss with the tips of your lips and that makes your head spin. All that life, in your hands, it's frightening. It gave you such pleasure to snuggle her in your arms, give her hugs, whisper sweet nothings to her. You thought that kind of love for a body could never happen, didn't you? So much love. You didn't think that existed. So much love.

CONSTANCE   Why are you torturing me?

THE WOMAN   I'm torturing you? No, that's not torture. I'm feeling no pleasure seeing you suffer. Only I consider that there are necessary kinds of suffering, "constructive" kinds of suffering. I'm tired. We'll carry on tomorrow.

CONSTANCE   No!

THE WOMAN   Do you want us to carry on? Good. Okay. What I'd like to know is what happened to Estelle. Do you still see her now and then?

CONSTANCE   Why are you doing this?

THE WOMAN   Why am I doing what…?

CONSTANCE   Do you want me to say it? You want to hear it? Okay, okay, okay! Estelle is dead.

THE WOMAN   Ah.

CONSTANCE   As you already knew. It was in all the news at the time. Everybody from the Marcellines was at the funeral.

THE WOMAN   No, I wasn't there. I didn't know. It must have happened after I moved with my parents out of the province.

CONSTANCE   She was hit by a car. A man lost control of his vehicle and hit Estelle. She was sixteen years old.

THE WOMAN   It's almost funny to die like that. How could anyone try to make sense of such a banal death? Poor Estelle!

CONSTANCE   I was the last person to see her.

THE WOMAN   Why are you telling me that? What difference does it make?

CONSTANCE   I don't know…

THE WOMAN   Do you glory in being the last person who saw her?

CONSTANCE   No, it's just that I said to myself that if…

THE WOMAN   Yeah, yeah, the little games about the minute that makes all the difference between life and death. If you had done something or other, perhaps she wouldn't have had the accident, blah blah blah…. Fine, it's the kind of guilt that doesn't cost you much. Your part is the good part in it.

The telephone rings.

(*shouting*) Go ahead! Answer! Do you need my permission to answer?

CONSTANCE   Hello, yes… no, well no, I have no news… yes… yes, I'm waiting for you.

She hangs up.

THE WOMAN   Your husband Antoine?

You told him about me. That's good.

I'll come back when you're alone.

Your daughter… I love her. So stop worrying.

Scene Five

ANTOINE   How can it be that you have no idea what she looks like. You've seen her twice. You must certainly have noticed the colour of her hair, how tall she is, her clothes, I don't know what else. It's impossible that you can't remember a thing.

CONSTANCE   I don't remember, Antoine.

ANTOINE   It's impossible that you can't remember a thing. That just simply cannot be.

This is driving me crazy. I demand that you tell me what's really going on.

CONSTANCE   …Listen. I know it's hard to believe, but I remember everything she said, but I don't remember what she looks like. It's like a blackout. I can't find any kind of a picture in my head.

ANTOINE   Do you think the police are going to believe that…! Listen, make an effort!

CONSTANCE   That's all I do, is make efforts. I spend my life making efforts. And now I don't want anyone speaking to the police about this woman…

ANTOINE   She told you that she had kidnapped Mathilde. So…

CONSTANCE   I've told you this three times now. Not directly, but she said to me that she loved her, and that all she wanted to do was talk to me, and after that she'd give Mathilde back to me.

ANTOINE   Are we going to submit to the rules of a mentally ill woman? There's no doubt she's deranged.

CONSTANCE   Yes, she's a madwoman. I'm afraid that if we don't do what she asks something will happen to Mathilde. I'm afraid, do you understand?

ANTOINE   We're not about to buy into her blackmail. We have to tell the police…

CONSTANCE   No, she'll know it if we speak to the police. She manages to know everything she wants to know. She knows a lot of things about me…

ANTOINE   What does that mean, she knows a lot of things about me?

CONSTANCE   She knows I hit Mathilde on Saturday…

Beat.

ANTOINE   What? What are you saying?

CONSTANCE   I hit Mathilde last Saturday. She said to me that she wanted to go on a diet.

ANTOINE   Hit? What do you mean by hit?

CONSTANCE   I panicked. I panicked. I went into a rage, such a rage, that I wanted to destroy her little face, make her stop looking at me, make her stop loving me…. When she said to me that she found herself fat and that she wanted to go on a diet, it was as though she shouted right in my face that my whole life was a monstrous failure. I wanted her to die, and I wanted to die. And then, it happened, just like that. I hit the beautiful face of my little girl. I couldn't hear her crying anymore; I was hitting.

ANTOINE   *(completely devastated)* Stop.

Beat.

How could you, how could *you*, you who spends hours, days, weeks patiently listening to strangers? You can't even tolerate a few meaningless words coming out of your daughter's mouth?

CONSTANCE   No, there was nothing meaningless in those words. All the world's suffering was in those words.

ANTOINE   And is that the way you remove suffering? You smash it?

CONSTANCE   I panicked.

ANTOINE   Is it panic that's making you lose the memory of the face of the woman who has kidnapped your daughter? Is it panic that prevented you from going to get her from school?

CONSTANCE   I can't accept your accusation. I can't accept…

I know that you're angry with me for not going to get her at school. But I understood that you were the one who was going to get her.

ANTOINE   I told you clearly, I remember, I said to you: tonight, I can't go to get Mathilde. Can you go? You said yes to me. And then I asked Mathilde again before she left if everything was arranged. She told me yes, it's Mommy who's coming to get me.

CONSTANCE   I didn't go. The books fell on top of me. I lost my head. I went out of the house, and then I started to run. I ran and ran for a long time, right to the end of the dirt road. I broke my heel. I came back to the house. And then I sat down on the lawn. I couldn't go in. I couldn't, not all alone.

ANTOINE   You should have called. All you had to do was call me.

CONSTANCE No, I didn't call you. I don't know what got into me.

We're not going to hurt each other this way, Antoine. We must stay together to face this. Believe in me.

ANTOINE You ask me to believe in you after what you just told me?

CONSTANCE Listen, you and I, we aren't like everyone else. We never have wanted to be like everyone else. Do you remember when we woke up together for the first time?

I looked at you, and I had so much love inside me that I was uncomfortable. I knew that you were me, and that I was you. I started to cry and then I asked you…

ANTOINE I can't trust you. I can't anymore.

CONSTANCE No, listen to me! I started to cry, and then I asked you, do you think we're going to turn into a couple like everyone else, a couple that can't see each other anymore, doesn't get along anymore…

ANTOINE Let go of me…

CONSTANCE You gave me the answer: no, because we're different.

ANTOINE Stop…

CONSTANCE We're different, because our love is sacred. Because you and I, we're the two sides of the same coin.

Beat.

We slept inside each other, welded together, and we dreamed of the life we could create together.

ANTOINE If you only knew all that's going round in my head. All the horrors I can imagine. All the terrible possibilities I don't want to see, but that my damn head can't stop playing over and over again. I've lost control of everything. I can't get hold of anything. The world as I know it no longer exists, Constance. I can't recognize anything anymore.

CONSTANCE Why, all of a sudden, can't you see me anymore as you used to? Are you imagining that I have become another woman? I care about Mathilde just as much as you do. My love, it's visceral. I panicked, but it's over now. That never happened to me before. And it won't ever happen again.

Beat.

I'm asking you to let me talk to her one more time. She said that all she wanted to do was talk to me. Just talk to me, and then she'll give Mathilde back to us. Let me see her for one last time, and then, afterward, if Mathilde hasn't returned, we'll do as you want.

ANTOINE   I'll give you one hour. I hope you know what you're doing, because if something happens to my daughter, I will not be able to forgive you. Not ever.

Look right at me. If Mathilde is not here at home by eight o'clock, when I come back, I'll do everything, everything, to find her.

CONSTANCE   Antoine, look at me, you can't leave like this.

ANTOINE   You talk to her and Mathilde comes home. If not, we'll do things my way. I have your word on it.

CONSTANCE   Antoine, talk to me really, look at me really.

ANTOINE   Stop!

She takes his face and tries to force him to turn toward her. He takes both her hands.

CONSTANCE   We're not going to be like everyone else.

She shouts.

Look at me, for Christ's sake!

ANTOINE   *(finally looking at her)* I'm in the process of going under. Do you understand? Going under.

CONSTANCE   We'll get out of this together, together. Do you understand?

ANTOINE   Together...

He leaves the house. The telephone rings.

CONSTANCE   Yes... I know, I'm late.... Listen, I have a major problem. I would like you to cancel my appointments for the rest of the week. Yes, I know that it will be difficult to reschedule them. Yes, but I have no choice. Is that clear...? Yes, yes, tell her that I've changed my mind. It's no longer possible for me to take her client. No, listen. I don't have time to explain this to you.

She hangs up. She sits on the sofa. She stands up, and faints.

Scene Six

CONSTANCE is trying to pick up the books. THE WOMAN enters softly through the window.

THE WOMAN   Just let that go.

We don't have much time to discuss.

CONSTANCE   *(jumps with surprise, is frightened, trembles)* We're going to talk and then you'll give Mathilde back to me?

THE WOMAN   Yes, that's what we agreed on. I always keep my word once I've given it. Quit trembling.

Beat.

What are you going to do with all those books?

CONSTANCE   I'm going to put them back on the shelves.

THE WOMAN   Why do it?

CONSTANCE   Because that's their place.

THE WOMAN   Why do you want to be surrounded with books? Why do you want to keep them? If you have already read them, why don't you give them to someone else? They take up so much, so much space for nothing.

CONSTANCE   I want to keep them for Mathilde, so she has the chance to learn through reading.

THE WOMAN   I understand.

Are you happy knowing all you know?

CONSTANCE   The more things you know, the freer you are. I want my daughter to be free.

THE WOMAN   Is that why you hit her?

Beat.

Have you read all these books?

CONSTANCE   I've read many of them.

THE WOMAN   What does that give you?

CONSTANCE looks at her watch.

If you look at your watch every five minutes, I'll have the impression that our conversation doesn't have much interest for you. I'll feel insulted.

Beat.

So you think that all these fine books have made a person of you who is more free. Is that what you said?

CONSTANCE   I didn't really say that...

THE WOMAN   It's funny, isn't it? For me you are one of the least free people I know. Are you free to think, Constance? Do you have the right to question what's called an inalienable truth? Are you free enough to do that?

CONSTANCE   You're trying to say that I'm not free. Is that it? Okay, I'm not free. Have it your way.

THE WOMAN   Oh, no! That's not the way things can work. Either you really talk to me, or else we stop everything right now. You will never see Mathilde again. Is that clear?

CONSTANCE   Yes.

Beat.

THE WOMAN   So then, I'll repeat my question. Are you free enough to be able to challenge an inalienable truth?

CONSTANCE   An inalienable truth?

THE WOMAN   Don't pretend to be an idiot.

Are you free enough to imagine that the earth is round and that it revolves around the sun, as Galileo did while everyone was saying that the earth was the centre of the universe?

CONSTANCE   I don't know.

THE WOMAN   It takes courage to defend an idea that goes against the grain of what everyone else believes and says. Are you courageous?

CONSTANCE   I don't know.

THE WOMAN   Well, if you know nothing, we'll stop our conversation here…

She goes toward the door.

CONSTANCE   *(shouting)* No!

THE WOMAN   So are you ready to have an intelligent conversation?

CONSTANCE   Go ahead. Ask me your questions.

THE WOMAN   In fact, I would like you to help me understand.

That's the sort of job you do. You help your clients understand why they are sick. Because understanding why is sort of being cured, isn't it?

CONSTANCE   It's a start.

THE WOMAN   I would like you to explain to me why you're sick.

CONSTANCE   Ah…

THE WOMAN   Yes, you heard what I said. I know that it's difficult for you when I treat you like a sick person, because you're usually called "doctor." It's the others who are sick.

Beat.

Your husband knows, of course.

CONSTANCE nods her head in the affirmative.

How long have you been sick?

CONSTANCE   Fifteen years.

THE WOMAN   That's a long time.

How did it start?

CONSTANCE   I left my father's house to go and study at the CÉGEP. I lived in a student residence. I had my own room. It was a big concrete building. Every room had its own toilet.

THE WOMAN   In other words, you could vomit inside four soundproof walls? Neither seen nor known.

CONSTANCE   I got my degree.

THE WOMAN   Bravo. And I'm sure that what's more you had the best marks in the class.

What did your family say about that?

CONSTANCE   I didn't see them very often.

THE WOMAN   And your friend Estelle?

CONSTANCE   I've already told you that Estelle had an accident and that she died.

THE WOMAN   Ah, yes. Estelle died. Was it very long after she died that you started to stuff yourself with food and then bring it back up?

CONSTANCE   Two months.

THE WOMAN   Poor you. That must have really upset you, the death of your best friend.

CONSTANCE   It's shocking to see someone die so young, for no reason.

THE WOMAN   For no reason, it's shocking, yes. Was it because of Estelle's death that you began to be sick?

CONSTANCE   No. But maybe that moved things along faster. Maybe.

THE WOMAN   So where does it come from?

CONSTANCE   From inside me.

For as long as I can remember, I think I've always had it in me.

THE WOMAN   What is "it"? An inferiority complex? A lack of self-esteem? Your parents didn't love you enough? You were physically or verbally abused?

One or several of these answers?

CONSTANCE   Are you expecting me to tell you that I don't have any valid reasons for being the way I am?

What are you expecting me to say to you?

THE WOMAN   Do all the women who are your clients have the same kind of past as you? Inferiority complex, lack of self-esteem, lack of love from parents, physical or verbal abuse, etc....

CONSTANCE   Yes, my clients often come from a dysfunctional environment! Yes!

THE WOMAN   So, is that your answer? You are sick because your mother and your father were rotten parents. Your mother drank and your father engaged in mental cruelty? Something like that? I'm not asking you to recount the details, all sordid stories sound the same.

What matters is that you know where it comes from and how to go about finding a cure. Obviously, that's not working for you. But surely it works with your little ladies? Are you successful in curing all of them?

CONSTANCE   It's not like a broken leg.

THE WOMAN   What's your rate of success?

CONSTANCE   I don't keep statistics on my clients.

THE WOMAN   You don't want to tell me?

CONSTANCE   You can be successful in stabilizing someone for several months, indeed even years. But that doesn't preclude the possibility of a relapse.

THE WOMAN   Are you one of the "stabilized" who has "relapses"?

CONSTANCE   It's not the same for me.

THE WOMAN   Ah, okay. What surprises me about you is that you have had no desire to go and look further, that you were satisfied with the obvious, expected answer: the dysfunctional family.

CONSTANCE   It's more complicated than that...

THE WOMAN   Of course. It takes a little girl with a very sensitive personality, an intelligent and gifted little girl, a perfectionist whose portrait is going to be perfectly arranged by her parents. Can't you see that you're wasting your time and your clients' time? Can't you see that you're in the process of wrecking your daughter's life? All the work you've done up to now is completely useless.

CONSTANCE   I have helped teen girls, and women...

THE WOMAN   You might have provided them with a little bit of comfort. I can agree with that. You gave them attention, human warmth. But as for the rest, your lack of concern is criminal. You've never thought that there might be something else. Something bigger than a sordid little story, something infinitely more powerful that swallows up everything in its way?

CONSTANCE   I can see the billboards with Kate Moss, Cindy Crawford, and the others. I live in the same world as you, with the images of women getting younger and younger, always thinner, always more beautiful... I know the pressure that weighs on all our shoulders...

THE WOMAN   That's not what I'm talking about. That's merely the consequence of something even more serious.

You're not seeing that the problem is elsewhere. You're not seeing that the problem's in the way your brain has learned to think. The problem is all the "truths" that have been implanted in your head ever since you've been in the world. That's what's making you sick, you and everyone else.

You know that when you name a thing you bring it into existence. Do you know that?

CONSTANCE It's the opposite. Words are there to describe reality.

THE WOMAN No, not at all. Reality does not exist. It cannot be described. It's we, with our words, who invent what you're calling reality.

Look, what's that?

CONSTANCE Ridiculous.

THE WOMAN What is that?

CONSTANCE It's a chair.

THE WOMAN It's a chair because it's been decided that that thing, it's called a chair. But there's no universal law that says to us that that thing, it has to be a chair. Can you see what I mean?

CONSTANCE There has to be agreement on the meaning of words if we want to be able to all live together and understand each other.

THE WOMAN *(impatient)* No! That's just it. Words send us the image of how it has been decided we should live together. For example, you use the formal pronoun "vous" with me. Why? Because you want to keep your distance from me. You don't want to create an intimate situation with me.

I would like it if you could force yourself to use "tu" when you're speaking to me.

CONSTANCE I have no desire to address you using "tu."

THE WOMAN *(moved)* You're going to see you have no choice. You and I are going to be close, very close.

CONSTANCE I am capable of judging what is or is not necessary for me.

THE WOMAN I doubt that! We have just now both discovered that your thinking is far from being free. How can you know what's necessary for you when you're not even capable of thinking freely?!

CONSTANCE I think as I like!

THE WOMAN No! You don't think as you like. You think as you have been learning to think for two thousand years. You see the world through all these books. And in most of these books, you don't exist. As a result you accept as reality a world where your existence is less or not at all.

CONSTANCE I exist. I have enough pain at this moment to know that I am alive!

THE WOMAN Yes, you're there in flesh and blood, a woman I could touch. But in your everyday life, whether you're walking in the street, writing a thesis, making love, being happy or unhappy, old or young, you exist less than a man. Your life is less real than a man's. If the reality of your existence could be reflected on your body, there's a part of you that would be transparent.

Take a look! The Bible, *The Odyssey*, *Don Quixote*, and all the others that history has decided to retain. Those books are extremely powerful, more powerful than the most invincible army of mercenaries. Those books are stronger than us because all the damned words that are in them have been shaping our heads and our way of describing the world for centuries. And you… you, the rest of us, we're living in that world. Tell me what you have learned about what it means to be a woman in those books. Tell me!

CONSTANCE You must be thinking that I'm an idiot. And that I didn't understand where you were taking me.

THE WOMAN So, tell me what you learned about what it means to be a woman when you were reading all that…

CONSTANCE Do you expect me to talk to you about all the horrors that have been thought and written on the subject of women? Do you want quotations? *(She bends over and searches frantically through the books.)* I could read Homer to you, or Plato, or Aristotle…. Oh, Aristotle, just wait a little. Yes, I think he was the one who began the story that women don't have a soul…. Ah, wait, St. Thomas Aquinas! If my memory serves me well, it was he who said that woman is impure, and that it's in her nature to be dominated by man. And it continues: Molière, Shakespeare, Racine, Goethe, who said that all women think about is screwing. It was Rousseau who said that men have to respect women precisely in order to protect themselves from their terrifying desire to screw around. Oh, yes… Hegel. I did a research project on him in CÉGEP. He supposed that woman is an inferior being, lacking in self-awareness, a bit like animals.

Of course, there's Freud. Good old Freud who tells us that we discover we are women because we are *lacking* something, a penis. Do you want me to put that down in writing for you? Yes? Should I continue?

Beat.

You're surprised? You thought I didn't know how to read?

THE WOMAN On the contrary, I always knew that you were a conscientious reader.

Okay. So then, what do you do with all that?

CONSTANCE Nothing. Because those days have come and gone. That's the past. I have always lived my life with the idea that nothing could stop me from reaching my goals. I studied what I wanted to. I have a profession respected by society. I have an excellent salary. If I decide I want to do something, I do it. If I decide to say something, I say it. I have a partner who shares household chores, and who would never come up with the idea of asking me to sacrifice a part of my life to let him be more successful in his.

I'm not a victim. I refuse that.

And so I would ask you to give me back my daughter right away, so that she might continue to live her life in freedom, like you, like me. So that she might exist as she wishes.

THE WOMAN She is going to exist, but she is going to exist like the *other*.

You exist, you too, but you are the *other*. You have the existence of the *other*.

CONSTANCE The other.

THE WOMAN The main thing is that for millions of people woman is a *lack* of something.

What defines us is that we are the *other*, she who is lacking something. We aren't allowed to define ourselves for ourselves. We are defined as a function of he who is the *one*, while we are the *other*.

And then, the fact of being the *other*, all women have that well implanted in their brain.

CONSTANCE You're dredging up the jargon of the 1970s?

I'm no fool. I know there are women who are living in difficult situations elsewhere in the world. That there are even some who don't have the same freedoms as me, who don't have the right to go out all alone, nor to vote, nor to speak, nor to work.

There's nothing I can do about that.

But here, I'm free to be the human being that I want to be.

I don't feel like the other. I feel like me.

THE WOMAN Myself, I'm not convinced of that. Do you feel yourself included when the word "man" is used to speak of the entire human race? When man's great march in history is spoken of? Do you feel that you are the one doing the marching?

CONSTANCE But those are just words. Vocabulary. That's all.

THE WOMAN But I said to you just now that words create reality. I disagree with you. This is very important. Your brain is fed with this damn vocabulary, with all the imprints of history, with all those examples of beauty.

She points to the books.

You can understand why, at this time, all the damn words that are in there wound me. Even the most beautiful, those showing the greatest genius and that make my spirit soar wound me. What's more, the more they're beautiful, the more they hurt me. I am always the *other* in all those versions of human experience, even when I have a leading role, even when I have been allowed to speak, I am the *other*.

People talk about man's experience on earth. And I ought to feel myself included in that definition of reality. But it doesn't work for me. It makes me so dizzy to look at that it's already made me weep for weeks on end. That's why, when it's rooted in somebody's heart and body that they're *one* or the *other*, it's hard for them to think freely.

But I don't want you to believe that I'm putting myself in the position of victim. No, that's not my way. It's just that I'd like more human beings to recognize the immense weight of all that beauty. That's all.

CONSTANCE   I know how I feel. I feel like a thirty-year-old woman, whose name is Constance Lussier, and who is certainly capable of thinking by herself, for herself.

THE WOMAN   Your thinking is taking place in a box that is already built by those fine stories. You're a woman. That means that whatever you create, whatever you say is less important, less meaningful for the universe. When you speak, it's the *other* who is speaking. Even the words you use reflect back to you an image where you exist less, since the masculine takes precedence over the feminine. You can easily see that there is nothing less free than your thinking.

CONSTANCE   These are insignificant details...

THE WOMAN   They're insignificant, the tools you use every day to communicate with others and to describe your world? Your way of thinking already dooms you to be less. Why do you think that you make yourself vomit, that you always find yourself either too much or not enough? The worst is that you don't even realize it. That makes it even more striking.

CONSTANCE   It's not true. I've always said to my daughter that if she made up her mind she could be anything she wanted. My daughter can dream of anything at all and make her dreams come true. The only person who can prevent it is you.

THE WOMAN   Do you really think that I'm the one who hurt her most lately? I would like you to trust me. You don't trust me.

You do the same thing with other women. Keep a good eye on yourself and then watch how your mind reacts when it's a man speaking, and when it's a woman speaking. Try to really listen to *what* is said and not *who* is saying it. Do just that. And afterward you'll be able to tell me if your mind isn't biased.

It's true that you have a fine career, a good husband, a little girl full of potential. There's just one little problem, isn't there? Just one. I apologize for coming back to that, but I can't get it out of my mind.

How many times a week do you stick your fingers in your throat? Two, three, five times, six times?

CONSTANCE I continue to work, to have a life.

THE WOMAN I'm sorry, but it's not a life you're having.

I do not call that a life.

But you're right. It's better to live, whatever the price.

> Beat.

You're looking at me as if you were going to eat me. You don't want to forget me?

Have to give a description to the police? I think there's a policeman outside. Take a look. But he didn't see me come in, otherwise…

Do you want to give him a signal to come?

CONSTANCE No.

THE WOMAN You trust me. I'm touched.

I trust you too.

CONSTANCE Where did you get the letter from Estelle?

THE WOMAN I told you that. Estelle and I were good friends. Before I moved she gave me her music, her paintings…

CONSTANCE You have Estelle's paintings?

THE WOMAN Yes. I must have at least twenty of them.

CONSTANCE Even the last one?

THE WOMAN The last one? What do you mean by the last one?

CONSTANCE The last one she painted before her accident.

THE WOMAN I must have it. What's it about?

CONSTANCE I don't know. I never saw it. Estelle never wanted to show it to me.

THE WOMAN Estelle hid quite a few things from you, as far as I can see?

CONSTANCE She didn't want to show it to me. I don't know why. She showed me all the others. How can it be that Estelle gave you her paintings…

THE WOMAN You're jealous?

CONSTANCE No, I'm not jealous, I'm astonished.

THE WOMAN Yes, you're jealous. That hurts you, doesn't it? But you must never show your suffering. It's a great weakness. Do you know what a scumbag you are? You're a damned scumbag.

It makes me wonder how you were able to do your medical program. Did you dissect corpses? I don't think so. Bullshit! You weren't even capable of seeing the dead body of your friend Estelle. Your nerves aren't very solid. You're rather the kind that needs to be cared for, the one that has to be looked after.

CONSTANCE   How is it that you know that?

THE WOMAN   You ran away. You checked out, as usual. You were afraid. Just admit it!

CONSTANCE   I wanted to go to the morgue to see Estelle. I wanted to go, but my father prevented me from leaving the house. I wanted to see her. But he threatened me and he gave me a pill to make me sleep. I wanted to see her, but I couldn't. I couldn't. I tried to run away. I ran down the lane, but he caught me. I couldn't see her.

THE WOMAN   No! You can't see anything. That's why you didn't even realize what you were doing to your daughter...

CONSTANCE   I told you I didn't want to hit her. That's the only time this happened to me.

THE WOMAN   In any case, you always feel yourself guilty of something. Listen, do you think you're nothing but a piece of shit?

I have the impression that deep down inside you don't think you're worth much. Right? Is that true? That you're just a piece of shit who doesn't deserve to breathe? Right? Is it true? That you're just a hole good to be filled? What do you say? Answer me.

CONSTANCE   Why are you doing this to me?

THE WOMAN   Because you're soft, because just as soon as someone gets in your way you fold, you're afraid, like when your father prevented you from going to see Estelle...

CONSTANCE   I wanted to go and see Estelle at the morgue. I wanted to go there more than anything in the world. I wanted to take her in my arms. I wanted...

THE WOMAN   *(very moved)* Your father was right. It was better that you not see me. I was no longer beautiful. When the car struck me, I was thrown into the air. I bounced onto the sidewalk, I fell back on my face. I no longer had a face. I died face down on the sidewalk. It hurt. But it's been over now for a long time. It's true that I would have liked you to take me in your arms. It's true that I would like that.

Scene Seven

ANTOINE and CONSTANCE are sitting beside each other as in Scene Two.

CONSTANCE   Antoine doesn't like to handle meat with his hands. It disgusts him.

Anything that's soft, cold, and bloody disgusts him.

ANTOINE Constance panics. It's her biggest fault. When she goes into panic mode she can't hear anything I say to her. She can't hear anything nor anyone.

It's as though she's inside herself, a prisoner.

CONSTANCE I have always thought that this disgust of raw meat had something to do with sex.

ANTOINE To tell the truth, I can't tell in advance what's going to make her panic. When Mathilde was a year old, I was playing with her on the sofa in the living room. I was tickling her. Mathilde was laughing hard, too hard because all of a sudden she lost consciousness. I froze. As for Constance, she took her by the feet, head down, and she shook her two or three times. Mathilde opened her eyes. We went to the hospital. The doctor spoke of vagal shock. I have to admit I was surprised by Constance's presence of mind.

CONSTANCE I have always had the impression that there are things in sex that disgust him. But we've never talked about it. I don't really have any desire to talk about it. Maybe it's just in my head.

ANTOINE After the ultrasound when we learned that the baby would be a girl, Constance panicked. She cried, said it was terrible, she didn't want a daughter, she didn't want her child to have to endure all that she had endured.

I remember her kicking the trunks of trees in the park across from the hospital. She shouted and raised her fists to the sky. I was happy to have a little girl. Afterward, she calmed down. Then she changed her mind. I have no doubt about that.

CONSTANCE I have fantasies that don't belong to me, fantasies of violence, but that's the way I have an orgasm. I want to be taken. The images are so strong in my head. They arouse my body, and at the same time they hurt my head.

You could say that there are things that make no sense to my thinking mind, things that are powerfully anchored in me.

Scene Eight

CONSTANCE and ESTELLE are twelve years old.

ESTELLE I'm not just what you see. I have ambition. I have talent. Even though I'm not like the others, they don't laugh at me. They can see that I am not the same as them. And they have no choice but to respect that because I'm brilliant. But I don't flaunt what I have in my head in front of everybody. No, I just look into their eyes, and they settle down. Constance is fragile. That gets on my nerves. There's a lot of force in her, I think, but fear gnaws away at her. She's so afraid sometimes that her brain isn't even capable of functioning. There are times when I feel inclined to hit her and to snuggle with her, all at the same time.

She's a good little girl.

I told her a month ago that she was a countess and that a countess had all the rights: the right to laugh, to faint, to shout, to order anyone she doesn't find pleasing killed. I am an archduchess. I run in the night when there are storms.

I tried to explain to Constance how I felt. She didn't understand.

We were sitting on the grass in the sisters' grounds. It was Sports Day. Constance is rotten in sports. She doesn't like to be seen in shorts. She thinks she has big thighs. It doesn't bother me to be seen in shorts, even if I'm as white as a sheet of paper. We had just finished the day with the javelin toss. Constance could have crippled all of us when she sent it flying into the group instead of throwing it out in the field. It's funny. Anyway, I think it's funny.

CONSTANCE I'm going to get changed.

ESTELLE Stay here for a bit. We're not in a rush. We have almost an hour before the bus gets here. And we have no homework. Sit down.

CONSTANCE I can't wait to get these horrid shorts off.

ESTELLE Sit down for two minutes.

> *CONSTANCE sits down. She's not comfortable, stiff in her body.*

I wrote you a letter. Take it. Read it right away.

CONSTANCE A letter from the archduchess?

ESTELLE Read! Go ahead, read!

CONSTANCE My dear Countess,

Ever since I had that red stain that soiled my pants and that humiliated me in front of everybody, ever since I became that disgusting thing, the universe has turned upside down.

I don't sleep any more.

I'm frightened. I'm very frightened. Because I have heard that when you become you know what it's normal to lose the ability to speak. Oh, not all of a sudden, but quietly. It sneaks up on you. Of course, the rest of your person expands and prospers in numerous mountains and crevasses that are increasingly noticed by those that are said to be of the other gender. But your voice, which was so strong and carried as far as the other side of the earth, becomes as useless and annoying as the squeaking of the most insignificant little mouse. In the beginning, you speak and the others close their eyes and lean their ears forward. They ask you to repeat. Then, in the end, they don't hear anything. And it does you no good to shout at the top of your lungs, scream hard enough to tear the wig right off you. No one listens any longer. They look at you, but don't hear you.

I don't want to alarm you unnecessarily, dear Countess, but watch out. This could happen to you soon. And I've been told that this disorder is incurable.

Signed, the saddened Archduchess of Mirepoix.

What does your story mean?

ESTELLE It means that I find it sickening to be like that, and to have that.

CONSTANCE You don't want to have a sweater?

ESTELLE Ooch! I know they're not very big, but I'm talking about my boobs and my pussy. Are you trying to act stupid?

CONSTANCE I'm not acting stupid. (*She pulls at her shorts as though to pull them down.*)

ESTELLE I just don't care at all about your jiggly thighs…! My skin's white and it doesn't matter to me. I want to talk to you. Are you my best friend, yes or no?

CONSTANCE Why are you saying my thighs are jiggly?

ESTELLE Ah! They're not jiggly! I just like to bug you!

Look! (*takes a sanitary napkin from her bag*)

Have you ever seen that!

CONSTANCE Well! Yes…

Hide it. There are people coming up the hill.

ESTELLE And they mustn't see that. That has got to stay hidden. It's like a huge, disgusting monster.

And you… are you afraid of it? Look at it!

Puts it in her face.

CONSTANCE Stop!

ESTELLE Ta da, ta da. Disgusting, smutty, dirty. Ta da, ta da.

CONSTANCE You're not funny, you know. (*crying*)

ESTELLE Shithead! You bawl and bawl. Sniff! Sniff! Sniff! Bawling all the time!

CONSTANCE I don't want to be your friend very much anymore.

ESTELLE I'm sorry, Constance…

CONSTANCE Why do you get angry with me?

ESTELLE I get angry, that's all. That's the way I am. I'm an angry person.

CONSTANCE So, you know, I don't get angry with you, not ever.

ESTELLE   I said I was sorry.

CONSTANCE   Does your stomach hurt?

ESTELLE   I don't want to be a woman. It's sickening to be a woman.

CONSTANCE   You want to be a guy!

ESTELLE   No, I don't. Are you crazy? I don't want to be a guy, for heaven's sake!

CONSTANCE   Gonna have to be something. They'll ask you to choose. Anyway, it's silly. You have no choice. You're a girl.

ESTELLE   They'll ask me to choose. So… who is that…. Who is it who's going to ask me to choose?

CONSTANCE   Well, I don't know, life, the world around. You're a girl. Okay, you're gonna have to live with that!

ESTELLE   I can choose to be everything *I* want to be, okay?

CONSTANCE   If you're not a woman, you won't be able to have children.

ESTELLE   Perfect! I don't want any. Babies, they ruin your life. That's what my mother says. *I* don't want to be tied to anybody.

CONSTANCE   Well, you'll be making nests every month.

ESTELLE   I'm not a sparrow.

CONSTANCE   My mother told me that it's like you're making a nest for the baby. And that it's dangerous to get pregnant.

ESTELLE   I hate that, that dangerous bit. It makes my dad go out of his mind, because that could happen to me, and if I got pregnant…

CONSTANCE   What?

ESTELLE   I don't know what. It's just that doesn't seem to work for him, like it would be a major drama for him.

I was picking up stones in the yard at our house. Does that upset your dad if you dig in his dirt?

CONSTANCE   Not at the edge on the side by the river. It's just old earth. Why do you ask?

ESTELLE   I want to bury Mathilde, and put stones on top, so she can't run away, and so the dogs can't dig her up like an old bone.

CONSTANCE   Don't you want her anymore? I really like your doll. I'll keep her if you want.

ESTELLE   Yes, you could. But I don't think that's what I want. I want to hide her. I'm afraid I won't love her anymore. I'm afraid I'll cut her hair or scribble all over her or pull her arms out. You know, when you get into your teens, you do bizarre things. I'm burying her. That's the right thing to do. That way I won't be able to demolish her.

CONSTANCE   Why would you do that?

ESTELLE   All of a sudden I think she's too much a baby, la la la, and sweet, and cute, and cuddly, don't you think. I'm growing up.

CONSTANCE   Come to our house after supper.

I'm going to change.

ESTELLE   Are you going to answer me, answer the archduchess? Well, are you going to answer the archduchess?

CONSTANCE   I always answer.

Scene Nine

THE WOMAN   You certainly wouldn't have been able to recognize me. I don't have the same body. I couldn't use my old mushed-up body. I would have frightened you.

You'll just have to take my word for it. I can't give you any proof. I'm asking you to take me on faith.

CONSTANCE   I lost faith long ago.

THE WOMAN   Go ahead and ask your questions. I'll try to answer them, but I don't know much.

You don't get to know all the secrets of the universe just because you're dead. All I know is that my memory of you came back to me and that I had to talk to you. I had to see you.

CONSTANCE   I would have thought that when you die you understand why...

THE WOMAN   No, I don't understand anymore. I understand even less than when I was alive. I have no secret to share with you about the other side. I don't know how I was before taking this body. I have forgotten. I don't know how long I have to be able to talk to you with this body, but I know that it's soon going to be over. I'm going to go back to the other state that I don't know or that I've forgotten.

CONSTANCE   I remember that Estelle had a doll called...

THE WOMAN   Mathilde....

CONSTANCE   Mathilde, yes. And that Estelle buried her in my dad's yard. I had forgotten that her doll's name was Mathilde.

Everyone is going to take me for a crazy woman if I say to them that I think you, the woman standing in front of me, you're my friend from childhood, Estelle Ménard, dead at the age of sixteen, struck by an automobile when she was crossing the street. Why would I believe that Estelle returned from the dead for me, and what's more, to speak to me about the place of women in the universe. It's ridiculous.

THE WOMAN Hm, ridicule… it's hard to accept being alone against everyone.

CONSTANCE And why would a phantom, a ghost—I don't know what you should be called—kidnap my daughter…. Estelle wouldn't do that to me.

THE WOMAN Estelle loves you. I love you. And I know that you need your daughter's love to exist. If I kidnap your daughter, I am putting at risk the very grounds of your existence. You must be at risk in order to understand what I want you to understand. You must agree to put your mind in emergency mode. You must think as you have never thought before. Otherwise, you won't be able to go out there. You won't succeed in imagining the unimaginable. That's all.

CONSTANCE I want to talk to her. Let me talk to her…

THE WOMAN No, not right away. Not yet.

CONSTANCE Not yet! What do you still need? Do you want me to get down on my knees to beg you…

THE WOMAN Your clients. Are they sick girls?

CONSTANCE Okay. Here we go again!

THE WOMAN What's the difference between your "sick girls" and the rest of women?

CONSTANCE My clients have an unhealthy relationship with food and with their bodies.

THE WOMAN What is a normal relationship with your body?

CONSTANCE That's simple. It's being comfortable in it, feeling good in your body.

THE WOMAN Yes, but most women go on diets, find themselves too fat, too tall, not enough of this, not enough of that. Is that normal or not?

CONSTANCE It's normal to find yourself a bit chubby and to want to go on a diet in order to feel better. The fact of going on a diet isn't a problem. It's when behaviour becomes extreme that we can speak of illnesses.

THE WOMAN Okay. If I understand you, you're saying that always being on a diet is normal. Always finding yourself too fat, not tall enough, too old, not blond enough, that's normal. It's just when you push your behaviour further and when you eat one apple during the day, or, indeed, when you gulp down three meals in twenty minutes and then make yourself vomit afterward, that's being ill?

CONSTANCE That's not really what I said.

THE WOMAN   It's funny that all these little teens and these intelligent women should be superficial enough to waste their time on their appearance, while there are so many things to deal with in the world, elsewhere, while there are so many things to think, to create, to build. You don't find that devastating?

CONSTANCE   Superficial girls…!

THE WOMAN   Well, it's not affectation and meaninglessness, all those little illnesses of pretty, spoiled little girls, brilliant little girls who have upsets while children are dying in Africa? Isn't that being superficial?

Yes… that all that beautiful energy, all that vital force, should be lost in trivialities. Just imagine all the time you've lost making your little food orgies. Yes, it's true that you work hard on your research, but what does that really change for you and the women you work with? You haven't even succeeded in curing yourself. You are a recognized scientist. But basically what defines you most adequately is that you find yourself fat and that makes you lose your head…. Why? What do you say to your clients when they ask you why they feel so bad, and why they always find themselves too fat, even at sixty-five pounds?

CONSTANCE   They don't want to lose weight. That's not it…

THE WOMAN   Ah! What do they want?

What are *you* doing when you make yourself vomit?

CONSTANCE   I…

THE WOMAN   What?

CONSTANCE   *(something in her has let go)* I have no choice.

THE WOMAN   Is it pleasant to vomit?

CONSTANCE   I have no choice.

THE WOMAN   Afterward, you have the impression of having regained a bit of control, eh? Do you like that, hurting yourself?

CONSTANCE   I have no choice. Do you understand? I'm dirty.

THE WOMAN   I understand. Why don't you kill yourself? You could rid the earth of something rotten. Problem solved.

CONSTANCE   I'm not able.

THE WOMAN   You're not able to blow your brains out? You're not able to jump off a bridge?

CONSTANCE   I'm not able.

THE WOMAN   You prefer to do it cleanly.

You are killing yourself politely. The *other* who slowly erases herself.

Instead of killing yourself in small stages, maybe you could start a revolution.

CONSTANCE   Revolution? My God, is that ever a ridiculous word, revolution! So ridiculous!

Stop saying that.

THE WOMAN   Yes, it's ridiculous. If you like, it's ridiculous. But I don't see any way other than the revolutionary way. You, little you, quiet little you, you're going to start the revolution. You're going to plant the seeds of revolution in the heads you meet. One person at a time. One person at a time.

CONSTANCE   That's completely absurd, grotesque!

THE WOMAN   No, that's false. Mathilde believes in the revolution. She told me so.

Mathilde wants to start a revolution.

CONSTANCE   Mathilde is a child!

THE WOMAN   Do you think that Mathilde doesn't know the weight of things? Do you think that Mathilde doesn't have eyes to see? Do you think Mathilde doesn't hear you bawling and vomiting? Ever since she's been in the world, you've been showing her the weight of things.

CONSTANCE   I didn't think I was showing her that much.

THE WOMAN   Precisely. It's for her that the revolution must begin. When I was twelve, I felt it in my body, but I wasn't able to give it a name. I didn't know what to do about it. The archduchess's letter was my very awkward way of expressing that.

I was being expected to take on big studies, to be competitive and aggressive. But I was also, also expected to be a lovely and mysterious ballet dancer, gentle and sensual.... All that. And I wanted all of that, the blood, and at the same time, I wanted none of that. I wanted to be something else.

CONSTANCE   What?

THE WOMAN   I didn't have the time to find it. Maybe Mathilde will find it.

CONSTANCE   Mathilde, my love.

I don't know if I'm in the process of seeing more clearly, or indeed, if I'm in the process of becoming completely mad.

THE WOMAN   You see, it isn't sufficient to have an education, work, and a husband who shares household work. The most difficult struggle is the one that you will be having inside yourself.

The telephone rings. CONSTANCE answers.

CONSTANCE   Yes, it is I. No... I told you that I was absolutely not available.

Who is it.... Ask Doctor Létourneau. Yes, I know that she wants to see *me*.

Ask Doctor Létourneau.... What... commit suicide.... Yes, commit suicide.

I don't give a damn if she wants to commit suicide, do you hear me? Let her commit suicide. Then there'll be one less…. Wait, wait, I'll be there in fifteen minutes.

She hangs up.

THE WOMAN There's still one thing that you have to understand.

Scene Ten

CONSTANCE, sixteen, and ESTELLE, sixteen.

They run in laughing. ESTELLE takes off her sandals.

CONSTANCE Look, there's glass everywhere. People are so filthy. Don't go in your bare feet.

ESTELLE Sucky! It's just a bit of glass. It won't kill me.

It's good to go in bare feet. I like that, feeling what's moving under my feet.

Let's sit here. There's still a bit of sun left.

CONSTANCE I don't like having the sun in my face. I can't get over how awful people act. I think it's so beautiful here. Why do they come and destroy everything, and empty their ashtrays, and break their damn beer bottles.

ESTELLE It's a party, Constance! People had a party! A *party*! That's what the summer festival is all about. It's to have fun.

CONSTANCE Yeah, but they don't have to…

ESTELLE Yes, Constance! That's what a party is! A party is just that!

CONSTANCE Parties are about spreading shit everywhere?

ESTELLE Yes. That's what they are, and so many other dumb things, possible and imaginable! A party is whatever! You let yourself go. You sing, you dance, you break bottles, you turn over garbage cans, you find the guys handsome, and you want to put your arms around all of them. And you could do it. All you'd have to do is decide to do it. Parties are whatever you decide.

CONSTANCE Put my arms around all the guys? Well, maybe not all of them!

ESTELLE Yes, all of them! All the guys, all the ones that you want to grab by the hair… and give them a kiss right on their mouths.

CONSTANCE *I* have no desire to do that to the guys.

ESTELLE Yes, yes. You do desire it.

I desire it. Just like I would desire to lie down on the grass. But seeing that people are filthy, as you say, I'm going to stay here sitting on the bench.

CONSTANCE   Yeah. Grass is lovely when it's green. It makes me feel bad to see the grass all dirty.

ESTELLE   You don't like dirt?

CONSTANCE   Talk about a strange question! Really, nobody likes dirt. Somebody that's dirty turns your stomach. Once I went out with a sweater on that had a grease stain from french fries. I didn't notice the stain before I went out. I was with my mother. We were walking to the drug store, and then halfway there in front of the convent for illegitimate babies, I saw it. I wanted to go back to the house. But Mommy certainly didn't want to. I put my hand over the stain. And I stayed like that all the way until we got back home. I was really ashamed.

ESTELLE   *(laughing)* You're such a nut! You get so upset about things that don't matter.

CONSTANCE   Can I ask you a question?

ESTELLE   No, you can't ask me any questions.

CONSTANCE   Well, after all…

ESTELLE   Ask your question, and don't ask me if you can.

CONSTANCE   You're such a drag!

ESTELLE   Fine…

CONSTANCE   I'm getting sick of the story about the painting.

ESTELLE   Are you ever stubborn!

CONSTANCE   Why do you refuse to show me your painting?

ESTELLE   I've already told you just now. I do not wish to show it. That's all…

CONSTANCE   Did you show it to Benoît?

ESTELLE   Benoît!

CONSTANCE   Do you trust him more than me?

ESTELLE   You don't understand anything. I did not show the painting to Benoît.

CONSTANCE   Ah…

ESTELLE   Nobody's seen my painting. I don't want to show it. I don't want to, I don't want to! Anyhow, not right away.

CONSTANCE   I'd like to see it. You've always shown them to me. Every time you do a new painting, you show it to me.

ESTELLE   Argh! Habits get on my nerves. I've changed. I do not wish to show it to you. That's all. Maybe when it's done. I don't know. You get on my nerves. I'll show it to you when I show it to you, and maybe that will be never!

CONSTANCE   You really are nasty!

It's okay for you to change, but the rest of us have to adapt!

What does your Benoît have to say about that?

ESTELLE Forget about Benoît! It's not like my whole life revolves around him. I go out with him. It's not the third world war. It's not just because we have sex in a cottage that the world is going to turn upside down.

CONSTANCE Whoa! Hey, whoa! You've had sex?

ESTELLE Well, yes. We did. So what?

CONSTANCE Wow! And you just tell me about it like that, any old way…

ESTELLE Okay, then.

I have big news. Wow, we did it! Me and Benoît, we had sex. Yippee! Are you happy now?

CONSTANCE Well, don't be such a drag.

Tell me about it? Don't pretend that it's just a piece of shit in your life. You don't have sex for the first time without being totally changed!

ESTELLE Who told you that? I'm the same person. Well, I'm not a virgin, that's all.

CONSTANCE So?

ESTELLE I liked it. We took our time. I wanted to know what it was like. Now I know.

CONSTANCE What's it like?

ESTELLE You'll see when you do it. I can't explain that.

CONSTANCE Ah…! Benoît's a nice guy. He loves you.

ESTELLE Yes, he loves me.

CONSTANCE You say that kind of funny.

ESTELLE Well, yes, he loves me. It's not the end of the world! It's not because a guy loves you that all the bad things in your life—the little ones, the big ones, the huge ones—are fixed all at once. It's a smooth moment, nothing more than a smooth moment. Do you think that because someone says he loves you that you're going to love yourself any more?

CONSTANCE I would have thought so. I would have thought that love is the only thing that matters.

ESTELLE No. That's not what's most important.

CONSTANCE Then what's most important?

ESTELLE I don't know. How would I know? But seems to me that there are more important things than love. Just take a look. We're both alive. It's unbelievable, all, yes, all that we could do. Why should I stop with the love of a man? Why would that be the most beautiful event that happens in my life? Eh? Why? Why would having children, why would that make me the happiest? That doesn't work for me. It doesn't work for me. It's not enough. It's far from being enough.

CONSTANCE   You'll have your painting. You're going to be a painter!

ESTELLE   No, I won't be a painter.

CONSTANCE   Why?

ESTELLE   Because that's not enough for me either.

CONSTANCE   What's "enough" for you, Estelle?

ESTELLE   I can't say. But I feel that it doesn't exist in this world.

I have the impression that I want something that doesn't exist.

I would like to speak and have everybody listen to me. I would like to go out in the evening without being afraid. I would like to not be forced to think about what I look like. I would like to not spend my life angry and frustrated like my mother.

CONSTANCE   You have wanted to not be a girl for a long time. I've already told you that you have no choice.

ESTELLE   It's not that! Then again, it's that…

CONSTANCE   Don't get angry. You get in a bad mood so often these days.

ESTELLE   Okay. It's true that I'm not… nice. Talk to me about you now.

CONSTANCE   Nothing's happening for me.

François is dumb. I don't want to go all the way with him.

ESTELLE   You don't want to? Why?

CONSTANCE   I don't like the way François asks me for it.

He pushes too hard. We went quite a ways the last time. He stroked my breasts, but I don't want him to put his hands in my pants. I said no. And that made him mad.

ESTELLE   He's a jerk.

CONSTANCE   Tell me how it was. Were you afraid? Did it hurt?

ESTELLE   Well…. It's not a mechanical shovel! It was fun. We laughed.

I was fine. Benoît is gentle, but not too much. It's funny because he's so much taller than me that…

CONSTANCE   That what?

ESTELLE It didn't hurt. Just a little, but that's normal... this is getting too personal. There are things that have to just stay between him and me. *(suddenly very emotional)*

CONSTANCE Well then, why did you even start to talk to me about it?

ESTELLE looks at her strangely and sadly.

I'm pleased for you that the first time was good. I'm happy for you.

ESTELLE *(getting up and walking on the path)* You can't be happy for me. You're happy with me. Yeah!

CONSTANCE I told you not to walk in your bare feet. There's a lot of glass here. Let me see!

ESTELLE Ouch. It's bleeding a lot. Don't look. You'll get dizzy.

CONSTANCE Oh, stop! I'm not that much of a scaredy-cat.

She feels sick.

ESTELLE I told you so. Give me some Kleenexes. It's funny how life can drain out from us, like that, with just a little red trickle. It's beautiful.

CONSTANCE I'm sick to my stomach.

ESTELLE You'll be all right. You're too fragile!

CONSTANCE I'm not fragile. Just because I don't shout like you doesn't mean I'm fragile.

ESTELLE Do you think I shout? I speak strongly. That's not a fault. Everybody makes *you* repeat when you speak. Oh, 'scuse me, I shouldn't have said that.

CONSTANCE Do you want to come and sleep at my house tonight? You could tell me the little things that aren't secret... it won't bother my mother.

ESTELLE No, I'm not tempted.

CONSTANCE Why?

ESTELLE I'm not tempted. I won't go.

CONSTANCE You're a drag. I'd like you to come. It's been a long time since we've been together and had a good time. It's nice now.

ESTELLE Don't push it. You don't like people who push it. I don't either. Anyways, I think we should see less of each other.

CONSTANCE See less of each other?

We're already not seeing much of each other, ever since you started going out with Benoît. Before, we were together all the time.

ESTELLE Aren't you fed up with being called the little pet dog?

CONSTANCE What does that mean? Who calls me a little pet dog?

ESTELLE   You know that Monique's gang calls you the little pet dog. You follow me everywhere. You do everything like me. You try to dress like me. You listen to the music that I like...

CONSTANCE   I like it too.

ESTELLE   Yes, but it's 'cause I got you to listen to it.

It'd be better for you if we see each other less. That way you could do things your own way, and have your own ideas.

CONSTANCE   Is it because of Benoît?

ESTELLE   Not at all. Benoît has nothing to do with this. Benoît isn't important. I'm the one who decides. And so... I think you should make other friends.

CONSTANCE   What have I done? I didn't do anything.

ESTELLE   Silly. You didn't do anything. It's just that I can't do what I used to do before anymore. Let me have some peace!

CONSTANCE   Why? I don't understand.

There's something you're not telling me.

ESTELLE   There are things you can't understand.

CONSTANCE   There are things you can't understand. You're not my mother. You'll find out I'm no dunce, Lady IQ.

ESTELLE   (*After a fairly long time, she looks at her and caresses her face very gently.*) I know that.

Well, I'm going home. I don't want to miss my bus. There are things that you can't understand.

CONSTANCE   I'm taking it with you. Then I'll transfer after.

ESTELLE   (*very stiff*) No. I feel like being alone (*softening*)... besides, it goes a whole lot quicker if you take the forty-three to start with.

You're my best friend. You always will be. Smile. We'll see each other at school on Monday.

CONSTANCE   Yeah, but maybe the little pet dog is going to be sick.

ESTELLE   Smile a bit for me, baboon. This doesn't suit you.

CONSTANCE   (*forced smile*) There!

ESTELLE   Don't be angry with me, please?

She puts her arms around her and gives her a hug.

CONSTANCE   Bye.

ESTELLE   See you, Constance.

Scene Eleven

ANTOINE is alone. He is sitting on a pile of books. The door opens. CONSTANCE comes in from outside.

ANTOINE   Where were you?

CONSTANCE   I went to the clinic.

One of my clients was in a crisis situation…

ANTOINE   There's no one who can replace you?!

CONSTANCE   No, there was no one available, no one.

It had to be me.

ANTOINE   You put your clients ahead of your daughter?

She looks at him.

So, where is Mathilde. You don't answer.

What did she say to you?

CONSTANCE   I don't know how to explain this to you. I don't even know if I'm going to explain it.

ANTOINE   Listen, I can't wait any longer. You said to me that if you weren't successful in convincing her to give Mathilde back to us we'd do things my way.

I'm calling the police. You're going to give a description of that woman.

CONSTANCE   I told you that I can't remember what she looks like. I can't give a description.

ANTOINE   This is impossible. I don't believe you. Not you. You who remember the slightest details of the front of a store. No, you're lying. I don't know why you're lying to me this way. What have I done to you to make you make me suffer this much?

CONSTANCE   Hold on, what are you saying?

ANTOINE   Do you want to take Mathilde away from me?

CONSTANCE   How can you think that?! No! No! Mathilde is our daughter. I'm not trying to steal her from you!

ANTOINE   No? So what am I supposed to believe? You leave me in the middle of a nightmare. You tell me nothing. You speak to a mysterious woman, who has no face, with features you can't recall. You tell me that this woman has our daughter Mathilde, but she just wants to talk to you and then she'll give Mathilde back to us after you've had a conversation that she's satisfied with. And you find that all right. You accept a stranger's conditions. I trust you. I say okay, go talk to her if you think that's the best thing to do to save our daughter.

And now I come back to the house. You're not there. You didn't leave me a note. You didn't phone. You come home and you say to me that you went to work!

I want to know what she said to you! It makes me think you don't care about what happens to Mathilde!

CONSTANCE   That's right, I don't care what happens to Mathilde. I want my daughter to suffer. Is that what you want me to say?

He slaps her.

ANTOINE   Stop!

CONSTANCE   Antoine, I have always believed that you were a respectful person. I've loved you because you've had a sense for the big and the little things in life.

There is nothing too childish nor too unimportant for you. Life was all of that, sometimes the big thing, and then the little things most of the time. And that was okay with you.

You showed me how to accept everything in life.

ANTOINE   I want you to tell me the truth and quit lying to me!

CONSTANCE   The woman who came to speak to me, I think that I know her. It's true that I don't recognize her face. Her face, I can't even manage to remember it as soon as she's no longer in front of me. I forget her features. That's the truth, I swear it. I don't understand what's happening to me. She knows many personal details about my life. At the same time I have the impression that I know her.

And then at the same time, she frightens me. She told me her name was Estelle Ménard.

ANTOINE   You know her name. You know her name and you're only saying it now!

CONSTANCE   Wait! Estelle Ménard was the name of my best friend in high school.

You know that I've often talked to you about her. I talked about her because she got hit with a car when she was stepping off the bus. And she died from that.

ANTOINE   A crazy woman who's passing herself off as a dead woman.

Beat. He looks at her and guesses.

What…? What? You're not going to tell me you think that woman really is your friend Estelle?!

CONSTANCE   I know that doesn't make sense. That's not what I think. But I can't help asking myself, what if it was true? Do you understand? What if it could be true?

ANTOINE   Are you in the process of losing your mind? You've lost your head. I should have realized before. I shouldn't have trusted you. I don't know what that woman has done to you, but from now on, I'm going to be looking after things... I should have realized before... I'm going to do everything, do everything, do you hear me, to find Mathilde.

If you refuse to tell us where that woman is hiding, I'll have you arrested.

I'm going to lay a complaint against you. Let me say this again. If ever you refuse to tell me where that woman is, I'll have you arrested. I couldn't...

I couldn't live my life if somebody kidnaps my daughter.

I'd be angry with everything, everything around me. I wouldn't be able to look outside anymore without being enraged because the weather is nice, and because there are flowers that dare to grow even if *I* can no longer take my daughter's hand!

CONSTANCE   I knew that we would come to this one day, what we are here, at this moment.

ANTOINE   It wasn't me that wanted it this way!

CONSTANCE   I'm going to lie down. Don't worry, I won't escape through the window.

ANTOINE   (*picking up the telephone*) Hello. Yes, Inspector Despins. This is Antoine Melançon. No, my daughter has not returned. No, I wish to lay a complaint against my wife, Constance Lussier. Yes, I have good reason for believing that she is hiding things. Yes, that is indeed what I'm saying. I think that my wife is implicated...

Yes, I am upset. But I'm thinking straight. No, I don't want time to think about it.... I know that it's a great shock.... I don't need to see a psychologist.... No, my head is very clear. Yes, I assure you that I have all my marbles.... Well then, listen. Will you accept my complaint, yes or no? Good, I can go look for a lawyer if you want it that way.... Good, yes, I understand, I understand. Good. I know that's normal procedure, but in this case you're not dealing with a madman. Yes, I would like that to be done as quickly as possible... yes.... You could come when? No, no, she won't leave...

Okay. Yes. Thank you, Inspector.

He hangs up.

Scene Twelve

ANTOINE is sleeping on the sofa in the living room. His sleep is troubled.

A white, dazzling light. THE WOMAN is now sitting beside him.

White, dazzling light.

This time the woman is holding a painting wrapped in brown paper in her hands.

White, dazzling light. CONSTANCE is in the living room. She is stupefied as she watches the transformation of the light. The light inundates the space with an indescribable whiteness. ANTOINE no longer moves.

CONSTANCE Why doesn't Antoine wake up?

THE WOMAN Quite simply, because he's sleeping!

CONSTANCE You won't hurt him?

THE WOMAN You haven't understood yet that I'm not a monster!

CONSTANCE I've told you that I didn't know what to understand.

THE WOMAN I've brought you the picture.

My last picture. The one I did before...

She starts to unwrap it.

CONSTANCE I don't know if I can. Estelle never wanted to show it to me.

THE WOMAN Estelle wanted to protect you. But now, you no longer need protection. You need to understand.

THE WOMAN unwraps the painting, showing a wide boulevard, with the body of an adolescent girl whose head is beneath a large rock. A border of blood flows in the gutter. CONSTANCE is thunderstruck.

So?!

CONSTANCE The boulevard where Estelle was hit.

THE WOMAN And...!

CONSTANCE Estelle... she's wearing the same clothes that she was wearing the evening she died.

THE WOMAN What else...

CONSTANCE Her head is crushed under a huge black rock.

THE WOMAN Something more...!

CONSTANCE There's blood coming from beneath the rock. There's an outline of blood flowing into the gutter.

THE WOMAN So?!

CONSTANCE Estelle drew her own death.

THE WOMAN How can that be possible?!

CONSTANCE Perhaps Estelle had a premonition. Maybe she felt her death was going to come, or that...

THE WOMAN   Or that…!

CONSTANCE   Or that Estelle decided her death was going to come.

THE WOMAN   Do you mean that Estelle committed suicide?!

CONSTANCE   I don't know. We can't ever know.

THE WOMAN   Ask me the question!

CONSTANCE   Why would Estelle have committed suicide. Her life was going so well. She wanted to study sculpture at CÉGEP. She had just made love with her boyfriend…

THE WOMAN   Benoît!

CONSTANCE   Yes, Benoît.

THE WOMAN   Does making love immunize you against the pain of living?!

CONSTANCE   No… but Estelle wasn't the type to commit suicide.

THE WOMAN   What is the type to commit suicide?!

CONSTANCE   Okay. Okay. I know that what I'm saying doesn't make any sense…

THE WOMAN   You feel guilty, still…!

CONSTANCE   What should I have understood? I didn't understand what she was trying to tell me.

THE WOMAN   Perhaps there was nothing she wanted to say to you, nothing!

CONSTANCE   Estelle spoke in parables. You had to guess.

THE WOMAN   No, I didn't speak in parables. I just wanted not to be like everyone else. Being like everyone else is the worst thing that could have happened to Estelle!

CONSTANCE   That's like me. I don't want to be like everyone else.

>   *Beat.*

We have to admit that it wasn't an accident.

THE WOMAN   So are you saying it was suicide?!

CONSTANCE   Yes, suicide.

>   *Beat. She looks her in the eyes.*

Why?

THE WOMAN   Are you asking Estelle?!

CONSTANCE   I can pretend to believe you, to see what you're going to make up.

THE WOMAN   Until the time when I was crossing the street, I didn't know if I was going to do it.

When I left you, I didn't know if I was going to do it. You remember we had seen each other just before…!

CONSTANCE   Yes, I remember. I told you that the second time you came here.

THE WOMAN   We hugged each other, and then I got on the bus. I sat down.

And I repeated in my head: I'm doing it, I'm not doing it, I'm doing it, I'm not doing it…!

CONSTANCE   Estelle was not a girl who couldn't make up her mind.

THE WOMAN   You don't know Estelle well.

I got off the bus. I still didn't know if I was going to do it or not. The sole of my foot was burning me. You remember that I had cut my foot?!

CONSTANCE   Yes.

THE WOMAN   I know that bothers you, the cut in the foot, doesn't it. Who else other than you and I could know that I cut the sole of my foot by walking on pieces of broken bottles?!

CONSTANCE   Someone else could have known it, heard us, seen us from far away…

THE WOMAN   It's okay that you don't want to admit that I'm Estelle.

I know that I'm asking you to travel the course of several lives in just a few hours.

I'm not upset with you. In exchange, I'm asking you to not be too upset with Estelle!

CONSTANCE   Why would I be upset with Estelle? It's you I'm upset with. It's you who's butting into my life and tossing everything down on the ground. Estelle hasn't done anything. Estelle died a long time ago.

THE WOMAN   That changed many things in your life when Estelle died.

Your life was turned upside down!

CONSTANCE   Yes, but that was fifteen years ago. I got over it.

THE WOMAN   If you're over it, would it upset you to know whether Estelle committed suicide or not?

Would it change something if it was an accident or a suicide?

CONSTANCE   I already felt abandoned. It couldn't get any worse than that.

I was just curious… unhealthy curiosity. It was her choice.

THE WOMAN   But what does it tell you, her choice? What does it tell you? It tells you that Estelle was weak, that Estelle had no backbone. It took a mere second. It wasn't a carefully thought-out decision. It was a matter of a second. That's all it took for Estelle Ménard to cease to exist.

I crossed. I had almost reached the other side of the street.

Then I felt the urge to stop for a second. I felt no urge to put my foot on the sidewalk. I had no urge to make the effort to lift my leg. I just wanted to stay there. I didn't want to hear anything more. And I heard nothing more. No more noise. I felt good. I bent over to see whether my cut was still bleeding.

A frightening noise went through my ears like an immense mouth opening up. I felt a mass in my back. I turned around, and I saw this car coming down on me. I knew that my face would be smashed when I fell. But even knowing that, I couldn't lift my leg to put it on the sidewalk!

CONSTANCE That's not a suicide. That's an accident.

THE WOMAN Maybe it's an accident from lack of courage!

CONSTANCE I wish that she had come to sleep at our house, and that we had talked.

THE WOMAN What did you expect her to say to you? On the contrary, I didn't want to say anything to you anymore. I didn't want us to see each other. I wanted to push you away from me. So that things would be less difficult for you...!

CONSTANCE My God! Hearing you talk, Estelle was a saint who killed herself because life didn't come up to her ideals and who, in addition, went to the trouble of pushing away her fragile and silly best friend so that she wouldn't suffer too much.

No, in *my* opinion it was egotism, pure and simple. Egotism and cruelty.

You didn't give a damn about me nor about my life. You don't give a damn about hurting me.

Hmm, what was it that you said to me? Oh yeah, the little pet dog.

I was your little pet dog, the stupid girl with neither ideas of her own nor personal tastes, the one who had be told what music to listen to and what clothes to wear.

Yeah, that's what a little pet dog is. So I'm just your pet dog, am I?

It's fun to have someone who admires you at no cost, who swallows every word that comes out of your mouth, oh genius. And, what's more, who likes being treated that way.

And then, when the archduchess is sick of her pet dog, she takes off her leash and gives her a good kick to make her run away. And the archduchess does her final big mortuary number, and everyone bawls.

THE WOMAN I couldn't stand having you around, with all your good little girl's dripping affection.

I love you, Constance, but even that love didn't manage to make me forget that I needed air, that I couldn't stand suffocating in my body anymore. This was a body that was growing stranger and stranger the older I got. I couldn't stand it anymore.

I wanted to be able to bury myself the same way I did my doll…!

CONSTANCE   Mathilde!

THE WOMAN   I wanted to remain a little girl with my two feet on the ground, not a woman who spends her life on a high wire.

I wanted you to know. I wanted you to know that I was wrong, and that you must continue to struggle. I want you to give yourself permission to think for yourself.

At least try. Make a little bit of a revolution every day. If *you* begin, maybe in fifty years it will be easier for others. Do that much for me!

CONSTANCE   I don't give a damn about that. I want my daughter.

THE WOMAN   I'm leaving!

CONSTANCE   My daughter!

> THE WOMAN *moves away. She is almost out the door.*

THE WOMAN   I hid her in the ground so she would be safe and nobody could hurt her. When she's ready, she'll come out. She'll have dirt in her eyes. Her eyes are going to be full of dirt, but you'll be able to get it out. She's going to ring the doorbell. It might be in five minutes, or two hours. It's up to her.

> *She leaves.*
>
> CONSTANCE *is crying. The telephone rings, the telephone rings. She doesn't move.*
>
> ANTOINE *wakes up. He's dozy and still only half awake. He gets up and looks around the room. He looks at* CONSTANCE, *is exasperated, and goes to answer the telephone.*

ANTOINE   Yes, yes, Inspector. Yes, you can come. No, I have…

> CONSTANCE *gets up to go out.*
>
> ANTOINE *throws himself on her and restrains her.*

Just where do you think you're going?

> CONSTANCE *does not answer.*

Here, you're staying here, are you listening to me?

> *To the person on the telephone.*

Yes, I'm waiting for you. Thank you.

He hangs up.

CONSTANCE   I want to go outside.

ANTOINE   My good God, I think you're crazy!

CONSTANCE   No, Mathilde will be coming back soon. I want to wait for her at the front of the house.

I'm anxious to see her. See if she's grown. See if she's changed.

My little girl.

ANTOINE   No, you're staying here with me. You're not going out!

CONSTANCE   I can wait for her here. It doesn't make any difference to me. It doesn't matter to me. I'm thirsty.

ANTOINE   I slept too long. I don't understand how I managed to sleep that way!

CONSTANCE   Do you want some water?

ANTOINE   No, you're staying here. You can drink later!

CONSTANCE   You're wrong. I'm not a madwoman. And I'm not a bad mother either!

ANTOINE   You can tell that to the police!

CONSTANCE   You want to have me arrested?

ANTOINE   Yes, I have no choice!

CONSTANCE   Mathilde is coming. And then you'll understand.

She gets up and goes to open the window.

ANTOINE   No, leave the windows closed!

CONSTANCE   I want air!

Do you know a love song, Antoine?

ANTOINE   I don't understand what's going on with you. But I have to follow my heart when it tells me what to do. I'm doing what I'm doing because I think that's what I have to do. I couldn't forgive myself if I didn't do it. Do you understand?

It's for Mathilde!

CONSTANCE   Yes, it's for her, Mathilde.

Mathilde, my love. Mommy's waiting for you.

CONSTANCE stands up and picks up a book from the pile of books on the floor. She rips a page out, and, picking up a pencil, she begins to write.

ANTOINE   What are you doing?!

CONSTANCE   I have to write a letter to a friend.

I'm going to say to her that I still don't have a lot of courage, but that I am starting to understand.

That perhaps I can begin to imagine a new language, and that perhaps in fifty or a hundred years there will be human beings who are going to write stories using this language. Perhaps.

It may be that I'll lose my nerve. It may be that sometimes I'll let it all go, because it's not easy being alone against the world. But I promise to try.

A knock is heard at the door.

The end.

Public Disorder
(Désordre public)

by Evelyne de la Chenelière

translated by Morwyn Brebner

Introduction to
Public Disorder (Désordre public)

The character who serves as the focal point in *Public Disorder* is a young, unemployed actor, who does not understand why he no longer has work, is never invited to auditions, and does not even have the opportunity of doing commercials. He is using public transportation in a large city, that is to say he is in a bus with several other passengers who get on and off as the play progresses. The *public disorder* arises on the bus from the ability he suddenly develops, and from which he cannot escape, to share the unspoken thoughts and feelings of those around him. His reaction and response to these thoughts and feelings, including their revelation of his own distorted view of himself and of the world, cause considerable upset for him and the others. In fact, the disorder is not only in him but shared in one form or another by everyone else. The dramatic conflict of the play derives from the resistance within himself and when confronted by others to such clairvoyance and to the enigmatic human solidarity it illumines.

Using this fascinating device, Evelyne de la Chenelière immediately evokes in her audience's mind the unspoken teeming underbelly of what is going on in this shared space: the experience we have all had in spots of crowded public transportation knowing that all individuals around us have their own unique concerns, doubts, emotions we cannot share and knowing as well we must not breach the imperative that we neither speak to strangers nor transgress the tiny bubble of private space they inhabit.

The theme of omnipresent solitude in the hearts of the anonymous crowd, accompanied by either the longing for affective and physical contact with another human being or fear of such contact, is compelling. The need for contact with others is dramatized by De la Chenelière as so compelling that in the absence of such contact and the words and compassion it brings, individuals lose a sense of their own existence. Max, the central character, comes to realize this in the end and to know this entails the use of words:

> I have to talk. If I'm talking, I exist, whereas if I'm quiet, it's like a conglomeration of strange words stuck in my head and then there's no room left for my thoughts [...] It's all stacked up: sweet things, the shiver of a first kiss, the relief of good news, reunions, forgiveness, a load lifted [...] But also the sick screaming out, your cries as ceaseless as the tides [...] (Scene 23)

De la Chenelière represents such longing dramatically on a continuum of intercourse that stretches across social encounters and friendship, love and care, erotic union, lucid awareness of catastrophe, and theatrical communion, taking in the mind, body, and spirit. Her "Avant-propos" in the French text, addressed ambiguously to a *vous* who could be anyone she is able to reach with her fervent appeal—a stranger, an intimate lover, an actor, or a spectator about to watch this show, opens this entire horizon and affirms the need to keep dynamically moving in it—physically, emotionally, intellectually:

> ...it's because I don't know where to put my body when you aren't there [...] it isn't content being alone. As soon as there are two of us, I can at least place my body in front of a fellow human being and that grabs it [...] I have a permanent lack of indifference because I *can't get over* and I shall never be able to get over our way of being together [...] In the disorder of our greedy melee, in the cruel climb to the top where some use others as stepladders, we somehow manage, in spite of our murderous will, to embrace each other, to warm each other, to accidentally snuggle up together one on top of the other, to find some comfort in the very violence that brings us together [...] if I plant my body in front of yours for no obvious reason, please be good enough to not leave right away.[1]

The English version, *Public Disorder*, has unique status as a translation in that a definitive and final original does not exist. Its elusive origin is not accidental; it goes right back to the moment in 2003 when Jean-Pierre Ronfard first conceived the idea for *Aphrodite en 04* of urgency. Ronfard, renowned for decades in Québec for his radical experimentation in theatre, commitment to originality, and support for young artists, playfully set the rules for Atelier Aphrodite. It was his intention to offer fresh opportunities to new theatre artists, urgently anxious to do things differently, and to the playwright, De la Chenelière, prepared to demystify the norms of writing a play script, by overturning as many theatrical conventions as possible. In order to do this, the company would rehearse only one day before each performance and the script would be transformed regularly in the course of the run by De la Chenelière, who attended every show and then produced her new pieces. The objective was not to try to move closer and closer to perfection but rather to incessantly challenge and renew the creative juices of all members of the Atelier through participation in a constantly evolving artistic project and to avoid the phenomenon, more or less universal in theatre practice, of a show being as fixed in stone as possible on opening night, with no subsequent changes.[2] Although Jean-Pierre Ronfard died on September 26, 2003, the show went ahead for its entire run as *Aphrodite en 04*, adhering to the experimental principles he, De la Chenelière, and all members of the company had planned, for nineteen performances in January 2004.

When Ginette Noiseux, artistic director of Espace Go, invited De la Chenelière and Alice Ronfard (one of Québec's major directors, daughter of Jean-Pierre Ronfard and famous writer and translator Marie Cardinal) to remount this fascinating show in 2006, the decision was made to change its title to *Désordre public* and to more or less fix its form so as to facilitate its publication. The published version contains nonetheless many variations dating from earlier shows, which offer the translator and others who might undertake a reprise a broad range of choices for the script that is actually staged. Thus the text in both French and English remains a work in progress, open to new creative and experimental initiatives, as both Ronfards and De la

Chenelière would wish. The play garnering the 2006 Governor General's Literary Award for Drama (French) is in recognition of the artistic quality and thematic richness of this highly original and important theatrical piece.

Public Disorder begins with the apparent thinking out loud of Emily, reading quietly as many tend to do on their regular commute on public transportation. The passage Max and the audience hear her reading is thematically relevant, in that it involves seeking to make eye contact rather than avoid it in public spaces and the sexual innuendo this might be interpreted to convey. Still, at this early point in the growth of his self-awareness, Max is thoroughly disgusted and confused by what he hears. Emily is the first in a series of individual passengers with whom Max interacts—like the actor playing Emily, all the actors are obliged to improvise as they play several roles or otherwise keep their place on the bus. The character Emily reappears in a later scene and is seen making a futile effort to have a meaningful conversation with Alex, a former lover. When Max overhears her wondering: "It's so funny that we slept together and we don't know what to say to each other. Where did the intimacy go?" the quiet desperation so many feel in their search for communication, love, and intimacy is palpable.

Immediately following his nasty encounter with Emily, Max is heard in alternating conversations in a coffee shop with Ariane, one of his former lovers and a fellow actor of whom he is jealous because of her current success as a theatre professional, and out jogging with his buddy Andre. These conversations, during which Max reveals the disorder he feels at getting into people's minds, serve to reveal his character. As he admits, he is superficial, thoughtless, and entirely self-centred. He lacks respect and compassion for others. As would seem unsuitable for the main character in this quest drama, for an actor wishing to understand the roles he's called on to play and for a man unsure of his own identity, he is not in any way a seeker of life's deeper meaning: "I'm not mystical! I'm not spiritual. I don't believe in anything. I'm not looking for meaning. I love that my life has no meaning" (Scene 2). However, like it or not, meaning is coming his way. Through the opening scenes he hears without making any comment the remarks of his fellow passengers about the windows of the bus, their observations of fellow passengers, their doubts and worries, their misconceptions, and their annoyance with him.

Max's first step at engaging with the others occurs when he takes the place of Estelle, the wife of whom Louis is thinking. For the first time, he responds to the thoughts he hears. This initiative causes, however, great panic, whether in Estelle or Max is unclear: "No, no! That's not me!" (Scene 7). Nevertheless, he slowly sets aside his reservations, exchanging lines with some of the other characters, becoming a fleeting presence in their lives, and thereby recognizing himself in them: with Stephane, whom he acknowledges as a passing friend, Pauline, who is nervously looking ahead to her first date, little Daniel, whose mother is worried about him getting off at the right stop. The next stage in Max's evolution is the acknowledgement and expression of his own desires, such as reconciliation with Ariane and a good look at himself in the mirror. This is accompanied by a panicked sense of losing himself as he has always known himself because he is becoming part of the thoughts and obsessions of others.

Having cast off his severe state of self-preoccupation and recognized that to be an actor one must be capable of compassion and empathy, Max is led to wonder whether he now has what it takes to be a fine actor: the ability to get into other individuals' mind and body and to reproduce their performance before the eyes of strangers:

> Ariane thinks it takes imagination to be an actress. Maybe it just takes memory [...] the memory that makes us tired for every human being, dead and alive. Now that I'm finally tired for other people, have become other people, am I an actor? Am I a great actor? I could probably be an amazing, imposing, transcendent actor. If I wanted, I could be a truly great actor, speaking for every human being like they'd never been spoken for, portraying them with every echo they deserve (Scene 23).

The possibility is interesting, but Max immediately sees it as an illusion. On the stage of life, all individuals must perform their own scenarios, even if they must always remain incompletely expressed and represented. Actors may be able to position themselves imaginatively and corporeally on the tightrope between self and other, but they can never make a full entrance into another's life. The theatre is the wonderful place where actors perform roles that allow them to be both themselves and others, to live their own lives while temporarily stepping into other stories in other places. Max is on the verge of realizing that great actors must not only exhibit the compassion to feel and think what others feel and think. They must also possess vanity and have a sense of their own individuality, personality and identity. It is urgent to find this tenuous balance in one's own life and in the theatre. There must be the sparks of extreme tension between who the actor is as an individual and the weight of expressing the human condition, whom all share, each in their own way:

> I can't be an actor because I don't have any vanity left. I almost miss it. I held onto my vanity, my personality, my identity. I loved existing for myself and by myself. I loved finding myself important. But I didn't measure up. Nobody, nobody measures up to thousands of human beings. [...] I don't know what it means (Scene 23).

The very trajectory of the several versions of *Désordre public/Public Disorder* and the demands of the play for incessant improvisation suggest that what Max needs to rediscover his zest for life and his talent as an actor is the collaboration of fellow performers and writers in a joint creative process demanding a sense of urgency, unlimited energy, and a willingness to keep on changing the lines of the story, as De la Chenelière and Ronfard have done, never saying the production is completely ready, even after the show has opened and is seemingly launched for a steady run.

There is an extraordinary lightness and playfulness in Evelyne de la Chenelière's dramatic writing. The unexpectedly quick turns of phrase she gives to her characters never fail to bring pleasure, whether on the page or the stage. Plays such as *Public Disorder* produce an exhilarating sense of openness. She has a wonderful gift for respecting the freedom of the directors interpreting her work and the actors playing the roles she has created to invent using their own imagination, gestures, feelings, places, and social conditions. While her work is built on an awareness of all that is dark in human experience and the devastations humans have created, her belief that individuals are capable of lucid thought, of love and compassion, and of creating meaningful lives for themselves and others through reflection, erotic energy, and the élan of creativity appears unshakable.

Notes

[1] ...c'est parce que je ne sais pas où mettre mon corps quand vous n'êtes pas là [...] il n'est pas content d'être seul. Dès que nous sommes deux, je peux au moins placer mon corps en face d'un semblable et ça le saisit [...] je manque définitivement d'indifférence, parce que je n'en *reviens pas* et je n'en reviendrai jamais de notre manière d'être ensemble [...] Dans le désordre de notre mêlée avide, dans la cruelle ascension où les uns servent de marchepied aux autres, malgré notre volonté assassine nous finissons pourtant par nous étreindre, par nous réchauffer, par nous lover accidentellement les uns sur les autres, par trouver notre confort à même la violence qui nous unit [...] si je plante mon corps devant le vôtre sans raison apparente, ayez la bonté de ne pas partir tout de suite. (*Désordre public*, 7–8, tr. LHF)

[2] See "*Aphrodite en 04* ou les caprices de Jean-Pierre" and "Printemps 2003. Atelier Aphrodite, janvier 2004," in *Désordre public*, 9, 128.

About Evelyne de la Chenelière

Evelyne de la Chenelière, author and actor, studied theatre at the École Michel-Granvale in Paris. She has written many plays that have been produced in Québec and elsewhere and translated into several languages. Her play, *Des fraises en janvier*, was chosen for the Masque du meilleur texte original in 2000 by the Académie québécoise du théâtre. It has been translated into English, German, and Scottish and was produced at the Edinburgh Festival in 2006. Whether one looks at *Des fraises en janvier, Au bout du fil, Henri et Margaux, Aphrodite en 04, L'héritage de Darwin, Bashir Lazhar, Le plan américain, L'Imposture* or *Les pieds des anges*, one is struck by the fluid originality and poetic precision of her language. Her work reflects meticulous observation of human nature as well as infinite tenderness for the frailty of the human species. She received the Governor General's Literary Award for Drama (French) in 2006 for *Désordre public* and was shortlisted for the same award in 2009 for *Les pieds des anges*, which was produced in 2009 by Espace Go. *L'Imposture* was produced by Théâtre du Nouveau Monde in November 2009.

A long-time member of the Nouveau Théâtre Expérimental, she often collaborated with the late Jean-Pierre Ronfard. As well, she works regularly as writer and actor in close co-operation with director Daniel Brière.

Published Works by Evelyne de la Chenelière

Au bout du fil. Théâtre (2003). Montréal: Fides. 68–108.

Bashir Lazhar. Au Bout du fil. Bashir Lazhar (2003). Paris: Éditions théâtrales. 51–76.

Culpa. Théâtre (2003). Montréal: Fides. 154–87.

Des fraises en janvier. Théâtre (2003). Montréal: Fides. 10–67. *Strawberries in January* (2004). Tr. Morwyn Brebner. Toronto: Playwrights Canada Press.

Henri et Margaux. Théâtre (2003). Montréal: Fides. 110–152.

Aphrodite en 04/Désordre public. Désordre public. Aphrodite en 04. Nicht retour, Mademoiselle (2006). Montréal: Fides. 10–79.

Nicht retour, Mademoiselle. Désordre public. Aphrodite en 04. Nicht retour, Mademoiselle (2006). Montréal: Fides. 80–127.

L'héritage de Darwin (2008). Carnières, Belgium: Lansman Éditeur.

L'Imposture (2009). Montréal: Leméac.

Les pieds des anges (2009). Montréal: Leméac.

The first version of *Désordre public*, entitled *Aphrodite en 04*, opened at Espace Libre by the Nouveau Théâtre Expérimental on January 6, 2004, with the following company:

Delphine Arnaud
Marcelo Arroyo
Émilie Bibeau
Jocelyn Caron
Francis Ducharme
Marie-Christine Lavallée
Patricia Ubeda
Erwin Weche

Directed by Jacques L'Heureux

. . .

A revised version of *Désordre public* opened at Espace Go on April 25, 2006, with the following company:

Sophie Cadieux
Maxim Gaudette
Jacinthe Laguë
Dominique Leduc
Didier Lucien
Jean Marchand
Marie Michaud
Édith Paquet

Directed by Alice Ronfard

Characters

Alex
Andre
Ariane
Brian
Chinese Person
Cop
Daniel
Emily
Erwin
Father
Jacqueline
Jocelyne
Lady
Louis
Man
Marie-Christine
Max
Mother
Nathalie
Old Man
Old Woman
Patrick
Pauline
Ricardo
Stephane
Woman
Other Characters

PUBLIC DISORDER

Scene 1

Eight passengers on a bus. EMILY reads a book. MAX sits behind her.

EMILY   It would be strange. The way you can smell a flood, a catastrophe, a natural disaster; at first it would seem like nothing. The usual anonymity. But this thing would make people greedy to look at other people; to seek *their* looks; like it was possible to grab humanity with their eyes; to swallow humanity with their eyes. Like, for no discernible reason, they all finally felt like part of the same species: thinking animal. This would be enough to make people viscerally interested in the eyes of others. They'd start to feel other people. They'd be so inside another person's skin they'd be able to move another person's arm. They'd begin to feel hot or cold for other people. This would create a collective uncertainty about reality. At first, this intensification of the senses would make people feel such violent and inexplicable desires they'd be sure it was sexually perverse. At first they'd wonder what was wrong, why do I want everybody this way? Then they'd become conscious of experiencing something extraordinary, perhaps even from an alien world. They'd feel sorry for anyone who wasn't on the bus with them at that exact moment. Because they would have experienced the true depths of compassion.

MAX   Could you please stop reading out loud?

EMILY   Excuse me?

MAX   Could you read in your head. You're bothering people.

EMILY   I don't understand…

MAX   Look, your airport paperback isn't all that interesting to your fellow passengers.

EMILY   It's none of your business!

MAX   Exactly, so kindly spare me the lecture.

EMILY   What are you talking about! I'm not bothering anybody. I'm reading!

MAX   You're reading out loud!

EMILY   No, I'm not!

MAX   And, it's a terrible book. What book is it? Who wrote it?

EMILY   You know, everyone thinks he's the voice of our generation.

MAX   I hate "voices of their generation." If you want to make a spectacle of yourself, at least read something tasteful.

EMILY   No one else is complaining.

MAX They're too shy.

EMILY They're minding their business.

MAX People here are terrified of confrontation…

EMILY People "here"?

MAX …because they don't have the intellectual tools to debate.

EMILY Where is "here"?

MAX Canada.

EMILY You're bugging me. Please let me read.

MAX My pleasure. But read in your head.

EMILY Of course, I'll read in my head. How else would I read?

MAX Maybe you haven't noticed, but you were reading out loud. I could hear you.

EMILY That's ridiculous! *(She talks to someone else.)* Excuse me, could you hear me reading?

> *The woman shakes her head no.*

Excuse me? Did anyone else hear me reading?

> *People shake their head no, amused.*

MAX Then how did I hear you?

EMILY Ask your doctor. Maybe you're sick.

MAX Wait! I can prove that I heard you! I can tell you exactly what your book is about. It's trash. It's about people on a bus who start wanting to have sex with each other, all at once, for no reason. See, I heard? It's about a kind of animalistic solidarity, or freak alien occurrence, on a bus. It's dirty. Okay, it does seem true that, in the face of dreadful things, human beings sometimes mysteriously, desperately, want to have sex as a final expression of life. I've heard of it. In war, among the corpses, but please, on a bus. Not here! So there, I heard, so admit you were reading out loud, whispering even, because you can't leave me questioning my sanity. You wouldn't do that to your worst enemy, make him doubt his sanity…

> *A man stops MAX when he tries to get too close to EMILY.*

MAN Take it easy there.

MAX I need to know what's happening to me! I'm usually a good citizen. I don't talk to people on the bus. I swear I usually take the bus without making trouble, but this woman assaulted me. She was reading in my ear. She murmured filthy words…

MAN Either get off or I'll throw you off.

Everyone claps. MAX gets off, uncomfortable. He runs to escape. The next scene is interrupted several times by the exchange between MAX and ANDRE. It's the same MAX but at two different times. MAX and ARIANE are in a coffee shop, while MAX and ANDRE are jogging in a park.

Scene 2

At the coffee shop.

ARIANE I made an agenda.

MAX What?

ARIANE Like a list of the issues we need to discuss.

MAX You made an agenda?

ARIANE Yes.

MAX How could make an agenda! We're having coffee, it's not a meeting.

ARIANE We have issues to deal with. And I thought that if I made an agenda, we wouldn't forget anything.

MAX Does your agenda allow us to talk about our day? Because something unbelievable happened to me…

ARIANE I'm fine. I don't feel like telling you about my life, and I don't want to hear about yours.

MAX You know, when you act tough, you lose all your femininity. You'll get wrinkles.

ARIANE I don't care if you think I'm cute anymore.

MAX Okay, Ariane, I need to talk to you. Something really weird happened…

To ANDRE. They're both jogging.

I think I'm sick. I'm telling you, Andre, I never felt so humiliated in my entire life. The people on the bus thought it was like invisible theatre, or something. You realize they clapped? It was so abnormal they clapped! That means they couldn't accept that what was happening was *real!*

ANDRE What's invisible theatre?

MAX It's where the actors make a kind of scene without telling anyone it's a play, then afterwards, when people are forced to take sides, or react, they tell them it was only a play. It's stupid. We did it when I was in theatre school, in a restaurant with a fake bum who was eating and a fake customer who didn't want the bum eating near him and a fake waiter who tried to calm him down…

ANDRE Kind of like *Punk'd?*

MAX   Kind of, with no celebrities.

ANDRE   …

MAX   I'm going crazy, I swear. My doctor sent me to a psychiatrist. The psychiatrist is convinced I'm schizophrenic. I'm going crazy. And you're as calm as if I told you I thought I was myopic. I'm awash in full-on paranormality, you don't even bat an eye. I'm afraid to leave the house. I won't be able to work…

ANDRE   You don't work…

MAX   That's not the point! I'm just saying I have to get better!

ANDRE   It's not a disease.

MAX   What do you know about it?

ANDRE   It happens to other people, you know.

MAX   Really? You've heard of it before?

ANDRE   Asians.

MAX   Asians what?

ANDRE   Remember my trip, two years ago…

MAX   Your spiritual pilgrimage?

ARIANE   *(at the coffee shop)* Okay, first…

MAX   …I can't believe you made an agenda. We've been camping together!

ARIANE   I don't see the connection.

MAX   Camping is symbolically important. I mean, you liked being afraid of bears so that I'd hold you in my arms. You'd snuggle up to me! In the morning, when I made a fire to make you toast, you'd snuggle up to me again. And now you need an agenda to talk to me!

ARIANE   I don't have a lot of time, Max.

MAX   You found my outdoorsiness virile.

ARIANE   You hated that camping weekend.

MAX   Exactly. That's how much I loved you.

ARIANE   You couldn't stop whining that we should have stayed in a hotel.

MAX   That's because we didn't have any gear. I'm all for equipped camping.

ARIANE   We were equipped.

MAX   We didn't have a ground sheet. We weren't equipped!

ARIANE   You're such a wimp.

MAX I'm not a wimp. I have back problems. If you had a lower back like mine you'd have more compassion.

ARIANE So.

MAX So. How's your mother?

ARIANE Since when do you care about my mother?

MAX I'm trying to be nice, that's all!

ARIANE Well I'm not used to it.

MAX Gee, it's so fun, seeing you again…

ARIANE Excuse me, but you've never asked me how my mother was. You always looked annoyed when I talked about my mother, when I needed to talk to you about my mother. And now, suddenly, you act all nice, asking after my mother, so excuse me, but it's a little destabilizing.

MAX I came here thinking we could be relaxed…

ARIANE I'm sorry, but I can't relax…. I feel like if I relax, you'll think I've changed my mind

MAX Are you afraid of changing your mind?

ARIANE No!

MAX Fine, then you can tell me how your mother is.

ARIANE Not well, as always, thank you.

MAX I'm also not well, and that's why I need to talk to you…

ARIANE Unbelievable! It's all about you! You ask me about my mother, but you can't wait to make it about your little problems.

MAX They're not little problems. They're huge! Ariane, I think I'm going crazy…

ANDRE *(to MAX, while jogging)* It wasn't a spiritual pilgrimage.

MAX *(to ARIANE, in the coffee shop)* You have to listen to me. Even if it sounds unbelievable…

ANDRE *(to MAX, while jogging)* Max? You listening?

MAX *(to ANDRE, while running)* What?

ANDRE It wasn't a spiritual pilgrimage. It was a mystical quest.

MAX It was because you were dating a Buddhist.

ANDRE She wasn't a Buddhist…

MAX No, but doesn't being in love make you do stupid shit? I once went camping without camping equipment. By the way, did you know I saw Ariane again? She made an agenda, if you can believe it. You know, she did everything to seem… impenetrable, but I saw through it. I saw through it.

ANDRE Oh yeah?

MAX I don't want to bother you with it. You were talking about your trip…

ANDRE Well, it happens to a lot of Asians.

MAX What?

ANDRE Hearing other people's thoughts.

MAX Are you kidding me?

ANDRE No. Haven't you noticed how, when you walk by a group of Asians, sometimes they'll all start laughing?

MAX Um…. Yeah, sometimes.

ANDRE It's because they heard what you were thinking. Or one of them heard it and then told the others. I can't walk through Chinatown anymore. Or if I do I'm careful about what I think.

MAX Chinese people can hear my thoughts?!

ANDRE Not all of them. Just the more mystical ones.

MAX But I'm not mystical! I'm not spiritual. I don't believe in anything. I'm not looking for meaning. I love that my life has no meaning, so why is this happening to me?! I don't want anything to do with their thoughts! If Chinese people can hear thoughts, that's their problem. I don't care about whatever's cluttering up the tiny minds of my depressed contemporaries. It's noise pollution! It's unbearable! Why me? There are cults full of people waiting for just that, a magical power, a sixth sense! I don't want it! I already get too much information from my five senses! I don't want more! Why is this happening to me?

ANDRE It's incredible.

MAX *(to ARIANE, in the coffee shop)* You have to listen, Ariane. I'm the victim of something.

ARIANE Again?! You always claim you're the victim of something, Max! Misunderstanding, persecution, plots…. I-CAN'T-DO-ANYTHING-FOR-YOU! I've given up, understand?

WOMAN Excuse me? Ariane Letendre?

ARIANE Hello.

WOMAN I used to watch your show, *Happiness Next Door*… I thought you were great.

ARIANE Thank you.

WOMAN Too bad it's not on anymore. Are you gonna do anything else on TV?

ARIANE Not really... I mostly do theatre.

WOMAN Oh yeah? Well, could be worse. Can I have your autograph anyway?

ARIANE Sure, thank you. Here.

WOMAN Thanks and good luck!

ARIANE Thanks.

MAX Why are you nicer to that poor woman than to me?

ARIANE What makes her a "poor woman"?

MAX Any woman who's a fan of *Happiness Next Door* is a poor woman. And, just between us, you weren't terrific in *Happiness Next Door*. Admit it, you made very safe choices...

ARIANE More contempt. That's why nobody will hire you, Max. Because you're totally negative.

ANDRE *(to MAX, while jogging)* Usually, it's a power that develops gradually. You have to work at it. It's a kind of quest.

MAX Are you saying there are Chinese people working to hear what I think? Doing it on purpose? That's a breach of my privacy! It should be illegal! It's spying!

ANDRE What amazes me is that it happened to you without even trying. There must have been a trigger.

MAX What amazes me is that you never told me.

ANDRE Told you what?

MAX That most Chinese people are listening to my thoughts.

ANDRE They don't exactly listen to what you're thinking. They catch bits from everyone, by accident. I mean, you're overestimating your importance if you think the Chinese are spying on you...

MAX I didn't say they're spying on me. I said they can hear what I'm thinking and it makes me anxious.

ARIANE *(to MAX, in the coffee shop)* You're totally negative! How do you expect anyone to want to work with you? You're completely self-centred!

ANDRE *(to MAX, while jogging)* If you were less self-centred, you'd be less anxious.

MAX *(to ARIANE, in the coffee shop)* It's not my fault. I'm very needy.

ARIANE Everyone's needy. You have no respect for other people. And you think everyone else is stupid. You never have compassion for anyone.

MAX   It's easy to respect people when they ask for your autograph!

ANDRE   *(to MAX, while jogging)* Look around. You'll see that you're not the only person suffering.

MAX   *(to ARIANE, in the coffee shop)* You know what, everyone is stupid! And I have too many problems to have compassion.

ARIANE in the coffee shop and ANDRE while jogging.

ARIANE & ANDRE   Everyone has problems. Besides, we have something to tell you.

MAX   *(to ARIANE, at the coffee shop)* Mine are more serious. I can't find work, my wife left me, my agent won't talk to me, I had to sell my car. I have to take public transit.

ARIANE   *(in the coffee shop)* Poor you. Forced to mingle with other human beings.

ANDRE   *(while jogging)* Public transit is great.

MAX   *(to ARIANE, in the coffee shop)* See? You don't have more compassion than me.

ANDRE   *(while jogging)* Take it for the good of the planet.

ARIANE   *(in the coffee shop)* I take public transit. It's not a big deal.

MAX   Public transit is great. But now, I'll always wonder if there isn't a Chinese person listening to my thoughts.

ARIANE   What are you talking about, Chinese person? What's the connection?

MAX   I wasn't talking to you.

ANDRE   I think he was talking to me. Chinese people are my thing.

ARIANE   What blows me away is that you don't ask questions! If you were the tiniest bit interested in other people you might be a good actor, and maybe we wouldn't have ended up this way.

MAX   You should have married a saint, not an actor. By the way, do you ever see Andre?

ARIANE at the coffee shop and ANDRE, jogging, together.

ARIANE   What? Once in a while. He's your friend, you know, I mean, I met him through you. That's how we see each other, because we were used to seeing each other with you.

ANDRE   *(to ARIANE)* See, it would be the perfect moment to tell him, the time to just tell him things. But you're not there yet, I respect that.

ARIANE   Why do you keep changing the subject?

MAX   What? I didn't change the subject. I don't even know what we're talking about.

ARIANE Everything you lost is because of too much navel-gazing. Don't you get sick from hanging out with yourself? And I hate it when you pretend you don't understand, Max!

ANDRE *(while jogging)* Okay, I have to go to yoga. For your own good, try not to obsess. It's like the kettle: watching doesn't make it boil any faster.

MAX What's the connection? Andre! What's my connection with a kettle?

MAX finds himself back on the bus. He hears people thinking.

Scene 3

On the bus.

ALEX *(He speaks to EMILY.)* ...So, like, the guy, totally fed up, goes to McDonald's. He chills, he waits in line, then he orders breakfast. Some kind of Egg McMuffin breakfast thing. And then the McDonald's girl tells him it's too late—they're not serving breakfast anymore. So the guy asks what time breakfast ends. She says: "Eleven." So then, the camera shows the clock, and it's five after eleven. So the guy takes a breath, he doesn't freak out right away, he tells her it's only five after eleven, and he wants a McMuffin. She tells him she can't give him one because it's after eleven. He thinks she's kidding, but she's not kidding. So the tension rises, and you can see the guy is freaking out, so like, dude pulls out his gun, a big freakin' gun that he stole from an army warehouse the scene before, and he tells her again he wants a McMuffin! So everyone goes nuts, falling on the floor, then the girl thinks he wants money, that it's a holdup, but he just wants a McMuffin. He even wants to pay for it! You understand, because of everything he's gone though in the movie, you understand that he would pull out his gun for a McMuffin, and you understand the whole social critique of America, and the absurdity, and everything. It's really great.

EMILY Does he get his McMuffin, in the end?

ALEX I can't remember.

EMILY Anyway. It sounds good.

They don't know what else to say.

(thinking) I can't wait until he gets off. I never know what to say to people I know.

ALEX *(to EMILY)* Do you ever hang out with Jean-Francois and those guys?

EMILY *(to ALEX)* Not really. But I saw his sister on the bus. She got married. *(She thinks.)* Everyone's married. I'm freaking out.

ALEX *(to EMILY)* Aside from that, how are things?

EMILY *(to ALEX)* Fine. I'm tired of school, it's endless. *(thinks)* It's so funny that we slept together and we don't know what to say to each other. Where did the intimacy go? The intimacy I felt with the first guy who touched my breasts. My God, don't think about that when you're looking at him!

ALEX   What's wrong?

EMILY   Nothing. I was thinking.

ALEX   *(thinking)* She hasn't changed. "Nothing, just thinking." She keeps everything to herself and I'm supposed to guess. *(to EMILY)* This is my stop.

EMILY   See you!

ALEX   See you, take care! *(He gets off the bus.)*

EMILY   *(thinks, referring to MAX)* Why is he looking at me like that?

> *Embarrassed, MAX looks away. He turns and focuses on different passengers. He hears them:*

CHARACTER 1   all he has to do is call her, is that so hard

CHARACTER 2   not in the magazine that said you should put beer in your hair

CHARACTER 3   wednesday seven thursday eight friday nine saturday ten sunday eleven monday twelve it's a monday dammit, the twelfth is a monday

NATHALIE   *(thinking)* Like Ariane Letendre.

CHARACTER 4   what exactly is cholesterol

> *MAX goes back to NATHALIE.*

NATHALIE   I stare at people. I've been told it's really embarrassing. It's like I need to compare myself to other people. I make a kind of chart of the person sitting opposite me. I try to guess if that person has a fulfilling sex life, a high-profile job, if she has kids, if she's smart, if she's fit. I have no sex life, a boring job, I don't have kids, I don't know if I'm smart, and I've never tried to be fit. Am I sad? I don't know if I'm especially sad or not. I've been living in a moderate state for so long I don't know what extreme emotions are anymore.

> *DANIEL sits/stands between MAX and NATHALIE, so close that MAX has to listen to DANIEL.*

DANIEL   …holds my hand. With the other, she holds my mittens so I can hold onto the pole with a mittenless hand so I won't slip. There are empty seats but I like to hold onto the pole so I can feel when the bus is turning and when it brakes. Later, I might try to sit so I can see out the big window. A lady asked if I wanted her seat but I didn't want to sit beside the man beside the lady, so I have to wait for two seats to be empty to make sure I can sit beside my mother or beside no one. My mother unzips my coat and unties my scarf, saying "It's warm." But I was fine. My mother is always deciding when I'm warm, when I'm hungry, and when I'm tired. She's afraid my health is delicate because I'm a genius. She's afraid of what might happen when I go to my father's house in Ottawa.

NATHALIE Maybe I'm depressed? I have no friends. I can't become friends with Ariane Letendre because I'll always be jealous of Ariane Letendre. I'm afraid to go to her place. I shouldn't go to her place. Why did I say yes? I shouldn't go through her things. I shouldn't do it, I know I shouldn't…

DANIEL People look at my mother. They smile to show her she's a good mother, and while they do, my mother ruffles my hair, like she's proving them right. She looks at me, and then looks at the people to make sure they saw her being a good mother and ruffling my hair. People usually end up looking away. Sometimes people talk to us. Usually old people because of nostalgia. But today, I'm taking the bus all alone and nobody's talking to me. I'm all alone on the bus.

MAX thinks as a way of blocking out the other people. We see him next in JACQUELINE's office.

Scene 4

JAQUELINE's office.

MAX …I tried to stay calm. Like the little boy, I said to myself, "I'm all alone on the bus." I kept repeating it. Trying to disregard the other people, to stop hearing them. I kept repeating "I'm all alone on the bus." But it didn't work. I still heard people, and what's more, one of them was thinking of Ariane! Can you believe the coincidence? Ariane is even haunting me in other people's thoughts!

JACQUELINE *(in her office)* Ariane's an actress with a lot of momentum. It's normal for people to think of her. I think she has a lot of fans from *Happiness Next Door*. We worked hard, and now she has momentum!

MAX Let's talk about momentum. I need work. The only way I stop this this is to concentrate on something else. It's crucial…

JACQUELINE Max, I'm your friend. You know that, I'm your friend first. But I don't think we can keep working together. I already explained it to you…. It can be hard to admit, but maybe you're not built for this business…. You're too delicate. I don't think I can keep representing you. You're not *representable*. If you want to act like a star, you have to be a star, Max…

MAX Jacqueline, you can't do this to me! Get me one audition. Okay? One last chance. Okay? One audition for anything. Just make it real.

JACQUELINE I'll see what I can do. But there's not much happening now.

MAX A commercial! I take back my vow. I agree to do commercials, all right? I'm changing, Jacqueline. Something triggered. I got it. It's inactivity that's driving me crazy, that's making me hear things. It's inactivity that's making me make things up. That's it. I have to be busy. I have to work, Jacqueline…

JACQUELINE I'm sorry, I have a meeting.

MAX Remember when you began the agency?

JACQUELINE Yes, I remember.

MAX Remember who trusted you when you were starting out?

JACQUELINE Yeah, yeah…

MAX I never made the agency any money. That's true. But I brought you actors who made you money! Actors who made you rich! I brought you Ariane Letendre!

JACQUELINE I'll try to find you something.

MAX Thank you.

JACQUELINE But don't expect miracles.

MAX Okay. Thanks, Jacqueline.

JACQUELINE See you, Max.

MAX Jacqueline!

JACQUELINE What?

MAX Are there any Chinese people at the agency?

JACQUELINE Huh?

MAX At the agency, are there any Chinese actors?

JACQUELINE Uh… yeah, one Chinese guy and two black ones. But they don't work much.

MAX Could you give me the Chinese one's number?

JACQUELINE Why?

MAX Just give it to me and I won't ask for anything else. I'll let you work.

JACQUELINE Okay, okay.

Scene 5

On the bus.

PAULINE *(She thinks and MAX hears her.)* It's all that matters. I have a date. Having a date is something. It means someone's going to wait for me. Wait to see me. This person will say, "Today I have a date with Pauline." And this day will always be the day this person had a date with Pauline. That'll be the title of the day. A title nobody can ever erase, even if some day the day itself is erased from every memory, it'll always have a title: the date with Pauline. And if I didn't go on this date, someone would be expecting me, annoyed at me, then worried for me. I would take up all their thoughts. I would represent their most intense desire in that moment, so much so I'm tempted not to go on the date, just so I know I'll be expected for a few more minutes. So I know someone was thinking, "Where can Pauline be?"

NATHALIE   (*She thinks and MAX hears her.*) That lady is breathing hard. It's intrusive. It's like she's stealing other people's air. She's not that ugly but she looks disguised. I can't believe she actually chose the coat she's wearing. Actually went to buy a coat, made a plan to buy a coat, looked at a bunch of coats, and then chose that one because she thought it was nice. Nicer than the other coats. It's hard to believe. She looks like an immigrant. Not her features, but her way of being. She sits like she's not at home. You wouldn't think it was *her* bus. People who feel at home have a tendency to spread out, even on a bus. You don't say, "I missed the bus," you say, "I missed *my* bus." But you'd think she was on someone else's bus. Breathing someone else's air.

PAULINE   It's like wanting to die so that people will weep for us, but the problem is that once you're dead, obviously, you won't witness the people weeping for you and then you can't even enjoy it.

NATHALIE   Ariane Letendre told me she always ate out because she's not hungry when she's alone. I wonder if she wanted me to invite her over for dinner. Be neighbourly. Now that she said that I feel like I have to invite her over for dinner. She gave me some theatre tickets. I don't know what to do with them. I don't want to see her talent. I never had any talent. In any field. I was dancing in a ballet class full of girls, we were facing a big mirror, during the *adage*, and I looked at myself in the mirror, and I thought I was a good dancer. I was surprised by my own grace, and then suddenly I realized I was watching the wrong reflection. It wasn't my reflection. I was watching another girl's reflection, and because we all looked alike, in pink with our hair in buns, doing the same movements, I thought it was me. I thought I was such a good dancer. But in fact when I located the right reflection, my reflection, I saw I had no talent and it depressed me.

PAULINE   (*She thinks.*) …body knows I have a date. Nobody suspects what's happening. They think I'm just a lady taking the bus like them. I say lady because I'm aware of being in the lady category, not the woman category, they're not the same. Or maybe they're not thinking anything about me. They certainly haven't noticed me. I'm just a shape in a coat. Not a body, a shape. Why did I agree to go on this date? Why, when I have no body? He's an anthropologist. A specialist in analyzing archeological digs. I don't know what it's called, what he does, it's not skeletologist, I would have remembered that. He digs up skeletons and that's why he doesn't see human beings the same way. I asked him if it was frightening when he discovered a skeleton, because of their macabre look. I hope he didn't think my question was stupid. He told me he was never afraid of skeletons because, when he finds one, the first thing he sees is a smile. When many skeletons are found all at once, it's like a bed of smiles, and it's beautiful. A skeleton smile is wide; we smile wider once we're dead. I was happy he told me the skeleton story, because he believed it would move me. He believed in my sensitivity when I barely believed in it myself. He didn't think, like other people, "How could that shape in a coat be moved by skeleton smiles?"

DANIEL *(thinking)* ...not here but I imagine her beside me, or rather above because she's tall and I'm small. I'm like the Charlie Brown cartoons, where they don't show the parents because they want you to focus on the kids. So I'm focusing on me taking the bus. My mother isn't worried because the bus is full. My mother wants me to be on a full bus, so that nobody assaults me. Especially not sexually. She told me to make sure the bus was full before getting on, and to stand beside the driver and to tell the driver if someone tries to sexually assault me. But since my mother didn't make any prior arrangement with the driver, I don't know if he's agreed to save my life.

EMILY *(She has to pass MAX to get off.)* Excuse me... *(She gets off the bus.)*

Scene 6

CHINESE PERSON Whoa, that's fucked up.

MAX Yeah, I really need your help. I need to talk to someone who understands these things...

CHINESE PERSON Why me?

MAX Because you're Chinese.

CHINESE PERSON Yeah, but I don't know anything about it!

MAX You've never heard of it before?

CHINESE PERSON No. Never.

MAX Sorry to have to ask, but you don't really seem Chinese.

CHINESE PERSON My father's Chinese, but my mother's from Trois-Rivières.

MAX Have you ever been to China?

CHINESE PERSON No.

MAX Do you speak Chinese?

CHINESE PERSON No.

MAX That's disappointing. Do you hang out with Chinese people?

CHINESE PERSON Not really.

MAX You don't have an old Chinese uncle? You don't know an old monk, anyone?

CHINESE PERSON No! You're a funny guy!

MAX It must be in your genes, somewhere? Spirituality and all that!

CHINESE PERSON *(laughing)* I don't know, but I sure don't hear voices!

MAX I asked to meet a Chinese person, a real Chinese person with Oriental philosophy! A real Chinese person with acupuncture and martial arts! Do you drink tea, at least? Do you at least know how to eat with chopsticks?

Scene 7

On the bus.

LOUIS *(He thinks, MAX hears him.)* Estelle cries when she watches television. I've tried to tell her it's not real. She cries if there's a sick kid, an alcoholic wife who's suffering, a man who never told his father he loved him. When I worry, she says she likes crying in front of the television. I take her in my arms anyway, during the commercials, but I suspect she looks over my shoulder, because sometimes, she hums the jingles while she's crying. Sometimes she confuses the characters' fates with the actors'. She'll say "Poor Meryl Streep!" or "Mean Sean Penn!" And when I try to set her straight, she tells me to let her dream. My wife isn't stupid. She's delicate. She watches so much television she's no longer sure she exists. She'll ask, "Do I exist, dear?" I say: obviously you exist. Why are you asking me that? She explains that she's not sure she exists because she doesn't see herself in the television. She tells me it would help her know she exists, if she saw herself in the television. She says *in* the television like it was an aquarium. And it's true that, with the sound off, it looks like fish. My wife isn't stupid. I talk about my wife with all the affection she deserves, and not existing means she deserves a lot. Once I bought a video camera so she could see on television that she existed. I filmed her and we sat down to watch it, but she didn't recognize herself. She says, change the channel, it's not a good channel. I say, but it is a good channel. She says, no that's not me. I say, but of course it's you.

MAX *(He takes ESTELLE's place.)* No, that's not me!

LOUIS Darling, look closely. There, you're sitting on one of our kitchen chairs. Look, that's our table, and above your head, the clock…

MAX I recognize the chair, the table, and the clock, but that's not me onscreen.

LOUIS Then who is it?

MAX I don't know, not me.

LOUIS Look harder. See how you exist, my love. See how you cover your mouth when you smile. See how you tilt your head and how you lick your lips because they're dry… and there, ha! Hear my voice? *(He listens.)* I'm behind the camera, and I'm saying: my love, let me lick your lips because they're dry. See, you're laughing, in the television! I made you laugh! You're hunching your shoulders so you won't laugh too hard…

MAX   I recognize your voice... but who's that woman in the television?

LOUIS   Estelle, it's you!

MAX   No, no! That's not me! That's not me! Shut up! I don't want to hear it! Shut up! Shut up, all of you!

Scene 8

At the commune.

MAX   Mom, I don't know what to do...

MOTHER   You should come back to the country.... You're too sensitive to live in the city. You're so pale.

MAX   Yeah, but...

MOTHER   ...Baby, there's always a place for you here. You know that. And you don't need money. We're self-sufficient. We finished our windmill.

MAX   No, Mom, no...

MOTHER   It would do you good. A little fresh air, garden vegetables, sheep's-milk cheese...

MAX   I dunno...

MOTHER   You know, a lot of young people have joined us...

MAX   That's good...

MOTHER   Ricardo!

RICARDO   Hey.

MOTHER   Ricardo, I'd like you to meet my son, Max.

MAX   Hello.

RICARDO   Welcome, Max.

MOTHER   Ricardo, you wouldn't find it inconvenient if Max shared your room?

RICARDO   No, no. No problem.

MAX   No! No! I don't want to! I mean, that's not why I came!

ERWIN   You're welcome to use our room if you like. Does that bother you, darling?

PATRICIA   Not at all.

MAX   It's all right...

RICARDO   Maybe he needs a more solitary retreat.

JOCELYNE   Yeah, we could insulate the shed and put tools in the henhouse...

MARIE-CHRISTINE   Great idea.

MAX   Thanks, but no, no thanks, I swear… I just came to talk to my mother about a minor problem…

MOTHER   Honey, you know you were brought up here, outside the system. So it's normal if the system seems harsh to you. But you still have a choice.

MAX   I think I better go…

ERWIN   Would you like to share our meal before you leave?

MAX   Ah…

MARIE-CHRISTINE   I'm about to kill a couple of rabbits. Anyone want to thank the rabbits before I kill them?

EVERYONE   Yeah! Me! I want to thank the rabbits!

Scene 9

On the bus.

STEPHANE   Hello.

MAX   What?

STEPHANE   Hello.

MAX   Hello…

STEPHANE   Are you getting off soon?

MAX   Yeah… I guess.

STEPHANE   Perfect. I was wondering if you'd like to become my friend while you wait.

MAX   Excuse me?

STEPHANE   Because I'd like to develop a short-term friendship. I.e., as long as a bus ride.

MAX   What?

STEPHANE   I would be fantastic. We'd become good friends, fast friends, you know the kind you can count on one hand, but right now and only for right now. It would be incredible. We would talk together, confide in each other, tell each other our deepest secrets. Maybe we'd get pissed of at one another, but we'd be so happy to make up after, we'd forgive each other instantly. We'd stand up for each other. I wouldn't let anyone hurt you because I'd be your friend. And afterwards we'd say goodbye and never see each other again. We would have been the best friends ever.

MAX   Why don't you pick someone else.

STEPHANE   No! No, come on, tell me about yourself. I'll listen, I'm very empathetic. You'll appreciate it during our friendship. Go for it.

MAX   I don't have anything to tell you!

STEPHANE   Then I'll confide in you. I'll betray my most secret secrets to you and only you, since you're my only trustworthy friend.

MAX   I don't want your secrets! You're a pain in the ass! Go look for friends somewhere else and leave me the hell alone! Why do I attract all the freaks?

STEPHANE   Why don't you want to get to know me? Do you refuse to get involved in human relationships?

MAX   No!

STEPHANE   Then what? Am I not worthy of your interest? Do you prefer superficial politeness to real man-to-man contact?

MAX   Quite frankly I don't care. Leave me alone now. I've been dealing with a very demanding agenda and I want to be alone.

STEPHANE   Was it very demanding? Your agenda?

MAX   Yes.

STEPHANE   I'm sorry. How?

MAX   …

STEPHANE   You don't have to talk about it. Friends can also just sit quietly, side by side, and understand each other.

DANIEL   *(He thinks.)* …Lets me take the bus alone but not the subway, because the subway's underground and that's dangerous, but I prefer the subway because it's a surprise, like when you come out of the movies and life seems different. In the subway there are also some notable musicians. There's a man on stilts who plays the flute, and since his pants go all the way to the ground, it makes his legs look impossible, like a stork or a praying mantis. Although I don't know much about praying mantises except that they eat their husbands. I could sit way at the back of the bus and watch the scenery go by. But the big window at the back made me sad last time because it makes you feel you're leaving somewhere for good. You feel like everything is slipping away, sliding through your fingers, while sitting up front looking ahead like the driver, you feel like you're arriving and it's better for your morale.

MAX   That little boy is bright.

STEPHANE   Who?

MAX   The little boy over there, holding his toque…

STEPHANE   Tell me about it.

MAX   He's really smart.

STEPHANE Don't you think it's presumptuous to decide who's smart and who's not?

MAX Maybe.

STEPHANE I'd like to call you on that like a real friend.

MAX Thanks.

STEPHANE Just how do you know that little boy is smart?

MAX I hear people thinking.

STEPHANE You hear voices?

MAX No, I don't hear voices. I hear what's happening inside people's heads.

STEPHANE Whose heads?

MAX People. People going by, when I'm walking. People sitting or standing on the bus.

STEPHANE Do the voices talk to you?

MAX No! I'm saying, they're not voices, they're people's thoughts. People aren't talking to me, they're thinking.

STEPHANE Yeah…

MAX And I… well, I hear their thoughts.

STEPHANE And they makes noise when they think.

MAX Yes. It's unbearable. I talked to a Chinese guy but it was useless. Nobody believes me. Do you believe me?

STEPHANE Sure, I'm your friend.

MAX Thanks.

STEPHANE Do you believe it's like telepathy?

MAX No. I think I'm suffering from compassion.

STEPHANE This is my stop.

MAX Thanks. You've been an incredible friend.

STEPHANE You've meant a lot to me.

MAX Goodbye.

STEPHANE Goodbye.

He leaves.

Scene 10

On the bus.

PAULINE *(thinking)* …either. Unless I arrive just a little bit late so he'll be just a little happier to see me. He'll have had time to worry about me a little, there'll be a little snow dusting his shoulders. He'll see me arriving from afar, because at first I'd be a little far away, blurred, a little fuzzy, and little by little he would recognize the shape of my coat, among the other coat shapes. And I'd keep moving, just a little quickly, showing him my willingness by arriving on time. I'd give him a little wave so that passersby know I'm meeting someone—that if I'm sharing their same sidewalk, it's only to meet someone who's waiting. When we're face to face, we'd be silent, to better look each other deep in the eyes, as if we'd just survived something, as if we'd each risked our lives, and that now, the lives we'd risked had finally brought us together. We'd need to touch each other to believe it, to make sure everything was really whole and as alive as before. Why don't I have a before with him? Why don't I have a before with anyone? I want a past with someone, but the truth is that nobody in the world could see how I move my coat in a special way because nobody ever watched me move the way you watch a person you love move. Even if I have a date with an anthropologist, it will never change my anonymous past. It's too late. Every time I think about it I decide not to go on the first date. That's why I miss all my first dates. The anthropologist will get added to the list of people I'm afraid to run into because I've missed my first date with the anthropologist three times. Soon I'll be afraid to leave the house. Even if I went, I wouldn't be able to talk about myself because nobody's ever listed my idiosyncrasies. I imagine it's the people who love you who notice your idiosyncrasies. That's it. I'll ask him if he noticed I had at least one idiosyncrasy before he asked me on a date.

MAX *(taking the anthropologist's place)* Pauline? I was beginning to think you'd forgotten our date…. Were you lost?

PAULINE Yes.

MAX Everything okay? You look strange…

PAULINE I want to know if you noticed I had any idiosyncrasies. Something that makes me seem unique to you.

MAX Sorry? What's happened? You seem panicked…

PAULINE What did you do in the time I was late? Did you hope I'd come more than anyone in the world during that time? Did you see me arriving from afar while recognizing that way I have of moving my coat? Did you want to shout at people passing by that they weren't the one? That they were blocking the sidewalk where you had your date with me? Did you want to climb something so you could get a better view when I didn't come? And now that I'm in front of you, are you moved to silence?

Would you like to bend my elbows and check my teeth to make sure everything is like it was last time?

MAX What last time, Pauline?

PAULINE I know we don't have a last time. That's what depresses me about first dates. The idea that time still hasn't incurably bound you to me.

MAX You have to let time pass…

PAULINE It'll be too late! I want a past right away! Good memories, right away. I want all your memories to be about me. I don't want to meet you, I want to have known you forever. I want to be the first, and the first forever, and for us to say "Isn't it crazy? After all these years, it still feels like the first time."

MAX People who say that don't mean it.

PAULINE I don't care. I'd be ready to be nostalgic for having lived.

MAX I can't change the past.

PAULINE *(thinking)* Oh well. I won't go on our first date.

PAULINE gets off the bus crying. Maybe everyone thinks: "Poor lady."

Scene 11

PATRICK *(thinking)* Poor lady. Why is she crying? Why didn't I rush over and comfort her? It's like you're not allowed to cry in public. Hey, that's not bad. There would be a woman weeping on the sidewalk, and everyone walks by without stopping. Some people step over her because she's collapsed on the sidewalk. Taking up space. All stretched out. Blocking the way. There's even an old lady who walks over her because it's the only way she can go. The woman cries so much a huge puddle forms around her. It goes on for hours. She cries so much that the police get complaints and a cop is called to the scene. He explains that she's not allowed to cry like that in the street.

COP Ma'am, you're disrupting public order, and if this continues, it'll be disturbing the peace.

LADY But where am I allowed to cry?

COP You're allowed to cry. Just be discreet and don't make too much noise.

PATRICK She replies that she wants to cry out all her sadness and rage because the man she loves dumped her…

LADY …and that the man who caused this desperate noise be arrested. Arrest him. Arrest him so he'll take me back and so the people can calmly walk the sidewalks without having to step over anything.

COP I can't arrest a man because he dumped a woman. It's not grounds for arrest.

LADY Really? Are you sure?

COP   The law is clear.

PATRICK   …And there they are. She starts crying again and the cop squats down next to her. He begins speaking to her so close that he's speaking to the inside of her ear, all gently, he's so far inside her ear that he's almost inside her head. He wants to call her by her first name, the way he learned in first aid. He remembers that you have to speak to survivors using their first names because often, after an accident, their first name is all a survivor has left. So the policeman asks for her first name, deep inside her ear. Do they fall in love after this? No, that's not it.… Damn. My story ideas are never any good.

Scene 12

On the bus. MAX turns to DANIEL.

DANIEL   *(thinking)* …Don't miss your stop. The other day I missed my stop and ended up at the station. And then I waited in the bus until it turned around to go the other way. When it turned around I missed my stop again and ended up in the other station. And so on, from one station to the other until it was dark out. My mother was sick with worry, and when she asked me why I stayed on the bus the whole time, did I fall asleep or what, I said no, I was just preoccupied.

MAX   *(taking the mother's place)* Preoccupied by what?

DANIEL   Things.

MAX   What things?

DANIEL   You wouldn't understand…

MAX   How would I "not understand." Why not just call your mother an idiot! Even if you think you're superior because you have a high IQ, you should know that I made that big brain of yours! You were in *my* belly when you were endowed with a brain! So I'm sure you can tell me what preoccupied you so much you travelled the entire bus route five times!

DANIEL   I was wondering what it's like to be a grandfather without being old. There's an illness that gives boys my age a grandfather's face. See, they have a grandfather's face and they're my age.

MAX   Daniel, I told you not to watch that documentary. I told you.

DANIEL   …Grandfather ears, grandfather knees, neck, missing teeth, grandfather everything, except that look that's seen everything because at my age you haven't seen much.

MAX   Sweetie, you have to stop worrying about other people's misfortunes.

DANIEL   And then I wondered if the hairless, toothless, little eight-year-old grandfather could fall in love with a real eighty-year-old grandmother.

MAX Your stop! You'll miss your stop again!

DANIEL In the documentary, they showed a gathering of these elderly children. A kind of party so they could all see they weren't alone in the world. That's a basic right. It was surreal. Old womens' legs in tiny pink shorts, wigs like Halloween costumes, glasses so big they looked like jokes. Quavering childrens' laughter. Long noses and big ears everywhere. And the parents, like smooth-skinned giants, watching their little monster mingling for the first time with other little monsters from all over the world. It's the first time their child isn't the ugliest so they're enjoying every moment of what looks like some alien carnival.

FATHER That kid's not normal.

DANIEL That kid is your son.

FATHER I know it, that's why I wanted to sign him up for sports! I figured it was normal for a father to sign his son up for a sport.

MAX But he doesn't like sports.

FATHER I signed him up for soccer. I thought: while he's playing, he'll stop thinking about weird things. Nope! Can't be like other kids! His first game, instead of running after the ball and trying to count goals like any normal kid, he just stood in the middle of the field commenting on the game! He held his hand out like there was a mic in it, then he played commentator! The coach nearly went nuts, then everyone looked at me like I should do something. He made his team lose, the yellow team, then the yellow team parents started getting violent. I didn't know what to do. What should I have done?

MAX He doesn't like competition, that's all.

OLD MAN Maybe he needs a more individual sport, like archery.

FATHER Yeah, you think?

MAX Archery?

OLD WOMAN Or classical ballet.

The OLD MAN laughs.

What? What is it? I find classical ballet dancers quite virile. But obviously, whenever I suggest anything…

She starts to cry.

FATHER Mom, don't cry…

MAX Anyone want tea?

FATHER Why is it that whenever you're uncomfortable, you offer people tea?

MAX I offer people tea because your parents are over and I'm polite, go figure!

OLD MAN *(talking to himself)* When I was his age, I loved sports.

OLD WOMAN *(to MAX)* Maybe he doesn't like sports because he watches too much television?

OLD MAN I was skinny, but I had guts!

FATHER If only he watched cartoons…

OLD MAN There were fourteen of us at home and…

OLD WOMAN Oh don't start with your stories!

DANIEL Mom…

MAX Haven't you left yet?

OLD MAN Daniel! Listen up. An old sportsman's trick.

FATHER Daniel, I want to sign you up for a physical activity.

DANIEL I don't want to…

OLD WOMAN What, no kiss for your grandmother?

DANIEL I can't right now… I'm going to miss my stop…

MAX You don't have to sign him up for anything, just play with him.

OLD MAN Take off his boots! He'll play sports! There were fourteen of us at home…

OLD WOMAN You've told that story enough!

OLD MAN …and there were only two pairs of winter boots. We had to walk three miles to school. We shared the boots. But when it wasn't our turn with the boots, how did we keep our feet warm?

DANIEL You walked on the fences.

OLD MAN That kid's a quick one!

OLD WOMAN He always tells the same stories.

FATHER Let him talk, Mom.

DANIEL Hey, I'm going to miss my stop!

OLD WOMAN Come here, give me a kiss before you leave…

MAX Don't force him…

FATHER Let him give my mother a kiss!

MAX Why aren't you ever on my side?

DANIEL Stop! I'm going to miss my stop!

FATHER Well, I'd better be heading back to Ottawa.

MAX Fine, go to Ottawa, join your bimbo!

OLD WOMAN *(to DANIEL)* The Rideau Canal's in Ottawa. You'll be able to skate.

DANIEL Damn! My stop.

He gets off.

MAX Damn! My stop.

He gets off.

Scene 13

LOUIS Estelle! Estelle! Estelle! *(He takes her in his arms.)* Estelle…

MAX I'm not Estelle! I'm not her…

LOUIS Estelle, why don't you ever recognize yourself?

MAX You can see that I'm not Estelle.

LOUIS Please, Estelle…

MAX I'm not her!

LOUIS Humour me.

He makes MAX dance. MAX gives in.

MAX Okay. Okay, my darling.

The people in the street slow dance together.

LOUIS I'm going to take you somewhere lovelier than any television.

CHARACTER 1 That's not Estelle.

CHARACTER 2 No. It's not her.

CHARACTER 3 Totally not her.

MAX Shhh… I want to humour him.

LOUIS We'll travel, gently, without ever moving, just spinning, and we'll become a planet amongst the other planets. We'll spin without ever moving. It will be a respite for us all.

CHARACTER 1 Estelle disappeared for a long time.

CHARACTER 2 Estelle never existed.

CHARACTER 3 Estelle's a character on TV.

CHARACTER 4 She doesn't really exist.

LOUIS You'll never doubt whether you exist again. My arms will enfold you so tightly, and in enfolding you I'll take the shape of your body, and then you'll never be able to doubt you're really here. Now do you know you're really here?

MAX Yes, darling.

CHARACTER 1 He wants to humour her.

LOUIS We'll revolve gently, you around me and me around you, a motion that can't be stopped. Like objects in outer space whose flight never ends, we'll extend towards each other into infinity, only moving to gravitate nearer each other, without ever drifting.

MAX Without ever drifting.

CHARACTER 1 It's not Estelle.

CHARACTER 2 Totally not Estelle.

CHARACTER 3 Yeah, we got it! It wasn't Estelle!

MAX Shhhhh!

Scene 14

MAX runs. He passes people and hears bits of thoughts:

EVERYONE
1. does it seem like a good idea, I asked him, does it make sense
2. six or seven years my God it goes fast
3. *(singing)* such a lovely place such a lovely place such a lovely face
4. peas or green beans, peas, no green beans
5. an angioplas an angioscop an angio
6. late fucking goddamn parking
7. $575 unheated, well you won't find anything cheaper
8. all he had to do was call
9. 812, 814, going up, 820…

Scene 15

He arrives at ARIANE's. He calls through the window.

MAX Ariane! Ariane!

NATHALIE *(opening her window)* Ariane's not here.

MAX Where is she?

NATHALIE Who are you?

MAX Who are *you*?

NATHALIE I'm her neighbour. I'm taking care of her things.

MAX What things?

NATHALIE Her mail, her plants, her cat.

MAX When's she back?

NATHALIE Two weeks. She's off doing a play in Ottawa.

MAX Right. What play is she off doing?

NATHALIE *Phaedra.*

MAX *Phaedra*? Isn't Viviane Lacroix playing Phaedra?

NATHALIE She's replacing Viviane Lacroix.

MAX Really? She must be ecstatic. Was Ariane ecstatic?

NATHALIE I don't know…

MAX So when did she leave?

NATHALIE You just missed her. She left to catch her bus.

MAX How long since she left?

NATHALIE I don't know…. Fifteen minutes?

MAX Thanks.

He leaves. But he hears what NATHALIE is thinking.

NATHALIE Did you want to leave a message? Hey! *(She thinks.)* Why does everyone love Ariane Letendre so much? Why don't I have any men calling my name underneath my window? Why don't I have any men running to catch the bus I took? Why don't I have any talent, so that people would look at *me*?

Scene 16

BRIAN appears. We realize we're watching a television show.

NATHALIE Can you really look me in the eyes and tell me you don't love me anymore, Brian? That that night meant meant nothing to you?

BRIAN Come on, Brenda. Let's not fight.

NATHALIE And you've been drinking! Who were you with this time?

BRIAN A friend from work, I told you.

NATHALIE Sure, a friend from work. Don't insult my intelligence, Brian!

BRIAN Stop being so suspicious, Brenda! There's nothing wrong with having a drink with a friend!

NATHALIE I don't believe you! There's lipstick on your shirt!

BRIAN That's insane! Brenda! What can I do to help you stop not believing me?

NATHALIE What?

BRIAN What can I do to help you stop not believing me?

NATHALIE   What?

BRIAN   What can I do to help you stop not believing me?

NATHALIE   What are you talking about? I don't understand anything you say! Admit you cheated on me again!

BRIAN   I didn't! I swear!

NATHALIE   Look me in the eyes.

BRIAN   I'm looking you in the eyes.

NATHALIE   Okay. I believe you.

MAX laughs.

BRIAN   What are you laughing at, Max? Haven't you left for Ottawa yet? You're just sitting there watching us instead of going to see Ariane?

MAX   What?

BRIAN   Yeah, I'm talking to you. Don't you think you'd be better off going to see Ariane in Ottawa?

MAX   Ariane…. My TV's talking to me! Ariane!

Scene 17

ARIANE's dressing room, in Ottawa.

MAX   Ariane!

ARIANE   Max! What are you doing here?

MAX   I've come to Ottawa because the last time you asked me to, I said no.

ARIANE   But I didn't ask you this time! Why did you come?

MAX   I came to apologize for not coming to Ottawa the last time. I'm deeply sorry.

ARIANE   Look, that was two years ago. You were working, you couldn't come.

MAX   I should have cancelled everything for you.

ARIANE   No. It was just a whim, I got over it.

MAX   You asked me to come to Ottawa with you. You begged me while wringing your hands, you begged me. I think you even got down on your knees.

ARIANE   I never got down on my knees!

MAX   "Max," you said, "come to Ottawa for opening night, please, I'm nervous, please come. If you don't, I won't know who to act for, who to bow to, who to do it all for again the next night. Max, look how I'm shaking. You'll help me learn my lines, and you'll lay your hand on me like a balm. My stomach hurts,

Max, and I'm afraid of the dark, and I'm afraid of spending last call with someone who won't be you. Come to Ottawa, please. I'm afraid I'll cheat on you if you don't come."

ARIANE   That's enough. You have to go now.

MAX   It wasn't a whim, Ariane. You needed me to come with you.

ARIANE   Yeah, well the difference is that now, I don't need you.

MAX   Can I see the show?

ARIANE   Sure, go to the box office. That's what you do if you want to see a show.

MAX   I know, but I want you to ask me to stay and see the show.

ARIANE   No. It's up to you.

MAX   Then I'll stay here.

ARIANE   Where's "here"?

MAX   In your dressing room.

ARIANE   You're not allowed to.

MAX   So what.

ARIANE   You can't stay here, Max.

MAX   I'll just wait for you. I won't touch anything. You didn't tell me you were replacing Viviane Lacroix. Congratulations.

ARIANE   Thanks.

MAX   You must have been ecstatic when they asked you to replace Viviane Lacroix. I know you admire Viviane Lacroix a lot. If we'd still been together when they asked you to replace Viviane Lacroix, you would have thrown your arms around me and shouted: "Max, can you believe it? I'm replacing Viviane Lacroix!" I'm sure you would have thrown your arms around me.

ARIANE   Enough already. You can leave.

MAX   No. I'm going to sit here and wait.

ARIANE   I have to concentrate.

MAX   So concentrate. I want to see what you're like when you concentrate.

STAGE MANAGER   Five minutes. Stand by.

ARIANE   Max! I go on in five minutes.

MAX   I heard. Are you becoming Phaedra now? It's a great part.

ARIANE   You're not allowed in the dressing rooms! I don't even know how you got here!

MAX What I wonder is when you start being Phaedra when you're playing Phaedra. On the bus? In the street? In the dressing room? In the wings? Or do you have to become Viviane Lacroix *first* to play Phaedra?

ARIANE Why did you come here?

MAX I'll never refuse to come to Ottawa again.

ARIANE Are you really going to make me call someone to throw you out!?

MAX I know you won't do it.

ARIANE How?

MAX You don't like scenes.

ARIANE Max, you're an asshole. Just go. I have to go on. We'll have a drink after if you like, but go!

MAX You offered me sexual favours if I'd come to Ottawa. Now here I am in Ottawa and you're not happy. It's funny how things change…

ARIANE What are you talking about, "sexual favours"?

MAX You were on your knees, in front of me, and you started undoing my belt suggestively while asking me to go to Ottawa.

ARIANE That's not true! That's not true! Okay, I'm going on stage. I'll be great. Even if you came here to ruin everything, I'll be great.

She goes.

MAX That's it, go be great for other people. Again! You've always been great for other people…! Don't worry, Ariane!

Scene 18

NATHALIE is at ARIANE's place in Montréal. She reads a letter addressed to ARIANE.

MAX *(to ARIANE, in the dressing room in Ottawa)* You're good. You're a great actress. You'll dazzle them all, the critics will rave, don't worry. I'm there, I'm there with you. I'm in Ottawa. I lay my hands on your belly like a balm. I love you, Ariane!

NATHALIE *(She reads the letter out loud, to herself.)* "You're good. You're a great actress. You'll dazzle them all, the critics will rave, don't worry. I'm there, I'm there with you. I'm in Ottawa. I lay my hands on your belly like a balm. I love you, Ariane…. Max."

Scene 19

MAX *(He looks in the mirror. The reflections speak at the same time.)* I couldn't go see Ariane in Ottawa. *(He hears himself with multiple voices.)* What? What the hell? Agh! What's happening? I don't recognize the voice in my head. It's not my voice talking in my head! I'm disappearing! I can't see my reflection! It's my mirror but it's not my reflection! I can't see my knees when I run! I can't see my knees! I'm disappearing! Ariane!

Scene 20

MAX *(calling up to ARIANE's window)* Ariane!

NATHALIE *(still reading the letter)* "I love you, Ariane…. Max."

MAX Ariane!

NATHALIE You're crazy! Stop yelling like that! The neighbours will call the police!

MAX Hello. The light was on.

NATHALIE Ariane's not here. I told you she'll be back in two weeks.

MAX I know. I wanted to see you. I yelled "Ariane" because I don't know your name.

NATHALIE Ariane's nicer but my name is Nathalie.

MAX Okay. Next time I'll yell "Nathalie." My name's Max.

Long silence.

NATHALIE Oh, it's you.

MAX She talked about me?

NATHALIE Yeah. A little.

MAX Affectionately, I hope.

NATHALIE Very.

MAX I'm disappearing, you know. My sense of importance is gone. My knees are gone too. I can hear everyone.

NATHALIE Did you want to leave a message for Ariane?

MAX …Maybe we could have a drink together?

NATHALIE What?

MAX …Would you like to ask me up for a drink?

NATHALIE It's just that it's not my place… I wouldn't be comfortable entertaining… I mean, they're not my things… tomorrow, maybe… I mean, tomorrow would be a better time…

MAX I understand.

NATHALIE Well… I'm going to head in… I'm not really dressed…

MAX Yeah, that's a pretty nightgown.

NATHALIE Thanks...

MAX I recognize it.

NATHALIE Yes.... So tomorrow, I would love to have a drink tomorrow.

MAX Okay, see you tomorrow. Good night. Don't stay up too late reading...

NATHALIE Good night...

> *MAX walks. He turns his back to NATHALIE while she is unable to go inside. She looks at MAX. MAX hears her think.*

Scene 21

NATHALIE I'm almost Ariane Letendre. I'm wearing her nightgown, I have her stomach ache and I'm reading the love letters you wrote her. I walk in her footsteps, from the kitchen to the bedroom. I walk on tiptoe so my eyes are level with hers, so I see exactly her view, I have her view of things. I have access to all the movies in her mind, and when I look at myself in her mirror it's her reflection I see. I'm almost Ariane Letendre. I'm Ariane because that's the name you called up to the window. I'm Ariane if you want me at all. I'll be Ariane for you while she's in Ottawa, while she's being great for other people, while she leaves us alone and desolate with nothing but memories of her shows, while she's busy being Phaedra, while she plays at confessing her shameful love and pretending she wants to die.

Scene 22

> *ARIANE bows, as though she's just finished playing Phaedra.*
>
> *Everyone applauds. ARIANE joins ANDRE and they kiss passionately.*

Scene 23

> *On the Voyageur bus heading to Ottawa.*

DANIEL *(thinking)* I don't like going to Ottawa. My father will pick me up at the stop and he'll want to do an activity with me. Activities really reassure him. I'm really too small to go to university. But I'm a genius and it's not my fault. They warned me I'd struggle socially and it's true. They'd never seen it before: an eight year old at university, so they saw me as a kind of alien and maybe that's why they couldn't have any compassion for me. I learned that in compassion class. I mean, philosophy. The philosophy prof took an apple, rubbed it until it became red and shiny. He held it up to us for a long time, then he took a big, crunchy bite out of the apple. Then he told us: "You don't suffer with this apple.

You can't recognize yourself in an apple, that's why you can bite into an apple, or see one being bitten into, without feeling compassion for it. Also, you can only have compassion for a human being if you recognize yourself in that human being." I immediately thought of the elderly child documentary. Children you can't see yourself in because you can't see yourself in an old man's skin when you're not old. Later, he ate the apple in front of us and we didn't even flinch. While eating his apple, he added that there are some animals, especially mammals, monkeys especially, that we feel more sympathy for than others. And it's precisely because we imbue them with human features, expressions, reactions and expressions. It's all about anthropomorphism, which we're not really conscious of. And because it's easier to anthropomorphize a dog than a fly, because of its features, we have more trouble killing a dog than crushing a fly. I really enjoyed that compassion class, but I became incapable of eating apples, because when I bit into one, I felt like its blood was running and I could hear it scream. I automatically anthropomorphize. It makes it hard to function normally. For instance, I can't downhill ski without thinking I'm digging into a mountain's wounds, opening its scars. I tiptoe so I won't weigh too heavily on the earth's back. It's hard to deal with. I told my mother, who said that I should play with children my own age.

ANDRE Max?! What happened? You look exhausted. Are you sick?

MAX Yes.

DANIEL *(continues to think)* When I get to Ottawa my father will pick me up and he'll probably want us to go see a movie for children. The fact that I'm a genius makes him anxious because he's afraid it's ruining my normal childhood. The hardest thing for me to hide is my attraction to women in their thirties. And to my father's girlfriend. Jennifer. Jennifer is very beautiful. Sometimes I get into bed with my father and Jennifer. I tell them I had a nightmare but actually it's so I can feel Jennifer's hot body, sleeping in her panties and bra. I fall asleep with my mouth glued to her breast, as if by accident, and I know they watch me, finding it funny, a little boy with his inoffensive little sex drive. But I have a genius's sex drive, and…. Why don't we say "copulate" for human beings? Oh right, because that makes it sound like there are no emotions involved but it seems like there are lots when people make love. What's implied is that animals have no emotions when making love. But what do we know about it? We don't know. Still, that said, I once saw two dogs doing it, one mounting the other, and they looked a little spaced out.

ANDRE Max, I have to tell you…

MAX Shhh, I'm trying to listen.

ANDRE What?

MAX Nothing. Everyone.

ANDRE Are you still hearing inside people's heads?

MAX Yes. More and more. From further and further away. Like a gangrene growing over me. I'm disappearing.

ANDRE ...

MAX I hear from so far I can even tell you what's happening in people's unconscious. But it's hard to understand, it's chaotic like a dream, it's as if the thought wasn't yet formed. It's the stage that precedes structured thought. It's a jumble of abstractions that will only reach the consciousnesses of certain very attentive individuals, that most people will never access. Maybe I'll go insane, like people prevented from sleeping and so from dreaming do, who become depressed because they can't empty themselves anymore. I don't dream for myself, anymore. I don't think for myself I'm empty of my essence to better become others I am others I am every other person I am the receiver of their recurring themes their obsessions I always have a headache, back ache, stomach ache, foot ache, I sweat, I give birth I'm born I come and I die with other people, inside them and in their skins, and mostly I'm very tired. Because what we don't know is that we drag around the tiredness of every generation that came before. Sure, your day makes you tired, your week, every second of your life, but actually you've been tired since birth, tired of having clear-cut the virgin forests, the jungles, the Gaspésie Park, of having sent thousands of children out into the world, of having killed thousands more, of scheming, of farming, of slogging, constructing, writing, inventing, tired of the lives of emperors and slaves, of mothers and hunters, we carry the tiredness of the Berbers and the Chinese, the Greeks and the First Nations, we're tired of the words of every individual who came this way, full of echoes themselves, echoes overlying everything ever said since Man first grunted and spoke, we're exhausted of being conscious that we'll die, conscious for millenia of heading toward death, not just our own, but that of humanity, so it shouldn't surprise us that we're tired, and still, I hear people say, why am I so tired? Andre, do you sometimes wonder why you're so tired? I'll tell you: we're tired of having so much memory. Ariane thinks it takes imagination to be an actress. Maybe it just takes memory. I'm not talking about the memory that memorizes lines, but the memory that makes us tired for every human being, dead and alive. Now that I'm finally tired for other people, have become other people, am I an actor? Am I a great actor? I could probably be an amazing, imposing, transcendant actor. If I wanted, I could be a truly great actor, speaking for every human being like they'd never been spoken for, portraying them with every echo they deserve. You'd wonder, what's so exceptional about this actor? What is it that moves me so much and that makes me like being moved by him so much? But I can't be an actor because I don't have any vanity left. I almost miss it. I held onto my vanity, my personality, my identity. I loved existing for myself and by myself. I loved finding myself important. But I didn't measure up. Nobody, nobody measures up to thousands of human beings. I loved loving Ariane, but specific love became impossible because the whole world took up that space, no ranking, no ordering of affection, just the world that I hear and whose every word seems to speak to me.

He looks at ANDRE.

ANDRE   *(thinks)* Jesus does he think he's God?

What comes next should be accompanied, punctuated, heightened, rhythmically emphasized, I'm not sure, by something that represents the sound of human beings. I mean, the sound that would result from combining every sound made by human beings, in every language and the absence of languages…

MAX   I have to talk. If I'm talking, I exist, whereas if I'm quiet, it's like a conglomoration of strange words stuck in my head and then there's not any room left for my thoughts. I'm going to start expressing indecipherable sounds, like spasms, like convulsions, because eternity is impossible to state. What will I become? Words don't belong to me anymore. Help, Andre. I thought I'd conquer the world, but the world overwhelms me, smothers me, strangles me, swallows me. I hear buzzing bells, sirens, every book to come, and deafening secrets, and suddenly I hear so far I can't hear a thing, anything I can identify because it all overlaps. All of it. It's all stacked up: sweet things, the shiver of a first kiss, the relief of good news, reunions, forgiveness, a load lifted, a drowned man who breathes again, water running down a dry throat, somebody late who finally arrives, a finger that tastes like jam, and it'll be nice out tomorrow, a hug for the beggar nobody will touch, a promise, a kind look, drugs running through veins, everything. But also the sick screaming out, your cries as ceaseless as the tides, piling up until I'm deaf, and still I hear you, I hear you, but I can't understand what I hear anymore. I thought I was powerful but I can't do anything, anything but listen, and out of thousands of years of your accumulated babbling, only one note is left. It's both low and sharp, a moan or a rapture, who knows, a grinning ear, a rictus of sound, and I don't know what it means. I don't know what it means.

The end.

Chinese Portrait of an Imposter
(Portrait chinois d'une imposteure)

by Dominick Parenteau-Lebeuf

translated by Crystal Beliveau

If I cannot influence the gods, I shall move all hell.
Virgil, *The Aeneid*

Introduction to
Chinese Portrait of an Imposter
(Portrait chinois d'une imposteure)

Dominick Parenteau-Lebeuf began the process of writing *Portrait chinois d'une imposteure* when she was writer-in-residence at Théâtre français de Toronto in September 2001. Commissioned before the events of September 11, she had agreed to write a play around themes associated with *Don Quixote*. The events of that month led her to raise serious questions about what could be said and dramatized right away in an environment that had so transformed personal, social, and cultural life everywhere. Parenteau-Lebeuf's play makes no mention of either Don Quixote or September 11. Yet, in its dramatization of a decisively turning moment in the life of a vibrantly creative artist who must rid herself of delusions and fears and take control of her own ideas, values, visions, and practice, there are echoes of Cervantes, along with a unique and compelling comment on the events of September 11, 2001 and the discourse surrounding them. This discourse has proven determining in setting the course of twenty-first-century life and shown how hegemonic ideas can play with your mind, as they do for Candice de LaFontaine-Rotonde, producing silly behaviour and paralyzing you with the demons of doubt, anxiety, and the search for absolute certainty.

Playwright Dominick Parenteau-Lebeuf has created in *Chinese Portrait of an Imposter* a double, Candice de LaFontaine-Rotonde, a young playwright like Parenteau-Lebeuf and fictitious author of a second-level version of the same play, *Chinese Portrait of an Imposter*. The play published here, *Chinese Portrait of an Imposter*, is playfully constructed around this fictitious show, De LaFontaine-Rotonde's *Chinese Portrait of an Imposter*, within a television talk show, *Chinese Portrait of an Artist*. Adding to the playfulness and contributing to the ambiguity and confusion among appearance, fiction, and reality, there is even, within the embedded *Chinese Portrait of an Imposter*, a surprise visitor (played by the actor also playing Candice) who gives her name as Dominick Parenteau-Lebeuf. This multi-layered, spatially fragmented, kaleidoscopic, and elusive spectacle is a richly original, fanciful, and forceful exploration for the twenty-first century of identity, theatricality, dramaturgy, popular culture, performance, and discourse underlying practices of representation. The culturally bulwarked systems upon which they are constructed produce a disconcerting psychic and socio-cultural context for women artists, who frequently find themselves unable to escape the categorization in today's society as *imposters*. The theme of imposture is enhanced from the beginning by the attention drawn to the use of makeup and the use of Arcimboldo-style masks for Candice. The play's title suggests that whoever female artists choose to be, whatever they decide to do, wherever the flights of their imagination take them, they are at risk of being seen as imposters in disguise, rather than major players on public stages.

The Chinese portrait game of the title is a personality test bringing to light usually unacknowledged or unrecognized blind spots in individuals' ways of seeing the world. In the game, the spontaneous answers given by individuals to questions, such as "If you were…" a person, an animal, an object, a place, a quality, a feeling, etc., reveal arbitrary although interesting and telling associations, hidden fantasies, and deep desires. The structural and thematic place of this game throughout *Chinese Portrait of an Imposter* allows Parenteau-Lebeuf to imaginatively project fantasies onto a whole cast of characters and to live several different lives at the same time through them. She thus enjoys, as she said during an undated interview with director Paule Baillargeon, one of Québec's most honoured actors and filmmakers, at the time of the first production of the play the opportunity to recognize some of her own, "previously unnamed inner demons: perfection, anguish, and doubt."[1] By creating Candice de LaFontaine-Rotonde as an alter ego for herself, Parenteau-Lebeuf uses in delightful ways theatre's rich potential to produce understanding on many psychic and emotional levels of what it means to be a creative artist. She says that De LaFontaine-Rotonde "is a playwright and the forces she has to combat are her inner demons. And where can you carry out symbolic combats? In theatre and television."[2] This personal reflection by Parenteau-Lebeuf offers more broadly a significant perspective on the place of women artists today, the relevance of their way of seeing themselves and the world, and the use they are in a position to make in their creative processes of personal, social, and dramaturgical values and traditions.

Chinese Portrait of an Imposter is a play with a prologue, eight scenes, and an epilogue, having seven characters on stage and the insistent voices of five additional characters. During her initial session with the makeup artist in preparation for her first television appearance, Candice hears off-camera the strident voice of Inès Lusine, talk-show host of *Chinese Portrait of an Artist* (the echoes between the two titles of *artist* and *imposter* are telling). Candice mistakes the host's voice for that of her dead mother, who, like Lusine, represents throughout the play the voice of arbitrary authority and the source of major constraints in the creative process. The mother's voice, the *Vox maternalis*, promotes traditional standards for recognizing a literary masterpiece. This voice has been determining since the time of Candice's earliest memories what she should write and how she should write: "form, function, metaphors, rhythm, structure, style, syntax, originality, accessibility, subtlety, humour, emotion, simplicity, avoiding self-indulgence." This is a terrible burden for the young contemporary writer simply in search of her own voice and seeking to explore her "relationship with words" (Scene 3). In fact, the message is close to paralyzing. The affected, opinionated, and domineering Lusine, grotesque parody and caricature of renowned French talk-show host Bernard Pivot, represents prevailing contemporary criteria for artistic excellence, none of which are encouraging for Candice. Candice is alienated by these voices of authority; she has heard them with great regularity throughout her life, and she has internalized them. They have served to make her doubt the beauty of her own imaginative visions and to censor her own authentic voice, even to make her unsure of who she is, causing her to cry and to feel useless (Scene 1). The *seizures* during the play are flashbacks that render vivid once again for Candice such decisive moments with her mother, as well as the voice of received knowledge and the mass media heard through Lusine's megaphone and even through the voices of the characters Candice herself has created. The seizures reproduce "states of anxiety, neurotic memories, lucid escapes that transform the world into a raw and abrasive place" (Playwright's Notes).

Candice resists these authoritarian voices that threaten to censor once again what she has to say with words, and she causes the action of the play to flip over onto the stage of her own play *Chinese Portrait of an Imposter*, where the audience meets the three characters she has invented, the three sisters who founded and currently operate the Window to the Soul Publishing Company. The irony of the publishing company's name is striking since, ironically recalling the commonplace notion of the eyes being the window to the soul, these women have lost the ability to see beauty, spirituality, or ideas. Their model for "literary brilliance" suggests strongly that their soul is close to having dried up. Under the dogmatic direction of perfectionist Doris, they insist they must be, in their evaluation of manuscripts submitted for publication, "Dogged," "Determined," "Decisive," "Ruthless," "Relentless," and "Heartless":

> [...] our humble enterprise has devoted itself to nothing less than the development of contemporary literary brilliance [...] We need masterpieces of the here and now. And it's not by glorifying the past that we're going to succeed in our endeavour. No, what we need is "objectivity and rigour."

As an *off-sync postmodern choir*, these characters are tyrants imposing their theories, clinging to their dogma despite the fact that they have no works of art left to either cherish or burn (Scene 2). It seems that the young playwright created these three sisters and their publishing company under the influence of prevailing values in the critical establishment and its experts whom, in her self-delusion, she wanted to impress by the excellence of her own writing. The three sisters are the demons of perfection, anguish, and doubt that taunt both Candice and Parenteau-Lebeuf in their creative endeavours. Parenteau-Lebeuf has represented them dramatically as mindless, egotistical clown figures, gaily ridiculing and trashing all that comes before them, even tossing off dismissive judgments regarding variations on Parenteau-Lebeuf's other real plays.

Yet, perfection remains out of reach, for, in fact, their enterprise is soul-stifling. Candice's work is seen to not meet the standard, even when the publishers do not go to the trouble of reading the manuscript. They simply reject it out of hand. Doubt and anxiety persist for the playwright, as represented by the two sisters who are less assured than Doris regarding their absolute criteria and decisions. Paradoxically, the contemporary standards required to meet the criteria for artistic excellence adopted by the Window to the Soul Publishing are so demanding that they have condemned all of the world's great literature and theatre to burn to ashes in their crematorium. They have been so diligent in this that there are no jars left for the ashes of another literary work with pretensions of literary brilliance.

The four sisters whose voices clamour to be heard by Candice from beneath the floor represent the richness of thought and beauty of poetry found in the works of the past burned by Doris and her two sisters. Two of the publishing-company sisters, as well as Candice, particularly regret the rejection of Chekhov's *Three Sisters*. The four sisters, banished because they did not fit the insensitive and autocratic views of Doris and her acolytes, are muses drawn from Greek mythology: Urania, Calliope, Thalia, and Polyhymnia. They represent the forces that have always surged energetically through the imagination of creative artists: poetry, music, eloquence, writing, knowledge, meditation, comedy, memory, and vision. In the end, the demands of the *Vox maternalis* for masterpieces, of Doris for perfection and rationality, and of Lusine for populist appeal and conformity to the opinion of contemporary experts are burned to ash through the intervention of the surprise visitor, that is, the character named Dominick Parenteau-Lebeuf. Along with the disappearance of these demands dramatized in the fabulous cast of characters, the demons that haunted the playwright in the form of paralyzing, self-censoring voices have gone up in smoke. As the surprise visitor is on the point of leaving behind this scene of anguish and turmoil in order to set out on her own unhindered creative path, she is heard to say: "I am taking control of this house. It's not a proposition, it's a declaration. Tell the others what you've seen." Candice, who no longer needs to ask "How do you put makeup on a writer?" (Prologue), has removed her mask. "She touches her face" (Epilogue). The four banished sisters representing beauty, poetry, joy, voice, and freedom are ready to take their place on the main stage out of their banishment: "You can hear the sound of footsteps coming up from the basement and women talking and laughing" (Scene 8).

Chinese Portrait of an Imposter by Dominick Parenteau-Lebeuf is a joyous and compelling theatrical exorcism of many of the demons that beset women working and creating in today's theatre. Like any ceremonial celebrant, she has summoned into full visibility and presence the negative forces that have invaded the playwright's mind, soul, and spirit, causing her to lose touch with herself, to feel intense doubt and anguish, and to set aside both her own vital inspiration and the very works of beauty that could serve to inspire her and legitimize her work. Collaborating with her alter ego, she has resisted these forces and shown the dangerous and abusive power of their sterility. The surprise visitor declares that she is taking control of this house. There are many myths and models that theatre written and performed by women must still invent, construct, represent, and celebrate. The vital energy and contagious joy of *Chinese Portrait of an Imposter* hold great promise for new forms, new stories, and new characters coming up from the basement where they have been silenced, no longer feeling themselves to be imposters when they position themselves as subjects and agents, in all their creative legitimacy.

Notes

[1] "*Portrait chinois d'une imposteure* m'a donné l'occasion d'identifier des démons que je n'avais jamais nommés avant: perfection, angoissse, doute." (Email containing unpublished interview sent by Dominick Parenteau-Lebeuf, September 18, 2006 to LHF. Translated by LHF.)

[2] "C'est une auteure dramatique et les forces à combattre sont ses démons intérieurs. Et où peut-on mener des combats symboliques? Au théâtre et à la télévision" (Program, Théâtre français de Toronto, February 2004. Translated by LHF).

About Dominick Parenteau-Lebeuf

Playwright, screenwriter, fiction writer, and translator, Dominick Parenteau-Lebeuf is the author of more than twenty plays for adult and young audiences. Her work has been performed in Québec, France, Belgium, the United States, Germany, Austria, and Italy, and has been translated into English, German, and Italian. Her plays and scripts have also been broadcast on radio and television. She has taught and given workshops in various international locations and has frequently been invited to speak about Québec playwriting.

Parenteau-Lebeuf was born in Saint-Jean-sur-Richelieu in Québec and has lived in Australia and France. She holds a diploma in playwriting from l'École nationale de théâtre. She founded and is currently artistic director of Baraka Theatre. Parenteau-Lebeuf has won a number of prizes for her writing including the Prix Cartes blanches for *Poème pour une nuit d'anniversaire* (Paris, 1995), the Prime à la creation du Fonds Gratien-Gélinas for *Dévoilement devant notaire* (Québec, 1998), and first prize in the short-story competition in the journal *Voir* for *Vive la Canadienne!* (Québec, 1998). She has been playwright-in-residence at the Théâtre français de Toronto, at CEAD's translation workshop in Orford, Québec, at the Royal Court Theatre International Summer Residency, at the Festival International des Théâtres Francophones in Limoges, France, and at the Carrousel in Montréal, a company specializing in theatre for young audiences.

Published Works by Dominick Parenteau-Lebeuf

Hamlette, conte à une voix de fille soûle comme une Polonaise in 38 (1996). Montréal: Dramaturges Éditeurs. 15–30.

Poème pour une nuit d'anniversaire (1997). Carnières, Belgium: Éditions Lansman.

L'autoroute (1999). Carnières, Belgium: Éditions Lansman.

Dévoilement devant notaire (2002). Carnières, Belgium: Éditions Lansman.

Portrait chinois d'une imposteure (2003). Carnières, Belgium: Éditions Lansman.

Filles de guerres lasses (2005). Carnières, Belgium: Éditions Lansman.

La Petite Scrap (2005). Carnières, Belgium: Éditions Lansman.

Portrait chinois d'une imposteure was written in residence at the Théâtre français de Toronto and had a dramatic reading at the Centre des auteurs dramatiques in Montréal on December 5, 2003. Its first stage performance was on February 4, 2004 by the Théâtre français de Toronto at the Berkeley Street Theatre, with the following company:

Milli	Mélanie Beauchamp
Doris	Lina Blais
Nil	Stéphanie Broschart
Inès Lusine	Geneviève Langlois
Vox Maternalis and Makeup Artist	Olivier l'Écuyer
Candice de LaFontaine-Rotonde/ Surprise Visitor	Patricia Marceau

Directed by Paule Baillargeon
Stage managed by Emmanuelle Langelier
Set design and lighting by Glen-Charles Landry
Costumes by Sarah Balleux
Original music by Yves Laferrière
Production management by Sean Baker

This production was subsequently taken to the National Arts Centre in Ottawa and the Théâtre du Nouvel-Ontario in Sudbury.

Playwright's Notes

1. A Chinese portrait is a series of questions beginning with "If you were" followed by answers beginning with "I would be." A simplified version of the Proust questionnaire.
2. The mask that Candice/Surprise Visitor wears in the play is inspired by the summer and fall characters in Giuseppe Arcimboldo's paintings *The Seasons*.
3. The seizures are states of anxiety, neurotic memories, lucid escapes that transform the world into a raw and abrasive place.
4. The excerpt of *Three Sisters* that Nil reads at the end of Act 2 (Welcome to Window to the Soul Publishing) is from Vershinin's tirade in Act 3.
5. The Pear of Anguish used by The Surprise Visitor in Scene 8 (Torture) is an instrument of torture, an iron gag device shaped like a pear that is forced into the mouth and expanded to the maximum aperture; it can be replaced by a fist shoved in the mouth.
6. The Vox maternalis can be played by the makeup artist or by a different actor or actress entirely.

Characters

Makeup Artist, an older man
Candice de LaFontaine-Rotonde (Surprise Visitor), a playwright in her early thirties
Inès Lusine, host of *Chinese Portrait of an Artist*, forty years old
Doris, eldest sister of Milli and Nil, ageless; the perfectionist
Milli, middle sister, ageless; the angst-ridden one
Nil, youngest sister, ageless; the doubter

Voices

Vox Maternalis, the voice of Claudette, Candice's mother

The Four Sisters, the voices of Urania, Calliope, Thalia, and Polyhymnia, the four sisters trapped under the floor; they can be represented by puppets, shadows, or some other device.

Setting

The dressing room is simply a chair. The public is the mirror.

The set of the TV show is furnished with an armchair for the host, a couch for the guest and a small table.

The office of Window to the Soul Publishing is a closed room (the playwright's head) with two windows (her eyes). Inside there are three chairs, the crematorium, and the giant jar.

Under the floor—a space that is evoked, suggested—is where Urania, Calliope, Thalia and Polyhymnia are held captive.

CHINESE PORTRAIT OF AN IMPOSTER

Prologue

Darkness. Knocking at the door.

MAKEUP ARTIST Yes?

Fade in on the dressing room. We see a chair, a door, and two hands. The rest of the MAKEUP ARTIST is in the shadows. The door opens.

CANDICE *(concealed behind the door)* Is this *Chinese Portrait of an Artist*?

MAKEUP ARTIST You must be Candice de LaFontaine-Rotonde.

CANDICE *(still hidden behind the door)* Um…. Yes, you could say that…

MAKEUP ARTIST Come in, come in, whoever you are. I'd almost given up on you.

CANDICE enters with a bag slung over her shoulder and an Arcimboldo-style mask on her face.

CANDICE I'm uh… sorry I'm late… I… I didn't know what to wear.

MAKEUP ARTIST I can see that. Have a seat.

CANDICE sits down.

CANDICE I've never been on TV before.

MAKEUP ARTIST And something tells me that makes you a little anxious. *(CANDICE nods.)* They told me your name, but not what you do. Or who you are.

CANDICE I'm—

MAKEUP ARTIST No. Wait. Don't tell me. You're… a writer. *(CANDICE nods.)* And what is it you write, Ms. Garden Party? Theatre, no doubt. *(CANDICE nods again.)* And what, may I ask, is the name of your play?

CANDICE *Chinese Portrait of an*—

MAKEUP ARTIST No! *Chinese Portrait of an Artist*? You didn't.

CANDICE Didn't what? My play is called *Chinese Portrait of an Impostor*.

Beat.

MAKEUP ARTIST Ah, imposture. My specialty. Yours too, it appears. *(beat)* But I'm afraid you'll have to remove your mask. I can't put your makeup on overtop. I'm all for layered meanings, but even so… *(He tries to remove her mask, in vain.)* Why did you come here?

CANDICE   What do you mean? Inès Lusine invited me. What? You don't think I'm interesting enough for people to want to watch me?

MAKEUP ARTIST   Relax. You're on an arts program. No one's watching you. *(beat)* May I ask what's putting you in such a state?

CANDICE   It's just that… I've never spoken… publicly as a… I've never written…. Well, it's not that… I've written, but you know how it is… my path has been really… well, there's this play…

MAKEUP ARTIST   *Chinese Portrait of an Impostor.*

CANDICE   Yes. And now there's a production. It's a bit of a risk, for sure. It comes with the territory, I guess. And the subject's a little…. It starts tonight… I'm not well known, you know… so I agreed to come here to talk about it to… what was your question again?

MAKEUP ARTIST   Just act like you've done this your whole life and don't give it another thought.

CANDICE   But what if I stutter, or I get all confused and start spouting nonsense?

MAKEUP ARTIST   You wouldn't be the first. But if it bothers you, pretend you're high on narcotics. I could even give you the pallor of an addict, if you so desire.

CANDICE   I don't know if…

MAKEUP ARTIST   Stop imagining that you're—

CANDICE   That I'm something I'm not.

MAKEUP ARTIST   That you're going to make such a mess of things. Inès has been hosting this show for five years. She's seen it all.

CANDICE   All what?

INÈS   *(offstage)* Five minutes!

CANDICE   My God…. Mom…. That's her voice…

MAKEUP ARTIST   Relax, it's only Inès. *(beat)* Unless you invited her.

CANDICE   Who? My mother? *(beat)* No. She died last year.

Silence. The MAKEUP ARTIST puts his hands on CANDICE's shoulders.

MAKEUP ARTIST   A word to the wise.

CANDICE   What?

MAKEUP ARTIST   Be yourself when all else fails.

CANDICE   *(after a beat)* How do you put makeup on a writer?

MAKEUP ARTIST   That depends. On whom is it being applied?

CANDICE removes her mask. Everything around her is plunged into darkness, except for her face and the hands of the MAKEUP ARTIST, who is busy at work. His hands disappear and for a moment all we see is the face of the playwright. Then, darkness.

Scene 1
TV Show

Set of Chinese Portrait of an Artist*: the host's chair, the guest's couch and the small table in between, on which we see the manuscript of* Chinese Portrait of an Impostor. *INÈS Lusine emerges from the darkness when the show's theme music begins.*

INÈS   Dear viewers, good afternoon. I'm Inès Lusine and you're watching *Chinese Portrait of an Artist*, your favourite arts show, where, for the past five years, I've performed cool-headed vivisections on hot-blooded artists. And yes, it's already the last show of the season. My fifth season! How time flies! The other day someone asked me: "What's five seasons, Inès?" and I said, "Nothing, nothing at all." Some say it takes its toll, but I say it's a fountain of youth! Especially when you know you're watched and appreciated by distinguished viewers like you, ladies and gentlemen. Not to mention all the love I feel from the artists who stop in. No, for me, the first show feels like it was yesterday. *(staring into the camera)* There. I've said my piece. Now. At the end of last week's show, I promised all kinds of surprises for our fifth anniversary, and a rare interview, an intimate Chinese portrait of the great actor Wilfred Fitzgerald. Unfortunately, my dear friend Wilfred had to fly off to New York to be on *Inside the Actor's Playhouse* with John Campbell. These things happen. So it was with a heavy heart that I started scouring the arts scene in search of an artist, someone who would capture my interest. And yesterday, at the end of my rope, I found her, a young lady by the name of Candice de LaFontaine-Rotonde—yes, that's her real name!—an obscure young playwright, who, so I'm told, is on the rise and whose most recent play, *Chinese Portrait of an Impostor*, will premiere tonight at the very trendy Velvet Vervet Cafe. So it is with great curiosity that I welcome her today. *(lights)* Good afternoon, Mademoiselle de LaFontaine-Rotonde.

CANDICE   Good afternoon, Ms. Lusine.

INÈS   *(counting on her fingers)* Ma-de-moi-selle-de-la-Fon-taine-Ro-tonde. An iambic pentameter! Very apropos for a writer, but in-an-ef-fort-to-save-a-bit-of-time—iambic pentameter—may I call you Ms. Rotonde?

CANDICE   Only if I can call you Ms. Zine.

INÈS   Well! I see someone is sensitive about her name.

CANDICE   My name isn't Candice Tracted.

INÈS   Can... distracted.

CANDICE   My dad called me that.

INÈS How cute. Can we agree on Candice? *(CANDICE nods.)* Great. Now, if we know so little about my guest, it's because she's not... very well known. What we do know is that she studied at the National Theatre Academy and has a few plays to her name. Two of them, the wonderfully titled *Warsick Girls* and *Miss Bernice and the Bombs*, were produced in underground theatres and seen by a handful of aficionados. At the time, critics called her writing "sumptuous and singular," "acerbic and spiritual." Then she went under the radar. Five years later, she's back with a new play. She's nothing if not mysterious, but fear not, dear viewers, by the time I'm through with her, we'll know what really makes her tick. Now, if I took an interest in this *re*-rising young playwright, it is, of course, because of her latest play, the title of which—*Chinese Portrait of an Impostor*—strikes a very, and I do mean very, familiar chord. First off, Candice, admit it: my show was an inspiration to you.

CANDICE Uh... no, actually.

INÈS No? *(momentarily baffled)* Well. I would have sworn.

CANDICE I'm not sure how to put this: I've never seen your show.

INÈS After five years on the air? You're pulling my leg! The entire artistic milieu has been interviewed by Inès Lusine.

CANDICE I know, but I don't have a TV.

INÈS No TV? No eighth art in your life? In our day and age, that's like admitting you're illiterate. Where on earth did you come from, Candice?

CANDICE Where did I come from? I... I'm not sure I understand what you mean.

INÈS I mean exactly what I said: where did you come from? Through which door did you enter into the cultural landscape?

CANDICE You want to know where I came from or how I got in?

INÈS Whichever. Just answer the question.

CANDICE Well, I got in through the door of the academy... then I came out... and now I got in through... through this play, that is, I've just come out from writing this play—

INÈS Okay, yes, fine. And why *Chinese Portrait of an Impostor* now?

CANDICE Some plays are a question of life and death.

INÈS Oh, no. Not that. Not you, Candice. You're too young! Please. Spare me the clichés. Surprise me!

CANDICE They aren't clichés, Inès.

INÈS Of course they are! Come now! If it's not because of my show, then why the title? Why the play? Why the impostor? Why?

CANDICE   *(after a beat)* May I sit down to answer your questions?

INÈS   *(laughing)* Oh my! I forgot to ask you to sit down. Dear viewers, you just witnessed a first in five years. *(touching her forehead)* Ah! The fever of the finale. We'll get back to your play later, Candice. Please, have a seat.

   They take their respective places.

   I presume you understand the principle of a Chinese portrait, so without further ado, let's begin. "Chinese Portrait of Candice de LaFontaine-Rotonde." *(jingle)* The first category, an opening salvo to warm you up, is called "the five senses of childhood." Candice, if you were an image from your childhood?

CANDICE   I would be a little girl watching her father disappear in the storm to get some wood.

INÈS   If you were a taste?

CANDICE   Ocean water.

INÈS   If you were a smell?

CANDICE   Cold ashes.

INÈS   If you were a touch?

CANDICE   The softness of the sheets on my bed.

INÈS   If you were a sound?

CANDICE   My mother's voice.

INÈS   Your mother's voice. And her name is?

CANDICE   Claudette.

INÈS   Claudette who is no doubt watching as we speak. Hello, Claudette! Let's move on to the second category. The writer's craft. Your craft, Candice. If you were an object?

   Seizure. Spotlight on CANDICE, as a child, who is writing her name.

VOX MATERNALIS   *(spelling)* C-a-n-d-i-c-e-d-e-l-a-f-o-n-t-a-i-n-e-r-o-t-o-n-d-e. Candice de LaFontaine-Rotonde, the object of my love.

CANDICE   The object of your love, Claudette? What does that mean?

VOX MATERNALIS   I told you not to call me Claudette. I'm not a camp counsellor, I'm your mother. Your mommy. And how do you spell "mommy"?

CANDICE   *(spelling)* M-o-m-m-y.

VOX MATERNALIS   Already literate at the age of five! You'll be a great writer one day, I can feel it. Now, the object of my love means that you are the one on whom I bestow all my motherly love.

CANDICE   All your motherly love.

VOX MATERNALIS Exactly. Are you finished?

CANDICE (*still writing*) Almost. It's long.

VOX MATERNALIS You don't say long, you say…?

CANDICE Majestuous.

VOX MATERNALIS Exactly. With majesty, you draw your father and I behind you.

CANDICE (*presenting the sheet on which she has written her name*) I'm all done, Mommy. It's for you. I give you my name: Candice de LaFontaine-Rotonde, the object of your love.

> *The seizure continues. INÈS appears, speaking in a megaphone. CANDICE is lying on the couch as though in a therapy session.*

INÈS So, Candice, have you come up with an object? No need to rack your brains!

CANDICE I'd be a sponge.

INÈS All this time to come up with a primitive, porous animal. Won't this be riveting! Let's move on, shall we? If you were somebody?

CANDICE That's one of the questions on the writer's craft?

INÈS Of course, you've got to be somebody to write. When I was a writer, I was somebody!

CANDICE When you were a writer?

INÈS I was somebody!

CANDICE When you were a writer?

INÈS I was somebody!

CANDICE When you were a writer?

INÈS I was… enough! Answer the question! If you were somebody?

CANDICE Do you mean somebody accomplished or somebody unknown?

INÈS Accomplished *and* unknown: that's you in a nutshell, isn't it?

CANDICE No. I'm just Candice de LaFontaine-Rotonde.

INÈS Fine, but who is Candice de LaFontaine-Rotonde?

CANDICE I don't know…

INÈS Well, that doesn't get us anywhere, does it? Tell me your name again at least.

CANDICE Candice de LaFontaine-Rotonde.

INÈS Again.

CANDICE Candice de LaFontaine-Rotonde.

INÈS   One more time.

CANDICE   *(with more difficulty)* Candice... de... LaFontaine...

   CANDICE breaks down and starts crying.

INÈS   I'm waiting.

CANDICE   It's useless.

INÈS   So your answer to the question, "If you were somebody?" would be "I'm useless," is that it?

   End of the seizure. Both resume their positions prior to the seizure.

   So, if you were an object?

CANDICE   By "object" do you mean a writing instrument like a pen?

INÈS   Exactly, Candice. What did you think I meant?

CANDICE   *(after a short beat)* I would be my fingertips.

INÈS   Your fingertips? As in *(imitating fingers on a keyboard)*? *(CANDICE nods.)* Wow, objects sure aren't what they used to be. Now tell me: if you were a play?

CANDICE   I'd be *Chinese Portrait of an Impostor*.

INÈS   Really? And not—I don't know—*The Learned Ladies*, *The Taming of the Shrew*, *Les Belles-soeurs*, *Three Sisters*?

CANDICE   *Three Sisters*?

INÈS   I'm just saying, you have all the choice in the world.

CANDICE   I wouldn't be someone else's play.

INÈS   Fine, but *Three Sisters* isn't such a bad play to be. Do you like Chekhov?

CANDICE   I think he's a master.

INÈS   Finally, a little outside influence. And if you were a character, Candice?

CANDICE   I would be...

   Fade-out on the set of the TV show while the four sisters under the floor cry out: "Me, Candice! Me! Me, Candice! Me!" Then we hear DORIS stomp three times, which silences the four sisters and corresponds with the three knocks of the staff that signal the beginning of the play. Then, silence and darkness.

Scene 2
Welcome to Window to the Soul Publishing

   DORIS, MILLI, and NIL—an off-sync postmodern choir—appear. They are in a transitional space on their way to work.

DORIS Good day. I'm Doris. And this is—

MILLI Milli. Enchantée. Good day.

NIL I'm Nil. N-I-L. Good day.

DORIS, MILLI, & NIL Welcome to Window to the Soul Publishing.

DORIS I'm the editor.

MILLI And we are her editing attachés. Nil and I. Milli.

NIL Window to the Soul Publishing…

MILLI Nil came up with that dramatic name.

NIL Because of what they say about the eyes…

DORIS, MILLI, & NIL "Eyes are the window to the soul."

DORIS Milli, Nil, and I read the work in the window's reflection.

NIL And everyone knows that when you read in a reflection…

MILLI You read backwards…

NIL But in the publishing industry, it's… a priority.

DORIS Don't forget that a writer doesn't like to be pinned down.

NIL A writer never says what she really thinks.

MILLI A writer vacillates.

DORIS Always. So, by reading in the reflection…

NIL We have a better chance of finding the hidden truth…

MILLI The full mystery…

DORIS Or the emptiness…

MILLI Behind the words.

DORIS The true quality of the writing!

NIL In that way, our judgment of the work…

DORIS Is always right. Always.

MILLI It may seem twisted, but with writers, Doris says that…

DORIS That's just how it is.

NIL We have to be…

DORIS Dogged.

MILLI Determined.

DORIS Decisive.

MILLI Ruthless.

DORIS   Relentless.

MILLI   Heartless.

DORIS   Exactly.

NIL   Window to the Soul Publishing…

DORIS   With me, Doris, at the helm.

MILLI   But let's start at the beginning.

DORIS   Milli, must we really go so far back in time?

NIL   It bothers you, doesn't it?

MILLI   Please, Doris. Before we get to the office. We have time to tell the story on our way. From the beginning. For kicks. For clarity. What do you say?

DORIS   *(after a beat)* For clarity, I'd do almost anything.

NIL   *(to herself)* To save face too.

MILLI   Okay. Let's return to the source. Because before the publishing house, there was the writer…

DORIS   Before the writer, there were the words…

MILLI   Before the words, there was the matrix…

NIL   And before the matrix, there were the progenitors and pandemonium.

DORIS   Yuck!

> *With sounds, lighting, and props, DORIS, MILLI, and NIL act out the creation myth. DORIS goes through the motions, more interested in her manicure than in the story.*

NIL   In the beginning, everything was there, but nothing was in order.

MILLI   It was original nothingness: chaos and confusion.

NIL   Then there was the mother and the father…

MILLI   Not a strong and charismatic mother like in other creation myths…

DORIS   Wouldn't that be nice!

MILLI   But a mother with a low cloud cover and a sombre smile…

DORIS   My God, such euphemisms!

NIL   Flanked by a strong and stable father…

DORIS   He wasn't so—

NIL   *(giving DORIS a sidelong glance)* Flanked by a strong and stable father…

MILLI   Riddled with worry for his wife who trembled from head to toe.

NIL   In a tent with nylon walls…

MILLI   In the heart of a municipal campground...

NIL   On the Atlantic coast...

MILLI   On a stormy night.

Change in lighting.

NIL   The mother and father were on summer holidays in the Maritimes...

DORIS   In the province of New Brunswick...

MILLI   They were drawn to the strange attractions of that part of the country...

DORIS   The province of New Brunswick...

NIL   *(giving DORIS another sidelong glance)* Cape Enrage...

MILLI   Magnetic Hill...

NIL   The Reversible Falls...

MILLI   The mighty tidal bore...

NIL   The Bay of Fundy with the highest tides in the world...

MILLI   Grand Falls, where the river water explodes at the bottom of the gorge...

NIL   Breathtaking beaches...

MILLI   Rivers with outlandish names...

NIL   Miramichi...

MILLI   Memramcook...

NIL   Restigouche...

MILLI   Petitcodiac, Scoudouc, Kedgwick...

NIL   In short, they were drawn to the aquatic and to—

DORIS   The province of New Brunswick?

MILLI & NIL   No! The rustic charm of camping!

DORIS snickers and continues with her manicure.

NIL   But the moon was in Pisces...

MILLI   And it was raining cats and dogs...

NIL   And the nylon wasn't waterproof...

MILLI   And the wind was blowing to beat the band...

NIL   And day by day, July turned into a bleak November...

MILLI   And it was indeed the month of death in the belly of the mother...

NIL   Who was three months pregnant.

DORIS   Risky business.

MILLI   Hour after hour, the water threatened to flood the campground…

NIL   And wash away the mythical family.

DORIS   And with it, the province of New Brunswick!

MILLI & NIL   Doris!

MILLI   And so the father was riddled with worry…

NIL   For since they'd "come to know each other" between the strangely patterned sheets…

MILLI   In a dull blue bedroom…

NIL   In a sleepy suburb on the banks of a polluted river…

MILLI   The mother's depressive state had only gotten worse.

DORIS   And it goes without saying that the violent weather system that was besieging the province of New Brunswick didn't help things much.

Urged on by MILLI and NIL, who are getting into position for the panic attack.

While the elements were unleashing their fury around her, the mother rocked back and forth, wild-eyed, her hands on her belly, whispering…

MILLI & NIL   I can't have it, don't want it, won't do it…. I can't have it, don't want it, won't do it…. I can't have it, don't want it, won't do it…. Aaaaah!

DORIS   Suddenly, through the howling wind, the father heard the cries of his wife.

NIL   He quickly secured the poles of the tent and dashed into the little nylon house.

MILLI   Seeing his wife in the grips of a deep depressive state, he took her by the shoulders and…

DORIS   Shaking her with all his might…

NIL   Whispered words that were stronger than the storm…

MILLI   Stronger than her prayer to the goddess of miscarriage…

DORIS   *(aside)* But not stronger than three months of depression.

MILLI & NIL   *(running out of patience)* Doris!

MILLI   And the father broke the spell by imposing his solid frame on the violent winds that were racking his wife.

NIL   And six months later, in the middle of an icy winter…

MILLI   And a blizzard that would go down in the history books…

NIL   Her back up against the hospital wall…

DORIS   Why can't anything be done simply in this family?

MILLI & NIL The mother gave birth to a little girl!

MILLI And this child, who carried within her the maternal drama of the Atlantic coast…

NIL And the paternal strength of tactical intervention, was none other than…

DORIS The one who penned us into existence…

MILLI Our very own matrix…

NIL Our mother.

MILLI & NIL *(after a short silence)* It's a very, very beautiful creation myth.

DORIS "A very, very beautiful creation myth." Ladies, please. Objectivity and rigour. Just because we're telling our story doesn't mean we can get all caught up in subjective sentimentality. Don't forget that literature is an exact science. No matter what anyone says. Facts, facts, and more facts. There is nothing beautiful about it. Beauty is not of this world. All we can do is reach for it.

NIL Without a doubt, Doris.

DORIS Without a doubt. What an ironic expression! Let's wrap this up, shall we? So…

MILLI From this little matrix made of solid earth and raging waters…

NIL We came into the world.

DORIS Yes. Milli, Nil, and I are sisters. Three sisters. An electric trio. Ladies: one, two, one, two, three!

DORIS, MILLI, & NIL *(dancing and singing)*
We share the same blood
We're from the same place
Three peas in a pod
Three legs in a race
In one hundred years
A team we'll be still
Three sisters, three peers
Doris Milli Nil
Do. Mi. Nil. Yeah!

All three keep dancing, and DORIS hums the song to herself.

NIL Doris? Isn't this song a little inaccurate? There's seven of us. Not three. Seven—

DORIS *(pointing at MILLI)* One, *(pointing at NIL)* two, *(pointing at herself)* three. Three. It's not inaccurate.

NIL We're telling the story from the beginning, Doris. In the beginning, there were seven of us.

MILLI Nil is right, Doris. In the beginning, there were seven of us.

MILLI & NIL *(pointing at DORIS)* One, *(pointing at MILLI)* two, *(pointing at NIL)* three, *(pointing at the floor)* four, five, six, seven. Seven! Seven! Seven!

> *Under the floor, the four sisters cry out: "Seven! Seven! Seven! Seven!" DORIS, who has stopped dancing, stomps on the floor, which silences the four sisters and brings the dancing to a halt.*

DORIS Seven! Seven little rocks she'd push up the mountain only to see them come tumbling back down, and she'd push them back up, and they'd tumble back down and on and on until one day she'd be crushed by her seven little rocks. There. Are you happy? *(She starts filing her nails again, with vigour.)* Carry on. Carry on!

MILLI From this little matrix made of solid earth and raging waters, we were born.

NIL Seven sisters. There was Doris the perfectionist.

DORIS Thank you. And Milli the angst-ridden one.

MILLI And Nil the doubter.

NIL And Urania the eccentric and Calliope the passionate.

MILLI And Thalia the extravagant and Polyhymnia the profound.

DORIS, MILLI, & NIL Doris, Milli, Nil, Urania, Calliope, Thalia, and Polyhymnia.

NIL Seven sisters who came into being in a pink space that was filling up with thousands of words…

MILLI Seven sisters, seduced by the fire in her belly, the secret…

NIL Seven sisters who, sensing that something big was in the works…

DORIS *(pointing at the windows)* Were constantly on the lookout.

MILLI And one day, from our special vantage point, seeing the matrix seized by…

NIL The desire to unleash the thousands of words and put them all in order…

DORIS She was full of potential back then!

MILLI Realizing how bright the fire shone…

DORIS Her instincts were good.

NIL Sensing that the future was in literature…

DORIS How could we not believe?

NIL I founded Window to the Soul Publishing.

DORIS There. It's out. Do you feel better now, deary?

MILLI Doris!

NIL   Usurper!

DORIS   One must wrest oneself from the abyss of doubt if one aspires to the pinnacle of perfection, Nil. You know very well. We've discussed this time and time again.

MILLI   Please... that's all in the past...

DORIS   Exactly. The past. An unproductive tense. Don't you think, Nil? *(NIL nods.)* Good. We agree. So, sensing that the future was in literature, Nil founded Window to the Soul Publishing—bravo, deary, and thank you—and the first manuscript arrived.

NIL   And that's when it all began.

DORIS   The work...

NIL   And the hostilities.

MILLI   *(holding her sisters' hands)* Of course, alliances were formed.

DORIS, MILLI, & NIL   And blood was spilled.

DORIS   Can sisters refuse to live together?

MILLI   Can sisters hate one other?

NIL   Can some sisters drive other sisters out?

DORIS, MILLI, & NIL   Yes.

DORIS   And that's how it happened.

MILLI   One by one.

NIL   Step by step.

DORIS   Manuscript after manuscript.

MILLI   Battled and banished.

NIL   Out the door.

DORIS, MILLI, & NIL   Urania the eccentric, ousted. Calliope the passionate, evicted. Thalia the imaginative, rejected. Polyhymnia the profound, ejected. To the basement, our emotionally extravagant sisters!

Under the floor, the four sisters protest.

DORIS   *(stomping throughout)* Out the door, those who find clarity a bore! Out of sight, those for whom all is not black and white! Out of mind, those for whom ambiguity is sublime!

Caught up in the hysteria, MILLI and NIL join in on the stomping and repeat DORIS's words. Under the floor, the four sisters quiet down. DORIS, MILLI, and NIL arrive triumphantly at Window to the Soul

> *Publishing, a closed room (the author's head) with two windows (her eyes), three chairs, a desk, the crematorium, and the giant jar.*

And that's how Window to the Soul Publishing has prospered over the past decade. And, for the past five years now, directed by me, Doris, with an iron glove, a stiff wrist, a sure hand, a righteous red pen…

MILLI & NIL   Et cetera. Et cetera.

DORIS   …And with the aid of my precious collaborators, who support my every command, our humble enterprise has devoted itself to nothing less than the development of contemporary literary brilliance. But enough about everyone else. Let's talk—

MILLI & NIL   About me.

DORIS   About me. I always start my day with a prayer. *(With a gesture, she invites her sisters to pray.)* "Best of the best, top of the top, cream of the crop/May my eternal mission in life/Be to reach the highest of heights/Optimum, maximum, summum, amen."

MILLI   *(whispering)* What excites me the most are early bloomers. That's why I always keep *(exhibiting her book)* my *Compendium of Literary Prodigies* in my desk.

NIL   *(whispering)* Personally, I can't step foot in here without wishing there were still seven of us. *(taking a book from her desk)* At times I tell myself that together we were better.

DORIS   *(coming out of her contemplative state)* That said, in my quest for the best, my generosity and sensitivity don't always come shining through. Not often, in fact. Rarely, even.

MILLI   *(leafing through her dictionary)* Emmanuel Carrère… Paul Claudel… Réjean Ducharme…

NIL   In fact, while rereading *(exhibiting her book)* *Three Sisters* by Chekhov recently…

DORIS   Knopf can hang up his hat. I'm exacting *and* ruthless.

MILLI   *(leafing through her dictionary)* Nancy Huston… Carson McCullers… Sylvia Plath…

DORIS   That's why people love to hate me.

NIL   *(caressing the book)* What a pleasure!

DORIS   But hating me is no great feat!

MILLI   It's so simple, all I do is open my dictionary and…

NIL   *(flipping pages)* I took note of…

MILLI Take note of a writer's date of birth, which I subtract from the publication date of his first book, let's say for example…

NIL *(looking in her book)* something extraordinary…

DORIS I dare someone to try to love me!

MILLI Rimbaud. Born in 1854, he published *A Season in Hell* in 1873.

DORIS Now that's a challenge!

MILLI 1873–1854=19. He was nineteen years old!

NIL *(looking in her book)* A line full of hope…

DORIS *(defiant)* Ah!

MILLI *(hand across her breast)* Ah!

NIL *(finding the line)* Ah! *(reading)* "Here there are only three of your sort in the town now, but in generations to come there will be more and more and more…"

DORIS What are you reading, deary?

NIL *(continuing to read)* "…and the time will come when everything will be changed and be as you would have it; they will live in your way, and later on you too will be out of date—people will be born who will be better than you…"

DORIS Never! Never, do you hear me? We will never be out of date! People will not be born who are better than us. We are the best! And then she wonders why I had to demote her from the head of the publishing house. *(ripping the book out of her hands)* Well, what have we here? *Three Sisters*? *(returning the book to her)* Burn it.

MILLI Burn Chekhov, Doris?

DORIS Yes indeed! What that whining Russian is still doing on everyone's top ten list is beyond me. The masterpieces of our time will be published by Window to the Soul Publishing. We need masterpieces of the here and now. And it's not by glorifying the past that we're going to succeed in our endeavour. No, what we need is objectivity and rigour. Objectivity and rigour, do you understand that, Nil?

NIL *(crying)* No, I don't understand, Doris…

DORIS That's why I'm the one in charge here, deary. Go on, burn, honey, burn. Take my word for it: this is how we're going to leave our mark.

> *Fade out while NIL, still crying, burns* Three Sisters*; DORIS, with a watchful eye on NIL, retrieves an empty jar from the crematorium; MILLI puts her* Compendium of Literary Prodigies *back with care, and the four sisters huddle silently under the floor.*

Scene 3
Disturbance

Set of the TV show. INÈS picks up the manuscript.

INÈS Well, well. So if Candice de Lafontaine-Rotonde were a character, she'd be her own version of *Three Sisters*. The proof that you can't escape other people's plays. Obviously it would have been easier if you'd answered Medea, Miss Julie, or Lady Macbeth, but I've got to work with what you give me, Candice. That you identify with these three… *(tapping the manuscript with her hand)* nobodies… is a bit… puzzling, but puzzles are your specialty, are they not?

CANDICE Puzzles?

INÈS Yes, puzzles. As in "to be puzzled" or "puzzling."

CANDICE I… I can be puzzled, yes, and no doubt puzzling…

INÈS Ah, the confusion of youth. The confusion that binds us to childhood. To the childhood of art, in some ways. You're young. How old are you, thirty? You're trying to find yourself, no one really understands you. It's normal, it's refreshing, it does us all good! *(returning to her notes)* But let's get back to—

CANDICE How old were you when people stopped telling you that you were young and refreshing and you did us all good?

INÈS Well, that's what I call having a bucketful of nerve and a ladle to spare!

CANDICE It's a legitimate question. You were thirty once too.

INÈS Ah! Writers. Masters of evasion. They think they can expose you by turning the question on you, but they all forget one thing: I'm the interviewer here, I'm the one doing a portrait of them. And today, Candice, you just so happen to be my subject!

CANDICE I know, Inès, but all I'm trying to say is that, between the refreshing that does us all good and the old that no one wants to see, there must be other combinations, and at thirty you'd think that—

INÈS All I know is that when I was thirty, I was as fresh as a spring breeze. I'd left the pipe dreams of my youth behind me. I had the wind in my sails. I was just starting in television.

CANDICE At least we have that much in common.

INÈS *(dodging the comment)* Candice, we haven't finished the questions on the writer's craft. So, tell me, briefly: if you were a time of the day to write?

CANDICE I'd be the morning because everything is still possible. Things go downhill after that. I hate afternoons.

INÈS Well! I could take that personally, couldn't I?

CANDICE No, no… it has nothing to do with you or with this afternoon…. What I meant was that afternoons for writers… well, for me anyway… *(beat)* It's in the afternoon that you see melancholy in people's eyes, don't you find?

INÈS Yes. I mean no…. It depends… *(beat)* If you were a leitmotif for the writer's craft?

CANDICE "Sufficient for the day is its own trouble."

INÈS Jesus of Nazareth. Obviously, after five years in the desert. Now if—

CANDICE Not in the desert. In the province of New Brunswick.

INÈS In the province of New Brunswick? Oh, so that's where you've been hiding. And what were you doing in the province of New Brunswick?

CANDICE I was looking for the source. And I found it. I wrote this play.

INÈS In the province of New Brunswick?

CANDICE In the province of New Brunswick. *(INÈS starts to laugh.)* What? What did I say? Why are you laughing?

INÈS The province of New Brunswick. Don't you find that the more you say it, the less it makes sense? *(She keeps repeating "the province of New Brunswick" and laughing.)* So, if you were a source of inspiration—that's my next question—you would be the province of New Brunswick?

CANDICE No. I would be my life and the dictionary. There's a bit of everything in there.

INÈS Yes, so it appears. And if you were the person who sparked your interest in writing?

CANDICE I would be God because… because I feel like I was born with the spark.

INÈS "Born with the spark!" And yet, if I'm not mistaken, you haven't written all that much. I have a few notes on you, and you aren't what one would call a writer tapping into divine inspiration. I mean, if God sparked your interest in the uterus, I think we'd know about it by now. I jest, but you see where I'm going with this.

CANDICE God is just a manner of speaking. It's that, when I was young…

INÈS What? Your mother?

CANDICE No, no, it has nothing to do with—

INÈS Are you sure?

CANDICE It's my relationship with words.

INÈS It's always about the mother, Candice.

Seizure. Spotlight on CANDICE, who is writing. The intercom—channel of the VOX MATERNALIS—rings.

CANDICE Yes?

VOX MATERNALIS sings "Happy Birthday" to CANDICE.

What are you doing here, Mom?

VOX MATERNALIS It's your birthday, Candice. I came to wish you happy birthday.

CANDICE But it's three in the morning.

VOX MATERNALIS That's when you were born, my child.

CANDICE It's also when people sleep, Mom.

VOX MATERNALIS Thirty years ago, you weren't sleeping anymore than you are now, darling. You were crying out for the first time.

CANDICE You should be at the hospital resting.

VOX MATERNALIS Thirty years ago, I wasn't resting. I was giving birth to you. Ah, thirty. The age of success. The age of achievement. For some, it comes sooner. For others, it never comes at all. Thirty years old. *(beat)* Candice?

CANDICE Yes, Mom?

VOX MATERNALIS Why don't you come see me at the hospital? I'm all alone in my room fighting this terrible illness and I keep asking your father: "Edmund, where is my darling daughter?" *(CANDICE starts crying.)* Let me come up. It's cold outside. And the sleet is falling like little knives.

CANDICE Here too, Mom. Here too. We aren't any more sheltered than you are.

VOX MATERNALIS We? Is someone with you? You're not alone?

CANDICE I'm working. There's people.

VOX MATERNALIS Ah, your characters. You're writing.

CANDICE Yes, I'm writing.

VOX MATERNALIS Oh, that's good. And it's going well? You're pulling it off? Form, function, metaphors, rhythm, structure, style, syntax, originality, accessibility, subtlety, humour, emotion, simplicity, avoiding self-indulgence? Is it working?

CANDICE It's working.

VOX MATERNALIS And what are you concocting for us? A little masterpiece of your own making?

CANDICE Yes, Mom.

VOX MATERNALIS Oh, I'm proud of you, Candice. Now, let me come up.

CANDICE   Go back to the hospital, Claudette.

VOX MATERNALIS   I have a present for you, honey.

CANDICE   I'll see you tomorrow.

VOX MATERNALIS   A *Compendium of Literary Prodigies.*

CANDICE   I'll come visit you—

VOX MATERNALIS   What if I die before you come?

CANDICE   Tomorrow afternoon.

VOX MATERNALIS   You know I'm going to die, Candice.

CANDICE   Yes, Mom, I know, but you're not going to die before tomorrow afternoon.

VOX MATERNALIS   Let me come up, please. I'll stay out of your way. I'll just smoke quietly in a corner and let you concoct your masterpiece.

CANDICE   Please, Mom, just go.

VOX MATERNALIS   I don't want to face the wet dawn all alone.

CANDICE   I'm working!

VOX MATERNALIS   Candice!

End of the seizure.

CANDICE   My mother didn't spark my interest in writing.

INÈS   If you say so... but while we're on the topic of family, do you have any brothers or sisters?

CANDICE   I have seven only children.

INÈS   Sorry?

CANDICE   I'm an only child.

INÈS   An only child, but of course. The last of your kind. It's not easy being at the end of the line, is it?

CANDICE   *(sarcastically)* You tell me.

INÈS   *(unnerved by her gall)* Well! Dear viewers, after the... commercial break, we'll continue our Finnish—sorry—Chinese portrait of... Candice de LaFontaine-Rotonde, author of *(clumsily holding the manuscript) Chinese Portrait of an Impostor*. It's certainly Chinese to me! *(nervous laughter)* After the break, I'll ask her: "If you were a profession?" *(She looks at her notes.)* That's right: "If you were a profession?" *(beat)* So. Dear viewers. Stay tuned. Don't move an inch. We'll be right back.

Theme music. The four sisters dance and sing along. Silence. CANDICE gets up.

Where are you going?

CANDICE To the bathroom.

INÈS You've got two minutes.

> *CANDICE disappears. INÈS stays alone with the manuscript on her lap. Blackout.*

Scene 4
The Manuscript

Window to the Soul Publishing. Afternoon light is coming in through the windows. DORIS is pacing. MILLI is sitting down. Both are holding a big envelope they don't dare open.

DORIS *(shouting)* Nil! Nil, where are you? *(She listens. Silence.)* Oh, she's always vanishing right when you need her!

MILLI Do you think she may have suspected *(holding up the envelope)* THIS?

DORIS Ah! Don't talk to me about her suspicions. I lose all sense of direction when I listen to her. Her doubt leaves me with a feeling of slapdash grooming, approximate hygiene, neglected nether regions. I'm finding it more and more difficult to count on her. I'm going to have to rein her in. *(to herself)* Beware of little girls with dirt behind their ears, Doris.

MILLI I don't like it when you talk about Nil like that. Don't forget: "In one hundred years/A team we'll be still." She's our sister, Doris.

DORIS Milli, must I remind you of the bloody scenes in which you took part when we banished Urania, Calliope, Thalia, and Polyhymnia? *(MILLI smiles viciously.)* All right, so let me bray what I need to bray and speak when the spirit moves you. *(brandishing the envelope)* Our author has never done this to us before. Never finished a project without our two cents worth. Or our 250 cents worth, for that matter. I'm dying to open it.

MILLI Let's wait for Nil. Give her the time to get here. Maybe she hasn't finished her lunch.

DORIS You're right. We should wait for her. *(a short beat)* We've waited long enough.

MILLI Doris, no!

DORIS Stop being Miss Nicey-Nice, Milli. It's past one o'clock. And professionalism takes precedence over digestion.

> *We hear footsteps running up the stairs.*

MILLI It's her!

DORIS Coming up from the basement…

DORIS grabs NIL's envelope. NIL appears.

NIL   Am I late?

MILLI   What do you think?

DORIS   Where are you coming from?

NIL   That's none of your business.

DORIS   From the basement?

NIL   That's none of your concern.

DORIS   You went to see our sisters, didn't you? *(beat)* We cut ties with them, Nil.

NIL   You can't really cut ties with your family, Doris.

MILLI   How are they doing?

DORIS   Are they plotting their return? They've been pretty noisy lately…

NIL   Not really.

DORIS   Not really? Not really? I'd like to see them try! Isn't that right, Nil?

NIL   That… that's right, Doris.

DORIS   Okay, let's proceed. *(handing her the envelope)* A manuscript awaits.

NIL   A manuscript. Well, well…

DORIS   You knew?

NIL   Without knowing.

DORIS   That's just like you. And you didn't feel like telling us about it?

NIL   If I opened my mouth every time I had my suspicions…

MILLI   Okay. Shall we?

All three frantically open their envelopes. They each take out a manuscript. A letter is attached to MILLI's copy.

Look. *(reading)* "Hello, you three. Here's a surprise play. I hope it will make you fall off your chairs. Sincerely, your author."

DORIS rips the letter from her hands.

DORIS   *(reading)* "I hope it will make you fall off your chairs." Pfff!

All three look at their manuscripts and read the cover page.

NIL   "*Chinese Portrait of an Impostor.*" Promising title.

MILLI   "Final draft." Definite aplomb.

NIL   *(measuring the thickness of the manuscript)* Fairly thick. Undeniable breadth.

DORIS   "A play by Candice de LaFontaine-Rotonde."

MILLI   It's like music. I never tire of hearing it.

NIL   *Chinese Portrait of an Impostor.*

DORIS   Who do you think the impostor is?

MILLI   *(singing to herself)* Candice de LaFontaine-Rotonde.

NIL   *(caressing the manuscript)* She must have a lot of hope in this one.

DORIS   *(smelling the manuscript)* Aw, that gives it a little *je ne sais quoi* that's almost touching.

All three turn the page, and NIL reads the dedication.

NIL   "To my father, Edmund de LaFontaine, for the strength and the confidence."

DORIS   Comments?

MILLI   Yuck, yuck, yuck!

NIL   "To my mother, the late Claudette Rotonde…"

DORIS, MILLI, & NIL   *(singing)* Late, late, late Claudette, your ardour makes us swoon; late, late, late Claudette in the afternoon…

NIL   "May her sombre lineage end with me."

DORIS   Comments?

MILLI   Her sombre lineage?

DORIS   Incredible! We're only at the dedication and it's already enigmatic. And what, pray tell, is a Chinese portrait? Is the nationality random or not? Chinese, Chinese…. Why not Slovak, Danish, or Mi'kmaq? It sounds neither better nor worse. Nothing simpler than to put "Chinese" in front of a word: it will please a quarter of the human race and voila! It's purely mathematical. Purely mercantile. Purely mass market.

NIL   Maybe, Doris, but if she wants to be… commercial, that's her choice.

DORIS & MILLI   Commercial! Stop, I'm going to sprout a cold sore!

NIL   Now hold on. Might I remind you that we haven't yet read this play?

DORIS   Fine, let's read it. I'm fine reading it, but have you ever heard of a Chinese portrait?

NIL   Uh… no, but… I like Chinese food, so why not a Chinese portrait?

DORIS   Well aren't you the funny one today, Nil!

MILLI   I wouldn't complain if I were you.

DORIS   Chinese portrait, sombre lineage… I can't make heads or tails of this!

NIL   Doris, get a hold of yourself. Keep an open mind.

DORIS It's the emotion. I'm tense. I have been waiting so long for this. For the masterpiece. Do you understand? And what if THIS is IT? *(She takes a deep breath and then places her hand on the manuscript.)* Chinese Portrait of an Impostor, I welcome you into my home.

All three turn the page, and MILLI reads the epigraph.

MILLI "A Chinese portrait is a series of questions beginning with 'if you were' followed by answers beginning with 'I would be.'" For example, "'If you were a fruit?' asks the hostess. 'I would be a pear,' responds the guest." *(laughing)* A pear!

NIL *(to herself)* Interesting...

DORIS *(to herself)* Fascinating!

MILLI *(after a beat)* I'd like to do a Chinese portrait of Candice.

NIL Don't even think about it, Milli! Right, Doris? We have a manuscript to read.

DORIS Yes, yes, of course. Objectivity and rigour, we mustn't stray from our principles...

MILLI Come on, Doris. Say yes! Say yes!

NIL Milli! Can't you see that you're only adding to our editor's tension? *(beat)* Although it could be to our advantage, Doris. We would have... inside knowledge of what a Chinese portrait is.

MILLI Oh yes! Inside knowledge! Inside knowledge!

NIL And doing a Chinese portrait of Candice could get us back into the swing of things.

MILLI Oh yes! Back into the swing of things! Back into the swing of things!

NIL For I doubt that we're ready to analyze a play of this... thickness. We mustn't forget that we haven't received anything of this... breadth for quite some time.

MILLI Oh yes! We mustn't forget! We mustn't forget!

DORIS Milli! Stop your bellowing and tell me why we should do her Chinese portrait.

MILLI Um... because... because this playful exercise could... uh... help us understand her and in so doing better... uh... grasp her writing... and could serve as a helpful guide in our analysis of the play. There's nothing like a personalized analytical template. *(beat)* Is there?

NIL And given that the work is no doubt autobiographical, it would be even more... relevant.

DORIS Upon consideration, I think I rather like Chinese portraits.

MILLI Let's begin! Let's begin!

NIL   I'll ask the questions, and you can supply the answers. I have no doubt that you'll be up to the task!

DORIS   Very well. Let's amuse ourselves! Ladies. Chinese portrait of Candice de LaFontaine-Rotonde.

NIL   If she were… a vehicle?

MILLI   A wheelbarrow… with a flat.

DORIS   No, Milli. Render unto Caesarine that which is Caesarine's. She'd be a Mercedes… with nothing under the hood!

MILLI   Yeah!

NIL   Now, if she were… an art form?

DORIS   Your turn, Milli.

MILLI   An art form? Uh… writhing?

DORIS   Oh, writhing! Ingenious!

MILLI   Thank you, thank you.

NIL   If she were… a musical instrument?

MILLI   A harp.

DORIS   Why a harp?

MILLI   Because she's always harping on!

DORIS & NIL   Bravo! Bravo!

NIL   If she were a body of water?

MILLI   A puddle!

DORIS   A puddle! Milli, you're a genius!

NIL   If she were a political regime?

MILLI   A banana republic.

DORIS   *(singing)* Yes, we have no bananas! We have no bananas today!

NIL   If she were a material?

MILLI   Plasticine… because it's easy to manipulate!

DORIS, MILLI, & NIL   Hours of fun! To play it is to love it!

NIL   If she were a sign of the zodiac?

DORIS   Capri-corny!

NIL   If she were a planet?

DORIS   Neptune.

MILLI & NIL Why Neptune?

DORIS Because it's about time she nep-tuned in!

MILLI Oh Doris, you're a natural!

DORIS Aren't I?

NIL If she were an atmospheric phenomenon?

DORIS A tempest in a teacup.

MILLI Or, lesser known, though no less offensive: a fart in a cyclone.

NIL If she were a monument?

DORIS The unknown soldier. Killed in an unknown battle. In an unknown war.

MILLI Oh! Such horribly anonymous suffering…

NIL Let's do a sprint.

MILLI A sprint! A sprint!

NIL If she were a sport?

DORIS Hurdles!

NIL A quality?

DORIS *(with a gesture that takes in the room)* Hospitality.

NIL A weakness?

MILLI Just one? How about *(pointing at herself)* one, *(pointing at NIL)* two, *(pointing at DORIS)* three!

They all burst out laughing.

NIL A dish?

DORIS Mixed nuts.

NIL A nun?

DORIS Sister Goody-Two-Shoes.

MILLI & NIL Pray for us.

NIL A weapon?

DORIS Me!

MILLI Me too!

NIL What about me?

DORIS You're the cornerstone of the whole arsenal!

Outside, a storm is brewing. Under the floor, the four sisters huddle in silence.

NIL   If she were a body part?

MILLI   She would be her beautiful eyes.

DORIS, MILLI, & NIL   *(pointing at the windows and laughing)* So expressive!

> *Outside it starts to thunder and rain. Under the floor, the four sisters start to shout.*

MILLI   It's raining.

DORIS   *(pointing at the floor)* And they're thundering!

> *All three stomp on the floor to silence the four sisters, their frenzy reaching a climax.*

NIL   If she were an end?

DORIS   She'd be sad.

MILLI   So sad. Sniff, sniff!

DORIS, MILLI, & NIL   Sad enough to make you cry!

> *All three laugh until they have tears in their eyes.*

DORIS   Ladies, let's have some bonbons. If we don't busy our mouths with something else, we'll never stop. Neither will she!

> *They each take a candy. They suck on their candies and look out the windows. The rain slowly subsides. A sense of calm returns and they go back to work. They reread the title page, the dedication, and the epigraph.*

Let's review.

MILLI   "Chinese Portrait of an Impostor."

NIL   "Final draft."

DORIS   "A play by Candice de LaFontaine-Rotonde."

> *All three turn the page.*

NIL   "To my father to my mother blablabla…"

> *All three turn the page.*

MILLI   "*Chinese Portrait* blablabla…"

> *All three turn the page.*

DORIS   List of scenes.

MILLI   "Scene 1. Welcome to Window to the Soul Publishing."

NIL   "Scene 2. The Manuscript."

DORIS   Is this a joke?

MILLI   "Scene 3. The Surprise Visitor."

NIL "Scene 4. Torture."

DORIS She can't be serious.

All three turn the page and read the list of characters.

MILLI "Characters."

NIL "Doris, Milli, Nil, the Surprise Visitor."

DORIS "Doris…"

MILLI "…Milli…"

NIL "…Nil…"

All three abruptly close their manuscripts.

It can't be!

MILLI What do we do?

DORIS We stay calm!

NIL This is an affront.

DORIS Worse: it's an outrage. I can't believe this. She doesn't write anything for years, and then all of a sudden we get THIS. I mean, I can take a joke, but there are limits!

MILLI *(on the verge of an anxiety attack)* She'll never be an early bloomer! Never!

NIL *(hitting her thigh)* I doubt her good faith. I doubt everything! Everything!

DORIS *(crying out of rage)* I was sure she had what it takes to reach the highest of heights. I was sure, but she doesn't! She doesn't!

MILLI I can't believe we believed in her!

DORIS I refuse to blame myself for any of this!

NIL It's all my fault. It's all my fault!

DORIS *(wiping her eyes)* Finally! Some words of wisdom.

All three get a hold of themselves and look at their manuscripts in silence.

NIL Um… it's just a suggestion, but… what if we actually read the play?

Beat.

MILLI Yeah. What if we let a masterpiece pass us by? What if THIS is IT?

A long beat.

DORIS No. No, no, no, no, no, no, no! I am Doris, and Doris is not a character. This is not a masterpiece. It's a lie.

NIL You're right. You're right.

MILLI opens her copy discreetly.

MILLI   *(after a beat)* Who do you think this Surprise Visitor is?

DORIS   Shut that vile manuscript this instant, Milli! And go get me the dustbin! And you, Nil, find me the lighter. *(to herself)* We're going to fight fire with fire. Again and again. History is repeating itself. *(looking at her manuscript)* This calls for an *auto de fé*.

> *MILLI and NIL come back with the metal dustbin and the lighter.*

We will not stand for this. Give me your copies.

> *NIL hands her her copy. MILLI rips a page at random from her manuscript.*

She can write something else if she so desires, but she will not make laughingstocks of us. *(She takes MILLI's manuscript from her.)* We run an honest publishing house that has offered, for the past five years since I've been at the helm, the most loyal of services, so if she's not happy with our work, good riddance! *(brandishing the manuscripts)* This is nothing but trash, and what do we do with trash?

MILLI & NIL   We burn it!

DORIS   And mark my words: a retort on her part will only fan the flames. Hostilities have been declared. The demolition derby has begun!

> *Fade out on Window to the Soul Publishing. The four sisters start dancing under the floor, DORIS burns the manuscripts and NIL watches. MILLI slips the page she ripped out into her pocket.*

Scene 5
Interruption

> *Set of the TV show. INÈS is drinking a glass of Scotch and leafing through the manuscript. CANDICE arrives, her bag slung over her shoulder. INÈS shuts the manuscript, sets it on the table, and, with a gesture, invites CANDICE to sit down. CANDICE remains standing.*

INÈS   Would you like me to call the makeup artist? *(checking her watch)* You have a little over a minute to compose yourself.

CANDICE   I didn't decompose.

INÈS   *(offering her a handkerchief)* Dab your eyes a bit, at least. *(beat)* There. That's better. *(taking her handkerchief back)* Now, let's get something clear, Candice. You are my guest here, and it is customary for a guest to treat her host with respect. What are these insinuations about the end of my line?

CANDICE   Rumours about the end of your reign.

INÈS   You don't watch my show, but you listen to rumours about it. Priceless!

CANDICE I don't listen to them, I just hear them.

INÈS How convenient! Nothing but hearsay!

CANDICE Spread by wise people, if you want my opinion. The fact is, after five years, even in a democracy, you think you can do as you please. Five years is a long time.

INÈS Especially in the province of New Brunswick.

CANDICE Scoff all you like. I'm not playing this game.

INÈS Ah! They all want to come on my show, but once they're here, all they want is to be pampered. Tear a little strip off them, and ooh la la! If you can't stand the heat, get out of the kitchen!

CANDICE What is that supposed to mean?

INÈS True artists are like chefs. They can take the heat without getting burnt. That's important, especially on television.

CANDICE This is an arts program, not a cooking show!

INÈS The same principles apply. Don't mess with the ingredients if you don't know the recipe. It could prove fatal.

CANDICE For whom?

INÈS Don't try to outsmart me, Candice. You're not in one of your plays where you can pull the strings as you see fit.

CANDICE Don't tempt me. You might be surprised.

INÈS Okay. *(sighing)* I haven't read your play. There. I said it. Happy? I didn't have the time. When Wilfred Fitzgerald leaves you high and dry to do *Inside the Actor's Playhouse*, that's what happens. *(beat)* Now there's no need to make a scene, Candice. Just do like me: be a survivor. And if you can't do that, just grit your teeth and enjoy the exposure.

CANDICE *(taking the manuscript)* You didn't read it at all?

INÈS I skimmed it a bit. Earlier. When you went to the bathroom.

> *Seizure. Spotlight on CANDICE holding the manuscript. INÈS, DORIS, MILLI, and NIL demonstrate around her, brandishing signs and shouting their lines like slogans. INÈS speaks through her megaphone, and the VOX MATERNALIS resounds through the intercom.*

It is not my cup of tea! It is not my cup of tea!

DORIS, MILLI, & NIL An outrage! Treason! A tall glass of poison!

VOX MATERNALIS I want my masterpiece! I want my masterpiece!

CANDICE But you didn't read it?

INÈS No need to make a scene!

DORIS, MILLI, & NIL   No need to make a scene!

VOX MATERNALIS   Is it working? Is it working? Is it working?

INÈS   And what was the title of this latest flop?

DORIS, MILLI, & NIL   *Chinese Portrait of an Impostor.*

INÈS   Impostor?

DORIS, MILLI, & NIL   Impostor!

INÈS   Was it really that bad?

DORIS & NIL   What do you think?

MILLI   Ashes to ashes, dust to dust…

INÈS   From what I could tell, it's far from a masterpiece!

DORIS   What good instincts! I like you. Give me a hug!

MILLI & NIL   Give me a hug! Give me a hug!

CANDICE   Who said anything about a masterpiece?

INÈS, DORIS, MILLI, & NIL   *(sarcastic)* "Who said anything about a masterpiece?"

INÈS   Don't lie. That's all you want. To have it hailed as a masterpiece.

DORIS   Top of the top flop! Cream of the rotten crop!

MILLI   Late bloomer! Late bloomer!

NIL   I doubt everything! I doubt everything!

VOX MATERNALIS   Is it working?

INÈS   Grit your teeth and enjoy the exposure.

DORIS, MILLI, & NIL   Shut your laptop and save us from another flop.

CANDICE   *(shouting)* You can't do this to me!

INÈS   Who's doing what to whom?

DORIS, MILLI, & NIL   Who's doing what to whom?

INÈS   Who's doing what to whom?

DORIS, MILLI, & NIL   Who's doing what to whom?

Everyone freezes. Beat.

VOX MATERNALIS   Is it working?

End of the seizure. Action resumes and everyone goes back to their positions prior to the seizure.

CANDICE   *(holding the manuscript)* You didn't read it at all?

INÈS   *(taking the manuscript from her)* I skimmed it a bit. Earlier. When you went to the bathroom. But I must say the title is very catchy. You've got a knack for titles: *Warsick Girls, Miss Bernice and the Bombs* and *(tapping the manuscript)* this. Irresistible. *(She sighs.)* In fact, titles happen to be my weak spot. And, regrettably, that's often the problem with plays. The title is promising, so you take the plunge, but with every page, you like it less and less, don't you find? What's more, we talk a lot about the strength of our playwriting, but how many really good plays are there? And you, Candice, how many really good plays will you write in your life? Maybe this is one of them. Maybe not. History will be the judge of that. *(She sighs.)* I took a big risk inviting you here, you know. So don't make me regret it. Today is a day of celebration. The season is coming to an end. And I will not let you spoil my finale. So have a seat and let's end this on a high note.

> *CANDICE sits down.*

I knew you could play fair if you wanted to.

> *INÈS sits down, picks up her notes, takes a sip of Scotch. Suddenly, in the silence before the show's theme music, the four sisters under the floor shout: "Please don't let us down! Save us from this eternal night!"*

Did you say something?

CANDICE   Yes. I said: nor will I let you spoil my opening night.

> *Blackness. Muted theme music.*

INÈS   *(shouting)* For the love of God, what is that?

Scene 6
The Surprise Visitor

> *Window to the Soul Publishing. Traces of smoke. The dustbin sits on its side. Next to it is a pile of ashes that DORIS and NIL are sifting through, DORIS with pleasure, NIL with guilt. In the background, her face and hands covered in ash, MILLI is reading from the page she ripped out of her manuscript.*

DORIS   Ashes to ashes...

NIL   Dust to dust. What a strange thrill! It's like a guilty pleasure.

DORIS   There's nothing to feel guilty about, Nil. It's a well-deserved treat after an honest day's work. *(beat)* It's a dirty job, but somebody's got to do it!

> *DORIS laughs. NIL follows suit. MILLI slips the sheet of paper in her pocket, gets up, and recites the poem while smearing ashes on her face.*

MILLI   Ashes to ashes, dust to dust
A sentiment akin to lust

Arouses me, in you I trust
The dark remains of my disgust
Ashes to ashes, dust to dust
The Phoenix rises from its fire
So must you, from an inked-stained snow
Falling from the wreckage of ruins below
Ashes to ashes, dust to dust
I chisel and you are my bust
I unleash and you are my thrust
I desire and you are my lust

DORIS and NIL applaud.

Octosyllables, ladies. I let myself go. Did you like it?

DORIS   It's a lovely piece of poetry, Milli. Ardent, lively. You surprise me.

NIL   Your recitation was convincing, sincere. And the subject matter: hotly topical.

MILLI   I thought I might write a collection.

DORIS   And where would you publish it? At Window to the Soul Publishing?

MILLI   Why not?

DORIS   You'd be in our hands, Milli. Do you think you'd make the cut?

NIL   Your poem is very beautiful, but I doubt that it's perfect.

DORIS   Let me clear that up right now. It's not perfect.

MILLI   What's wrong with my poem?

DORIS   Your octosyllables don't all work. For example, *(quickly counting the beats)* "Falling from the wreckage of ruins below" is ten syllables.

NIL   And to be perfectly frank, "ink-stained snow/falling from the wreckage of ruins below" is a virtual impossibility. Snow falls from up high, not from something on the ground. The image is weak.

DORIS   And, while we're at it, "wreckage of ruins" is a little redundant, Milli. *(putting her hands in the ashes)* You should know better.

MILLI   Stop it, all that can all be fixed!

NIL   And, unless I'm mistaken, you used "lust" twice as a rhyme.

MILLI   But that's of no…. Agh! What do you want her—me—to do with must, crust, or gust?

DORIS   That's not our problem.

MILLI   You're sadistic.

DORIS   Relentless.

NIL   Don't take it that way.

MILLI   How am I supposed to take it?

DORIS   You wouldn't want us to give you special treatment now, would you? We must take action before the publication, Milli. After, the harm is done. How many books are published because of self-indulgence or, worse, grant money? No, we will not partake in the "publish quick, forget quick" business. *(playing with the ashes)* We are not complacent nor are we accountable to anyone. Is that clear?

MILLI   *(after a beat)* Yes, Doris.

DORIS   Very well. Now, forget your poem and go get me the potting materials. *(to NIL)* Give her a hand, deary, would you?

NIL   Right away, Doris.

> *While DORIS puts the ashes in the dustbin, NIL and MILLI look through the crematorium.*

DORIS   Be careful not to mix up the jars. I've put a lot of time in that. It's my work. My life's work.

NIL   *(after a beat)* There aren't any jars left, Doris.

MILLI   No more jars.

DORIS   Impossible, dearies. I always have some on hand.

NIL   I'm telling you we have a jar problem.

DORIS   That's absurd! Check the whole office.

> *NIL goes to the desk and MILLI keeps looking in the crematorium.*

MILLI   Nil is right, Doris. We have a jar problem.

NIL   *(looking in the desk)* Affirmative. There aren't any here either.

DORIS   Keep looking, I tell you there are some!

MILLI   *(reading the labels on the jars)* "Hamlet," "Tartuffe," "Exit the King." Wow, Doris, you really went wild with the incinerator.

DORIS   I had a bout of insomnia. There was nothing else to do. I had to keep myself busy.

> *NIL reads the jar labels aloud and removes them from the shelf.*

NIL   "Medea," "The Vagina Monologues," "Three Sisters"…

> *NIL holds the jar containing* Three Sisters *close to her heart and then hides it in her pocket.*

MILLI   "Provincetown Playhouse," "The Orphan Muses," "Six Characters in Search of an Author"…

NIL "*Warsick Girls* by Candice de LaFontaine-Rotonde, 1996." "*Miss Bernice and the Bombs* by Candice de LaFontaine-Rotonde, 1997." *(holding both jars in her hands)* You burned the plays we published when I was editor?

MILLI You did that, Doris?

DORIS *(getting up)* Yes. So what? Frankly, they were mediocre.

NIL Doris, you're playing with fire.

> *Furious, NIL sets down the two jars containing CANDICE's plays. At the same time, we hear two knocks at the door.*

MILLI & NIL Doris?

DORIS Quiet!

> *Knocking at the door. All three freeze.*

DORIS, MILLI, & NIL Is someone there?

> *More knocking.*

NIL Someone's there. Without a doubt.

DORIS Who could it be?

MILLI The best way to find out is to open the door.

NIL *(panicking)* Open the door? But we never open the door to anyone. No one ever comes here. How do you know that the best thing to do is to open the door? What if it's better to leave it closed?

MILLI What do we do?

DORIS *(to NIL)* Did you talk to Urania this morning? *(NIL nods.)* None of my business! None of my concern! See where your sympathy visits to the basement and your talks with an underground eccentric get us?

NIL It might not be her.

DORIS Then who? Who? If it's not her, it's Calliope, Thalia, or Polyhymnia. How will I know which one it is? I haven't seen them for—

> *More knocking.*

Ahhhhhhh!

MILLI & NIL Doris, what do we do?

DORIS I don't know! The only people I could possibly recognize are you two. I wouldn't even know my own mother if I saw her!

> *The knocking is more insistent. MILLI goes to the door, her anguish palpable.*

MILLI I'm opening the door.

DORIS & NIL No, Milli! Wait! We don't know if—

Impatient knocking.

MILLI We have no other choice.

> *MILLI opens the door. With her bag slung over her shoulder, the SURPRISE VISITOR arrives, wearing an Arcimboldo-style mask.*

SURPRISE VISITOR Well, that took you long enough! It's very bad manners not to open the door straightaway, you know. And it indicates an extraordinary lack of openness, if you'll excuse the pun. Normally, such a lapse of time means that one is sleeping on the job or up to no good. You obviously weren't sleeping. So what were you plotting? This place is a mess and so are you. Black as soot. Not very lustrous for a publishing house. We're off to a bad start. And here I came with a proposition to make. Well, we'll have to see now. *(beat)* I'm thirsty. Are you going to offer me something to drink?

> *Silence.*

DORIS Urania? Calliope? Thalia? Polyhymnia? Is that you?

MILLI Have we met before?

NIL Who are you?

SURPRISE VISITOR What, no "Welcome to Window to the Soul Publishing"?

MILLI I feel like I know you.

SURPRISE VISITOR That could be.

MILLI There's something familiar about you.

DORIS Who are you?

SURPRISE VISITOR Do we ever know who we are? *(beat)* Actually, I'm a fan. I'm passionate about who you are. Or what you do. If you know what I mean.

DORIS You've heard of us?

SURPRISE VISITOR In the wonderful world of writing, you're known and renowned.

DORIS, MILLI, & NIL Really?

DORIS Known *and* renowned.

MILLI That's very flattering.

NIL And your name is…?

DORIS Yes, with whom are we dealing behind this vegetable disguise?

SURPRISE VISITOR Is it necessary to know to whom one is speaking? Is it not more important to know what's being said?

DORIS What one says depends on to whom one is speaking.

SURPRISE VISITOR   Oh! In that case, it means one is speaking with one's interests at heart.

DORIS   Who are you?

SURPRISE VISITOR   You're tenacious, Doris.

DORIS   If you know my name, I have the right to know yours. Since you seem in no hurry to show your face.

SURPRISE VISITOR   *(after a beat)* If it will reassure you. My name is Dominick. Dominick Parenteau-Lebeuf.

MILLI   I think I've heard that name before…

DORIS   And what do you do for a living, Dominick Parenteau-Lebeuf?

SURPRISE VISITOR   I'm a playwright.

NIL   Is that a pseudonym?

SURPRISE VISITOR   You've got to be kidding.

MILLI   Have you ever sent us your manuscripts?

SURPRISE VISITOR   I haven't had the pleasure. So, is someone going to offer me a drink or shall I fetch it myself?

MILLI   "Fetch." Oh, you *are* a writer.

DORIS   Coffee?

SURPRISE VISITOR   Water. *(pointing at her mask)* For my vegetables.

DORIS   Milli, go "get" Ms. Parenteau-Lebeuf a glass of water. And bring me a coffee while you're at it.

NIL   Me too, Milli.

MILLI   Why me?

DORIS   Because you're the one who's so enamoured with "fetching."

MILLI   But—

DORIS   Who's in charge here?

SURPRISE VISITOR   You heard your boss, Milli.

MILLI   Yes, madam. Right away, Doris.

SURPRISE VISITOR   And make it a tall glass, Milli. One in keeping with my stature.

MILLI   It's as though you were drinking it already, madam.

MILLI disappears.

DORIS   She obeys you better than she does me!

SURPRISE VISITOR I know how angst works. *(She winks at DORIS.)* The trick is to get them to drink from their own source. May I look around?

DORIS There's not much to see, you know. Window to the Soul Publishing is a modest enterprise.

SURPRISE VISITOR And there's just the three of you who work here?

NIL Well, actually, there used to be sev—

DORIS Yes, just the three of us. Us three. Working away. In this little room. Day in and day out. With sharpened pencils and sharpened minds.

SURPRISE VISITOR You seem a little tense, Doris, preoccupied. Is everything all right?

DORIS No, everything is fine. Yes, perfectly fine. Everything is perfect. I feel perfectly relaxed.

SURPRISE VISITOR If you say so. I've surprised you in the midst of your work, haven't I?

NIL *(looking at DORIS)* It's just that…. Yes, yes. This is part of our work.

The SURPRISE VISITOR goes to the crematorium. She picks up a jar at random and reads the label.

SURPRISE VISITOR "*The Burnt House* by Candice de LaFontaine-Rotonde, 1999."

DORIS Put that back please.

The SURPRISE VISITOR puts the jar back and picks up another. DORIS wants to stop her, but doesn't quite know how.

SURPRISE VISITOR "*Blessed Peace and Other Unattainable Ideals*, unfinished play by Candice de LaFontaine-Rotonde, 2000." *(She puts the jar back and picks up another.)* "*Enigmatic Afflictions*, unfinished play by Candice de LaFontaine-Rotonde, 2001." *(She puts the jar back.)* My my, this Candice woman is a house favourite. What is this?

DORIS The Crematorium of Rejected Plays.

SURPRISE VISITOR A library…

DORIS Of ashes, yes.

SURPRISE VISITOR How interesting!

NIL Do you think so?

DORIS It's my idea.

SURPRISE VISITOR What an original take on preserves.

NIL There was a stash of empty jars in the basement. Doris thought—

DORIS   Yes, so, um, when you... surprised us, we were just about to pot the ashes of our latest "rejection."

SURPRISE VISITOR   *(approaching the garbage can)* And what was this "rejection" called?

NIL   Chinese Portrait of an Impostor.

SURPRISE VISITOR   Was it really that bad?

DORIS   What do you think?

SURPRISE VISITOR   And what was it about?

NIL   Well, actually....

SURPRISE VISITOR   Actually, what?

DORIS   We... *(nervous laugh)* We didn't read it.

SURPRISE VISITOR   Didn't read it at all?

NIL   Only the first five pages, from the title page to the list of characters. It was quite... edifying.

SURPRISE VISITOR   What a strange method! Do you often burn plays without reading them?

DORIS   Almost never. It's just that, well, you see... *(She stomps on the floor to silence the four sisters, who have begun to protest.)* Sorry. The downstairs neighbours are noisy. So I was saying that the playwright—

NIL   Candice de LaFontaine-Rotonde.

DORIS   Made Milli, Nil, and me, Doris—

NIL   Characters.

DORIS   Can you visualize that? Us, her editors, as characters?

NIL   And maybe even impostors?

DORIS   Deary, please. Impostor is singular in the title.

NIL   Yes, but... individually... we—

DORIS   *(covering NIL's mouth with her hand)* Can you visualize it?

SURPRISE VISITOR   That's rather bold.

DORIS   Ridiculous and unacceptable, in my books. We are not characters!

NIL   *(removing DORIS's hand from her mouth)* Or impostors!

   NIL puts DORIS's hand back on her mouth.

DORIS   You're a playwright. Would you do such a thing to your editors?

SURPRISE VISITOR   Never. So when I surprised you, you were getting ready to pot the ashes of your latest rejection. *(touching DORIS's ash-smeared face and* *inspecting her finger)* You're going to be missing some. Can I give you a hand while I wait for my water?

DORIS That's very kind of you, but we're out of jars.

SURPRISE VISITOR *(pointing at the giant jar)* What about that one?

NIL *(removing DORIS's hand from her mouth)* Oh no. That's Doris's. It's for—

DORIS My anthology, my life's work. When the crematorium is full, we'll transfer all the ashes of the rejected plays into this giant vessel, and my work shall be complete.

SURPRISE VISITOR How creative! You'll invite me to the launch?

DORIS *(flattered)* With pleasure.

NIL That doesn't solve our jar problem.

SURPRISE VISITOR I may have something that will do the trick.

> *The SURPRISE VISITOR takes a small urn from her bag.*

DORIS What is that?

SURPRISE VISITOR My mother's ashes.

DORIS & NIL What?

SURPRISE VISITOR I haven't had the time to dispose of them. It wouldn't bother you to mix the ashes of your latest rejection with those of my mother, would it?

NIL It's… my condolences… so for you…

DORIS For me, ashes are ashes and what's dead is gone.

SURPRISE VISITOR Good. So shall we get potting?

NIL I… uh… I'll go "fetch" the funnel.

DORIS I'll "get" the label. What was her name?

SURPRISE VISITOR Just write "Mom." She liked it when I called her that.

> *DORIS writes the label. The SURPRISE VISITOR kneels down beside the dustbin. NIL comes back with the funnel.*

NIL *(kneeling down)* May I call you Dominick?

SURPRISE VISITOR *(touching her hair)* Why not?

> *NIL takes the SURPRISE VISITOR in her arms.*

NIL I'm sorry, Dominick. I don't know what came over me.

SURPRISE VISITOR Come on, Nil, let's get potting.

NIL Yes, Dominick, let's get potting.

The SURPRISE VISITOR places the funnel on the urn and NIL, holding the dustbin, pours out the ashes.

SURPRISE VISITOR *(whispering)*
Ashes to ashes, dust to dust
The Phoenix rises; so you must
Above your pile of ink-stained flakes
The black snowfall of your mistakes

DORIS, who has finished writing the label, lifts her head, stunned. NIL, who has just finished filling up the urn, does the same.

DORIS *(approaching the SURPRISE VISITOR)* What did you just say?

SURPRISE VISITOR I was reciting a poem. *(taking the label from DORIS and sticking it on the urn)* I doubt that you'd know it. It's one of mine.

DORIS And what is this poem of yours called?

SURPRISE VISITOR "Ashes to Ashes."

NIL Are you sure?

SURPRISE VISITOR Nil, please. A writer may have doubts about what she's writing, but not about what she's written.

She recites her poem. DORIS and NIL listen, spellbound.

Ashes to ashes, dust to dust
A sentiment akin to lust
Arouses me, in you I trust
The dark remains of my disgust
Ashes to ashes, dust to dust
The Phoenix rises; so you must
Above your pile of ink-stained flakes
The black snowfall of your mistakes
Ashes to ashes, dust to dust
Enter me in a wondrous gust
Ravish me, yes, set me on fire
O dark object of my desire
Ashes to ashes, dust to dust
I chisel and you are my bust
I unleash and you are my thrust
I demand and you are my must

I initially wrote a shorter version, but the octosyllables were flawed and some of the images were weak. I think I've fixed it now. *(closing the urn)* At least, I hope so.

DORIS faints and NIL rushes to her side. The SURPRISE VISITOR slips the urn into her bag. DORIS lies with her head in NIL's lap, stunned.

NIL Get a hold of yourself, Doris. We'll work this all out with Milli later.

SURPRISE VISITOR What's the matter, Doris? Poetry makes you weak in the knees?

DORIS No, I mean, yes. Your poem is magnificent. I'm just a little… preoccupied, Ms. Parenteau-Lebeuf.

SURPRISE VISITOR Just as I suspected.

DORIS You were right, Ms. Parenteau-Lebeuf.

NIL Dominick.

DORIS I'm preoccupied, Dominick. By intestinal problems.

SURPRISE VISITOR You have colon issues?

NIL Doris meant "internal" problems. A few small internal problems, right Doris?

DORIS Yes, that's it. I had a lapse there. A few small internal problems.

SURPRISE VISITOR No good publishing house can avoid them, Doris. In fact, a few small internal problems can be very hygienic. They allow a business to identify *(whispering)* little girls with dirt behind their ears.

DORIS Now that's an image that speaks to me. Are you a good manager, Dominick?

SURPRISE VISITOR I've made great progress lately.

NIL Could you give us… a hand?

SURPRISE VISITOR Gladly. That's what I came for. In fact, I have a proposition to make.

DORIS & NIL A proposition?

MILLI arrives with the coffee and water.

SURPRISE VISITOR Ah! The best things come to those who wait. Set that down, Milli.

MILLI Doris, What's going on?

NIL You're asking us?

MILLI sets down the drinks while NIL helps DORIS back up.

DORIS Come here, Milli.

MILLI What? I don't like the look on your face.

DORIS "Ashes to Ashes," Milli?

NIL You let yourself go, Milli?

DORIS And you wanted to write a collection. *(beat)* Plagiarist!

NIL Impostor!

MILLI No! I wanted to tell you, please!

NIL The author could sue you!

DORIS At least you put your flair for literary prodigies to use. You had the cheek to plagiarize one! Too bad you didn't steal her final draft. She corrected everything. Everything. There's nothing to fix. "Ashes to Ashes" is a perfect poem. Ah! It's not the kind of thing Candice de LaFontaine-Rotonde could have concocted.

MILLI What are you talking about, Doris? It *is* Candice's poem. I ripped it out from my copy of *Chinese Portrait of an Impostor*.

The three sisters turn to face the SURPRISE VISITOR, who has removed her mask.

SURPRISE VISITOR So, I wouldn't be capable of writing something like that?

DORIS *(after a stunned silence)* Candice?

MILLI Matrix?

NIL Mom?

SURPRISE VISITOR Yes, children?

DORIS This is a joke. This can't be. Where are we?

SURPRISE VISITOR At the theatre, deary.

DORIS, MILLI, & NIL *(taking note of the audience)* Ah!

SURPRISE VISITOR *(to MILLI and NIL, pointing at the giant jar)* You two, pot her.

DORIS What? You can't do that. You can't do that to me!

SURPRISE VISITOR It's my play. I can do as I please.

Darkness.

Scene 7
Deconstruction

Set of the TV show. Theme music. INÈS is frozen, one hand on her heart, the other holding her glass of Scotch. She is staring at CANDICE, who is wearing her Arcimboldo-style mask. End of theme music. Silence.

INÈS Dear, dear, dear, dear, dear, dear viewers.... Welcome back to *Chinese Portrait of an Artist* for this final segment of the season, which will end on a high note—yes?—with my guest, the playwrong… playwright…

She takes a sip of Scotch, surprised that she forgot to get rid of the glass before coming back on the air.

Would you look at that? I'm drinking on the air. Haven't seen that since the sixties. How time flies!

> *INÈS sets her glass down on the table. CANDICE picks it up and empties it in one gulp.*

CANDICE Ha! That's not mouthwash you're drinking, Inès. That's good. It takes the edge off. *(beat)* So, Inès, where were we?

> *Beat.*

INÈS Before the break, I didn't have the time to ask you: if you were a profession?

CANDICE You'd know better than I would. I just got here.

INÈS Just answer the question.

CANDICE What composure! You're not easily flummoxed. I admire you. That's why, to answer your question, I'd have to say: the host of an arts program. The stakes are high. It has a kamikaze side. I like that.

INÈS Answer the question, Candice.

CANDICE Ah. It's *her* answer that interests you. Well I'm sure if she were here, she'd say: a playwright.

INÈS *(after a beat)* *Your* play, *your* characters, *your* profession… *(getting worked up)* It's no fun if you're everything you want to be!

CANDICE What a perfectly appalling thing to say.

INÈS *(trying to cover her gaffe)* I mean in the context of *Chinese Portrait*—

CANDICE But the worst thing is, you're right!

INÈS Really?

CANDICE Really. Authenticity is such a bore. Such a dreary display. No, what's interesting is the performance. *(slapping her forehead)* It's so simple, really. Down with reality. Down with truth. Long live the game and the players. So I'm playing, Inès. I'm playing. You ask me, "If I were a profession?" and I answer, "The host of an arts program." That's playing. *(beat)* From the looks of it, Candice really sent you spinning. I should have been more insistent. To do this interview. With you. From the beginning. And I almost made it, but in the dressing room, I cracked. Candice got the upper hand.

> *For a moment, INÈS is speechless.*

INÈS Who are you?

CANDICE I thought you'd never ask! *(extending her hand)* I'm her right-hand woman. Like a right-hand man, only a woman. Doer of dirty work. That's why I'm here. Which is pretty rare. Usually, I'm confined to her room. In reality, I work in fiction. *(She mimes typing on a computer.)* Does that answer your question?

> INÈS, *sitting in her chair, terrified, no longer knows how to react.*

That said, I'm starting to wonder why she summoned me. You're so calm, sitting there in your chair. So attentive. Who could possibly want to torture you? You look more like someone who needs to be wrapped up in a blanket and warmed with a fire. *(beat)* But here I am going on and on, and you have a portrait to do, a show to finish, and maybe even personal projects, what do I know? So, you want to end it on a high note? I'm ready.

> *Beat. Suddenly the music for "Happy Anniversary" starts playing. A cake with five candles arrives from the ceiling or the wings.*

INÈS Oh! Thank you. How thoughtful! Thank you. Thank you, thank you, thank you… dear viewers, dear members of the crew. It's with heartfelt emotion and, above all, a boundless, infinite gratitude that I blow today… that I blow out today, these five… *(beat, a sigh)* Oh, I don't know anymore.

CANDICE You're not the only one.

> *CANDICE removes her mask. They look at each other without saying a word. Then CANDICE leaves.*
>
> *Silence.*

INÈS Well. Dear viewers, you are cordially invited to the Velvet Vervet Cafe to see *Chinese Portrait of an Impostor* by Candice de LaFontaine-Rotonde. The show premieres tonight and is up every night this month. *(beat)* Well, that concludes our final show of *Chinese Portrait of an Artist*, your arts program. I'm Inès Lusine wishing you… wishing you… oh, whatever. Until next time. *(jingle, silence)* I'm Inès Lusine. *(beat)* Inès Lusine. *(beat)* Inès Lusine. Inès… Lusine… I… nès… I…

> *INÈS blows out the candles. Spotlight on the manuscript lying on the table. Darkness.*

Scene 8
Torture

> *Window to the Soul Publishing. The crematorium is empty, as are most of the jars. DORIS is gagged and buried up to her chin in the giant jar, which is full to the brim with ashes. MILLI and NIL each empty a small jar into the giant jar. With one hand in the form of a gun and the other holding her mask, the SURPRISE VISITOR supervises the operation.*

SURPRISE VISITOR The extermination camp has just been liberated by the tactical intervention force, brilliantly orchestrated by General Candice de LaFontaine-Rotonde *(holding the mask like Hamlet holds his skull)* with the support of her right-hand woman, Dominick Parenteau-Lebeuf. Thank you, comrade, *(kissing the mask)* but I shan't be needing you anymore.

The four sisters under the floor shout "Bravo!" and jump for joy. The SURPRISE VISITOR follows suit. MILLI and NIL pick up the last two jars, which they empty into the giant jar.

(looking at the "army of jars") Ah! My jars. The ones from when I was a baby. If only I'd known they could be recycled to such hateful ends. I used to imagine I had a different jar in my belly for each kind of food. When my jars were empty, I'd eat whatever I could get my hands on. If I came across a turnip, I'd swallow it whole. If I came across my children, *(looking at MILLI and NIL)* I'd take a big bite out of them. *(chasing them)* Yum! Yum! Yum!

MILLI and NIL run away, shouting. They set their empty jars down with the others and take refuge near the giant jar.

So, my wretched creatures, all finished? Sure you got them all? *(She takes the jar marked* Three Sisters *from NIL's pocket.)* What have we here?

NIL *(her hands joined in prayer)* Please, no! Not *Three Sisters*!

SURPRISE VISITOR Double agent! Traitor!

NIL I'm weak…. Teach me how to be strong… I beg you…

SURPRISE VISITOR You beg me? *(She slaps NIL across the face.)* Go empty this. *(while NIL follows the order)* And then go sit and think about you've done. That'll teach you where ambivalence gets you. Your head between your legs. That's an order!

NIL puts her head between her legs. MILLI cries out.

Voila! *(pointing to the empty jars)* Five years of cruel disservice. Our Doris didn't take her job lightly, did she? It's a real crematory oven in here. "My anthology, my life's work." *Mein Kampf*! Let's see if she's come around to a more noble sentiment.

The SURPRISE VISITOR removes her gag.

DORIS You'll regret this!

SURPRISE VISITOR That's highly unlikely, Doris.

DORIS You're nothing but a—

The SURPRISE VISITOR puts her gag back on.

SURPRISE VISITOR And to think you used to be my favourite. But I'm sure the last thing you want to do is sift through the past. That would be far too… Chekhovian.

DORIS's swears are muffled.

(removing her gag) You were saying?

DORIS *(with difficulty)* You could have been one of the greats…

SURPRISE VISITOR That's not for you to decide.

DORIS   But instead you're just a failed writer using us as a way out of your literary misery.

The SURPRISE VISITOR spits in her face.

SURPRISE VISITOR   Actually, I quite like hearing your muffled shrieks. It's like a postmodern swan song. It's… beautiful. *(She turns to MILLI.)* Come here.

DORIS   Don't do it, Milli!

SURPRISE VISITOR   I said come here.

MILLI goes toward the SURPRISE VISITOR. DORIS chokes. NIL lifts her head ever so slightly to watch the torture.

Thanks for the glass of water, Milli. I know someone who could use a sip, but too bad for her *(drinking the water in one gulp)* it's all gone. Now… *(putting down the glass and stroking MILLI's cheek)* angst. You can never get your fill, can you, my little junkie? Even Doris can't keep you in full supply. Stealing unfinished poems to get your high. How pathetic! But fret not, dear addict; in this bag, I've got the dose that's going to give you the trip of your life. *(She takes a Pear of Anguish from her bag.)* Do you know what this is? *(MILLI shakes her head.)* That's like the ocean not knowing what salt tastes like! *(She slaps MILLI across the face.)* This is a Pear of Anguish, you fool.

MILLI   A Pear of Anguish…

SURPRISE VISITOR   Do you want one?

MILLI   *(with desire)* Do I want one?

SURPRISE VISITOR   Then open your mouth. Mommy has a delicious pear purée for you.

DORIS   Milli, don't do it!

MILLI opens her mouth. The SURPRISE VISITOR brings the Pear of Anguish to her mouth like a little airplane; every time she says, "A bite for…" she puts the Pear of Anguish in MILLI's mouth and then takes it right out. DORIS has trouble expressing herself because of the ashes.

SURPRISE VISITOR   A bite for Mommy…

DORIS   I'm the one who gave you your greatest thrills!

SURPRISE VISITOR   A bite for Doris…

DORIS   Shut your mouth and give her the anxiety attack of her life, Milli, do you hear me?

NIL   We can't, Doris…. It's Mommy…

SURPRISE VISITOR   Lift your head and say that again, Nil.

DORIS   You are the cornerstone of the arsenal, Milli.

NIL   *(getting up)* I'm the cornerstone! I am!

DORIS   Shut up, Nil!

NIL   We can't use her weapons against her! She's our mommy!

DORIS   Of course we can!

SURPRISE VISITOR   A bite for Nil…

NIL   When in doubt, you've got to listen to your mommy.

DORIS   For the love of God, would you be quiet! Can't you see that I'm trying to—

DORIS chokes again.

SURPRISE VISITOR   Do you hear that, my dearies? Doris wants to muzzle you. Show her that you won't let just anyone control you. Go on, show her!

NIL   *(shouting)* Mommy! Mommy!

MILLI   *(shouting)* I want my Pear of Anguish! I want my Pear of Anguish!

SURPRISE VISITOR   Get them to drink from their own source, Doris. That's the secret. And a bite for Milli!

The SURPRISE VISITOR forces MILLI to put her fist in her mouth. MILLI looks like a mute, open-mouthed statue. She can only express herself with her eyes.

NIL   *(frozen)* What should we do, Mommy? What, Mommy, what should we do? *(ad lib, in whispers)*

DORIS   You can't just get rid of me. You'll have to push me up… like a little rock… and down I'll come tumbling… and you'll push me back up… and down I'll come tumbling and on and on and on… until one day… I'll crush you…

SURPRISE VISITOR   Yes, my dear Doris, but for the time being, we're at the theatre, and I'll have the pleasure of watching you die every night for a month.

DORIS   You forget that… every night… I'll rise from my ashes…

SURPRISE VISITOR   I know, but there's nothing like a traumatic event to change the course of things. *(beat)* Nil… your sisters…

NIL   Yes?

SURPRISE VISITOR   Go get them and bring them up here.

NIL   What about Doris?

SURPRISE VISITOR   That's none of your business. That's none of your concern. Go!

NIL *(saluting)* At your command, Mommy! *(She runs off. We hear her shouting in the stairwell.)* Urania! Calliope! Thalia! Polyhymnia!

In the office of the publishing house, all is calm.

DORIS I'm ready to hear what you have to say. What was your... proposition?

The SURPRISE VISITOR takes the urn with the ashes of "Mom" and "Chinese Portrait of an Impostor" from her bag and empties it into the giant jar.

SURPRISE VISITOR All you had to do was read the play, deary. It was all written down. Every last detail. Right up to the end.

The SURPRISE VISITOR sets down the urn and puts the lid on the giant jar.

DORIS Nooooooooooooooooo!

Silence.

SURPRISE VISITOR And Doris the perfectionist disappears into the ashes of contemporary and classic playwriting. And into the ashes of her grandmother, Claudette Rotonde. The Surprise Visitor blows a goodbye kiss to the jar. She then turns to Milli and says: "I am taking control of this house. It's not a proposition. It's a declaration. Tell the others what you've seen." The Surprise Visitor goes to the door—you can hear the sound of footsteps coming up from the basement and women talking and laughing—and then she leaves Window to the Soul Publishing. In fact, she leaves her own play.

The SURPRISE VISITOR disappears. Fade out on the office of Window to the Soul Publishing. Darkness.

Epilogue

Dressing room. The hands of the MAKEUP ARTIST are resting on the back of the chair, where CANDICE sits, lost in thought.

MAKEUP ARTIST There. What do you think? *(beat)* Candice?

CANDICE Huh?

MAKEUP ARTIST What were you thinking about?

CANDICE Do you have a few hours?

MAKEUP ARTIST *(after a beat)* So, do you like it?

CANDICE It's perfect. *(She touches her face.)* I feel more... less... thank you.

MAKEUP ARTIST It's nothing. It's my job.

Silence.

CANDICE Do you think we find our way in the end?

MAKEUP ARTIST   I only know one way in and one way out. Okay, off you go now.

CANDICE   Will you come see my play? No. Wait. Don't say anything. You don't like theatre.

MAKEUP ARTIST   Break a leg, Candice.

Only CANDICE's face is lit, like at the end of the prologue. We hear the seven sisters whispering, "Break a leg, Candice! Break a leg, Candice!"

Blackout.

The end.

Rock, Paper, Jackknife...
(Roche, papier, couteau...)

by Marilyn Perreault

translated by Nadine Desrochers

Introduction to
Rock, Paper, Jackknife... (*Roche, papier, couteau...*)

The moving beauty of *Rock, Paper, Jackknife...* comes from the intricacy of its words, the humanity of its adolescent characters, and the terrible truths of the story it represents. It is a tragedy of universal significance that is happening in the lives of the young. The teens of the play take us into the experience of forced emigration when their country of origin has exploded in violence, their parents are dead, their crossing was unbelievably difficult, and they find themselves in exile in a new country where they do not know the language, they are without means, and the reception in the community is one of distance and distrust. Along with these horrendous challenges, the teens make us confront the experiences and feelings of adolescence in a northern community—it could be Inuit or First Nations—where despair and boredom are rampant. In this suffering community, the sparks of friendship and meaning in life have been extinguished, even for its own young people. As in all tragedies, the adolescent characters of the play are victims of forces against which they struggle in vain, lucid playthings of social injustice and an implacable destiny, as well as agents of their own fate. Right to the end, we share the teens' hunger for love, a place to belong, a language to express themselves and communicate with others, and a life with hope. Right to the end, we wish to believe with them and their fragile teacher that, as their grasp of the challenges of their situation grows, this can happen. However, when the play ends and we realize that the finale was already anticipated in both the play's title and the opening scene, it becomes clear that the characters' struggle was futile from the start.

Rock, Paper, Jackknife... addresses the human challenges faced by refugees and makes palpable the alienation and threats of violence produced by exile—the insurmountable condition of always being an outsider, loss of homeland and culture, loss of language, solitude, financial insecurity, hostility of physical, social, and mental landscapes. Simultaneously, *Rock, Paper, Jackknife...* represents life in small communities in this country's *farthest north*, where poverty, addiction, suicide and other forms of violence, hopelessness, and despair, reflected in the icy landscape, are too frequently the order of the day. The young people in the play, who have for support only each other and their alcoholic and ill-equipped, although well-meaning, teacher, find themselves obliged to face simultaneously the devastating consequences of both forced emigration and the distress of northern communities. Perreault confines the characters on stage into a dingy space, from which they are not meant to escape. When they do get out, they are poorly equipped to handle the cold physical and moral environment. The desperate search for the right words to express meaning, love, security, and a place to belong is movingly represented in the play by two books. Seventeen-year-old Taymore, an intelligent young man who was well educated during his previous life, has lapsed into silence. He exercises his control over the group through rough physical means, and he conveys his thoughts to his twelve-year-old sister, Ali, who expresses them for him. Taymore clings to and pores over a telephone book from a large southern megacity and a dictionary, both of which were brought to the community by their teacher Mielke when she moved north. The significance of these books is open to interpretation. However, for me, they are the symbolic representation of the community and its language in which Taymore longs to find his place. Ironically, they remain for him empty, symbolic shells of an inaccessible home.

The play depicts the arrival in "an undefined Farthest North" of a pathetic group of young people ranging in age from five to seventeen, who have just spent a month in the dark dankness of a freighter container. The children have come from the harsh country of Harshenia, a fictitious land suggestive of eastern Europe. They have arrived in a place where life is no less harsh. The play takes place in a small warehouse, converted into a makeshift classroom and sleeping area. The cold and stormy space outside is felt to imprison in its inhospitable and menacing grip those inside the classroom. They are confined; yet there is nowhere else that is safe to go. The isolated community responded to their unexpected and threatening arrival by improvising an opportunity for them to learn the local language so they could be quickly assimilated and brought to work in the mine. Whenever the mine is mentioned it is represented as a dangerous place, a place for death. It is presumably an enterprise for the extraction of valuable minerals brought to the community by outside investors seeing an opportunity for profit. The poorly paid local workers who go down in the mine fortify their courage using substances such as alcohol or glue. To the end of preparing the teens for life in the impoverished community and for work in the mine, Mielke, who speaks the children's language thanks to her ethnic heritage, has been relieved of her duties at the local clinic and assigned to them as teacher. She commits herself to teaching them the language and the culture and affirms on Day 1: "I've adopted the mission of turning these four little identities into true-and-through Northans." Until the arrival of the teens, Mielke has been functioning in the community, although with difficulty. Her fear of the outside world and her alcoholism are signs of the inner turmoil that already played havoc with her life. Meeting the teens from the harsh country of her family's origins and communicating with them has unleashed in her memories of the violence that traumatized her childhood. She remains caught in dread at the end of the play.

Rock, Paper, Jackknife... covers a period of thirty-two days moving from late summer to fall, during which time the arctic days grow shorter and stormier. The play begins with the final day while the wind is howling outside and something is banging at the classroom door, as Mielke listens to a mysterious recording made by Taymore. In the recording Taymore is, ironically, promising to return. After this short opening scene, the action of the play flashes back to the past, to the day the teens emerged from the container, dazzled by the unfamiliar sun and "covered with everything a body can spew out with the force of nature." The youngest character, Ali, was dragging the lifeless body of her small brother, who died during the crossing. The freighter that brought the children also brought an illicit load of particularly strong vodka, to which, we learn, the people in the community are addicted, as is Mielke. Bottles empty and full are a constant accompaniment throughout the dramatic action.

During the first part of the month covered by the play's events, much is learned about the traumatized adolescents, two girls and two boys, each unique in character and behaviour, each having their own survival strategy. Their interactions and verbal jousts with Mielke dramatize their fears, the absence of affection and security in their lives, their inability to communicate directly, their claustrophobia, and their distorted relation with their sexed bodies and the desires they stir. Their eyes are blank and their words ring strangely hollow. Their restless need to escape impairs their ability to learn. Each in her or his own way exhibits the spontaneous instinct to fight or flight that so frequently characterizes severely traumatized children who have endured sustained abuse in their lives. Despite their psychic wounds, they initially give some evidence of an ability to adapt to their new situation. They show a desire to relate to Mielke, to learn the letters and words of the new language she is trying to teach them, to think of a future with a job in the mine. The usually silent and violent Taymore haltingly expresses through the use of a tape recorder nostalgia for a time of lost joy and life with parents. The urgent regret heard in his voice and shared by the others moves them to a state of panic.

The moment when this occurs, along with thirteen-year-old Nox's frenetic search for sexual gratification approaching the point of rape and fifteen-year-old Sola's epileptic seizure, signal a turning point in their lives. Violence, death, and addiction grow increasingly intrusive as their relations with the community and their understanding of themselves and each other deteriorate. The bottom of the mine where the ashes of Ali's younger brother have already been placed becomes an increasing obsession as the site of death. The outside community grows fearful and considers Mielke and the new arrivals responsible for the deaths and misfortunes with which they are dealing. The characters remaining inside the classroom are threatened, persecuted, and ostracized. The Harshes are not wanted by the community. A plane is coming to take them away. As events of the play move starkly toward their conclusion, the suffering of the characters becomes more and more gripping. The significance of the play's title, representing a transformation from the childhood game of rock, paper, scissors to rock, paper, jackknife, reveals its awful meaning.

Rock, Paper, Jackknife... gives dramatic representation to a grim story that is close enough to reality in many parts of the world, including Canada, to send chills down one's spine. Its immediacy is rendered that much more compelling by the language Perreault gives her characters. Their words and sentences are distorted in ways that evoke the kinds of mistakes made by children when they imitate and try to capture the meaning of adult expression. Their transformation of received clichés, social formulas, and common sayings is particularly telling. This fanciful, ludic play with words, which is sustained throughout the text, creates the impression of taking us into the minds of these alienated and isolated young people. It also has the powerful effect of awakening adult imaginations so that audiences, stirred to greater awareness in an effort to understand what the "usses" are saying, will see intimately and differently the tragedy in the lives of children and adolescents whose voices are not usually well heard and understood, particularly if their first language and culture are not the dominant ones. An example among so many of Perreault's poetic originality and mastery, using the most everyday of words, can be heard in the following lines spoken by Ali early in *Roche, papier, couteau...* where she explains to Mielke why they will not allow themselves to be locked into the classroom and insists that they will listen to her only if she understands that. She makes amusing yet telling errors in French:

> Les intérieurs font la peur dans nous, la Madame. On reste, on fait l'accord de ça; mais faut toujours nous laisser voir dans le dehors si les nuages fendent le ciel [...] On voit bien que vous avez les deux yeux dans la même bottine; vous pouvez faire le repos de votre bouche" (p. 12).

One smiles, with complicity and some measure of discomfort, at Ali's charmingly idiosyncratic use of words to introduce the group to their new teacher. Nadine Desrochers's virtuosic translation captures the earnest yet alien tone, the mistakes and the playfulness of these words, while finding or inventing alternative expressions and images:

> Interiors make fear inside of us, Miss-Miss. We stay, we make the agreement of that, but we have to be able to see in the out-there if the clouds are still piercing the sky [...] We can tell you've got your peepers in a knot, so you can take a breather for your mouth (Day 2).

The deceptively infantile words capture so movingly in both French and English the sustained disjunction between the characters' reality as children and the tragedy of the unmitigated horror in their lives. One hopes that the sprightly and multi-layered dialogue, that moves the action forward and captures the swell of emotions and confusion contained within the characters while bringing into full view the hopelessness produced in the lives of many by practices in today's society, offers fresh ways of listening to adolescent voices whose desperate circumstances make suicide appear attractive.

About Marilyn Perreault

Since graduating from the acting program of the Option-Théâtre at the Cégep de Saint-Hyacinthe, Marilyn Perreault has been pursuing a dual career, as an actor and as a playwright. She is the author of *Les Apatrides*, *Roche, papier, couteau...*, and *Britannicus Now*. As a dialogue writer, she has contributed to two of the Théâtre de la Dame de Coeur's productions, *Les dinosaures ne savent pas lire* and *La montagne qui marche*. *Rock, Paper, Jackknife...* is the first of her plays to be translated into English. As an actress, she has performed in many of DynamO Théâtre's productions, including *Mur-Mur*, *Lili*, and *Faux Départs*. In 2005, she was nominated for a Masque for her performance in a leading role as the character H. Da! in *Faux Départs*. She has also acted in *Les Apatrides*, *La Cadette*, and *La Robe de Gulnara* for Théâtre I.N.K., *8 femmes* for Productions Jean-Bernard Hébert, *La Migration des oiseaux invisibles* for La Compagnie Mathieu, François et les autres... and *À quelle heure le punch?* at the Théâtre St-Sauveur. Since 2002, she has been co-director, with Annie Ranger, of Théâtre I.N.K., a theatre company whose work is based in imagery and movement.

Between 1997 and 1999 Perreault headed up a project to introduce physical theatre to young people in Puvirnituq and Kangiqsujuaq (Nunavik) in collaboration with the Québec Ministry of Education, Section de la "Coordination des affaires autochtones," and the Kativik School Board.

Published Works by Marilyn Perreault

Les Apatrides (2005). Montréal: Dramaturges Éditeurs.

Roche, papier, couteau... (2007). Carnières, Belgium: Lansman Éditeur.

Roche, papier, couteau... was first produced by Théâtre I.N.K. and presented at the Théâtre d'Aujourd'hui's Salle Jean-Claude Germain in Montréal from November 6 to November 24, 2007, with the following company:

Iourded	Éloi ArchamBaudoin
Lonely	Catherine-Amélie Côté
Nox	David-Alexandre Després
Mielke	Eve Gadouas
Ali	Annie Ranger

Directed by Marc Dumesnil
Set design by Vano Hotton
Lighting design by Martin Gagné
Sound design by Martin Marier
Costume design by Sarah Balleux
Assistant direction and stage management by Emanuelle Langelier
Technical direction by Nicolas Fortin
Artistic direction by Annie Ranger and Marilyn Perreault

...

Rock, Paper, Jackknife... was first produced in Montréal in October 2009 by Talisman Theatre and presented at the Centaur Theatre as part of the Brave New Looks initiative, with the following company:

Ali	Stefanie Buxton
Nox	Rockne Corrigan
Sola	Lucinda Davis
Mielke	Julie Tamiko Manning
Taymore	Alex McCooeye

Directed by Emma Tibaldo
Set design by Lyne Paquette
Lighting design by David Perreault Ninacs
Sound design by Michael Leon
Costume design by Fruzsina Lanyi
Movement design by Rasili Botz
Stage management by Bonnie More
Publicity and marketing by John Custodio
School outreach coordination by Elysha Enos
Assistant direction and teacher's guide coordination by Jana van Geest
Technical direction by Tanner Harvey
Set building by Jean Letendre, Martin Berry
Costume assistance by Fanny Volcsanszky
Graffiti art by Lucas Ferguson-Sharp

Translation dramaturgy provided by Playwrights' Workshop Montréal
Artistic direction for Centaur Theatre by Roy Surette

...

Roche, papier, couteau... was remounted February 2 to 13, 2010 at the Salle Fred-Barry of Montréal's Théâtre Denise-Pelletier.

Author's Note and Thanks

I would first like to say a huge thank you to Jeannie, Susie, Mary, Eva, Denise, Alacie (and those I may be forgetting) for making me discover a Far North country I had dreamed of without knowing it.

The warmest of thanks to my friend and ally Nadine Desrochers, who has achieved, with this translation of *Rock, Paper, Jackknife...*, a meticulous work of Herculean proportions, an accomplishment that speaks to both her literary and human sensibilities. Thank you to Louise H. Forsyth, Annie Gibson of Playwrights Canada Press, as well as to the Canada Council for the Arts for giving the young author that I am the opportunity to be discovered in English. Thank you to Roy Surette of the Centaur Theatre and to Emma Tibaldo and Lyne Paquette of Talisman Theatre for giving the play such a beautiful English production in the fall of 2009. Thanks to Émile Lansman for the French publication; a thousand thanks once more to CEAD; to Annie Ranger, forever my partner in crime, and our Théâtre I.N.K.; Marie-Thérèse Fortin and the Théâtre d'Aujourd'hui; Pierre Rousseau and the Théâtre Denise-Pelletier; Playwrights' Workshop Montréal; Marcelle Dubois and her Festival du Jamais Lu; Michèle Rouleau and Claude De Grandpré at the Festival de Théâtre à l'Assomption; Gill Champagne and the Théâtre du Trident; José Pliya and the team at ETC_Caraïbe; and to the devoted actors and directors who all worked so well on the public readings and productions of this script.

Translator's Note and Thanks

I would like to first acknowledge the support of the Canada Council for the Arts. I would like to thank Talisman Theatre and Émile Lansman for accepting Marilyn's choice of translator; Louise H. Forsyth for choosing this beautiful piece for her anthology, and Annie Gibson and Blake Sproule at Playwrights Canada Press for all of the backstage work; the Centaur Theatre and Roy Surette for taking a chance on eighteen pages; Playwrights' Workshop Montréal for giving me the opportunity to see that we could, indeed, make music; the wonderful production team, Emma Tibaldo, Lyne Paquette, and all the designers, who made such stunning work of bringing the play to life; our amazing actors, Alex, Julie, Lucinda, Stefanie, and Rockne, for the elegance with which they crammed this Harsh language down their throats; Éloi ArchamBaudoin for his insightful, respectful notes; my family and friends for their unwavering faith in me; Karen Fricker, to whom I turned for counsel when I first got the call and who reassured me that I could absolutely do this; and Marilyn, for the friend that she is, the plays that she writes, and the laughter she brings to all that she does.

Characters

Mielke, woman in her thirties
Ali, young girl, twelve years old
Nox, young boy, thirteen years old
Sola, young woman, fifteen years old
Taymore, young man, seventeen years old

Setting

A warehouse, converted into a makeshift classroom. Enormous lamps hang from the ceiling. Somewhere, a rickety clock: it positions the events in the time of days. Around this warehouse-school, we can imagine a town, ghostly in an undefined Farthest North. It is cold and the hours of daylight, fairly normal at the beginning of the play, will shorten with the onset of fall. A second area is alluded to (and may be visible or not): outside this classroom is where the lurking occurs. A hard-to-reach window provides an uneasy access to this outside world.

ROCK, PAPER, JACKKNIFE...

Day 32 — 10:15 a.m.
Fall

MIELKE is sitting next to an improvised bed, her head bent over a tape recorder. There are childrens' desks scattered haphazardly throughout the warehouse-school. Bottles of an unknown intoxicant litter the floor. A tempestuous wind howls outside, and an unseen object can be heard banging against the classroom door. The sound of a plane taking off outside...

VOICE OF TAYMORE ON THE TAPE RECORDER   I will return—

MIELKE rewinds the tape.

I will return—

MIELKE   What? Speak again to me.

MIELKE rewinds the tape a second time.

VOICE OF TAYMORE ON THE TAPE RECORDER   I will return—

MIELKE   Oh. I was mistaken in my listening.... And the storm in the out-there that won't stop draping its snow.... It knocks at my door as though I really might give it an answer.

MIELKE picks up a very heavy heap of blankets and goes to the door. There are bloodstains on the blankets and on her clothing.

VOICE OF TAYMORE ON THE TAPE RECORDER   I will return—

Blackout.

Day 1 — 9:45 a.m.
End of Summer

MIELKE is alone in the classroom. She rearranges a desk or two, doesn't quite know where to position herself in this environment.

MIELKE   I've only met them once, they had just come out of the freighter. Their compass was out of tune with the north, and the flat-footedness of dry land made them vomit all over. They looked at the sun and seemed surprised to find that life still existed... for the sun. They were covered with everything a body can spew out with the force of nature. *(beat)* I was told they're doing better.... They managed to eat... *(beat)* A strange postcard they painted, with this country's sub-zero beaches in the background. The youngest of the four was dragging what we thought was a big teddy bear. From afar. We were wrong.

A little boy, it was, with no more breath in him than an apple in a still life. *(beat)* They will be here soon.

In their mouths lies the tongue of my ancestors and I… I am the only one in this village to know what it says. That's… that's why I'm here. I—usually—I hand out help at the clinic, not lessons. I… I have Harsh origins. It's because of my father. He graduated from childhood in Harshenia and the war exiled him to the south of this continent, where each new city gets bigger than the other. I—for my part, I couldn't live there. I came to survive here, after… after my parents' "accident." But… *(beat)* it's fine, here. When the snow plummets, the hands of minutes and horrors don't care about the order in which they're supposed to dance. Each day brings a slice of eternity… and that's just fine. Up here, we don't self-interrogate. *(beat)* Soon, they will be here.

These four young aliens, we… we can't report their presence to the governance because they arrived at the same time as a whole shipment of vodgur. Vodgur: a "light-years-percent-more-proof" version of vodka. Absolutely prohibited, but our people here can't live without it. Their efficiency at work depends on the drink that loiters around the gates of the not-so-artistic galleries of the mine. We… we've lived through the apocalypse a few times recently: the vodgur vessel put too much lateness in the moment of its arrival in the bay. When the captain finally dropped anchor and saw what lay in his hold… the rancid little boy and the other four who had sort of lost track of life… he took a step back, forwent the layover, left the five little scraps and the vodgur on the icy beach, and… and went to curl up in the arms of the sea with his big boat. Not responsible, he said. He won't be back so soon…. Now that—that puts panic in the village's near future. *(beat)* They should be here.

And the days played peekaboo with three suns before the aliens spoke again. Woe onto me who understood what they were saying. The people of the village turned to me. There aren't enough workers in the mine: vodgur has wreaked havoc in the winter without sunlight, which is now behind us. They need noses to the grindstone. They know I don't want to look again upon the cruel South and its sky-scratching buildings. *(beat)* I've adopted the mission of turning these four little identities into true-and-through Northans. That's for in case the governance agent should come round the rosy and fall into an investigation. Not that he comes much, nowadays…. We… we are quite alone amongst ourselves… here.

> NOX, SOLA, TAYMORE, and ALI *come in slowly, their quartet an almost eerie presence at the back of the classroom. They are wearing second-hand coats that are much too large for them.* TAYMORE *is the clan's silent chief. There is something wild in the way they consider* MIELKE.

They are here… armed with the stare they've been wearing for six days. Four pairs of eyes with no external imprints on their retinas. Irises constantly turned inwards, where it's comfortable, where it's the realm of the familiar, and where there was warmth once. They are always cold. We've installed big lights above their desks. Maybe one day, they'll be done incubating and the small mountain of fear inside them will melt a little... *(beat)* Okay. Introductions. *(to the four)* Hello. My nam—

The four bolt from the classroom.

Well. That was... predictable. We'll, uhhm... we'll try again tomorrow.

Blackout.

Day 2 — 10:30 a.m.
End of Summer

The four kids are in the classroom. They are waiting. MIELKE is not there. Rather, she is observing them from the window while trying to stay out of sight. She is holding a bottle of vodgur. She is drinking. A little.

NOX *I* wants to leave, Taymore.

TAYMORE ...

NOX Taymore, *I* wants to leave.

MIELKE *(outside, to herself)* The fear is there of that which I do not know. That's why I'm not so big on big cities. That's why I traded the megacity for this little village of five hundred ghouls stuck between forever and ever. Here, usually, you know all of those held inside the village. *(a little laugh)* I have to go in, not lose my job. *(beat)* Relax a little. *(A little sip. A grimace.)* Not too much.

NOX *I* says that the Miss-Miss won't come here inside this day. So *I* is leaving.

NOX stands up hurriedly, ready to leave. TAYMORE sits him back down firmly. NOX sees MIELKE looking into the classroom.

MIELKE *(outside, to herself)* Besides, in the megacities, I got fed up of hearing the waiters ask: "Will someone be joining you, miss?" No, sir. Many people think they know me, but I... I... don't know anyone.

NOX *(softer)* The Miss-Miss is here in the out-there; *I* thinks she's talking to herself...

MIELKE *(outside, to herself)* Before them, I knew, one by one, all the people who live here. I am the one who arrives at either end of their lives, the one who helps them be born and/or die... often...

NOX *I* tells again, for those of you who have shut your ears with deafness: the Miss-Miss will soon not know how to walk a straight line. *(He imitates someone who drinks, and laughs.)*

MIELKE But those four… they bother me, being here, scuffing up my well-learnt landscape. A whole day, already…. They should know the first letters of this place's alphabet.

NOX *I* says that the Miss-Miss puts her eyes on us like a lens box of surveillance…

> *NOX hoists himself up to the window and comes face to face with MIELKE. She disappears. NOX laughs. TAYMORE puts him back in his place.*

I says we here are in the observations, but we here don't know what's in the experiment. We here are stuck. *I* doesn't like it. Make some words, *I* hates making the monologues.

TAYMORE …

ALI Taymore says shut your mouth when you talk.

MIELKE *(outside, to herself)* Empty the whole bottle to put an SOS message inside…

NOX The Miss-Miss is surely making the thoughts—

MIELKE *(outside, to herself)* …toss it all out on the ice.

NOX —that we are monsters, all the usses together.

MIELKE *(outside, to herself)* Wouldn't help much.

TAYMORE …

ALI Taymore makes the agreement of that: we won't chomp at our bits like some rats, we're out fast.

> *NOX runs to the exit. TAYMORE stops him.*

MIELKE *(outside, trying hard not to stagger)* March straight ahead, not let it show…

ALI *(in a whisper)* We leave like real civilization, our heads high on the spinal. We remove the noise from our steps—

> *Just as the four are about to leave, MIELKE enters. They all sit back down in their seats. Sound of a latch: MIELKE has locked the door.*

NOX No!

> *NOX hurls himself onto MIELKE, who falls backwards. She stops moving. Droplets of blood appear on her forehead.*

ALI *(softly)* We make the apologies for that, Miss-M—We didn't mean—

SOLA *(whispering to ALI)* Why do that? Always making the apologies.

ALI *(whispering)* This Miss-Miss doesn't have threat in her height…

TAYMORE ...

NOX *(too loud)* I says that the Miss-Miss—

ALI & SOLA Shh...

NOX *(more softly at first, but the volume rises as he speaks)* If the Miss-Miss doesn't make surveillance with her eyes, I can go run his feet in the out-there of here. I wants to go see the snow hanging from the clouds. The key, where is it?

> *NOX runs toward MIELKE, but TAYMORE stops him. MIELKE comes to abruptly and retreats to a corner of the classroom. Silence.*

MIELKE Okay. Okay. I don't want any kind of drama.... I—I didn't mean—I'm awkw—I'm unlocking the— *(MIELKE nervously unlocks the door and stays near the entrance.)* Life is good in this country of which I admit the love. *(beat)* The worst I could do to you is to cram a tongue you don't want to speak down your throats, to remove a few of the Harsh crumbs which drag their feet inside of you.... You... you could be happy here.

> *TAYMORE stares at MIELKE, who moves from the door. The other three look at the bottle she dropped when she got hit.*

That, in the bottle, it's to warm me up... *(She leans forward to pick up the bottle, but SOLA takes it first.)* I... I know what I'm doing... *(beat)* My name is Mielke. *(beat)* Uhhm... you understand what I'm saying?

> *ALI whispers something to SOLA, who whispers in turn to NOX, who whispers to TAYMORE, who nods in agreement. Reverse to ALI.*

ALI Yes. *(ALI takes the key from MIELKE and gives it to NOX.)* There, better? *(NOX nods. To MIELKE.)* Interiors make fear inside of us, Miss-Miss. We stay, we make the agreement of that, but we have to be able to see in the out-there if the clouds are still piercing the sky.

> *Beat. All four sit down at their desks.*

MIELKE *(to herself)* Okay, where do I start...

ALI We can tell you've got your peepers in a knot, so you can take a breather for your mouth. You don't have the need to start, we can make it to be capable of that. So what is it you have the need to know? Identification? Okay. That there is Sola, and that's Nox, and that, in the far over-theres, that's Taymore. And the one that's not in his body like an envelope that I held in my arms before, that was Mute. Mute got death in his face because—

SOLA That's Ali. Her word bank never reports a loss. Ali's role is to fill the void. Plus she's the smallest of us so she's the first we'll talk about for you. *(NOX whispers to SOLA.)* "We" doesn't always include all of us. That's a fact. It's good I should mention it; that's what Nox says I should say... *(beat)* Ali is always a little grimy. She likes to get into things. If you don't make the supervision of her, Ali often finds herself in the swamps, running after the tails of cats. I don't know if there are swamps or cats here, but I tell anyway. Ali was once drowned after being almost burnt. Finally, she bounced back. Also, Ali knows camouflage. She's in the corners. Ali. She makes believe she's dust, she'd like to be antique furniture, but she's not old enough yet.... Ali smiles a lot and laughs too, as though there was no end to life in the opposite of reality. I like Ali, but sometimes she bothers with her clinging to me. She leaves traces on my dress. I'm not in the agreement of that... *(louder)* She can go see her big brother Taymore... *(correcting herself)* But, now... I'll say no more because I'm entering in the introduction of someone else.... What I finish telling is that since she's small, she tries to fit in the arms of those who are the all-arounds of her. That's Ali.

NOX   If *I* tells, can *I* leave?

MIELKE   Uhhm...

NOX   Then *I* wants to tell now, can *I* tell now?

MIELKE   Wait.

NOX   If *I* doesn't tell all things, *I* is going to explode.

TAYMORE   *(looking at ALI)* ...

ALI   Nox, Taymore says shut up.

MIELKE   Wait—uhhm... Ali?

ALI   Yes?

MIELKE   *(to NOX)* You—

NOX   *I* wants—

MIELKE   Yes, I know you want, but uhhm... you are...

NOX   Not me, *I*...

ALI   That one's Nox. N-O-X. *(whispering to MIELKE)* His self-being got lost in the dark of the freighter. Nox became "*I*." We still call him Nox in case Nox should want to come back.

MIELKE   And you are Tay...

ALI   ...More.

MIELKE   Sorry?

NOX   *I*—

ALI   *(to NOX)* Shhh! *(to MIELKE)* More. But that's the nickname the father from before gave him. Taymore, that's his name. He likes both, so you can say both. The family name is too long because of, well, all the families in our lives' curriculum, so we don't say it anymore.

MIELKE   Right.

Silence.

NOX   *I* is ready, Miss-Miss, *I* can make someone's portrait. Of whom *I* speaks, who *I* interviews, for whom does *I* intervene? *I* wants to make some action. *I* can tell the dictionary of proper nouns and dirty nouns. *I* can introduce everyone, throw a party, and clean up afterwards. In fact, *I* is going to go ahead with *I* because *I* knows *I* really well. *I* has been living in close quarters with *I* since many years went by, even if *I* was called something else back then—

MIELKE   Whoa, whoa, whoa... a little slower... Nox.

NOX   *I*!

MIELKE   I don't understand, your words get lost in the flow and undertow. I—

NOX   Like the days in the freighter, huh?

MIELKE   Uhhm—

NOX   *(panicking)* *I* doesn't want words in his mouth like the days in the freighter! *I* wants to run in the out-there with the wind at his back! *I* doesn't want to kill his time being a plant caught in a pot. *I* follows Nox. *I* is leaving. *(NOX tries to get out. TAYMORE catches him.)* *I* doesn't want to be caught.

NOX manages to struggle free and leaves. TAYMORE follows him.

MIELKE   *(toward outside)* At least put on something warm!

ALI   The world would still be cold, Miss-Miss.

SOLA   *(to herself)* Not speak of the freighter, Nox, he...

SOLA goes to the window with their coats. Beat.

ALI   The sorrow fills me that we have difficulty telling you the words. The darkness of the freighter gave the cat our tongues to swallow. When they came back, our tongues, they were still Harsh, but they had visited the interior landscape of each of all the usses. *(Beat. To SOLA.)* Sola? Sola, come here. *(SOLA doesn't move. To MIELKE.)* Can I talk about someone too?

MIELKE   Uhhm... sure, but we'll wait for the others first.

They wait in silence. SOLA is still looking outside. Slowly, ALI starts to speak.

ALI   See, I don't wear the skirts anymore. I gave them all to she who is Sola. She's become a big girl now. She likes clothes that don't clothe very much. That's why she wears mine. When she was small, she could still be controlled. Now, she can choose when she gets dressed in the morning whether or not to put panties under her skirt. That's a clear... uhhm... social advantage she now knows she's got. I tell of her, but Taymore's the one who knows her by heart. They've played doctor many times together.

MIELKE   Any talking?

ALI All the time, she's always telling the things I am to everyone—

MIELKE No, Taymore. Does Taymore ever do any talking?

ALI No, not Taymore. His head told him to go on word strike because if not they hurt. He's established a customs filter in his mouth for sentences. Besides, no need for him to talk: I get the meaning, and I tell.

MIELKE Oh.

ALI Where was I in the history?

MIELKE The social advantage…. Panties under the skirt.

ALI Oh, yes. Sola, despite her angel-fallen-from-hell look, she's dreadful, and generous. She lets her existence scatter everywhere.

MIELKE She doesn't mind you talking about her like this?

ALI Right now, she can't hear me, she's far away. Where we were in the world before, Sola was one of the most village beauties. The freighter got to her. She now has teeth that won't answer roll call and some of her features are leaning towards the not-so-nice. The thing with Sola is that she leads a strange life. She has little deaths. One moment, she stops talking, and the next, she's on the floor with her mouth foaming up like a volcano in a bathtub with too much soap in it. She spills out. She has the shame of that. So you shut the trap on the truth I'm telling. Sola… when she drops in the clouds like that, you have to wake her. If not…. But I'm a little tired of beating her daylights so that she comes back…. It always breaks her a little, she gets blueses. *(pause)* Is this in the bottle very strong, Miss-Miss?

MIELKE No! Don't take that!

ALI I make the apologies for taking it, but if it's good for you, it might work for Sola. *(MIELKE runs toward ALI to take the bottle back by force.)* You don't touch me if I'm not the one who decided you could. Here, Sola, drink.

ALI gives the drink to SOLA, who awakens abruptly.

SOLA Leave me alone. Not a baby.

Beat.

ALI Well, I say they've gone around the world. I know how to read between the skylines. They won't be back in the here-and-now. Nox sure can run. In the country where we use to belong, we could be bored like this for the length of days, so much so that what happened was we started digging a hole and came face to face with Atlantis. The other peoples of the village told us that that country was supposed to play the part of legend, so we filled up the hole and buried the rumours. Miss-Miss, can we dig wherever we want here?

MIELKE Uhhm… sure… but you won't get very far, it's all frozen stiff.

SOLA   Not so interesting to wait. I too suffocate in the indoors. I'm getting the hellebore outta in-here to go wait for the others.

ALI   You stay here or I go with you.

SOLA   Go with me.

MIELKE   Yes, but… you haven't learned a single letter and I don't want—

ALI   Miss-Miss, tomorrow there is more life? *(MIELKE nods.)* We will have room for that.

MIELKE   Yes, but—

SOLA   Ali said, tomorrow there is more life…. We will have room for that.

MIELKE   Yes…

ALI   In any of all the ways, we don't want the exile to run any further than here. We have the weariness of always being in transit. *(Without warning, ALI cuddles up to MIELKE.)* We establish our new life here and we'll take your last name. We remove all the ones that link their wagons to the given names of all the usses and we put yours in their place because you're the one who takes care of us now. What is the name?

MIELKE   Mikailshva.

> *Discreetly, SOLA takes the bottle of vodgur, puts on her coat, and takes MIELKE's as well.*

ALI   Ali Mikailshva. Works for me. Sola?

SOLA   Sola Mikailshva. Works too. Let's go.

MIELKE   But, I…. If you find the running boys—

ALI   Don't make worries for yourself. We'll see them in the night if we don't find them before. The peoples here are strange: the beds where we make our sleep, well… they separated them. Too far. We can't hear each other's dreams. And then, in today's morning, the peoples who make the fostering of us screamed when they saw that a bed had cracked because we all made our sleep in it together.

MIELKE   Oh.

ALI   It's costumary for us to do that, to prevent the chill from taking hold of our bones…

SOLA   We put the others like clothing around us. That way, not so cold. Let's go now.

ALI   Ah, but you know all about that, eh, Miss-Miss? The mommy with these things here *(She indicates the breasts.)* all warm in front of her…. The daddy with his big, hairy arms on the skin of all the usses—are you okay, Miss-Miss?

> *MIELKE leaves the classroom and vomits. SOLA takes the bottle of vodgur hidden in her coat and drinks.*

(to herself) She left. The vodgur gave her potion sickness… *(to SOLA)* Sola, stop drinking all the swallows.

> *ALI grabs the bottle from her and puts it on the desk.*

SOLA   Or maybe it's because the Miss-Miss has caught the belly swell.

ALI   What?

SOLA   See, you're the type of human who is too small to hear about that affliction.

ALI   *(grabbing onto SOLA)* No, I want to be a human bigger than strife. Tell me again the explanation of the affliction.

SOLA   Let go of my perimeter, Ali! Taymore will tell your ears again if you have the Ps and Qs to find out more.

ALI   Fine, no need to paint me a tincture, my brain's got enough chemical reactions. *(MIELKE comes back.)* All right now, your affliction is gone?

> *SOLA puts the bottle of vodgur back in her coat.*

SOLA   Not stay here till the morrow, our footsteps let's go follow.

MIELKE   Yes…. Okay… but tell the boys that I would like them to introduce their person the way you did.

ALI   When? In today's morrow? That will be the difficult task for Taymore because in actual practise—

SOLA   Ali's the one who tells what Taymore has thought. Nothing to say about that? Okay? Later.

ALI   Miss-Miss, you can't get the rattle-and-rolls over this. I'm gonna find the way to fixate this in a spec of a sec.

SOLA   We fare you well.

MIELKE   Right. Sure.

ALI   Make some care for the vertigo in your stomach.

MIELKE   I will.

> *ALI and SOLA leave. MIELKE, exhausted, sits at one of the desks. She looks for the bottle of vodgur, can't seem to find it.*

Where did I put it?

> *She frantically looks for the bottle. Not finding it, she heads for the exit, but her coat is also missing.*

(opening the door just slightly) Ali! Sola!

> *The echo of her call fills the landscape, becoming weaker and weaker.*

SOLA *(from outside, imitating MIELKE)* Ali!

ALI *(from outside, also imitating MIELKE)* Sola!

MIELKE Ali! Sola! This isn't funny, my coat…

SOLA *(from outside)* Ali! Not funny, my coat.

ALI *(from outside)* Sola! This isn't funny, my coat.

> *New echo of the two girls' voices, then laughter. MIELKE re-enters the classroom. We hear a whisper: ALI is playing rock, paper, jackknife.*

Rock, paper, jackknife…. Ha! Rock, pap…. No, I don't want to play right now. Nox has run away again, it's in the best that you take care of him.

> *SOLA and ALI continue to hang around the classroom. They laugh.*

MIELKE The laughter of children lurking in the flatlands like early school memories. A forsaken time when my skin showed its Harsh colour and a few extra bruises. Other memories too, of cruel games to which I was summoned…. My body like a pawn positioned by kicks and blows. Causes, effects, and behaviours that become mature and dangerous with time.

> *ALI enters.*

ALI It's all good, Miss-Miss, we have found the tools for Taymore to make his introductions. *(She presents a little tape recorder.)* Oh, and I'm bringing back this, and this… *(ALI gives back the coat and the missing bottle of vodgur.)* It's… it's Sola, she can't have the sight of it. She watered the snow with it, she says it'll make the flakes grow. Now, I don't believe her, because it's not the earth underneath, is it, it's rock. *(beat)* Miss-Miss, Mute… where did the peoples of the village put him? Even if he's writing his final decomposition now… well, I had the wish to have him before my eyes. When I was in the country from before, they'd put the envelopes of those who had finished their life-part in the earth; here, it's frozen… you just can't.

MIELKE We make ashes with them. And the ashes, we put in a little pot we hide at the bottom of the mine—

ALI Oh, no…

MIELKE But Ali, Mute—who is he, exactly?

ALI Mute is the last affliction of the woman who had the care of us before. But—

MIELKE Your brother.

ALI No—

MIELKE Taymore, though, he's your brother.

ALI Yes. But Mute—

MIELKE And Sola is also your sister?

ALI And just who the hell are you?

SOLA *(from outside)* Ali!

> *ALI runs to prevent SOLA from entering the classroom by holding the door handle.*

MIELKE I'm asking the questions: is Sola your sister?

ALI No!

SOLA *(from outside)* Ali, I want to come in.

ALI No, she's not a sister to me. *(to SOLA)* You can't come in, you're all dirty! *(to MIELKE)* Sola is not from the clan of usses. She's the one who will have afflictions with Taymore. Taymore, he calls her his necessary evil. And Nox isn't a brother to me either. Don't look any further for our ties: when the ghetto burnt down, we all adopted the same family, Mute's… *(beat)* But I don't understand the ashes. How can that come to be?

MIELKE We put the envelope, like you say, in the fire.

ALI But no, I don't want Mute in the fire! Mute was the most beauty-filled child in the village from where we were. Before the time when he made the stopping of his tongue in the freighter, he had the name of Cute. Mute can't have the fire lapping up his skin, lighting up his eyes…. That's not in Mute's life-part!

MIELKE Mute is dead, Ali…. If we don't want the dogs to eat the envelope, we don't have a choice but to—

ALI I don't want the dogs to swallow Mute whole either.

SOLA *(from outside)* Ali!

ALI *(to SOLA)* Shhh, Sola! We're done playing echoes. And right now, I'm talking to the Miss-Miss.

MIELKE Let her in!

ALI She'll put dirt everywhere. For once that I'm not the one staining her. Besides, as long as she's talking, we're good.

> *We can hear SOLA repeating, "Not funny, not funny." ALI speaks louder.*

Mute's hiding place, Miss-Miss, where is it? It hurts, the fire-lapping. The fire eating up the ghetto, the shacks of all the usses belching out fire, the flames making a new home with my pieces of clothing…!

MIELKE *(trying to control ALI)* Hold on, stop—

ALI I have made the warning: I don't want to be caught by you, Miss-Miss. If you don't want to say things as they are, I will go get Mute, even if I have to walk alone, down the fields of cobblestone.

ALI struggles free, opens the door, and leaves. MIELKE follows her. Beat. SOLA, seemingly a little lost, enters. She has dirt on her legs, her face. She takes the last swig from the bottle of vodgur ALI has brought back, and exits. Blackout.

Day 2 — 11:30 p.m.
End of Summer

NOX enters the classroom running, with TAYMORE in close pursuit. They are both out of breath.

NOX   Ali, Sola, and the Miss-Miss. They're in a state of disappearance.

TAYMORE   ...

NOX   If *I* had not run so much, we would have been back in due time and place not to miss our shot? Eh? That what Taymore wants to say?

TAYMORE   ...

NOX   And *I* would not have made the trials of riding the girls who protruded from the village's houses. That what you want to say, eh? What words can you produce for the reply? *(TAYMORE pins NOX to the ground.)* What *I* does... it's what we call going to "swell and back."

NOX laughs. TAYMORE pins him to the ground again, violently.

Give Sola to *I*. *I* says no more doing things like today.

TAYMORE grabs him by the collar. MIELKE comes in with their coats. TAYMORE releases NOX, who runs outside. TAYMORE makes for the door, but MIELKE holds him back.

MIELKE   Wait! Here... the coats... I was waiting for you to come ba—

MIELKE and TAYMORE look at each other. Something materializes in that glance.

Let him go, he has enough energy to make the earth spin counter-clockwise... *(nervous laugh)* seems... to me. *(beat)* He probably doesn't even know he's cold...

TAYMORE tries to wriggle free. Awkward moment. MIELKE releases her grip, slightly. SOLA appears at the window. MIELKE and TAYMORE don't see her.

How long will you keep your tongue from moving?

TAYMORE   ...

TAYMORE turns his head toward the door.

MIELKE   Don't give yourself worries; he's found his way once, he.... A jungle of snow can be tamed quickly. We'll.... We'll see each other in the morrow—

uhhm, see you tomorrow. Ali has the tape recorder; tell me about yourself, tell me what Harshenia has become… it inhabits me, but… I don't know this which inhabits me now… I, uhhm…

> *SOLA tumbles from her window. TAYMORE runs off. MIELKE sighs. Blackout.*

**Day 14 — 3:30 p.m.
Early Fall**

The four are sitting down, quiet. TAYMORE has a phone book and a dictionary in front of him. MIELKE is teaching letters from the Northan alphabet at the blackboard.

MIELKE   *Inar-ziaak.*

SOLA, ALI, NOX   *Inar-ziaak.*

> *TAYMORE writes in the dictionary.*

MIELKE   *Deeoumz-shou.*

SOLA, ALI, NOX   *Deeoumz-shou.*

MIELKE   *Etsouvarjeek.*

SOLA, ALI, NOX   *Etsouvarjeek.*

MIELKE   *(still pointing at letters on the blackboard)* The only thing I brought back from the megacity: the phone book. All the people I don't know contained in a singular space… smaller than a village. It's reassuring. They are less noisy, accuse less, create less fear. Taymore found it. He's reading it. He's also holding the dictionary hostage. Barricades of paper. My eyes fly above them… *(Her eyes meet TAYMORE's by accident.)* Taymore doesn't speak. His eyes cry out something which I hold on the tip of my tongue…. His pupils painted with charm…. What colour is the voice he wears? The words that surround him come in and out of his head like wind through a house… by the seashore… during a furious summer. He doesn't study, he has other blank pages to fry… but which? Who knows…

ALI   For the questions landing in your head, Miss-Miss—in case you're wondering—Taymore, he knows intelligence. He's been through universatility. Taymore's brain on a plate serves up a clever mix of knowledge and brilliance. You stick that in the oven, Miss-Miss, and you get a soufflé so big his head stops fitting through doors. *(ALI, SOLA, and NOX guffaw.)* Inar-ziaak, deeoumz-shou, etsouvarjeek. If we learn enough lessons, will we be able to do the work in the mine, like the other peoples of the village?

MIELKE   Yes. *(continuing with the lesson)* *Leel-aou-tchavay-z.*

ALI, SOLA, NOX   *Leel-aou-tchavay-z.*

ALI   But we won't lose our Harsh like you, huh? It's because you make the disavowal of the country that you don't speak—

MIELKE   To speak Harsh is to *be* Harsh. *(pointing to another letter)* Mioumek-srenz.

ALI, SOLA, NOX   Mioumek-srenz.

ALI   So you're not entirely Harsh.

MIELKE   I'd rather not answer that. *(another letter)* Seeza.

ALI, SOLA, NOX   Seeza.

ALI   It wasn't a question.

MIELKE   Rooma-ee.

ALI, SOLA, NOX   Rooma-ee.

ALI   We're not barbarians.

MIELKE   *(seeing that TAYMORE isn't paying attention)* Taymore? Are you okay?

NOX   Taymore? Are you okay?

NOX, ALI, and SOLA laugh. TAYMORE throws them a look; they quiet down immediately.

ALI   The word to say yes like the answer, how do we make that?

MIELKE   Ley.

ALI   Well then, Taymore says *ley*, he's okay.

MIELKE   Ali, let Taymore speak for himself!

A persistent stare from TAYMORE to ALI.

ALI   It's no care of his. Taymore asks why don't you want to go back to the South?

MIELKE   I'm afraid of people.

ALI   Isn't it more that people are afraid of you? *(furious glance from MIELKE to ALI)* Hey, it's not me, it's Taymore.

MIELKE   Let him ask his own questions if he wants me to answer.

Beat.

ALI   All right. Now that's the kind of word that breaks the comment's back. You don't want me to tell. Then let's ask the little box. *(to TAYMORE)* The Miss-Miss wants to hear you tell things. *(to MIELKE)* But you asked for it.

ALI tears the tape recorder from TAYMORE's hands and presses play. The track is glitchy, as though someone recorded it bit by bit.

VOICE OF TAYMORE ON THE TAPE RECORDER   I. Like. Lists I. Like. Collections of. Words. All. Woes too. I Like. No sound at the. End. Of woes.

I. Don't like. Telling. Of. Me. I tell. Of those who are the all-arounds. Of me. Those who made. Parents for us. The smile. Of them with life. I want. The joy of them to put. All over my. Face. Open up the smile. From one ear to the.

A big glitch in the tape.

VOICE OF ALI ON THE TAPE RECORDER What, that's where you stop?

Voice of TAYMORE on the tape in the background: "Say the parents."

No, Taymore, I don't speak in the box— *(He hits her.)* Ow! It's for you to make the continuity…

Voice of TAYMORE on the tape in the background: "Tell of widening the smile. The jack—"

No!

Another big glitch in the recording. ALI stops the tape.

ALI Taymore is right: it's no good the voice in the little boxes; so I'll make the continuity of it. The father loved all numbers and calcultraitors. He opened up his "busy-ness," he could tell it like he saw it. He sold the water from the snow of the country where we were to the Smartipans. He gave them belief that there were minerals in it that extended youth on the skin. And plus there was Mute… Mute, I was the best who loved him. He knew my arms that were warm around him.

MIELKE Ali, forg—

ALI *(louder)* Before we had the freighter for a house, Mute was called Cute, the most beauty-filled child—

MIELKE Ali—

ALI *(practically shouted)* See, I may be palatable, but I'm not potable. Big people can't swallow me up to stop the flow of my words. They know I'll just keep babbling in their bellies. So there…. He was so small, Mute, that he could only tell numbers. He's the one who counted the drops that told the number of minutes that were dripping from life in the freighter. And then, there came the day—or night, I didn't know anymore because we couldn't tell where the sun it had gone—

MIELKE All right, enough—

MIELKE throws herself toward ALI. TAYMORE protects ALI.

ALI Well at one moment in time, Cute, he just stopped talking; and then, we didn't like that he didn't talk, so we called him Mute. And then, he stopped smelling nice, just like the parents of us who had gone before we left—

MIELKE Ali, what are you saying?

TAYMORE plays the tape from the start at the highest volume.

ALI See, I'd rather forget when I tell the words, they only live once and it's all they deserve.

MIELKE Stop the tape, Taymore. *(beat)* Taymore, the tape!

NOX takes the tape recorder.

NOX Miss-Miss, *I* thinks the tape has stopped stopping. It's going to talk until the morrow. *I* can go bury it outside.

NOX tries to leave. TAYMORE stops him. MIELKE takes the tape recorder and removes the batteries. A long pause.

MIELKE Okay. Okay. Let's all… calm… down. *(beat)* We'll just…. We'll just place a word or two in your heads; it'll be a start. *(She writes on the blackboard.)* Mey-ee-shoo…Na, which means: I am, or me. Very useful when you need to identify yourself to other people in the village. *(The four don't answer. She repeats.)* Mey-ee-shoo…Na. I am, or me.

MIELKE, NOX, SOLA Mey-ee-shoo…Na. I am, or me.

MIELKE writes another word on the blackboard.

MIELKE Mey-ee-tay…Na. You are, or you.

MIELKE, NOX, SOLA Mey-ee-tay…Na. You are, or you.

MIELKE Okay. *(realizing that the four youngsters are in a state of panic)* That's… that's enough inside this d— That's enough for today.

ALI and TAYMORE leave. NOX and SOLA linger at the door.

NOX *(taking SOLA's hand and placing it on his chest)* Mey-ee-shoo…Na. I. *(NOX places his hand on SOLA's chest.)* Mey-ee-tay…Na. Sola.

MIELKE *(louder)* That's enough for today.

SOLA and NOX leave. MIELKE takes a bottle of vodgur and a glass from her coat. She drinks in small, tight sips. Since she could be observed from the window, she moves out of sight. She puts the batteries back in the tape recorder and presses play.

VOICE OF ALI ON THE TAPE RECORDER —you stop?

Voice of TAYMORE on the tape in the background: "Say the parents."

No, Taymore, I don't speak in the box— *(He hits her.)* Ow! It's for you to make the continuity…

Voice of TAYMORE on the tape in the background: "Tell of widening the smile. The jack—"

No!

MIELKE rewinds the tape and turns up the volume.

—you stop?

> *Voice of TAYMORE on the tape in the background:* "Say the parents."

No, Taymore, I don't speak in the box— *(He hits her.)* Ow! It's for you to make the continuity...

> *Voice of TAYMORE on the tape in the background:* "Tell of widening the smile. The jack—"

No!

> *MIELKE rewinds the tape and turns the volume up again.*

—you stop?

> *Voice of ALI outside. MIELKE stops the tape to listen.*

ALI *(outside)* Rock, paper, jackknife.... Ha! *(laughter)* Rock, paper, jackknife.... Ha! Rock, paper, jackknife.... There.... Fine. Nox; Nox runs all the time; and also, he carries two people inside of him, he must be exhaus—

> *We hear a very loud banging at the door and then a voice in Northan. MIELKE puts the vodgur bottle and the glass in her desk and answers the door. A short discussion in Northan, then she leaves. The tape recorder is left on the desk. Footsteps are heard moving away. The stage is empty. Different footsteps are heard approaching.*

Day 14 — Immediately After
Early Fall

> *SOLA comes in, she is carrying a small bag of sniffing glue. She searches for the vodgur, finds it, and drinks directly from the bottle. NOX appears at the door and locks it with the key he then puts back in his collar.*

NOX *Mey-ee-shoo...Na....* That's another nice name for *I. Mey-ee-shoo...Na* wants to have *Mey-ee-tay...Na* Sola in his shadow.

> *NOX puts his hand on SOLA's chest. She casually removes it.*

SOLA Not a thing of the possible, Nox.

NOX Mustn't say Nox. *I. I* is stronger. *I* survived the days of the freighter.

SOLA This what I say: "Not a thing of the possible for me to be in your shadow, *I*." See, I will be Taymore's womanifesto and he will be my manifesto. And not a reason that we're not in the country we were to put the rules six feet under. I stay clean for Taymore.

NOX *I* knows the games you make to put the little bags in your hands. Staying clean is a gone reason...

SOLA *(trying to wriggle free from NOX)* I know Nox's interior well. Nox has the good heart in him, he can't do things to me. I want to go in the out-there—

NOX   Nox isn't here to make your defence. You stay here with *I*. *(indicating the outdoors)* They were setting up play, we don't have much time to get ourselves under control. *I* needs you, to taste the other things that are in life… *I* wants to know the bliss of boys with you. We get on like a louse on fire. *I* can feel it.

SOLA   Not…. Not with you…

>*SOLA tears the key away from NOX's neck and puts it in the lock. NOX catches up to her before she manages to open the door.*

Taymore! Taymore!

>*SOLA struggles against NOX.*

NOX   *(trying to control a struggling SOLA)* Shh! Taymore didn't say no when *I* asked to be given you.

>*SOLA freezes in NOX's arms, announcing an epileptic seizure.*

I made patience for a long time in the freighter. *I* was waiting for Taymore to catch his death. But no, he never reached his expiration. *I* can't wait any longer. Here, you, all for *I*.

>*NOX takes the bottle from SOLA as she succumbs to the epileptic seizure. He lays her down on the floor and turns her head sideways.*

I can't touch your lips with his mouth when you are spitting like that. It's not pretty in your mouth. *(NOX lifts SOLA's clothing.)* But it is pretty how you are made under here.

>*NOX spoons SOLA's body and puts his hands under her clothes.*

ALI   *(outside)* Rock, paper, jackknife…. Ha!

NOX   As long as we hear them play, they don't know we're gone.

ALI   *(outside)* Rock, pap— No, that's not in the rules…

NOX   Did Nox also have love for you? *I* would be jealous of that.

ALI   *(outside)* What? No, I'm not making up rules…

NOX   *I* still has the need of those things in front of you. *I* has the need of them in his hands, against his cheek.

ALI   *(outside)* We said: "Not twice in one here day."

NOX   Nox has the longing of an envelope like yours.

ALI   *(outside)* You want to understand nothing, I'm going.

NOX   You're warm yourself alone even without the others in bed.

>*TAYMORE tries to get in. The key is still in the lock.*

Shh…. Shh…. *Mey-ee-shoo…Na* fares you well.

> NOX *leaves through the window. With a knife, TAYMORE manages to make the key drop out of the lock. He comes in, picks up the key, sees SOLA, puts the knife down on the floor, and slaps her in the face. Her first instinct is to grab on to him.*

SOLA   No… no other hands that graze the skin… also, I'm thirsty, to make all the snow melt in the out-there… and me, so clean, absorbed in it… to drink the snow… Taymore…. You…. Don't leave me in this solitude…. Take me to the end of ice…. You and me at the end of snow like two figures on the cake at a wedding…. The eyes of you that plummet onto me…. Not…. Not pretty the new eyes on Nox…

NOX   (*outside, in a panic, his voice coming from afar*) May-ee-shoo…Na I… Nox.

> *Outside, cries in Northan. TAYMORE tries to break free from SOLA's grasp.*

SOLA   I have the faith of you, of your hands that stay inside your realm. No defence on my own…

NOX   (*outside, his voice getting closer to the classroom*) Mey-ee-shoo…Na…Na… I has gone too far. I is scaring Nox! Taymore! Ali!

> *TAYMORE picks up his knife and leaves.*

(*outside*) Taymore!

> *Muffled sound of someone getting hit in the stomach.*

Taymore!

> *More shouts in Northan, sounds of a fight, and loud thumps against the door. Blackout.*

Day 15 — 9:30 a.m.
Early Fall

> *SOLA and ALI are alone in the classroom.*

ALI   Sola, wake your eyes, we're in the classroom. We're the first ones in the same place, same time. Taymore is making some sleeping in. Poor Taymore, all broken up in his bones, he is. Okay. We have to keep learning if we want to go find Mute at the bottom of the mine.

SOLA   Nox… I—

ALI   The peoples of the village, they sure took care of Nox. Me, it's of you I take care. Huh, Sola, I may be in the minors, but I know how to be a tutor to your grown-up when she forgets how to make her steps, how to take a breath, and how to say: "Fine, thanks," with a huge exclamation point, to those who ask her "How are ya?" You can't show that nothing's fine to strangers; so you're going to be the big girl with her backbone straight and her eyes wide open. I told you that your manner of clothing that don't clothe very much isn't so good if you want to be clean for Taymore. Nox, he sort of jumped on the occasions you gave him.

SOLA I—

ALI *(lifting a bag of sniffing glue to SOLA's nose)* Here, the kids who are of our age tell us that this helps to solve sicknesses.

SOLA *(pushing the bag away)* I know that. Nox not alone in having little ideas in his head and in his hands. The young peoples of the village…. Ali, it's cold behind the warehouse.

ALI Yes, it's cold everywhere here.

SOLA Also, I am Sola, Ali. Friend of the boys here. The soul, the half, the me of whom. And rather than a half of me, I'd rather be the *la-si* of someone and sing the whole scale. Not easy to be one body for five hundred lost souls, it leaves traces bigger than the ones you put on my skirt when you hold on to me, Ali. But I am useful. My belly takes in a litre of love for two bags of glue, I can handle that. Also, when I get my headaches, it's because I turn into a unicorn, huh? I am fantasy and I take flight, Ali.

ALI You don't have any wings, Sola. You will trip and fall if you lose your marbles, too.

> *ALI puts the bag of sniffing glue up to SOLA's nose again. MIELKE comes in.*

MIELKE Ali, the snow is all red outside— *(seeing the bag)* What are you doing?

ALI I'm putting a gag on Sola's little deaths so that they don't have the last word.

> *MIELKE abruptly takes the bag from ALI.*

MIELKE *(to ALI)* Where are they? Taymore? Nox? The sound of a brawl last night, the people of the village gathering, the young girls screaming as though life itself had been stolen from them. They asked me a lot of questions. You saw what happened? And what's with Sola?

SOLA Miss-Miss, here I have found the remedy to keep my head from making little deaths. The glue in my nose rises to my head and sticks all my ideas together, and my head it likes the feeling because it makes less thoughts all the time.

ALI Sola is unloading.

MIELKE Ali—

ALI Don't touch me.

SOLA Also, the memories drift like the fog that makes a cradle for the boats on the ocean. Miss-Miss, I feel like sludge on a frozen lake's floor.

ALI Sola is making survival poetry, Miss-Miss.

MIELKE Stop joking around, Ali. Footprints that walk in and out of here. Red footprints. Who is dead? The people speak of one of Mielke's boys, which one? They made a prison of my house yesterday, with me in it.

ALI takes MIELKE aside.

ALI *(to MIELKE)* Mind the words. If you speak them too fast, they bounce everywhere and you stop hearing them. First, you will sit the butt you carry behind you right here and I'm gonna explain. *(beat)* I had predicted that this was something of the possible in Nox's future.

SOLA *(to herself)* When I had less years, I would put my ear against the bathtub's abyss.

ALI *(to MIELKE)* The peoples of the village found him with his hand in the cookie jar that a young girl had between her legs, so they say.

SOLA *(to herself)* Also, I would make a sure thing of putting water in the bathtub first.

ALI *(to MIELKE)* Nox thrust into a young girl what he'd been wanting for a long time to put into Sola and that he couldn't go all the way.

SOLA *(louder)* The young girl cried her lungs ou— *(beat, to herself)* It is the joy one calls being out of self. Also, there was so much peace in the aquatic realm. The more I went there, the less I swam. And then, in the afterwards of the moment, there was no more bathtub, and no more fins. I am like a fish in the sea. How many lives to a fish, I wonder? If the cats fill their bellies with the fish, then it must be that the fish have more lives than the cats. *(to MIELKE and ALI)* How is the number "nine," in Northan?

MIELKE Sorry?

SOLA How is the number "nine," in Northan?

ALI *Auf-feeveek.*

SOLA *Auf-feeveek* lives for the cat, how many for the fish?

MIELKE ...

SOLA *Auf-feeveek* lives for the cat, how many for the fish? *(to MIELKE)* Why do you make the lessons if you can't match the answers to the questions?

ALI *(to SOLA)* Shh... *(to MIELKE)* A people of the village came and saw Nox in his birthday suit below the waist. The other peoples of the village weren't happy about that. Nox ran to here. When he arrived by the door, Taymore was there. Taymore took Nox in his arms to make some comfort for him. He knew that "*I*," inside of Nox, hadn't done it for the bad deeds because "*I*" only knows the hard-knock life. So the peoples of the village made Nox's heart explode in blood. That's just the way. You're not nice, you lose life.... Just like in the home of ours from before. One more human-without-a-trace who sinks into disappearance. Nox had been warned of the price to pay for the flip side of his coin.

SOLA Right. So this class, is it time for it?

MIELKE Taymore, he—

SOLA My head is here waiting for feeding. The letters of the alphabet can come in and do the rhymes and reasons.

MIELKE Sola, wait—

SOLA Also, I want to see them in my soup, the letters of the alphabet... I—

MIELKE Ali, what about Taymore, is he—

SOLA *(coldly)* Taymore's a-okay. I saw him. He's gone to bury the memory of Nox in the mine.

ALI Not true. He had made the promise that I go with him.

MIELKE How many times do I have to tell you: the mine is not for you!

ALI You said that we could do the work in the mine if we learn. I have learned: *Deeoumz-shou. Etsouvarjeek. Mey-ee-shoo...Na* Ali! *Ley*?

MIELKE *Ley*! But when I said it, I meant Nox and Taymore. Only big men go in there.

ALI Nox is gone; and you know, giants don't give me fear because I can sneak through the legs of them. I can camouflage in the corners. I can't dig the earth to go get Mute, so I'm going to go through the mine—

MIELKE Ali.... They're all imbued with vodgur, they can't even tell where to dig so that the galleries hold up—

ALI How can I believe you, Miss-Miss? Your tongue makes a sponge for the vodgur too.

ALI leaves. SOLA keeps MIELKE inside.

MIELKE Let me get through, Sola. *(beat)* Why are you always running, eh? Let me get through.... Why is there always a gust of wind around you? That's no way to live, you know!

SOLA We don't live, Miss-Miss, we survive. Like you.

MIELKE Ali!

SOLA Ali, Taymore, Ali, always! What about Sola, eh? Taymore will take care of Ali. Me, it's of you I take care. *(beat)* You shouldn't fill your head with ideas, Miss-Miss: Taymore will never have the need of anyone.

MIELKE What?

SOLA I'm no moon. You caught one of Taymore's glances in the other day. *(beat)* How did you do it? I gave my body to the science of these here boys, I put millions of baby beginnings in my belly for Taymore, so he would glance at me.

ALI *(outside)* I want to go!

MIELKE Ali!

ALI *(outside)* Okay.

SOLA *(grabbing hold of MIELKE)* Ali won't come. Ali loiters around Taymore like an imaginary friend in denial. But… no changing of the subject, Miss-Miss. What is the secret of Taymore's eyes falling on you? *(She takes a knife out of her pocket.)* You tell or I draw flowers of blood on your blouse, Miss-Miss.

MIELKE It can't be told, Sola, it happens…

> *SOLA freezes.*

ALI *(outside)* Rock, paper, jackknife…. Ha!

MIELKE Sola…

ALI *(outside)* Rock, paper, jackknife…. Ha!

MIELKE *(slapping SOLA)* Sola…

ALI *(outside)* Rock, paper, jackknife…

MIELKE Sola… Sola, wake up!

ALI *(outside)* No, not her. I don't want that…. That's not fair! Yes, I need to go to the mine!

> *The knife falls out of SOLA's hands as she has an epileptic seizure.*

Okay, fine. Sola.

MIELKE Ali! *(TAYMORE comes in.)* Where's Ali?

TAYMORE …

MIELKE Why didn't you— You take care of Sola, I'll go get Ali.

> *MIELKE leaves. TAYMORE turns SOLA sideways and puts his coat under her head. He picks up the knife and stands. Blackout.*

Day 15 — 10 a.m.
Early Fall

> *It is dark inside the classroom. Outside, ALI is grabbing on to MIELKE, and TAYMORE holds a bag of glue. Opening the door is impossible, as the key is in the lock and TAYMORE doesn't have his knife.*

MIELKE *(outside)* You left her there alone?

TAYMORE ...

ALI *(outside)* I have fear, I have fear in me, lots. Labyrinths of darkness... my eyes lost in the rocks of the mine... a freighter of stone... catastrophobia...

MIELKE *(outside)* It's over... calm down.

> *MIELKE tries to put ALI down.*

ALI *(outside)* No! Don't let me go!

MIELKE *(outside)* Sola, open the door... it's freezing out here. Open up! Taymore has brought you something.... It will help y—

ALI *(outside)* Taymore says he couldn't wake her. The seizure was stronger than in Sola's customs. He thought of vodgur, he only found glue.

MIELKE *(outside)* Sola, this isn't funny. Ali, climb on Taymore's shoulders, you can—

ALI *(outside)* Nooooooo! I want to stay in the calm of the arms that are yours, Miss-Miss. It's good here, it's warm here, it's a shelter...

MIELKE *(outside)* Taymore...

ALI *(outside)* Taymore?

> *TAYMORE breaks the windowpane and enters. He turns on the light. SOLA is lying on the floor. She holds a knife in her hand. Her wrists have been slit. TAYMORE freezes.*

MIELKE *(outside)* Taymore? Taymore, what's happening? *(to herself)* As if he would answer... *(to Taymore)* Taymore, open the door... Taymore!

> *TAYMORE opens the classroom door. Blackout. A cry in this darkness becomes an echo.*

ALI *(outside)* Rock, paper, jackknife—no, no, no. I know it in Northan, now... *Trayqasz, vwem, soujvao*.... Ha! *Trayqasz, vwem, soujvao*.... Ha! *Trayqasz, vwem, soujvao*.... We have to stop... *(beat)* Okay, okay.... Let's see: who has pains to stand up straight? Touhdash, Insdiou, Psdotee. Yes. You're right, Taymore.

Day 26 — Noon
Fall

> *MIELKE and ALI are alone in the classroom. Makeshift repairs have been made to the broken window. ALI is playing teacher to three little urns. A bottle of vodgur lies on the ground.*

MIELKE How long since Sola and Nox have gone? I've lost track. The emptiness has taken hold of the classroom. Calm, too. No more cries, no more tears. The people of the village have replaced me at the clinic so that I take "better" care, as they say, of the two I have left.

ALI Me, it's of you I take care; you're going to be the big girl with her backbone straight and her—

MIELKE Thank you. It's fine, Ali. It's okay.

ALI returns to her game.

Since her adventure in the mine, she follows me everywhere like a little dog. Those little things become endearing with time. She makes warmth around me, and I go on teaching her. We barter, we're human. *(beat)* We hardly ever see Taymore. He's still refusing to talk. He started working in the mine when Sola passed away. The people of the village give him a lot of work. He spends the rest of his time reading the dictionary and the megacity's telephone book.

ALI He's learning them by heart.

MIELKE Sorry?

ALI The dictionary and the phone book, he's learning them by heart.

MIELKE Hum. Yesterday, he added a missing word, "traumutism." I kept telling him that that word doesn't exist in the tongue that moves here. "Traumutism" is now in the dictionary in big, fat black marker, solidly cradled between "trauma" and "travel." The definition is held somewhere in Taymore's head.

ALI It gives me worry that Taymore is not here on his way back.

MIELKE Since the last cave-in, every day the same old song: Ali awaits Taymore's return. Her "it gives me worry" like a nagging tune. Ali now knows what lies in a sound barrier. She is building a solid one between herself, the silence, and the emptiness. There are now words in every square centimetre.

ALI Why did you make the rescuing of me? Nobody's done it before, except Taymore. He's my brother, it's in all normalcy that he does it. But you—

MIELKE I like when you're—

ALI Why the vodgur if I'm here to warm you up?

MIELKE You're still a child, you don't yet give out quite enough warmth.

ALI Oh. *(beat)* Taymore's lost his childhood. He might be able to make you some war—

MIELKE Well, you are losing your mind. Don't say things like that.

ALI takes NOX's urn, tops it with a tiny dunce's cap, and brings it to a corner of the classroom.

To stop Ali from constantly harassing Taymore when he leaves for work, I brought the three little pots of ashes back to the surface of the classroom. Nox, Sola, and Mute are now here with us. Ali clowns around, she teaches the little pots. Today, she's teaching Mute's ashes how to say his numbers in Northan so that he can count the sands of eternity's time.

ALI *(addressing MUTE's urn)* Mo-ah. No! It's not *Auv-veeveek*. It's *Auf-feeveek*. "Nine," my brain tells me it's not that difficult.

MIELKE At times, she gets angry.

ALI *(talking inside MUTE's urn)* Don't have much between the ears, buddy? If you keep this up, I'm throwing you to the dust bunnies. *(ALI puts the urn to her ear, satisfied.)* Good… *(beat)* You remember the other week's lesson, the names of the peoples of the village: Touhdash, Insdiou, Psdotee…

MIELKE Ali's even taught Nox, Sola, and Mute the game of rock, paper, jackknife… in Northan. She hummed it "with them" a few days ago, adding the names of certain people of the village. *(beat)* Like a premonition, the ones she named died in the mine the very next day. The men perish amongst the stones. The women keep the memories of their lost ones afloat in the drink. Children are already wandering in the village. And they forbid me from working at the clin— It's the end of a small world. Ali, Taymore, and I, we stand in the middle of it all, like an island drifting away.

ALI *(addressing MUTE's urn)* See, it might be that Taymore's not doing good enough work of throwing rocks on the peoples of the village. The little voice in Taymore's head is pretty greedy, isn't it, Mute? It got you right in the kisser, that little voice, and it put red all over the place, huh? Me, I didn't want that.

> *TAYMORE comes in, drops a big bag on the floor, and looks at ALI fixedly. MIELKE starts leaving.*

The peoples of the village have had enough, they're going to send us to the South. Between now and the end of one calendar line, the planes will stop tearing through the clouds for winter. The peoples of the village will take the advantage of the situation to give us flight towards the unsettling peoples of the South.

MIELKE No, they can't send you there, you don't even have—

ALI You too.

MIELKE …

ALI They're saying that the Harshes are a real curse, that it's all the usses' fault if the village is losing its inhabitants …

MIELKE I'm not Harsh, I'm part of life here.

ALI They're no fools, they remember the number of many persons who passed away while you were making help in the clinic. *(beat)* They have a hostage hold on your house… axes are attacking the wood in the right now. If I were you, I'd stay right here, 'cause they've gone right mad.

> *MIELKE leaves. TAYMORE sits ALI on a chair.*

Aren't you tired of this, Taymore?

Beat. Then she begins the game of rock, paper, jackknife in Northan.

Trayqasz, vwem, soujvao.... Ha! *Trayqasz, vwem, soujvao....* Ha! *Trayqasz, vwem, soujvao....* Ha!

TAYMORE slaps her. Beat. She begins again.

Trayqasz, vwem, soujvao... Sdygut, Bixzeeat, Monraw, Loyutat.

Pause. TAYMORE slaps her again.

Enough, Taymore. That's enough. In any of all the ways, how will it work? Soon, we won't even be able to go out, they're already watching. *(beat)* Tonight? Here, it's always night.

Blackout.

Day 27 — 1 p.m.
Fall

ALI is lying down, alone, in a corner of the classroom. She is sleeping. Commotion. MIELKE enters. She is carrying pieces of sheet metal and a bag full of blankets.

ALI   You've come to make existence with us? You're going to become Taymore's womanifesto. *(MIELKE continues to bring the sheet metal into the classroom.)* *Moooo-ah*! No! No barricading the classroom! We're gonna leave.... Taymore says a new life in the South!

MIELKE   Believe me, you don't want to go there. *(MIELKE forces ALI to breathe into a bag of glue.)* I "make the apologies," Ali, but it's every man for himself. If I go back to the South, it's like putting bars up all around me. The eyes of all the people accusing, "It's her, she's that young woman who did the slaughter in her house. Blood everywhere. The father on one side, the mother on the other." If I hadn't killed he who was my father, he would have killed me, I—it was self-defence. I defended my mother. Ali, you understand!

ALI struggles.

ALI   When this here village becomes a field of very precious, but very tomb-stones, what will you do then, huh? Stay in solitude? Go deep into the white desert which surrounds all the usses like a suffocation? With this here country repeating all the time, with its bottomless winters, that it doesn't want to give hospitality to the human race?

TAYMORE enters, pulls MIELKE away from ALI and threatens her with his knife. Brutal fight between TAYMORE and MIELKE.

MIELKE   Can't I just be left in peace, Taymore? Come on, Taymore.... Show what you're made of.... Speak with your fists, your hands, anything you like! Know what? This, a knife to the stomach, or going back to the South, or staying here with you, or whatever else, it'll all add up to the same thing. It'll split open my belly. It'll capsize the bowels. Make a real solid noose with them, hang myself with the noose. Come on, Taymore, stick it in real good, right where the skin was broken while I was being born. *(beat)* So whatcha gonna do, Taymore? You've prepared your decision? Bring Ali to the South? Over there, it's the straight and narrow, you're gonna need an identity you don't even have on paper. Do you even exist? You'll be one of all the Harshes nobody wants around! Once you get there, you'll leave on another ship for another exile priced at another life. Ali's, or your own? Who will take care of her? Eh, Taymore? Who will love her enough to hold her in their arms until she's got all the years she needs to stand on her own? *(beat)* I can do that! I've got nothing better to do! *(Beat.)* Could you move your feet out of my way, I've got a classroom to barricade…

Blackout.

Day 32 — 5 a.m.
Fall

A storm is raging outside. The power is out. A candle gets lit. MIELKE is sitting on a small, improvised bed. In the centre of the room, another, larger improvised bed, where ALI and TAYMORE are sleeping. MIELKE is in rough shape.

MIELKE Sleep has escaped me for five nights, yet I resist. I'm cold. I'm scared. A winter is settling in. My world is shrinking. The plane leaves tomorrow. *(beat)* I went out of the classroom one last time to see freedom run wild… I could've hid in the rubble of my wind-built house, but Ali was waiting. Someone was holding on to me. We hide out in what we now call our freighter-classroom. All the planes in the world could take off from this place, never would we be on board. Taymore is Ali's buy-one-get-one-free. She married me to him yesterday. We became, the three of us, a little family. She did everything she could to make me comfortable. *(indicating SOLA's urn)* She put Sola next to my bed to keep me company. *(a smile, beat)* They sleep soundly…. Taymore's slow breathing hovers…. No more vodgur to keep me warm. *(beat)* My yearning to go be the clothing around them. Ali… so tiny, and… Taymore. My heart as big as a tank. Taymore hides the vodgur. Must simply hold my breath.

A wobbly MIELKE moves toward TAYMORE's side of the bed. While she rummages through a bag next to the bed, TAYMORE awakens.

TAYMORE *(handing a bottle to MIELKE)* This. You're looking for. In desperate times. And measures.

MIELKE grabs the bottle and takes refuge in her improvised bed. She drinks.

MIELKE *(to TAYMORE but without looking at him)* You're talking, Taymore…

TAYMORE   I talk. When it's. Important.

MIELKE   Tonight, it's important?

TAYMORE   Yes. *(a long silence)* In the other. Life before when you. Made teacher. You knew how to. Relieve the peoples who suffer. *(MIELKE nods.)* Do you. Treat. *(beat)* Traumutisms?

MIELKE   I don't know what traumutisms are, Taymore.

TAYMORE   Nightmares that make reality even through. The day. The little. Voice like Ali that. Gets angry, talks when it wants. Like someone. Who. Follows the back of my mind. Someone. Who yells at me.

MIELKE   It's the wind, Taymore…

TAMORE   *(indicating the bottle of vodgur)* That. In the bottle. It resolves the wind. That blows. In the mind?

TAYMORE reveals all the vodgur bottles he has hidden under the bed.

MIELKE   …

TAYMORE   Yes?

MIELKE   *(giving up)* Yes.

TAYMORE   …

TAYMORE takes a bottle and drinks. MIELKE watches him insistently.

Something. Written on. My forehead?

MIELKE   No, it's the first time there is sound on your face.

Beat. They look at each other and drink. A lapse of time. One last candle's flame flickers from the excess of wind. We hear laughter in the semi-darkness. MIELKE and TAYMORE are drunk.

TAYMORE   I can't stand… gnawing pain… or overwhelming joy…

MIELKE   I try to keep the pain from crying its existence from the rooftops…

TAYMORE   …by suiciding… those who are sick… inside themselves…

Beat.

MIELKE   Why do you say that?

TAYMORE   I don't tell many words… but I hear the rumours lurking…

MIELKE   In Harshenia, euthanasia is the legal right of those who suffer.

TAYMORE   But… it isn't like that here. *(beat)* You shouldn't regret what you do… shouldn't deny… where you're from, you shouldn't… stop speaking…. Harsh… really…

MIELKE   To speak Harsh is to remind myself of my barbarism.

TAYMORE   There's beauty in... a barbarian woman.

A long pause.

MIELKE   Taymore, the cold inside of me is gone, you... you don't have the need to place your arms on the perimeter of me... to place your lips on the steam that comes out of my mouth... that your hands take a stroll between my legs. Has the frost also made a hostage of you? My fears, go play hide-and-seek in the trenches of some unfinished war... control... is escaping from my hands like the sands of a seashore I have yet to know...

Day 32 — 7 a.m.
Fall

MIELKE sleeps in the large improvised bed alongside ALI and TAYMORE. The following scene will happen in whispers.

ALI   Taymore, it's cold inside of me... I'm full of hypothermia.... No...

TAYMORE   Just one last time before we go.

ALI   No, I know what you want.

TAYMORE   After, I'll let you make more sleep.

ALI   What I wanted was a family, I've got one.

TAYMORE   Okay?

ALI   ...

TAYMORE   Say yes?

Beat.

ALI   Okay.... But you asked for it.

TAYMORE   Rock, paper, jackknife.... Rock, paper, jackknife... *(ALI lets out a small laugh.)* Rock, paper, jackknife.... Ha!

ALI   Ali.... It's Ali's turn to go night-night.

ALI laughs.

TAYMORE   You're cheating. It should be her.

ALI   No. I lost. It's done.

TAYMORE   You lost...

ALI   That's the game, Taymore: first name spoken. We're done. *(beat)* Yes?

TAYMORE   Yes. I understand. It's what you want.

ALI   Yes.

Beat.

TAYMORE Sleep tight, Ali.

ALI Put Mute next to me.

TAYMORE I already feel the absence of you…

Blackout.

Day 32 — 10:15 a.m.
Fall

Blinding lights of a northern morning. The wind is still howling outside. An unseen object can be heard pounding against the door. MIELKE wakes up. She is confused and covered in blood. ALI is lying next to her, half-conscious.

MIELKE Ali… Ali…

ALI He's gone. Taymore. No one was spared: Mute… Nox… Sola… he's relieved the village of part of its inhabitants… he played rock, paper, jackknife… with me, and this time, when I lost, I lost. I could've gotten away…

ALI faints.

MIELKE Speak again to me…. What were you saying? Ali, Ali, what were you saying? Keep telling me the words…

MIELKE tries to stop the bleeding with pieces of blanket.

ALI You speak our Harsh…. Taymore has had the success of convincing you. He has persuasion like a talent… *(beat)* See, before, I was the little voice that spoke the loudest in the head of him. Rock, paper, jackknife… is a dangerous little game we made the invention of together. The persons who are the all-arounds of us play without knowing. I lost control of the game, and of Taymore. I lied. Yesterday, strictly spoken, you're the one who should have lost, not me. But you saved the life of me in the mine, you took the care of me. I would have liked to continue this life, to collect even more of this love of yours…

MIELKE Hold on tight, I'm taking y—

ALI Let me go. Life is too heavy inside me. I lost yesterday and I want to continue losing today. I'm suffering, I have a right to die. But now Taymore is running. He's taken a liking to this need to kill and it comes back and it's in him. I'm almost gone, he doesn't need a game to get there. This he left as yours. *(She is holding the tape recorder.)* He left with the dictionary and the megacity's telephone book. Chase after him, he's a fast-running danger. The plane, it's today…

MIELKE *(trying to cover up ALI as best she can)* Ali? Ali. Taymore made the preparation of his itinerary… is that it? Ali? Answer me!

ALI Now, I say no more. Now, I am tired.

ALI dies. The tape recorder falls from her hands and starts playing. The sound of a plane taking off outside.

VOICE OF TAYMORE ON THE TAPE RECORDER   I will return—

MIELKE rewinds the tape.

I will return—

MIELKE   What? Speak again to me.

MIELKE rewinds the tape a second time.

VOICE OF TAYMORE ON THE TAPE RECORDER   I will return—

MIELKE   Oh. I was mistaken in my listening.... And the storm in the out-there that won't stop draping its snow.... It knocks at my door as though I really might give it an answer.

MIELKE picks up ALI's body and walks toward the classroom door, where the pounding was coming from. MIELKE opens the door and freezes. TAYMORE has hung himself there, the dictionary and the telephone book at his feet.

VOICE OF TAYMORE ON THE TAPE RECORDER   —but when next you see me, I will have conquered my exile and even changed my name. I will have become *Je-suis-mort*. I will have become greater, having ended the life of all the little voices that won't stop the arguing in my head. I will finally speak freely without encrypting my words. I will finally be alone.... While you are listening to this, you are probably alone in the middle of this white nowhere, have you any idea what you will do? My fears of seeing the suffering told me to kill those who were the all-arounds of me. I hope your own fears will be more understanding towards humanity...

The end.

Jouliks
(Jouliks)

by Marie-Christine Lê-Huu

translated by Crystal Beliveau

Introduction to
Jouliks (*Jouliks*)

Jouliks[1] is a darkly tender drama exploring the vast, bumpy, and treacherous terrain of love. The brilliant lights it projects on this terrain are harsh and terrible, yet, at the same time, they often stir gentle smiles of complicity, as they are refracted through the eyes and voice of a seven-year-old girl, the Little One. The play dramatizes a few days in the life of a family: grandparents, parents, child, and neighbour. The grandparents, Mam and Pappy, have come for a visit after seven years of estrangement, in which time they did not see their daughter, Vera, her partner, Zak, or the Little One. From the very moment of her arrival, Mam sets to work reconstituting her daughter's home and family so they conform to her extremely conventional sense of propriety. Vera left the family home ten years before in order to escape the narrow values, constraints, and hypocrisy of such propriety. She and Zak have chosen to live in a "dilapidated wooden house at the end of a dusty country road," where social constraints are non-existent and where poverty "doesn't give a damn—happy, sunny poverty" (Setting). They and the Little One are the *jouliks* of the title, social outcasts for whom freedom in spirit and body and respect of others' freedom is a primary consideration. As the clash between the conflicting value systems of the two generations grows increasingly acute from scene to scene, a sense of dread develops. The audience can see that Vera's parents' visit will inevitably lead to "big trouble" (Prologue). This is a family in the process of bursting apart.

The conflict between world views is not an abstract or theoretical argument in *Jouliks*. It is a conflict that is played out in the memory, emotions, and guts of each of the characters, since, despite all their differences, they have shared experiences and they love each other—each in their own way. The difficulty of finding words to express their love runs through the play, where no one is able to say "serious things" like "I love you" and where addressing serious issues directly is like "walking on eggshells" (Prologue). The play makes one know that life without love and friendship is not worth living. And yet the dynamics of love are so complex that the search for it cannot be anything more than a work in process. *Jouliks* is an anatomy of love in all its inescapable contradictions. The characters of the play show that in its positive manifestations love is compassion, understanding, communication, rapturous intimacy, joy, respect, and freedom. The characters' lives are, however, a complex amalgam of these experiences that they embrace and the extreme pain love causes when it gives rise to moral policing, guilt, self-doubt, silence, separation, loss, bitterness, abuse of power, and death.

The perspective on love developed by Lê-Huu is brilliant. She has created the character of the Little One, who is both witness and participant in the family drama. She speaks on two wavelengths in that she slips back and forth between a narrative mode, in which, detached from direct involvement in the action and dialogue, she talks about what is going on in the other characters' actions, minds, and hearts, and a playing mode when she interacts with the others as the child in the family. Although the Little One is a compassionate and perspicacious observer, she does not analyze in any depth what she sees around her, nor does she make moral judgments of others' behaviour. Lê-Huu has written lines and created actions for her that are delightfully childlike, using words that are direct and simple and finding solutions to problems that only a child could invent. Her words would be received initially by the audience as the spontaneous thoughts of a child. However, their multiple levels of meaning and the serious questions they raise quickly come to mind, particularly when visual images enter the picture. The Little One often speaks of the inadequacy of words, whether for purposes of communication or to understand events.

The disproportionate distance between the Little One's childlike understanding of characters' relations and the terrible ripping that is going on in the lives of those she loves provides surprisingly moving insight into the ways in which love can thrill or wound. As she moves fearlessly through the dangerous minefield of family politics, she reminds one of Voltaire's Candide, who provides probing insight into a vast range of social ills and awful violence while he himself remains quite detached from the horrors he sees by virtue of his innocence. An example of a question posed by the Little One which remains with me because of its inexhaustible resonance occurs at a moment when she is playing on the floor beside Mam and Vera. The members of her toy marching corps that were not killed are returning from war, and she is counting their steps. As she is apparently making errors in her counting, Vera corrects her. The Little One explains that she is accelerating her counting because they are in a hurry to get home, and she asks "How many steps does it take to come back from the war?" (Scene 8). It is, of course, a child's naive question for which there is no clear answer because of all the variables involved. However, for me, the question takes an incisive look at the impact of war on all those who have lived through its violence in any way. Does one ever come back from war? Other one-liners tossed out by the Little One, giving understated emphasis to the thematics of *Jouliks*, occur throughout the play, as, for example, when she asks after Mam observes that Zak's "life was going nowhere," "But who says life always has to be running after something?" (Scene 4)

Jouliks begins with a prologue and ends with an epilogue, both delivered by the Little One. These framing moments allow her to introduce herself to the audience and to provide the information that there have been deaths and she is now in the institutionalized hands of her grandparents. Since we soon learn that Mam plays to the full her maternal role of designated keeper of love as she understands it— constructed by dominant values, prevailing proprieties and conventions, and hegemonic discourse of patriarchal and materialistic society—this is a chilling announcement. The Prologue and Epilogue remove any element of suspense regarding the final outcome of Mam and Pappy's catastrophic visit. They thereby leave the audience free to accompany the Little One and her family on the path that leads to such tragedy.

The Little One tells us that Vera is a woman with an extraordinarily beautiful body "when Vera's inside it" (Scene 7) who demonstrates an ability to love her child and laugh with her without putting limits on her freedom. Her refreshing approach to mothering offers the child explanations and protection when protection is needed, without imposing rules or restrictions when they would be arbitrary or superfluous. At the same time that Vera assumes joyfully the role of mother, she is dramatized as a sexual human being, having and claiming gratification for her own urgent desires. She loves her partner Zak with an erotic joy and sensuality that is spontaneous and unconstrained. Her naturalness is reflected in her usual way of dressing and keeping her hair, which reflects no concern about the dictates of the socio-cultural norms propagated by the conventions of the beauty myth. One can sense the richness of her psychic and spiritual energy, her pleasure in life.

It would be a mistake, however, to see Vera as an untroubled free spirit. She and Zak both have a past. They carry memories, stresses, fears, and doubts inside them. She is a complex character, forging a new path for herself as a woman and facing serious challenges in her determination to be true to herself. Vera's agitation, sadness, and obsession with arranging the house, of which the Little One speaks (Scene 1), show her anxious to be seen living up to her mother's expectations. In effect, as subsequent scenes show, Vera's past has continued to weigh on her, even though it has most often been set aside in her memory. The parents' visit is the return to the surface of the unhappiness of her childhood. The visit has placed her in a position where she is: "just walking around in her head, in memories that make her sad" (Scene 7). Vera has rejected all the values, practices, and roles she was required to learn as a child, but she has not lost the love she felt for her parents, nor the guilt that haunts her as a result of the conflict between such love and her absence from their lives.

The Little One's narration also reveals that all is not peace and harmony for Vera in her relation with Zak, particularly when his unbridled anger explodes and he speaks "in his road language." Unlike Zak, who has been coming and going as he pleases, Vera has not been free to ask him questions about his rambling: "[…] she knew she couldn't ask questions, that if she opened the door with questions, her Zak would suffocate and she'd lose him" (Scene 4). When her irrepressible anger bursts out in Scene 12 as a result of Zak's departure just before her parents' arrival and his morose silence following his return, it becomes clear that his egotism in not thinking at all about the impact on her of his exercise of total freedom can and does hurt her deeply, leaving her alone and unhappy. In this case, his inconsiderate departure has significantly aggravated the intense guilt she has been made to feel under her mother's gruelling questions.

Mam's mode of mothering comes immediately into view at the beginning when she takes over Vera's house, fails to notice Vera's week-long efforts to make it nice, starts to wash the windows, and makes sure that Vera knows she has done so. Mam is a stock character in Québec theatre, incarnating all the stereotypes surrounding mothering and femininity: the domineering wife and mother, talkative and opinionated, incapable of seeing others for who and what they are, constantly surveilling, judging, and correcting others' behaviour, spouting moral platitudes, demanding apologies and explanations, bitter and incapable of relaxing or enjoying any kind of pleasure. She is obsessed with her memories of the past. They represent for her nothing more than a relentless series of incidents when someone treated her poorly. Her view of love shows itself to be based on duty, conformity to social values and religious dogma, and not at all on a spontaneous show of affection. When the Little One becomes aware that she will be judged on her appearance at the time she is required by Vera to put on a dress and comb her hair, Lê-Huu has her observe dryly: "They mustn't love us very much." Mam's thoughtless judgments of Zak, whom she calls a "dirty, good-for-nothing, womanizing bum" (Scene 9) are particularly cruel. Mam's love-demolishing world view is an entire package that she felt compelled to impose on her daughter when Vera was a child, and that she immediately reactivates upon her arrival in Vera's home. The first half of the play shows her taking her daughter on the entire trip of feminine propriety: proper clothes to wear, the house spotlessly clean, the right techniques for preparing food, control of children, selection of husband, financial situation in society, regular observation of the rituals of religion.

Pappy is a moderating influence for the negative impact of the grandparents' arrival and Mam's devastating behaviour. Like Vera, he is constantly bullied by Mam's jibes and taunts; he regularly makes short retorts that deflate the validity of her hot air; he takes quiet steps to express his compassion and love for Vera. Still, he is not at all a worthy adversary of his wife's dangerous interference in the lives of those she claims to love. Despite his awareness of the family's dysfunctionality, he is either unfailingly compliant, dozing off, or walking away; he fails to take any decisive steps that would correct problems or put an end to Mam's repetitive scenario. In many ways, the role he has assumed in his relation to Mam and his concern for Vera is one of aggressive passivity.

Zak's wordless and unapologetic return and the brutal confrontation between Zak and Mam ensuing from it precipitate the crisis that has been building in Vera's head, heart, and body. She explodes at Mam, affirming her absolute right to live her own life and to love as she wishes:

> I never asked you for anything! Nothing! Not your advice, not your help, not to come judge me here, in my own home! Can't you just love us the way we are? [...] You're gonna shut up and let me live! You're gonna shut up and let me live my life, you got that? (Scene 12)

Vera follows this powerful affirmation of her own right to choose and her detachment from all the negative stereotypes of mother-daughter relations with an equally powerful outburst at Zak: "Leave me alone. Go away! You don't care about anyone else! It's you, you, and always you" (Scene 12). The Little One listens to what she takes to be the "sound of our house shattering" (Scene 13).

Vera's powerful and direct expression of her need for his love to contain a caring component is enough to slowly bring Zak out of his shell, confront directly his memory of his abandonment by his mother, recognize the force of his love for Vera and his need to respect her freedom, and acknowledge the devastating effect on her of his lack of consideration. The situation is excruciatingly painful for Vera, yet in the end the possibility of reconciliation and a newly found frank basis for love hovers in this modest house. However, the haunting mention of death that has also been hovering around this family throughout the play cannot be washed away. Great damage has been done, and tragedy occurs. It is the Little One herself who, knowing the intensity of the happiness brought to her parents by the total love they share and running her beautiful memories through her head as though it were a movie she will not erase, is the unwitting cause of their deaths.

Jouliks is a gentle and terrifying reminder of the complexity and fragility of love, the beauty of the human body, the inadequacy and absolute necessity of words, the dangerous contingency of social convention and the inevitability of misunderstanding, separation, and death. As in the plays of Perreault and Lebeau in this volume, Lê-Huu has created a memorable child character who faces the most difficult and urgent problems human beings have to address. These problems are usually represented in drama and theatre through the lives of adults, as though tragedy did not exist in children's lives. Theatre, movies, and television programs in today's culture often endow shows for children or with child characters with Disneyesque qualities, as though all children existed in lands of sweetness, light, sprightly images, and frolicking music, far removed from such realities as others' incomprehensible behaviour, suffering, loneliness, death, meanness, displacement, violence, loss of love and security, words that don't say enough, the disappearance of memory, the fragility of hope.

Jouliks introduces all these—credibly and strikingly—into the life of the seven-year-old Little One without suppressing the childish charm, resilience, and humour of her irresistible behaviour. Lê-Huu, Lebeau, and Perreault join a number of Québec women playwrights for whom the curtains drawn between theatre for adults and theatre for young audiences are tossed aside, such as Anne Hébert, whose *Le temps sauvage* (1963), *L'Île de la demoiselle* (1979), and *La cage* (1990) all dramatize the lives of adolescent characters dangerously threatened by the obsessions and violent behaviour of abusive adults. Carole Fréchette, Lise Vaillancourt, Abla Farhoud, Geneviève Billette, and Evelyne de la Chenelière have all created child characters with experiences and words that cast a powerfully fresh light on human affairs, while themes of mother-child relations are well-developed and thematically integrated in a majority of the Québec dramaturgical corpus by women.

The world view of Lê-Huu, Perreault, Lebeau, and Jasmine Dubé, another wonderful Québec playwright specializing in theatre for young audiences, embraces centrally the perceptions, experiences, and observations of children and adolescents. This inclusion is interesting thematically and philosophically, but also theatrically, in that the plays of these writers are richly experimental as they use images, develop dialogue, and invent techniques whereby the full and complex humanity of the young is put on stage for both child and adult audiences. The work of Lê-Huu, Lebeau, Perreault, and Dubé is particularly exemplary from an artistic point of view in its deceptively simple yet richly layered poetic language, use of non-verbal languages, amazing exploitation of narrative on stage (a development of the monologue that has also been a major component of women's theatre), and playful destabilization of traditional play structures and the flow of time.

Notes

[1] The word *joulik* appears in some French dictionaries, where it is defined as a synonym of *voyou*. An English equivalent for the word seems impossible to find. Crystal Beliveau has chosen "outcast" (Prologue) to evoke the situation of those who live on the margins of society. This is probably the best choice, even though it does not quite capture the idea of vagabond and stranger contained in French. Of eastern European origin, the word *joulik* captures the lifestyle of the Roma tradition.

About Marie-Christine Lê-Huu

Trained as an actor, Marie-Christine Lê-Huu now divides her time between playwriting and acting. She is the author of ten plays for the theatre, including *Faust, pantin du diable* and *Les disparus, chronique de la cruauté*, both of which were shortlisted for Best Original Play at the Gala des Masques. Her play *Jouliks* was produced in Québec by the Théâtre d'Aujourd'hui, as well as in France and Belgium. *Jouliks* received the Prix Sony Labou Tansi des lycéens, and was shortlisted for Best Original Play at the Gala des Masques and for the Governor General's Literary Award for Drama. She has also written two plays for young audiences for the Théâtre de l'Avant-Pays: *Une Forêt dans la tête* and *Le Voyage*. She directed her first production, *Le Voyage*, in the fall of 2009.

As an actor, Lê-Huu has participated primarily in new Québec plays, including *La Crise* by Hélène Ducharme at Théâtre Motus, *2025, L'Année du serpent* by Philippe Ducros at the Théâtre du Grand Jour, and *Jouliks* at the Théâtre d'Aujourd'hui. On television, she was a member of the cast of *4 et demi* and of the children's program *Cornemuse*. She was nominated Best Actress, Children's Program, at the Gemini awards for the role of Tibor in *Cornemuse*, and, more recently, for that of Alia in the children's program *Toc toc toc*.

Published Works by Marie-Christine Lê-Huu

Les disparus, chronique de la cruauté (2002). Montréal: Dramaturges Éditeurs.

Jouliks (2005). Carnières, Belgium: Lansman Éditeur.

Jouliks was first performed on March 8, 2005 in Paris at the Théâtre des Sources by D'Après la pluie, co-produced by La Scène nationale 61 and Le Rive Gauche, with the following company:

The Little One	Catherine Verlaguet
Vera	Catherine Le Henan
Zak	Patrick Azam
Mam	Geneviève Penchenat
Pappy	Louis-Basile Samier
William	Xavier Kuentz

Directed by Gérald Chatelain
Set design by Sylvia Goubern
Lighting by Alain Vincent
Music by Pierre Gaudin
Assistant director Isabelle Lusignan

...

Jouliks was first performed in Québec on April 5, 2005 in Montréal at the Théâtre d'Aujourd'hui, with the following company:

The Little One	Marie-Christine Lê-Huu
Vera	Suzanne Clément
Zak	Patrick Goyette
Mam	Catherine Bégin
Pappy	Aubert Pallascio
William	Guillaume Champoux

Directed by Robert Bellefeuille
Set design by Jean Bard
Costumes by Sarah Balleux
Lighting by Etienne Boucher
Music by Louise Beaudoin
Assistant director Diane Fortin

Characters

The Little One, seven years old, intelligent, free-spirited, left to her own devices but happy that way, loved.
Vera, her mother, a wild and beautiful woman.
Zak, her father, a rambling man who has always lived on the road.
Mam, Vera's mother, a woman who loves all wrong but with good intentions.
Pappy, Vera's father, a man who is loving but uncomfortable expressing love.
William, the neighbour, the one who desires and waits.

Setting

A dilapidated wooden house at the end of a dusty country road. Drafty windows with warped frames. A hole in the roof that lets in the rain. Mismatched objects, a clothesline outside, sheets that are threadbare but clean, a red dress, old but pretty. An impression of poverty, but poverty that doesn't give a damn—happy, sunny poverty.

Note

The Little One is wearing old clothes, pants for running through the tall grass and splashing around in the nearby stream. She is the one telling the story. Sometimes she is part of the action and sometimes she watches the others from a distance, simply turning to face us and addressing us directly.

JOULIKS

Prologue

THE LITTLE ONE is alone on stage. The lighting is on her only and is spare. She addresses the audience in the narrative mode.

THE LITTLE ONE   I'm seven. I'm Skindiana. My mom always called me skinny but I like Skindiana better. I think it's prettier.

They came here earlier. There were three of them. My mam, my pappy, and Number Three. I call him Number Three because I don't know who he is. Never seen him before. But he came here with my pappy and my mam and we all cut the silence with a butter knife.

They came here looking like death, because there was one. Two actually. I'm telling you that because there's no way you could know but it's important so why not say it right off the bat. They were here looking for words to tell me things people never know how to say. Serious things like "I love you" or "I don't love you anymore even if we spent seven years under the same ceiling and I told you every day we were for keeps but, what can I say, no one really knows how long for keeps will be."

Three of them came here. Maybe they thought that with more of them looking, it'd be easier to find the words, but it wasn't. And since my pappy came from another country when he was little, I don't think he was much help. They spent fifteen minutes preparing me, with a bite-your-nails kind of silence, and walking on eggshells. And I was the eggshells.

They were here to tell me about a disaster. The kind that makes kids un-normal after finding out, if they were normal before. But that's another story and I'm staying out of it.

They were here to tell me about my parents being dead but I already knew about my parents being dead since I'm the one who did it. And don't go thinking I'm a criminal because this is really a love story, but people don't understand things like that. So it's better not to say anything or they put you in some kind of prison place. It's better to say things they can understand. And how life works isn't one of those things. I guess no one ever explained it to them.

You I can tell what happened. Then you can believe whoever you want because in the newspapers there might be newspaper truths, the kind that sometimes lie so they'll sound even more true. But our real lives won't be in their words. They'll be in between the lines, where it's white, where they don't let us speak.

There was a Vera and a Zak. And I know that because they were my mom and my dad and that's because they loved each other.

William's in our story too, but that's a coincidence. He came into our lives one movie night and he couldn't get out. It's not our fault but you can't come near us. We've always been jouliks, and in Zak's language, that means outcasts. Zak used to live on the road. He was in an acrobat routine and there was a beautiful woman who played violin to help people cry because it was a sad acrobat routine. I know because he told me. That was before life happened to me, and that was an accident, but that's how life works.

The real story of my parents being dead started like this, with the old folks. They arrived in our lives that day, and our lives ended up in big trouble.

1. The Dress

Daytime, in the house. VERA is tidying up. She seems nervous, unable to sit still, never satisfied with the position of any single object.

THE LITTLE ONE It's been a week now that Vera's been acting strange. Because all this scrubbing and rubbing and putting flowers in the bedrooms and moving things ten times to make sure they're in the right place, I've never seen her do that before. She tells me it's because Pappy and Mam are coming soon. I'm happy because I've never seen them before. They came when I was really little. I know because Pappy made a tiny cradle just for me and it's made of wood and it's still in my room and my mom always tells me it's a present from my pappy because he loves me. And there's lots of glue on it, but it's glue you can't see because Zak worked really hard so no one can tell it's broken. I remember that, it happened the day Zak got mad, and Vera and him were shouting and shouting and Vera was crying and Zak went and got the little cradle in my room and started smashing it to pieces. And he was shouting things in his road language, the one from before us, and I couldn't understand a word he was saying but it sounded pretty serious. It took a long time for Vera to forgive him. I could tell she wanted to but she was holding back because the cradle was the only souvenir she had of her dad. And breaking a souvenir like that deserves a lot of guilt, so she gave Zak a whole week to let his grow, and when it was big enough, Zak took all the pieces—and there were a lot because it was an anger that needed to make a big mess—and he went into the yard and started gluing it all back together and sanding it and making it look exactly like it was before. That was when Vera decided to forgive him. And she forgave him a lot. They forgave each other all night and the whole week after. I even had to make my own food all by myself because when they forgive each other like that, it's not like they can get up for little things like eating or getting dressed or hanging sheets on the line. So I took care of everything because it's not like I had anything important to do and I was happy they were forgiving each other properly because they are my mom and my dad after all.

Vera dusted the cradle from top to bottom. It's so Pappy'll see that we take good care of it. Then she went to the hairdresser in town but I don't know why because she's never gone to the hairdresser in her life and she doesn't need that to be beautiful. Actually, I think she's way prettier when her hair is messy and falling all over the place. But I'm not gonna tell her that because today she kind of looks like someone whose feelings you don't want to hurt.

VERA   I have a surprise for you.

THE LITTLE ONE   What is it?

VERA   Open it.

THE LITTLE ONE   *(opening it)* What's it for?

VERA   It's a dress.

THE LITTLE ONE   Oh. What for?

VERA   Do you want to put it on?

THE LITTLE ONE   No.

VERA   Put it on.

THE LITTLE ONE   Why a dress? Dresses are for girls. Girls with dresses can't run fast because the dresses always want to fly away.

VERA   It's only for today. Will you just try it on?

THE LITTLE ONE   No.

VERA   Please.

THE LITTLE ONE   No. Because I'm not a girl-who-wears-dresses kind of girl. I'm a pants-runners-bruises-on-my-knees kind of girl.

VERA   Just this once.

THE LITTLE ONE   No.

VERA picks up a comb and a ribbon.

VERA   Come here for a minute.

THE LITTLE ONE   *(apprehensive)* Why?

VERA   Come here.

THE LITTLE ONE   What are you going to do?

VERA   Comb your hair.

THE LITTLE ONE   What for?

VERA   *(trying to appease her)* Look. I bought a ribbon.

THE LITTLE ONE   What for?

VERA   For your hair.

THE LITTLE ONE No. I'm not a combed-hair kind of girl. I don't want to dress up as a combed-hair kind of girl.

VERA (*impatient*) Hurry up. They're gonna be here soon. We have to go meet them.

THE LITTLE ONE That's why?

VERA What?

THE LITTLE ONE It's for that?

VERA What?

THE LITTLE ONE It's because of them that we have to wear costumes?

VERA Stop it! Putting on a dress and combing your hair isn't a costume. It's normal.

THE LITTLE ONE Why can't we be like we usually are?

VERA Because we're having company. It's to welcome them.

THE LITTLE ONE But I can welcome them with pants on.

VERA Okay, that's enough! Get undressed and put this on.

THE LITTLE ONE begrudgingly puts on the dress.

THE LITTLE ONE They mustn't love us very much.

VERA Why do you say that?

THE LITTLE ONE Because if they loved us, we wouldn't have to do all this.

Then my Vera brought her hands to her face and started crying. She wasn't crying like she usually does. Not like when Zak and her make each other sad. She was crying as though she was really little. Like she was a wet little bird that had fallen from her nest and was scared her mom wouldn't come and get her. She was crying like she'd forgotten she was my mom. That's why I forgot I was little and I took her in my arms. But that was a terrible idea because instead of comforting her, it made her cry kind of even harder. And I was scared there'd be a flood because she was making almost as much water as when the rain comes in through the hole in the roof. But I didn't go get the bucket because it's not like you can catch sadness in a bucket and it probably wouldn't have helped things any.

Because of Vera's sadness, we missed the train. When she saw the time, we started running and running and I could tell I shouldn't have put the dress on but I didn't say anything. When we got to the station, Vera's hair was all messy and I thought she looked beautiful but she tried to redo it like the hairdresser had. And I don't think she'd watched him very closely because it ended up looking like a kind of lopsided mountain on the top of her head. Then we sat down and waited, but we were actually waiting late, which wasn't very helpful because while we were doing that, the old folks were walking to the house. And when they arrived, there was no one there to greet them and that wasn't good for the circumstances. And the circumstances were that we hadn't seen them in seven years and Mam thought she'd be greeted like a queen with a red carpet and a big WELCOME banner and that we'd be there with Zak and a car for their suitcases. And for Mam, that was kind of a big disappointment.

2. The Train Station

MAM and PAPPY are at the station. Standing tall and proud on the platform, they wait for VERA.

MAM Well! Quite the reunion this is!

3. The Road

The old folks are walking to VERA's house. We can sense that the trip was long and they are tired. MAM is carrying the suitcases.

MAM It's up ahead. We're almost there.

PAPPY Yes.

MAM It's not that they're heavy, but they're still suitcases aren't they, Pappy?

PAPPY Yes.

MAM Still, I'd say they're not as heavy as they sometimes can be.

PAPPY Yes.

MAM I'm talking about the weight of the suitcases.

PAPPY Yes.

MAM You don't give a hoot about the weight of the suitcases!

PAPPY What?

MAM You could care less about the weight of the suitcases! I know, I know, for you, it's humdrum. Like talking about the birds in the sky. You want me to say I don't care about the weight of the suitcases either. And yes, I think it's humdrum, oh yes I do. If I weren't the one carrying the suitcases, I wouldn't even bring it up...

PAPPY Mam?

MAM Yes?

PAPPY Are you sure you don't want me to take the suitcases?

MAM No no, Pappy. That would tire you out. You don't have the strength for it, do you? But honestly, they could have been there. I always said that man was… I mean, really, leaving an old pair like us to walk. You have to have no heart! Not to mention that their house…. Did he have to cart them off to the boondocks? Not a house for the past two miles. Not even a dog! Not even the skinniest little dog! Nothing but dry hay and trees, trees…. He never did know how to live like the rest of the world. And when you don't know how to live like the rest of the world, that's what happens, you have to hide out. You see what I'm saying…

PAPPY Yes.

MAM I mean… you know…

PAPPY Yes, I know what you're saying.

MAM Good.

PAPPY Everything you're saying, I know.

MAM Good.

PAPPY Because everything you're saying, you've said it before.

MAM Is that so? *(a beat, then apologetic)* Must be getting old, Pappy. Must be our lives that are already lived. Must be our lives that are already so lived, there's nothing new to add.

PAPPY I guess so, Mam. But lay off on the "must be's," will you? Because your "must be's" are depressing. Not to hurt your feelings but they're depressing.

They arrive at the front door of the house.

MAM Okay, here we are. Straighten up, Pappy. Straighten up so I can brush you off. *(brushing him off)* All this dust! No way am I walking into my daughter's house looking like something the cat dragged in, oh no! *(She hands him a hankie.)* Here, wipe your brow. And stand up straight. She'll see we're better than this. We made it to her place all by ourselves, didn't we?

PAPPY Mam?

MAM Yes?

PAPPY You want to give it a bit of a rest?

MAM Give what a rest?

PAPPY We're not even inside yet and already I smell trouble.

MAM And you're gonna say it's my fault, I suppose? Because maybe I'm the one who let two senior citizens hoof it for an hour on a dusty old road in this sun…. Don't you find this sun's a little…. Must be the air that's no good or something. This sun, it beats down like it wants to dry you right up. It's not the same as our sun back home, that's for sure!

PAPPY At the risk of disappointing you, Mam, it's exactly the same.

MAM Would you stop, Pappy! It's like you're trying to get under my skin! If you weren't always trying to get under my skin, I'd be in a better mood, oh yes I would! So please, try not to spoil our reunion. Come on!

She knocks at the door.

THE LITTLE ONE Mam knocked and knocked, but because we weren't there, we didn't answer. We only arrived after. And Mam had already made herself at home, so it almost felt like we were disturbing her. Vera even knocked before going in and Mam came and opened the door like it was totally normal, wiping her hands on a rag she'd been using to wash the windows. At first, there was a butter-knife silence.

4. Reunion

VERA and THE LITTLE ONE are inside the house.

MAM *(after a long beat)* I washed the windows.

VERA You didn't have to, Mom.

MAM Oh yes I did. Just look at all the dirt I wiped off! Look! And to think I raised you in a house with—

VERA Okay, Mom!

MAM That's all you can say? You couldn't possibly say thank you, oh no!

PAPPY Now Mam…

MAM What? I can't talk to my daughter now, is that it? You remember, Pappy, that even if she hasn't exactly requested to see her parents in seven years, she's still my daughter, and I still have the right to give her my opinion!

VERA goes to her dad and gives him a hug and a kiss.

VERA Hi Dad.

PAPPY is touched. He gives her a few awkward taps on the shoulder.

MAM So there's the Little One! Well!

She looks at the child but doesn't really know what to say. She would like to be warm but doesn't know how. She looks her over from head to toe. THE LITTLE ONE is uncomfortable. She tugs on her dress.

VERA Give your grandma a kiss, sweetie.

THE LITTLE ONE gives her a kiss and sits down on the arm of the chair where PAPPY is sitting. They look at each other for a while without speaking, then start to laugh for no reason, a hearty and irrepressible laugh. THE LITTLE ONE pulls gently on the old man's ears, a tender language between the two of them, an awkward and sincere affection.

Between VERA and MAM, it's quite the opposite: an uncomfortable silence.

I'm sorry, Mom. We got there late.

MAM Oh, that's all right. Your father and I aren't that old! You think we can't walk anymore?

VERA No…

MAM It's not an hour out in that sun of yours that's gonna get the best of a woman like me. I've seen worse, oh yes I have! To get rid of your old mom, you'll have to get up bright and early, my dear!

PAPPY Now Mam!

MAM What? Have I or have I not seen worse? Did I not look after your old mother for ten years? Did I not wash her every single day when she couldn't even move the toes on her feet? Did I not raise our two children all by myself for two years because you got it in your head to find a better opportunity in that godforsaken city? What was the name of that city again? Never mind, I'd rather not remember anyway. *(She turns to VERA.)* Because after two years, the only opportunity he brought back was a pile of shirts that needed mending. That, and a hard drinking habit. Your father who'd never had a drop in his life!

PAPPY Here we go…

MAM I'm just saying, Pappy, if you'd always toed the line, my bringing it up wouldn't bother you so much, oh no it wouldn't! But what can you do? We make our beds, it's up to us to tuck in the corners. *(talking to THE LITTLE ONE, a little hypocritically)* And your daddy? Where is he? It would have been nice to see him. I thought maybe he'd come to the station to say hello… and we sure wouldn't have said no because the suitcases are a little on the heavy side! Did he go out? *(to VERA)* He could have at least left you the car, no? I mean, the station's not exactly next door. Leaving you and the Little One to walk like that…

VERA We don't have a car, Mom.

MAM What do you mean, you don't have a car? My poor girl! It's not like I didn't warn you. The moment I saw him. Remember? I said, "My dear, that boy will not make you happy." Did I or did I not say that?

PAPPY Mam, in front of the Little One?

MAM Oh, he probably had better things to do than come get an old pair like us.

VERA He… went to work.

MAM Is that right? He has a job? Something good?

PAPPY Let it go, Mam.

MAM My poor dear, good or not, we can see plain as day he hasn't made life easy for you. This house is about to fall to the ground! And you and the Little One are both so skinny. *(to THE LITTLE ONE)* Here, I brought you some candies.

THE LITTLE ONE No thank you.

MAM What do you mean, no thank you? Do you know what these are? They're candies. Pralines! Caramels!

THE LITTLE ONE No thank you.

MAM *(to VERA)* Is she sick or something?

VERA She's perfectly fine!

MAM Okay, okay…. So will he be home late? I don't want to impose, but your dad and I are a little peckish. Right, Pappy? With the trip and all. And you know your dad, he's always had a delicate stomach. When it's time to eat, it's time to eat!

PAPPY No it isn't, Mam.

MAM Oh, he's just saying that to be polite, but I know your dad. Known him fifty-seven years, since our school days! So he's not the one who's gonna tell me when he does or does not need to eat. *(beat)* So, will he be back soon?

THE LITTLE ONE The problem was Zak, we didn't know when he'd be back. That's how it was sometimes. He'd need to get away, like before, when he was free, when he didn't have Vera holding back his heart. He usually left on rainy days because the rain brought him bad memories, and he'd suddenly have the urge to take off, to go drown his sorrows on the road, to make secrets for his return, secrets that would drive my Vera crazy, crazy with love and sadness because she knew she couldn't ask questions, she knew that if she opened the door with questions, her Zak would suffocate and she'd lose him. Not because he didn't know how to love but because he was born like that, on the road, with the jouliks.

This time he didn't leave because of the rain but because of the old folks. My Zak, he knew Mam didn't like his life. She never thought it was good enough for us. She said his life was going nowhere. But who says life always has to be running after something?

VERA He'll be back late. He said not to wait.

THE LITTLE ONE Vera, she's used to not waiting. She knows there's no sense waiting, that she just has to let time go by. Her Zak has always been that way so she knows what to do, don't think she doesn't.

When Zak's away, sometimes William comes over. The three of us stay here and we don't say anything because it's not like talking doesn't make the time go by. And on those days, I can tell William is trying really hard not to take her in his arms because Vera, she's the love of his life. It's not a problem for us, but for him it kind of is. But that's his business because it's not like I didn't warn him.

William I met the day I went to the movie. He was surprised I was there by myself because he thought I seemed a little young.

5. The Movie Theatre

An evening, in town, at the entrance to the movie theatre.

WILLIAM   How old are you?

THE LITTLE ONE   But I had money, so surprised or not, he had to let me in. So he sold me a ticket. William was the ticket seller, but I guess you already got that. When I came out of the theatre, it was dark.

WILLIAM   It's dark.

THE LITTLE ONE   He said that to make a conversation because it's not like I hadn't noticed.

WILLIAM   Isn't anyone coming to pick you up? Do you want me to walk you home?

THE LITTLE ONE   Are you afraid of the dark?

WILLIAM   No. Are your parents coming to pick you up?

THE LITTLE ONE   Nope.

WILLIAM   Then I'll walk you home. Your parents let you stay out this late? Where are they?

THE LITTLE ONE   How should I know? I was at the movies. You want me to tell you something? The only thing I'm scared to do by myself is sleep, so you don't have to walk me home. *(beat)* Do you have a girlfriend?

WILLIAM   No.

THE LITTLE ONE   Then you can't come to my house. Because my mom, it's dangerous how beautiful she is. She even used to be public. But that's not because she was a slut, it's because life wasn't giving her work and she was hungry. So sometimes men took her to the restaurant, but the restaurant was in a hotel and she could sleep there but only if she pretended to love them. Vera's so beautiful, you can't even imagine. You can even die of it. That's why you can't come to my house because once you see her, you're gonna dream her all the time. Vera does that to people. It's like a madness that gets in your head. If you see her once, you'll want to see her again and again, you'll want to fly her away, you'll want to tear the petals from her lips, you'll want her wind in your hair and her rain on your roof, and you'll want death too, because there's no coming back when you love that far. And I didn't say that, some kind of poet guy did and he was very handsome but Vera already had Zak, and that's how life works. And the truth is that other guy's dead because he wanted to be. And it's love that does that.

WILLIAM   Let's go. I'm taking you home.

THE LITTLE ONE   Even death doesn't scare you? Vera and Zak are gonna like you.

That night, Vera and Zak got home really late, and William was still there because he was watching me sleep. He'd become a friend too, but mostly so he could spy on my mom. I always thought a spy tried to stay out of sight, but William's kind of spying involved showing himself all the time: morning, noon, and evening, and sometimes even at night when he watched me sleep. That way he knew everything: what time Vera and Zak came in from loving each other, how she tied up her hair when it was hot, how she laughed when Zak came back and how she took him in her arms, how beautiful she was with her sweat and her red cheeks, and how easy she was to love.

6. Sardines

Seven o'clock at night, in the kitchen. VERA is preparing sardines. MAM is watching her. We sense that she's been hovering for a while.

MAM   Now, Vera, that's not how you fillet fish. First you take the knife, and believe you me, I know my fish, oh yes I do! You make a cut right here and you gut it like so.

VERA   You know what?

MAM   What?

VERA   I haven't lived under your roof for ten years, and we eat fish at least twice a week, so why do you have to come shove your method down our throats?

MAM   I'm not shoving. I'm helping.

VERA   Well then just take the bag of sardines and fillet them.

THE LITTLE ONE enters.

THE LITTLE ONE   Mom, can I help?

MAM   Come here, Little One, your old mam'll show you how to fillet a fish. First, you cut it open here and then with your thumb you just—

THE LITTLE ONE   That's not how Vera does it. *(to VERA)* That's not how you do it, is it?

VERA   No, it isn't. And tell your mam what my fish is like.

THE LITTLE ONE   It's the best.

VERA   There you have it.

MAM What's the matter with you two? I'm just trying to help. But if that doesn't suit you, just say the word, because Pappy and I can always go to the hotel.

VERA Yes, I know.

PAPPY enters.

PAPPY Is that or is that not sardines I smell? I always did have a nose for sardines. Oh, and they're the nice big ones! When I was little, my mom would take them by the tail, dunk them in a pail of ice water, and without a knife or anything, just with her thumb, she'd split them open like so…

He splits the sardine open with his thumb.

MAM Oh Pappy, stop being a pain in the backside! We know perfectly well how to gut sardines. And it's not because your mother had her method that…. We don't give a darn about her method! You have to keep up with the times, oh yes you do! So enough about your mother, especially since she's dead and gone and good for her.

PAPPY What do you mean, "good for her"?

MAM What? Was it or was it not good for her? It was very good, if you want my opinion. Very dignified, and I can attest to that because it just so happens I was there. I was right there, at her bedside, when death came upon her. Not like Pappy here who went out to get the doctor and came back drunk.

PAPPY Here we go…

MAM Dead drunk, but alive and kicking. And making a terrible racket with this trumpet he got from God knows where and hollering, "Dust and decay! Dust and decay!" loud enough to wake up the whole neighbourhood. All this, I gathered, in honour of his poor mother. Poor old woman! Let me tell you, even dead, a mother has her fair share of worries… *(beat)* Okay, the fish! Come here, Little One. See what I'm doing? You make a cut here, and then you split it open with your thumb. And if you learn to do it like your old mam…

VERA Mom, are you just about finished? When it's time for her to fillet fish, she'll do it however she likes.

MAM *(to PAPPY)* What was I telling you? Kids nowadays. Won't listen to anyone. They just do as they please!

VERA Seven years. Seven years I haven't seen you. And it's only been a couple of hours and already…

MAM Already what?

VERA Already I feel like putting you back on the train!

A long beat. MAM turns her attention to the fish and sheds a few tears.

PAPPY That's fish, Mam, not onions, so how about giving the tears a rest.

MAM   I'm not crying.

THE LITTLE ONE   So why are your eyes running?

MAM   It's… it's because of the fish. Because of this poor fish…

PAPPY   *(a bit irritated)* Mam, are you just about finished?

MAM   Yes, I'm finished!

> *MAM goes into the bathroom and slams the door behind her.*

PAPPY   *(accustomed to such behaviour)* Now she's gonna lock the door and stay there for hours.

THE LITTLE ONE   What's the matter?

PAPPY   *(making light of the situation)* If you want my opinion, she's crying.

THE LITTLE ONE   Why?

PAPPY   Oh you know, your mam's getting a little sensitive in her old age. *(to VERA)* Go talk to her, Vera.

VERA   What? Why should I go talk to her? Me? Now? And say what?

> *A beat. VERA is annoyed. MAM's strategy has always been to lock herself in the bathroom to get an apology out of someone. This time, there won't be one.*

(to PAPPY) Here. Finish the sardines!

> *VERA exits.*

PAPPY   *(to THE LITTLE ONE)* Come here. See this fish?

THE LITTLE ONE   Yes.

PAPPY   I'm gonna tell you a secret, but it stays between you and me. This is how my mom used to do it. She was real good with fish. And sardines, we used to eat them raw. We'd split them open, squirt a little lemon on, and ta-da! Open up…

THE LITTLE ONE   Raw?

PAPPY   Go on, open up.

THE LITTLE ONE   *(chewing the sardine)* That's really good, Pappy!

7. Night

> *VERA is sitting in the kitchen alone.*

THE LITTLE ONE   My Vera's been like this for hours. Hours and hours like this, not sleeping, just walking around in her head, in memories that make her sad. It looks like her body's crying, like she abandoned it on the chair and good riddance. But I can see her body isn't doing well all by itself. It isn't happy. When my Vera's inside it, it's so beautiful it sometimes makes me want to cry because she's my mom. I know that's a silly reason to cry, and I try to hide it so no one can tell, but still. And Zak too, sometimes I've seen him cry from finding her so beautiful and I've seen him turn fast, really fast toward the window because tears like that, if other people see them, sometimes they want to protect you, and Zak has always done that by himself. Since he was eight he's been all alone to protect himself. So he never got used to letting other people give him some time off.

Vera's thinking about Pappy and Mam. I know because I saw her before they arrived, scrubbing and rubbing our life so they'd find it good. But she put all her energy in that. She stored up seven years of love waiting to see them again and she spent it all before they got here with her housecleaning and washing everything and turning everything upside down. That's why by the time they arrived, my Vera, she was already empty. She didn't have any more stored up. She could look and look, but she had nothing left to put in the hole that needed to be filled. And I could see that's what Mam was expecting: for Vera to fill the hole. Mam didn't put anything in. Sometimes parents are like that: they just decide it's not their turn anymore. But how can a person possibly fill a hole like that all by themselves?

Vera's sitting like that on her chair. And I can see there are dark forests and monsters in her head. I can see she feels lost, my all alone Vera. And I understand that because I know monsters. Sometimes they catch me in my dreams, and on those nights, Vera and Zak come to my bed and start singing.

> THE LITTLE ONE starts singing a lullaby.

Rouma tchéna, louma roussa
Coï fa noussa tché-é-ré
Louba réka, laïrou coma
Messa doura bélé né
Houm maraï la ya
Houm maraï la ya
Sé coréfa na
Moulouj maï ié da
Koulda mé ta, zlous ti véna
Ré-ï maï lou ksé-é-mé
Soussa méla, rouma tchéna
Vlaïko réfaï lou ma né

> VERA stays sitting like that for a while without moving, then PAPPY arrives. He is a bit uncomfortable and does everything slowly so he won't disturb her. He comes close to her and sits down without a word. They both sit like that for a while without looking at each other or talking or doing anything. We can still hear THE LITTLE ONE singing. After a while, VERA starts weeping. PAPPY, uncomfortable, lets her be. Then he

reaches out to her, a small, hesitant gesture, his hand on her shoulder, almost nothing, just to say, "I'm here."

8. Early Morning

The next morning. The remnants of breakfast. MAM, PAPPY, and VERA are still at the table. THE LITTLE ONE is playing on the floor.

THE LITTLE ONE One, two, three, four, here comes the marching corps! Forward, march! Not all at once, you'll die of boredom! One, two, three, four, five, ten, twenty…

VERA After five, it's six.

THE LITTLE ONE I know.

VERA So say it, or we'll think you don't.

THE LITTLE ONE That's okay. I know that I know. One, two, three, four, five, ten, twenty…

VERA Three, four, five, six…

THE LITTLE ONE I know but I'm making them go faster or they'll never get there.

VERA Where are they going?

THE LITTLE ONE Home. Because they lost the war but they didn't die, so they're going home. Ten, twenty, thirty, forty, fifty, sixty-four…

VERA Sixty, not sixty-four.

THE LITTLE ONE Why?

VERA Thirty, forty, fifty, sixty…

THE LITTLE ONE Yeah, but they're going really fast because they're almost home and they can't wait to get there. Sixty-four… sixty-five… that's because one of them has to stop and tie his shoes, so the others are waiting for him. Sixty-six… sixty-seven… one hundred and fifty! How many steps does it take to come back from the war? More than a thousand?

MAM You can count to a thousand?

THE LITTLE ONE I can count to a thousand thousand!

MAM You're a smart little one, oh yes you are! *(trying to sound casual)* And Zak, is he… still in bed?

Beat.

VERA He didn't come home.

MAM Didn't come home?

VERA No, didn't come home.

MAM Well! *(beat)* But I won't interfere, will I? I won't interfere.

VERA No, Mom. Exactly. Don't interfere.

PAPPY That's right, Mam. Don't interfere.

MAM What's the matter with you two? As if I don't know how to mind my own business! Of course I won't interfere. And God knows what an effort that is! Because…

PAPPY Effort or no effort, Mam, all we're asking is that you don't interfere.

9. Heaven

The same day, later in the morning. MAM enters the kitchen in an elegant outfit. She has a hat in her hand.

THE LITTLE ONE Where are you going?

MAM It's Sunday, Little One! Go get dressed.

THE LITTLE ONE What for?

MAM For church.

THE LITTLE ONE Why church?

MAM Because today's church day!

THE LITTLE ONE No thank you. I'm like Zak and Vera. I don't believe in church.

MAM But church isn't about believing or not believing. It's about… you have to go, or you can't have heaven. And heaven is very good.

THE LITTLE ONE What's heaven?

MAM They haven't told you about heaven?

THE LITTLE ONE No.

MAM So, in your mind, what happens when you die?

THE LITTLE ONE I saw a dead cat once in the middle of the road. It was the body of a cat, but there wasn't any cat inside.

MAM And that's death to you?

THE LITTLE ONE And it makes me think of your baby too because Vera told me the story about your baby who died when he was really little. But that happened before he knew how to talk, so maybe he never knew what "dead" meant. I had a dog once and I always told him, "Play dead!" so of course I know.

MAM Do you want me to tell you a story? It's the story of a little girl like you. She had a grandma, a grandpa, a mom, a dad, and they all had religion.

THE LITTLE ONE   What for?

MAM   To… to learn how to be kind to others… and every week, the little girl went with her family to reflect on religion, and every day, when the sun was up high in the sky, she'd also stop to reflect. And one day, she understood that she was going to die.

THE LITTLE ONE   I don't like your story. Your story has no imagination.

MAM   Sure it does! You'll see. So the little girl dies…

THE LITTLE ONE   That was fast! What kind of death did she die of?

MAM   A disease. And then…

THE LITTLE ONE   What kind of disease?

MAM   A disease of… the plague or something. Anyway, she dies, and everyone thinks her life is over. But all of a sudden she wakes up and sees her family crying and all the people she loves, and she can even see her little body in a little box. And she can fly and see everything. She can't talk and her loved ones can't see her, but she can land on their shoulder and console them. And that's heaven. That's the gift religion gives the little girl for being good.

THE LITTLE ONE   That's bull.

MAM   What?

THE LITTLE ONE   What you just said. It's make-believe.

MAM   But it's the truth, oh yes it is! And I know because when it happened to my little boy, he landed right here on my shoulder. The day he died, I was crying and crying and he landed on my shoulder and I felt him there.

THE LITTLE ONE   You're making that up. The truth is that death is worms. Zak told me that because I have a right to know about the food chain!

MAM   When you don't believe in anything, maybe it's the food chain, but when you pray…

THE LITTLE ONE   That's not true! Zak told me it was the food chain, with trees that grow from us, and flowers too!

MAM   Good heavens no!

THE LITTLE ONE   Yes! What you're saying isn't true! Those are all religious lies, and I know because Zak never tells me lies!

MAM   That's enough! *(calling)* Vera! Vera!

   VERA and PAPPY arrive.

VERA   What's going on?

MAM   That heartless man!

VERA   What's going on?

MAM Putting stories in her head about the food chain! Telling her about worms, disgusting worms that pick at our bones! What kind of a future is that? That dirty, good-for-nothing, womanizing bum!

THE LITTLE ONE Stop! Stop! Stop! Stop! Stop!

VERA *(Taking THE LITTLE ONE in her arms. To MAM.)* Never again, do you hear me? Never again in front of the Little One!

MAM No religion. What kind of life is that? And did you see how rude the Little One was to me? But you: not a word, not one word of reprimand. You raise children to think they're above the law, and it'll come back to haunt you, my dear!

She locks herself in the bathroom. VERA and PAPPY don't say anything for a moment.

VERA I suppose you think I should go see her? Do you want me to go?

PAPPY No. If you want my opinion, I say we go for a little walk.

VERA and THE LITTLE ONE look at each other and share a small smile. All three leave. A few seconds later, MAM opens the bathroom door, looks around, and sees that they have left.

MAM Well!

She hesitates for a moment, then grabs her bag and hat for church, smoothes her clothes, and exits.

10. Remember When?

Late at night. PAPPY, MAM, and VERA are in the kitchen.

MAM *(to PAPPY)* Reminds me of the old days, remember, Pappy? When we first met? You lived so far away, and every Friday…. I never missed one, not one! Every Friday, for three long years, I'd take the train to come see you in that apartment… in that place… oh, I'll never forget that place! It was awful! Do you remember, Pappy? Just awful! Three boys in that shack… in that… hovel… in that dump…

PAPPY You're still talking about that? Is that what you're still talking about?

MAM What I'm talking about is love. Because say what you will, it was love! And that is where we conceived Vera after all.

PAPPY Didn't you say it was on our trip? Didn't you say it was in the country, the night we saw those goats?

MAM No, Pappy. It was in that rathole, oh yes it was!

PAPPY You said that according to your calculations, it was…

MAM I said, I said…. A person's allowed to spice up the past a bit. Where's the fun in reminiscing if it's always the same story?

> *Beat.*

PAPPY Do you remember our Vera when she was young…

MAM Oh, she was something! *(to VERA)* You always went out without worrying whether your hair was done or your clothes were ironed or your rouge was applied right. All the things a mother likes to see. No, none of that. Oh, you used to drive me crazy! And still they followed you everywhere. Men, women, children—all fascinated! Like in that story, you know? The one about the pied piper. Except you didn't need a pipe, did you? You had this nonchalance that floated around you, everywhere you went…. You remember what she was like, Pappy?

PAPPY Of course I remember, Mam.

MAM But how, I'd ask myself, how do you make sure she turns out good?

PAPPY Now, Mam. Your daughter turned out just fine. Remember our holidays, Vera? Remember how you wanted to capture the blue of the sea? You'd take a jar and fill it with water and then wonder why it wasn't blue like the rest of the sea. And out you went in the water, always further out, to try and bring back the blue.

MAM Oh! Even then you couldn't do things like the rest of the world, oh no! Never like the rest of the world! *(VERA is distracted by something outside. ZAK has come back.)* And instead of playing, I don't know, like other girls your age, you got it in your head that…

> *MAM follows VERA's gaze, sees ZAK, and stops talking. ZAK enters. He stands facing VERA. Both of them look at each other for a while without speaking. ZAK nods to PAPPY and MAM, and goes into the bedroom without a word. A long silence.*

Well! If that's how it is, that's how it is. *(A beat. She continues in a harmless tone, as though what she is saying has nothing to do with the situation at hand.)* I always insisted on an explanation. The number of times that… oh no, I insisted on an explanation. Apologies too. Remember, Pappy? Remember that day you went and got yourself lost? Oh, he'd gone rabbit hunting in the morning and at eight o'clock that night: nothing. No news, no Pappy, nothing. Oh, I was livid! I'd invited Mrs. Webster over for rabbit stew and I had to give her bologna. Fried bologna! To Mrs. Webster! She already looked down on us from her high horse. Fried bologna! Can you imagine? Let me tell you, there were apologies that day, oh yes there were! Apologies and then some! And the next day, flowers. *(to PAPPY)* Remember the flowers, Pappy? *(to VERA)* A huge bouquet! I had to keep them outside because they made poor Pappy here allergic. Remember, Pappy? Remember your allergies? So I sat outside with my flowers for three days because you don't let an apology like that go to waste.

THE LITTLE ONE starts her narration while MAM keeps talking under her breath.

Oh no! You wouldn't get away with that with me! Say what you will, but people don't know common courtesy anymore. Right, Pappy, they don't, do they? Just the other day there was this young man, a strapping young man, not a puny old fart or anything, that I would have understood, but a young man! He passes me on the stairwell, and there I am loaded up with groceries… no offer to help me with my bags, nothing! He was probably going to see that girl, what was her name again? Remember, Pappy, that young girl? Anyway. That's how it is. What can you do about it? It's not us old folks who are gonna tell the young ones how to live, oh no!

THE LITTLE ONE Mam kept talking and talking and talking. And all my Vera wanted to do was go to the bedroom and see Zak, but she didn't want to look like she was in too big of a rush, so she waited for Mam to finish. But Mam was un-finishable, she couldn't stop making her noise, it was like she was trying to make our heads spin, except that didn't happen. What did happen is that Pappy fell asleep at the table and Mam only noticed because he started snoring, and that's when she decided it was time to go to bed.

When the old folks were gone, Vera opened the bedroom door and leaned up against it. And then she didn't do anything because it was kind of up to Zak to do something. And my Zak, he's never been very good with words and that's because before us, he was almost always on his own and his life didn't need explaining. That's why he always said things plain, without any frills. And that didn't always make him easy to forgive.

11. Saying Things Plain

VERA is leaning against the door. A long beat. ZAK finally appears from the bedroom.

ZAK That's how it is. I leave. I come back. That's how it is. Can't pretend. Hello, ma'am. A pleasure, ma'am. Can't do it. They want to come, they come. That's it. Don't want to be here, I'm not here. That's all.

THE LITTLE ONE Clearly, things weren't off to a great start. I was scared my Zak was gonna make a mess of things. He'd have to sweeten up his talking or the night would never be long enough to get forgiven. And because at the end of the night, Mam would be in the kitchen bright and early making breakfast and sweeping and moving this here and that there like she couldn't just leave our life where it belonged, he needed to get a move on. So he leaned against the door, next to Vera. He was there in the smell of her hair and it was driving him crazy and because he wasn't looking at her, wasn't looking in her eyes, words started popping into his head, and they were flowing and flowing just like that, without any effort, everything she's wanted to hear him say for so long.

ZAK Out on the road, I thought about your hair. And all the rest of you. Can't do different, you know that. If I could, I'd leave. My life's out there, on the road. Can't live in a life with no air. In a yard with no weeds. In a house with no cracks. Me, it's rainwater, tracks in the mud, fresh-cut hay, ditches, the sweat of horses. Then she shows up, reminds me where you come from: everything proper, everything paved. Comes and closes our windows and to please her, you become a clean and quiet little house. I look for you. Scared. Can't find her, the Vera who dances in the rain in her red dress. Vera who falls to the grass, drenched in her sweat and the storm. Vera who drives me mad in the night, a she-wolf howling with her wolf. Vera who trembles, capsizes, drives the men in town crazy with love, drives life itself crazy with jealousy. Vera who holds me here, holds me here with love, when no one before ever could.

THE LITTLE ONE He said all of that in his head. It's crazy how long it went on. And because Vera didn't want to make an effort, she didn't hear a single word. She stood there waiting and waiting for the words to come out, and then she got sick of waiting, and for Zak it was too late. She went to the bed and laid down, turning her back to him like when there's nothing more to say, and pretended to be asleep. And Zak believed her but that's because he doesn't really understand women. And he didn't insist, but that's also because he doesn't understand women. They didn't forgive each other all night. And I know because they didn't close the door, and you don't forgive each other with the door open.

12. Efforts to Communicate

The next morning. VERA and ZAK are in the kitchen.

THE LITTLE ONE The next morning, my Vera and my Zak were in the kitchen really early. And I could see that Zak was still walking on her eggshells. And that he wanted to be done with all this, so he could take her in his arms and hold her tight, bury his nose in her neck and pull on her ears to make her laugh. But Vera kept her grumpy-day face on. And then Mam came in the kitchen. And she started making efforts to communicate, and that was kind of not a huge success.

MAM enters.

MAM *(overly cheerful)* Well, well. Another day, another dollar. Who wants tea? *(beat)* I'm gonna make some tea. Not that I'm forcing anyone. I'm offering is all. A common courtesy, to be polite. Nothing wrong with being polite, is there?

VERA We're good, Mom. We don't need anything.

MAM Oh I can see very well that you fend for yourselves. No, that's just fine. You do as you please. The last thing you need is an old bat like me giving you advice. No, you young people, you do as you wish. It's none of my business anyway, is it? *(A beat, then she starts up again, incapable of holding her tongue.)* My only concern is the Little One. What kind of future is this for her? This life way out here, sheets you can spit through, doors never locked, clothes all washed by hand… I mean really, dear, almost everyone has a machine nowadays! You were made to live in luxury, in the lap of luxury. Servants, the good life.

VERA   Mom…

MAM   Have you looked at your hands? Ah, you used to have such class! You were a queen, my dear. A queen! When you walked down the street, you held your head high. You could have had anyone! *(to ZAK)* Anyone. Oh, she was something. You should have seen her. The best suitors lined up at her door. Has she told you? How she came this close to living in society?

VERA   Mom!

MAM   They met. A very nice young man. From a very good family. With servants going back five generations. He asked her to marry him, and that was very, very good. And the day of their wedding—*the day of their wedding*—do you know what she does to us? She's up in her room getting ready and the clock's ticking and I'm not about to show up at the church with my hair a mess and all clammy from rushing off in that heat. So I say to Pappy, "You wait for her, I'll go now and I'll meet you there." And when the two of them walk in…. Oh, I swear, it was almost the death of me. In front of everyone! One of the best families in town! In she walks, and she's cut off all her hair. It looked like a bunch of stairs. Nothing the same length! And she's wearing a suit. A man's suit! *Who does that?* When she walked in, you could have heard a pin drop. It was plain as day something was wrong. She walked slowly up to the altar where her fiancé was standing, and I have to say that in spite of everything, I don't know how she did it—with her man's suit and her hair all hacked off—she had this grace, it took your breath away. And when she got up to him, she looked him right in the eye and slapped him across the face. In front of everyone! A family with servants going back five generations! *Who does that?* That night she left town, and no news for nearly two years. *(to VERA)* Did you know he's married now? Two gorgeous little girls. A beautiful family. A huge house, and so well kept up. And all that could have been yours. *(to ZAK)* You're a lucky man, you know. Very lucky.

ZAK   I know.

MAM   If you say so.

ZAK   Yes, I say so. And I don't need you to tell me so.

VERA   Zak!

ZAK   You see her, your Vera? In a big house? Inside varnished walls? Becoming an old woman like you? A dried-up old woman who dreams of servants? You know where I met her, your Vera? You know where?

VERA   Zak!

ZAK   You know what state I found her in, your queen?

VERA Zak!

ZAK Queen of the dumpsters. A filthy, fallen queen. Had to be crazy to love her like I did. And I'm still crazy. You agree, you don't agree. We don't ask. Don't ask you to understand. Just to keep quiet, to leave us alone, to pack your bags and stop looking down on us. Not good enough for you. No, never good enough. Never looked at her, your daughter. Never really saw her. She's wild. Like horses. Wild and beautiful and untamed. Not a doll for the drawing rooms. If that's how you want your daughter, I spit in your face. I spit and spit in your face.

MAM Well then spit, go ahead and spit! Spitting's about all you're good for! He waltzes in, can't bother to say hello, can't bother to be just a little bit polite. For us, what difference does it make? Why should we care? But Vera, it's her whole life. Her whole life! You have to be a monster to leave a woman like that, stay out all night, and when you come back: not a word, not an apology, no explanation. A monster! And I know very well my daughter can't be tamed or I would have dragged her away from here a long time ago! You're nothing but a bum. Nothing but a dirty bum! Oh! I pity the poor mother who gave birth to such a son!

VERA Mom!

MAM What? You're going to take his defence, I suppose? Well go ahead, my dear, if you're heart's so set on it! Go right ahead! Keep your life of waiting around until Mr. I-do-as-I-please decides to come home or decides to talk to you or decides to say he's sorry. And here I am wasting my time trying to help you. But no thanks from you, ever!

VERA I never asked you for anything! Nothing! Not your advice, not your help, not to come judge me here, in my own home! Can't you just love us as we are? We always have to be how you want us to be: proper, well-behaved, no dirt behind our ears. I don't just exist in your plans for me. I exist in my own dreams! I live, I make mistakes, I start again. That's how it is. So don't you come and judge me. Don't look down on us like we've failed you, like we've shamed you. I don't need a mother to knock me down to size, life's done a pretty good job all by itself. It's dished out all it has to dish out. And someone came and took me away from all that. And it wasn't you. No, you weren't there, so now you're gonna shut up. You're gonna shut up and let me live! You're gonna shut up and let me live my life, you got that?

A long beat.

MAM So, that's how it is. You live your life as you please, my dear. But don't expect me to approve of it, oh no! If you need us, your father and I will be there for you. But clearly you don't need anyone. Oh, don't worry about it. I shan't get in your way. Pappy and I, we know how to live.

She exits. VERA sits down at the table, holds her head in her hands, and stays like that, quiet and withdrawn. ZAK doesn't know what to do. He tucks a piece of her hair behind her ears but it falls back in her face.

VERA Leave me alone. *(He doesn't move.)* Go away! *(He still doesn't move.)* You don't care about anyone else! It's you, you, always you. Was it too much to ask you to just say hello when you came in, to just sit down with us? Once in seven years, was that too much to ask? Was it too much to ask you to think about me for one second? To make things easy, to be there when they arrived? To spare me the questions, the comments, the awkward silences? You couldn't do that just because it mattered to me? Because I wanted things to change, I wanted to start fresh, for them to think you're okay, to think we're okay. But no! What do you care what she thinks? You could care less if she likes you or not. But what about me? You don't ask if it's important to me. Of course not. A little effort, that's too much to ask. It's not up to you to make a little effort. It's not up to you to think a little bit about someone else. You just hit the road and who cares, leave your problems behind and come back when you feel like it. Well, I'm not a problem you leave behind! I've had it with you coming and going and no questions asked, staying alone for nights on end and never asking where you are, never asking, "Do you love me? Am I still beautiful? Do you think you'll always have to leave to be happy? Do you think one day you'll love us enough to be happy here?" Maybe you think a woman can just wait around nibbling on the scraps of your love without one day leaving to find someone who loves her better— maybe with less fever, but who loves her every day, every day of her life.

You want to leave? Go. Go back on the road and follow it right to the end, and forget the way home while you're at it! Forget it, okay? Get out! Get out!

THE LITTLE ONE Zak left. And Vera: not a word, nothing to hold him back, not even with her eyes. And yet she knew it wasn't like the other times. She knew that what she said, Zak couldn't just get over it. He couldn't come back after, like every other time. Before he left he came and hugged me, too hard. And then he told me a story, like a parting gift. He told it without looking at me. But that's because he was crying. So I closed my eyes to help him not be embarrassed and I listened really hard because it would be my last story from Zak, for always.

13. Laüda

ZAK is sitting on the bed. THE LITTLE ONE is listening to him with her eyes closed.

ZAK This is the story of my mother. Laüda was her name. I was your age when my dad died. My mother became old, old that day. She had a new face. I wanted to console her but couldn't. I wanted to be everything for her and erase. Erase my father gone. I was crazy with jealousy. I took my dad's baggy clothes, put them on. With coal, I made a moustache above my lip. My father's moustache.

I took a cigar from the box he kept for special occasions. There in the trailer, I started walking, limping like my father, because of the war. My mother watched my foolish parade. My grotesque parody. And she was crying, howling. And suddenly she throws herself at me, slaps, slaps, and slaps again. Pushes me into the armchair. Rips the cigar from my mouth. "You want to act like a man? Go on! Go on and smoke! Put it in your mouth and inhale. And out your nose, the smoke! Out your nose!" And she was miming it, with crazy gestures. She lit the cigar. Handed it to me like this. I took it. She watched me continue my funeral march. Watched me smoke the cigar to the butt. Then she collapsed on the bed. That night, I threw up my meal. Didn't eat for three days. Laüda in bed almost three weeks. She got up skinny, old, quiet. Then she said, just like that, "We're leaving the trailer. That's it." And that was it. We emptied the trailer, and at the bottom of a drawer, a dress. A pretty dress. Cream chiffon. My mother puts it on. Her eyes come back, her eyes from before that shine. Her mouth, her legs, her breasts. She becomes a young woman. Dances in the living room. To see her like that again, I laugh. Hug her, kiss her. Her, nothing. Doesn't see me. I hold her tight, talk to her, shout at her. Doesn't see me. I watch her leave, leave the trailer in the sunshine, run like a little girl, twirl to make the dress dance, run and disappear. That evening, nothing. Then the downpour. Hammering rain in the night. I think about my mother's dress. About my mother in her dress in the rain. About the dress clinging to her body. I wait outside. For my mother. For hours. The hammering rain. Night fallen long ago. Then nothing else, ever. My runaway mother, never to be found.

THE LITTLE ONE   I keep my eyes closed really tight so I won't drop a crumb of his words. I keep them closed while my Zak leaves, tears himself away from us. And maybe it's just in my head, but I swear it makes a sound you can hear. The sound of Zak tearing himself away from us. The sound of my Vera breaking into a thousand pieces on the kitchen chair. The sound of our house shattering, blowing away in the wind. But when I open my eyes, there's still a roof, walls, windows. And that hurts me because I can see that our disaster isn't an end-of-the-world one, that there are still things that hold up, that there will always be things that hold up.

14. The Departure

In the kitchen the next morning. MAM and PAPPY are standing by the door with their suitcases.

THE LITTLE ONE   Mam and Pappy took the first train out in the morning. Because it's not like there was any sense pretending anymore. I was looking at Pappy sitting on his suitcase. You could see he wanted to say something but he didn't know what. It was so often Mam talking that naturally he didn't really have the hang of it. He didn't know how. So, again, Mam was the one who spoke.

MAM That's how it is.

VERA Yes.

MAM And we're taking the train back and…

VERA Yes.

MAM I was wondering…. What he said…. When he was talking about the dumpsters and the state you were in…

> *A beat.*

VERA It's true.

MAM I'd heard some things but… so it's true?

VERA Yes.

> *Another beat.*

MAM We don't know each other very well anymore.

VERA No.

MAM That's how it is.

VERA Yes.

THE LITTLE ONE Mam's looking at Vera. She's looking at her and it's like she's seeing her for the first time. And then it comes over her, the desire to take her in her arms, to say something nice to her. Something like "I love you" but with easier words. "I love you," Mam never really knew how to say that. So she's looking at Vera, trying to figure out how. They're standing there, small, looking at each other like two birds who've lost their feathers. Like when the nest is too far away, so there's no point even going "Chirp! Chirp!" And then finally, Mam says something.

MAM You coming, Pappy?

PAPPY Yes.

MAM *(to VERA)* There's no sense coming with us. It's fine like this. And it's not like we don't know the way.

VERA As you wish.

> *MAM hugs VERA. She exits. PAPPY stays behind. He looks at his daughter, tugs at his hat.*

PAPPY I… I… I'm proud of you.

> *He exits.*

15. The Flood

VERA is crying. She is lying on the floor under the hole in the roof where the rain comes in.

THE LITTLE ONE   They left. And that's when the downpour started. My Vera lying on the floor, and all the water in her body rushing out of her eyes. At first, I didn't do anything because it's true that sorrow has to flow out, it has to drip away or it stays jammed like a rock in your throat and then there's no getting rid of it. So I waited and waited, but her sorrow was like a spilling-over sorrow. Like a sorrow that wanted to cause a flood. And when night came, it started to rain, and with the water coming in through the hole in the roof, I started to get scared there'd be a drowning. I wasn't scared for me because I know how to swim, don't think I don't, but for Vera, because she knew how to swim too but it kind of looked like she didn't feel like it. That's why I thought of William. Because I was too small to get her out of there but William, he could do it. So I ran and ran in the night and I woke him up.

16. Rescue

At WILLIAM's house. THE LITTLE ONE is outside in the rain.

THE LITTLE ONE   William! William! Open the door! I have to show you something. William, get up! I want to show you Vera. She's got sorrow. It's time for you to be useful!

We ran and ran. But as far as consoling goes, William was kind of a disaster. When he saw Vera like that, all he could do was start feeling sad himself. So he got in on the production of tears like we didn't have enough with Vera and the rain that wouldn't stop. And as usual I had to take matters into my own hands and I started with a bucket, because on top of all the crying, the rain was coming down harder and harder.

Get up, Vera! Stop playing sad and dead! It's pouring through the roof. I need you to get up and help me!

With that, Vera got up and she saw William, but he's over so often that she wasn't even surprised. And I was there wringing out rags over the bucket and I was starting to get tired of it.

I've had it! I've had it with your problems! They're all sopping wet disasters so I'm moving to another life because enough's enough! If you love me, follow me, because I'm leaving!

Then I got a little scared because "If you love me, follow me!" was kind of a bit risky. I mean, Vera's love was Zak, and that was obvious, seeing that she was completely devastated with devastation. So maybe I should have just said, "Follow me!" but I'd seen, "If you love me, follow me!" that time I went to the movies and for me that was the ultimate act of courage, so I couldn't help myself. But no one moved, so I said:

Love or no love, I'm not leaving you here to drown!

That's how we ended up outside.

17. Bad Movie

Night. WILLIAM, VERA, and THE LITTLE ONE are outside. Downpour.

WILLIAM Now what?

THE LITTLE ONE It's true we had to think fast because it was already a downpour inside, so imagine outside.

We could go live the good life.

WILLIAM What?

THE LITTLE ONE Vera, say yes to the good life, please! William, tell her it's a good idea! I want us to live the good life because in the rooms they have bottles filled with blue and green alcohol, and when you put them around the lamp, it makes all kinds of colours. Except I broke one once and then we had to put the good life on credit because we only had money for the room and to order my orange juice. And they bring it right to the room, and they call me miss and they call Mom madam and they look at her a lot, but they still have manners. Oh, say yes, William! Tell Vera you agree!

WILLIAM I'm taking you to my place.

THE LITTLE ONE We walked to William's and it was pouring so hard that Vera's dress started to stop doing its job of covering her up. It was all stuck to her and you could see her skin through it, so she was already pretty much naked when we got there. And William couldn't help but look at her really hard. It's not that he wanted to take advantage of the situation, but he'd been trying to not love her for so long that it kind of wasn't possible anymore.

WILLIAM I want to kiss you.

VERA I know.

THE LITTLE ONE There's still the danger of a drowning but they don't seem in any hurry to go in. They're both standing outside sucking on each other's mouths. Pressed together so tight that the pouring rain can't even trickle between their bodies. They're trembling all over but I'm pretty sure it's not from the cold. There's a soft whispering and I know it's not the wind. I watch them in the downpour. I think I'm crying but maybe it's just the sky that won't stop drowning on me. Or maybe it's that I'm thinking about my Zak because I see them loving each other with their mouths, breathing all deep, and all of a sudden I can't take it anymore. William keeps saying, "I love you, I love you" like a bad movie. Vera keeps keeping quiet because she's a silent movie. I take off running because I already know the end. I've seen a movie at the theatre. He's gonna take her in his arms, he's gonna carry her to his bed, he's gonna take off her dress, they're gonna love each other with noises that sound like it hurts, but really they like it and they're just doing it to show off.

I walk back home. I start singing. I always do that when I don't want to hear anything. If I didn't sing I'd start talking in my head. That would give me ideas but I don't want any. I know my ideas would make me cry. I get home and it's a shipwreck, a tidal wave in all the rooms. But I'm tired of rescue missions. I lock the door, climb into bed, hide my head under the pillow, and fall asleep.

18. Jouliks

The next morning. It's sunny. ZAK is outside at the front door.

ZAK   Vera? Vera!

THE LITTLE ONE   My Zak woke me up with the sunshine. My Zak outside calling for Vera. I could feel my heart ballooning, because Zak back home, I didn't think it was possible. But he kind of didn't choose the best time for a miracle since Vera hadn't come home yet.

ZAK   Vera? The door, you can keep it closed. If that's what you want, that's how it is. I came back, just in case. To apologize. If you want. I didn't know what it was like to wait. Didn't think about it. It was to come back. To come back that I left. To come back to you. On the road like that, not going anywhere… what for, I don't know anymore. I need to arrive. Not like before where anywhere I stopped I said, "Here is my life, here is my home."

THE LITTLE ONE   It was beautiful what Zak was saying. And I think Vera would have been happy to hear it. So I stopped him right away so it wouldn't go to waste.

She's not here.

ZAK   You're all alone?

THE LITTLE ONE   Yes.

ZAK   Where's Vera?

THE LITTLE ONE   Not here.

ZAK   Where is she?

THE LITTLE ONE   I didn't know what to say but it was kind of their fault, because if they weren't so complicated, I wouldn't have to get involved.

ZAK   Is she at William's?

A beat. THE LITTLE ONE opens the door.

THE LITTLE ONE How did you know? *(a beat)* You're not gonna say anything? I cried. They're kissing. William's loving her with love and Vera's letting him. You're gonna go over there, aren't you? You're gonna run over there and bring Vera back, right? I want her to come back. I want her to love us like before.

My Zak didn't go. He decided to wait. Because it was his turn, he said. His turn to wait and not ask questions. He waited all day until the sun fell down. She only came home after.

My Zak's running outside. Vera's walking up the lane like an exhausted person, like a woman emptied of love, like a little girl who only remembers when the light goes out that it's time to be afraid of monsters. Zak's running so fast he finally reaches her. Vera's falling into his arms. Zak's getting beautiful. It's always like that when Vera's in his arms. Vera's wanting to love him. To erase the memory of William. As though she'd cheated on love all night and all day too.

VERA I just wanted to…

ZAK I know.

VERA But it didn't warm me up, not even a bit. In his arms, I was thinking… maybe I'll be cold all my life…

ZAK Forgive me.

VERA In his arms, I was thinking…

ZAK It's okay.

VERA I love you.

ZAK Forgive me?

VERA Yes. Yes.

THE LITTLE ONE She was in his arms but it wasn't a bad movie. He carried her to the root cellar at the far end of the yard where they like to love each other because they think I don't know. I stretched out on the floor in the kitchen, right under the hole where you can see the sky. I was singing but this time it wasn't because I was sad. It's because I didn't want to picture them loving each other. Some things it's better not to. It makes you too happy, like your heart will explode in your chest.

It happened in the night. Right in the middle of the night. I felt water dripping on my forehead. It was the rain. I thought about my Zak, about the rain that brings him his bad memories. I ran out to the yard and locked the cellar door because no way was he leaving us again. No way was my Vera getting ruined by the rainwater, the tidal wave in her eyes. I'd had it with shipwrecks.

It rained for days and days. Then the sun came back out. I opened the cellar door.

Up and at 'em! It's summer. And I'm tired of making my own stuff to eat. We could go pick strawberries. I even know where we can steal some for free in the big field, there's so many no one will even notice. Zak, come race me! My shoes aren't dry yet but that doesn't mean I won't win, you'll see!

When they brought them out, they were all dead. I was at William's so I wouldn't see. It was something about not having enough air and once the air was breathed in, it wasn't good anymore so you go dead.

Epilogue

THE LITTLE ONE   After that, Pappy, Mam, and Number Three came to the house to walk on my eggshells. They stayed for two days. It was because of my tears that wouldn't come. Number Three was a specialist in repairing people after a disaster, and I needed repairing, and I could see he was making a big effort and I was kind of a disappointment because I wasn't a good result. But Mam was already crying her eyes out, so it's not like there was a shortage of tears. And I'm not gonna start downpouring just to make them happy. And anyway, I don't want the tears to come. I want to be alone with the pictures in my head, because it's true there was a tragedy, and that's what a tragedy does: it puts pictures in your head that keep flashing and flashing. And I know because I've been to a movie, and at the movies, they can show the inside of a person's head. It's a technological thing. And in the movie, there was a kind of tragedy. They always put one in because it makes the movie better. And in the tragedy someone died. And the person who made that person die always had pictures of him in his head, and I'm not making that up. They call it reliving the event but I kind of don't get that, because it's redying in your head all the time.

In my head, I have really beautiful pictures. I have pictures of Vera in Zak's arms, and pictures of Zak holding her tight and dancing, twirling her so fast she starts screaming, "Stop, stop!" but you can tell she wants him to keep going. With pictures like that, you can't cry. So they can wait. There's no way. Because maybe if I make too much water with my eyes, my pictures will get erased, and I don't want that. I want to keep them. I want to remember them like that. Forever. Happy.

The end.

My Mother Dog
(Ma mère chien)

by Louise Bombardier

translated by Leanna Brodie

Introduction to
My Mother Dog (Ma mère chien)

My Mother Dog dramatizes the final thirty-six hours in the life of a seventy-year-old woman who is dying of cancer. Her oldest daughter, an aspiring novelist, is with her throughout this time, even through the night, either sleeping on a small sofa in the hospital room or lying down beside her mother in order to hold her close and ease her suffering. Despite her pain and difficulty in breathing, the mother is determined to hang on until the arrival from Mexico of her other daughter, an aspiring actor. The play thus produces and maintains a sombre mood as death inexorably draws closer and closer, while mere mortals seek to hold it at bay long enough for them to come together in one last embrace. At the same time, and despite the horror produced by suffering and a character breathing her last breath, the powerfully mythic significance of the mother's death reaches our awareness as Thanatos and Eros dance together throughout the play in the spirits and bodies of individuals who grow increasingly aware of the force of these determinants of the human condition, yet who, in the final analysis, are unable to resist their demanding thrust.

The sombre mood caused by death's inevitability is enhanced by flashbacks to memories and glimpses of dreams that reveal the harshness of the lives the three women have lived, their insecurities, and the troubled relations among them. This thirty-six hour period is an interval when the linear regularity of time is transformed. At certain moments when the mother and daughter are particularly anxious for the sister to arrive, it feels like time is standing still or even backing up. At other moments, when memories and conflicting emotions come rushing in, time explodes and grows complex through the fusion of multiple incidents that occurred on various occasions in the past, with powerful intensity. Louise Bombardier thus captures magnificently the gripping and unforgettable out-of-time, out-of-space experience many feel as they sit with their memories and overwhelming emotions at the bedside of a dying mother. Is that once-in-a-lifetime experience ever without feelings of doubt, regret, powerlessness, guilt, and anger?

My Mother Dog is a play in forty-three short scenes that alternate regularly and rapidly between "Reality" and "Dream." It has, therefore, a syncopated rhythm that plays out between two stage areas, with events, characters, words, and images in one enhancing the meaning of what is happening and being said or done in the other. Directors and designers will enjoy meeting the artistic challenge of staging this play in ways that invite audiences to enter into the fictional reality of lives painfully lived, while letting themselves be carried away imaginatively in dreams and memories from other places and other times.

The "Reality" sequence, which does not always follow chronological order, evokes moments in the lives of the three characters and the sisters' father, who left the family when the girls were small children. Most of the "Reality" scenes show the progression of the mother's illness over the past year and take place frequently in the hospital room where she has spent the past three months in palliative care. The storyline that emerges from the "Reality" sequence of scenes is one of an extremely dysfunctional family where the father acknowledges he never loved the mother, the mother admits she so ardently did not want the children that she tried to drown them when they were about five, the sister, who has explained to the mother that the problem in her life: "It's you—it's me" (Scene 34), calls the mother a "fucking pleasure-sucking black hole of misery," and the daughter calls her a "fascist" (Scene 36).

In contrast to this representation of a family torn apart, *My Mother Dog* ends with a final "Reality" moment, with the sister bursting in, the mother and sisters embracing, the mother delivering just before her death a monologue in which the words are incomprehensible but the love is strong: "It is a birth. A luminous ascent" (Scene 43). In the play's last line, the sisters affirm in unison: "My mother was beautiful." Does this final reconciliation mean that all the conflict has been resolved, the cruelty forgotten, and the dissension dissolved into an explosion of enduring harmony? Perhaps. This final scene highlights the importance of living one's life as fervently as one can, and it rings an echo of the "Incantation" in the opening scene where the daughter and the sister perform a sort of eulogy for the mother, already dead, and celebrate her ascension as "that giant comet,/that soaring vessel of vaporous light,/until a hole opened in the sky/and breathed her in" (Scene 1).

The conclusion of *My Mother Dog* is, however, more complex and problematic. I am rather inclined to interpret this final moment of apotheosis as that kind of wishful thinking that develops when the unthinkable has happened and cannot be reversed. That is to say, that I am inclined to agree with the sister, who says in her final line: "Mum, *no one* could stage a death scene like you" (Scene 43). The sister thereby problematizes the *real* authenticity and sincerity of their thoughts and emotions, including the mother's. Is this scene primarily a matter of fiction and performance? The sister's dry comment highlights the constructed nature of even this ultimate and unavoidable event in life's experiences. Most of the "Reality" scenes of *My Mother Dog* up to this point have portrayed the difficulty for love and compassion to show and speak themselves, have even evoked the extreme violence that sometimes broke out among the characters. Undoubtedly, these troubling memories, the stress they produced and the embodied negative emotions to which they gave rise, will remain with the sisters beside the thrill of the final shared moment of love. Like the play itself, the sisters will alternate in their own feelings between love and understanding of their mother, their sense of having shared an indescribably transcendent vision of the human condition, and resentment for all the harm she did.

The six scenes entitled "Truncated Reality," scenes that seem to derive from actual experience but that explode into disturbing representations of fear, violence, obscenity, and monstrosity, are particularly powerful in capturing the inescapable undercurrent of distrust and misery produced over many years in the past and standing in the way of lasting harmony.

The first three scenes of *My Mother Dog* introduce the characters, Mother's terminal illness, the larger family context and history, and the wait for the arrival of the sister, which provides the anecdotal storyline. The fourth scene then shifts to the first of eighteen "Dream" scenes. The "Dream" scenes introduce front and centre the theme of aggressive eroticism that accompanies the theme of death that is so powerful throughout the play, showing both the complementarity and opposition of these two powerful forces. With the exception of the dream sequence of Scene 12, which depicts the sister's fantasies of sexual encounters, bulimia, and taking flight at the time of her fortieth birthday, all the "Dream" scenes appear to be a dramatic representation of the terrifying nightmares that haunt the daughter. The interweaving of these scenes as the daughter stays right at the mother's bedside throughout the play suggests that they are going through her mind and intruding into her sleep, even as she cares for her mother and does her best to find comforting words. They further suggest that the mother's treatment of the daughter over more than forty years is the source of the nightmares, as well as the daughter's solitude, introversion, and inability to find erotic satisfaction.

The wealthy mother and gynecologist son of most of the "Dream" scenes are shown cruelly and sadistically torturing the daughter, in complicity with both the mother and sister. Their torture is powerfully driven by the sexual obsession of the promiscuous son, as well as his stance of superiority as a medical doctor, and is shown in its terrible violence to be so successful that the daughter is taken in these nightmares to the loss of a breast through irresponsible surgery and to the brink of suicide and the suggestion of death.

The strange and mysterious woman who appears in the "Dream" of Scene 27, and who restores the daughter's vitality, offers compassionately a return to the life force of the earth and the animal world and a sense of security in one's own body. She does not, however, offer a solution to death, as is dramatized in Scenes 38 and 40, when the daughter shows the woman the bones of the two children she discovered in the vegetable garden and receives a violent slap for her find.

That traumatic moment seems to produce an enhanced sense of reconciliation in the daughter as she expresses greater compassion for her mother's suffering, says for the first time "I love you, Mum," "breathes deeply with her Mother" (Scene 41), and sings "a very, very beautiful and very, very ancient lament" (Scene 42). She says in her dream a simple "I know, Mum…" as Mother and Daughter are both heard acknowledging frankly to each other the mutilation, abandonment, and violence that has characterized both their lives. The cheerful puppy who is able to quench his thirst without difficulty at the end of *My Mother Dog* suggests a new dawn in her life and perhaps that of her sister.

There is a presence of dogs, either real or toys, throughout *My Mother Dog*, and, of course, in the title. The daughter is told by her mother in a scene of "Truncated Reality" that her mother is a dog: "You *should* love dogs, he's the one who saved you, not me. I was… I was…. Your real mother… is a dog… your mother… dog" (Scene 39). Since the dog characters are consistently male in the French text, the play is not suggesting that the daughter was actually born from the body of a female dog. The enigmatic image of a canine maternal force appears to be more symbolic than literal. It lends itself to many interpretations, starting, of course, with the comforting presence in children's lives of stuffed toys and pet puppies. However, as dogs appear, bark, and growl in several scenes through the play, I am struck by their subtle association with or reminder of death. I am led to think of the gods of death in mythology, Anubis (Egyptian and Greek) and Cerberus (Roman), who have at least the heads of dogs and who are frequently represented as protective. Cerberus was said to have guarded the gates of Hades to prevent those who had crossed the river Styx from returning.

Mothers—dogs—death? The association is puzzling, and yet on psychic and mythic levels, when one lets one's imagination and dreams take flight, one realizes the profound insight *My Mother Dog* provides on human mortality, on the search for love and life lived with meaning and authenticity, on the fragility and necessarily limited nature of human relations, even, and perhaps particularly, with one's mother or child. The mysterious sentence uttered by the mother, written down at the beginning by the daughter, and reiterated in the daughter's spring dream (Scene 35): "It's good to be elsewhere" rings like a refrain that could be a consolation on the separation death always brings or a simple expression of the joy of life as long as it lasts and offers the hope of renewal.

About Louise Bombardier

Louise Bombardier was first an arts student, and then studied acting in the Option-Théâtre de Saint-Hyacinthe. She began her career as an actor in the 1970s. This career has led to her remarkable creation of more than thirty new roles, which include Lise Vaillancourt's *Billy Strauss* and *Tout est encore possible*, Reynald Robinson's *La salle des loisirs*, the text she co-wrote at Le Petit à Petit, *Bain public*, Normand Chaurette's *Le petit Köchel* (played in the Festival d'Avignon) and his *Les Reines*.

Bombardier describes her career as a playwright as an adventure, and considers herself a long-distance runner in that role. Having initially written and collaborated with several companies, including Le Sang Neuf, Le Gyroscope, and Le Petit à Petit, she has written about thirty plays, most of which have been successfully produced on stage by various theatre companies in Québec, France, English Canada, and Mexico. She is also the author of several radio plays (Radio-Canada), television scripts for young audiences, two short film scripts, and several collections of short stories. *Petits fantômes mélancoliques* (stories for autistic children), first performed September 17, 2007 at L'Agora de la danse during the Festival International de Littérature in Montréal, was remounted in Munich in March 2008, then remounted in Montréal by Pigeons International at L'Usine C in 2009. Bombardier is also co-author with Élise Turcotte of *Jubilation noire*, which was presented at the Festival Voix d'Amériques in February 2010. She is currently writing a play for Le Théâtre Incliné, which will be created on stage in 2011, as well as two novels for young readers.

Published Works by Louise Bombardier

Sortie de secours (1987). Montréal: VLB Éditeur.

Hippopotamie (1994). Montréal: VLB Éditeur.

Le champ (1998). Montréal: Lanctôt Éditeur.

Contes-gouttes (2002). Montréal: Lanctôt Éditeur.

Pension Vaudou (2003). Montréal: Lanctôt Éditeur.

La cité des loups (2005). Montréal: Lanctôt Éditeur.

Ma mère chien (2005). Montréal: Lanctôt Éditeur.

Petits fantômes mélancoliques (2008). Montréal: Les 400 Coups.

Ma mère chien was first produced at Théâtre d'Aujourd'hui in Montréal on September 13, 2005, with the following company:

Markita Bois
Julie Vincent
Anne Caron
Robert Lalonde
Patricia Nolin

Directed by Wajdi Mouawad

Translator's Notes

The original text clearly sets the play in Montréal. However, in the event of future productions, the author is open to adapting these references.

P. 380: Jeanne Bourin, writer of a bestselling series of romance novels set in the Middle Ages: roughly as popular in French as Ellis Peters and her Brother Cadfael series of medieval mysteries in English.

P. 381: raï—Algerian raï music (political folk music that has absorbed everything from Bedouin melodies to hip-hop beats) is an established world-beat idiom, as well-known in *la francophonie* as reggae might be to an English-speaking audience.

FLQ: The Front de libération du Québec, an extremist separatist group best known for the murder of politician Pierre Laporte in October 1970.

P. 381: TV5—The French equivalent of the BBC or Bravo, this arty channel should be read as "Tévé Cinq."

P. 398: Jean Coutu, a Québec-based chain of pharmacies.

P. 400: The Aboriginal Woman speaks a dream dialect that follows the French system of orthography. So, for example, "oshné" is pronounced "osh-nay" and "gouch" (on p. 401) is pronounced "goosh."

The translator wishes to thank Playwrights' Workshop Montréal, which generously hosted a workshop of this translation in June 2009. She is indebted to the actors (Susan Bain, Domini Blythe, Susan Glover, Marcel Jeannin, and Danette Mackay) and the director (Emma Tibaldo) for their insight as well as their skill. This translation was dramaturged by Linda Gaboriau, whose advice was invaluable.

Characters

Reality

Mother (Madeleine Marjot), of humble origins, age seventy, with a mixture of charm and violence peculiar to eternal childhood.
The Older Daughter (Laure Frappier), introvert, age forty-eight, author.
The Younger Sister (Mylène Frappier), extrovert, age forty-seven, actress.
Father (Jean Frappier), the girls' father. Divorced. Attractive, debonair, bon vivant.
Dr. Dumas, physician, in the death business, age sixty, with the compassion of those accustomed to caring for the dying and those around them.
Nurse (Alejandro Rodriguez), charismatic nurse, working in palliative care and therefore equally accustomed to the rituals of death. Has a Spanish accent.

Dream

Wealthy Mother, refined and attractive woman of the world, in love with her son. Toxic.
Her Son (Jean-Marie), experienced seducer, madly charming, worldly, alcoholic. Toxic.
Aboriginal Woman, ancestral figure, healer, mineral presence. Animal mother.

MY MOTHER DOG

Scene 1: A Locket

About one year before our story, the MOTHER, age sixty-nine, beautiful, happy, and as yet healthy, sings "Parlez-moi d'amour." Her two daughters are at the piano, playing a duet.

DAUGHTER Mum will be happier recovering here.

SISTER Let's hope so… but you know how she is…. I'm not holding my breath.

DAUGHTER Yeah, I know…. How are things with you?

SISTER Good. I just got a really good gig…. I'm going to do a show in Mexico.

DAUGHTER Yay! *(pause)* Will you be gone long?

SISTER Pretty long. I can't say no. I'm like her, I love to travel.

DAUGHTER I know. *(pause)* I went to see Dr. Dumas yesterday.

SISTER Which one's Dumas again?

DAUGHTER Her gynecologist.

SISTER Right. And?

DAUGHTER One in ten chance of survival, if there are no complications.

SISTER Really… *(pause)* Okay, look, you only live once, she's fine for now, I'm going. It's now or never.

DAUGHTER You're right—but I'm scared.

SISTER Me too, but… *(a shrug)* If I stay here, it's her or me! *(pause)* How are things with you?

DAUGHTER I'm trying to finish my novel.

SISTER Yay!

   Piano finale.

Incantation

This incantation has all the emotional immediacy of a funeral eulogy or a letter being read at the burial of an urn. The sisters may trade words back and forth, as each in turn finds herself unable to go on.

DAUGHTERS My mother was beautiful
   her eyes
   two

bright blue
slightly faded
streams of vaseline.
She was very thin
a sacred knucklebone
a precious stone
the kind you carry with you
wrapped in linen
for fear of damaging it.
We all wanted
to polish her
and we didn't hesitate
to touch her
to stroke her
our talisman.
Even while alive
she was already dead
a lit candle
gleaming
in mid-November.
And oh, the tears she'd weep,
in torrents,
at regular hours,
around seven p.m.,
like pressing a button.
Dried off with a towel
she was led back
to her basket
where Yappy the dog
would lap up her liquid eyes
ad nauseam.
My mother and Yappy
in the dog basket.
Watching them remake the world together
with their lunar alphabet
while the scent of mandarins
surrounded us.
Eyes were everywhere
inside the darkness.
And oh, the fear it caused us.
Beneath my skin,
I felt the coming of disaster.
The setting of fires,
rumours of deportations,
hordes of the homeless.

My mother
touched the pulse of the world
and it withered her.
One day I brought the bread
to the basket
shared by Yappy and my mother
and *she* bit me.
I still have
the scar on my wrist.
It was near the end,
I was about to extricate myself
from this story,
my mother was no longer leaving the basket
and Yappy had certainly shrunk beneath her terribly,
becoming almost invisible.
My mother
lay down,
her throat poured forth
a cough from the crypt,
her eyes rolled up to the sky,
white,
lots of white,
someone even captured the moment for posterity.
Ever since then I've been bleeding from the wrist
and Yappy has disappeared forever
into the depths of the basket.
That's where my mother gave up the ghost,
coughed it up like a banner in the wind,
and her lifeless maiden smile
made her open her mouth up wide,
swallowing the earth
and our bodies leaning toward her.
She touched the sky
and left us feeling sorry
to be so pathetically alive,
little bundles nailed to the ground,
staring upwards, open-mouthed,
at that giant comet,
that soaring vessel of vaporous light,
until a hole opened in the sky
and breathed her in.

Scene 2: Reality

The present. Hospital. Palliative care. A woman (the older DAUGHTER), very agitated, enters the room of her dying MOTHER, a little intubated mummy who breathes with difficulty. Winter coat, luggage.

DAUGHTER   Mum, sorry, I couldn't get here any sooner, I was in Québec City for my book launch when I got the mes—as a matter of fact, here it is!

She feels uncomfortable.

Hang on, it's in here somewhere...

She busies herself with her packages, her winter coat.

Hey! They even have poinsettias! I brought you some soup...

She realizes how preposterous it all is: her MOTHER is near death.

MOTHER   *(weakly)* Stop fluttering...

Silence. The DAUGHTER sits down, tensely, at her MOTHER's side.

DAUGHTER   Are you thirsty?

The MOTHER nods.

You don't even have any water, let me get you a...

She does.

Here, drink...

The MOTHER can't quite manage it.

Want your teeth?

She tries to give her her dentures, can't quite manage it.

You need a straw...

She searches.

I can't find them.

MOTHER   *(barely audible)* In the drawer...

DAUGHTER   Oh, right. Here—drink...

The MOTHER is too weak.

Okay—aha!

She finds the sponge-sticks.

Here—try this...

The MOTHER sucks on the sponge-stick.

That you can do! Good...

Silence.

Is there anything you'd like?

> *The MOTHER shakes her head. Long silence. Laboured breathing. The DAUGHTER cries discreetly.*

Is there anything you'd like to say to me?

MOTHER   *(very hard to understand)* It's good… to be elsewhere…

DAUGHTER   What—what—what are you saying to me?

MOTHER   It's good to be elsewhere…

DAUGHTER   Oh! *(for herself)* It's good to be elsewhere…

> *Silence.*

MOTHER   *(almost inaudible)* When… coming?

DAUGHTER   When? Huh? Who?

MOTHER   Don't make me repeat myself… your sister…

DAUGHTER   Oh right! She's arriving tomorrow night, her flight's at noon.

> *The MOTHER groans. Silence.*

Would you like me to stay with you tonight?

> *The MOTHER nods. Silence.*

MOTHER   What time?

DAUGHTER   Huh? The time? It's five o'clock.

MOTHER   Night?

DAUGHTER   No—afternoon. Rest, I'm here.

> *The MOTHER is no longer moving: she seems unconscious, breathing with difficulty. The DAUGHTER touches her sweat-soaked MOTHER, goes to get her a cold cloth, and dabs at her gently. She talks to herself, holding back tears, quietly singing a lullaby: "Duerme, duerme, negrito… y tu mama esta en el campo… negrito." Several times. She blows her nose, tidies up the hospital room, paces, goes back to her MOTHER, rummages in her purse, gets her book out, goes to place it on her MOTHER's bedside table, realizes that it's too late, puts it back in her purse, paws through the purse, gets herself a piece of chewing gum, drinks water, takes out her pack of cigarettes, looks at her MOTHER, touches her, puts the pack back in her purse. She takes out a notebook, writes in it: "It's good to be elsewhere." Tries to write, can't. She goes out for a moment, comes back with wet hair. Peers into the hall outside the room. Comes back. Paces back and forth, trying to calm down.*

> *Then she lies down on the little palliative-care sofa.*

Anxiety ensues: her MOTHER's breathing and bursts of sound make her periodically start up and spring to her MOTHER's side. She touches her and her breathing eases for a moment. The DAUGHTER goes to lie down again, does some deep breathing, contracts her solar plexus. The MOTHER's laboured breaths and the beep-beep of medical apparatuses dominate the soundscape. With the help of relaxation exercises, interrupted by moments of anxiety, the DAUGHTER gradually manages to fall asleep. The room shifts.

Scene 3: Reality

Years earlier. The SISTER (Mylène) is stretched out on a sofa, smoking a joint. The FATHER enters: attractive, in winter clothing, two enormous gift boxes in his arms.

FATHER Merry Christmas, little girl!

SISTER Oh man, it's Christmas! Dad! What are you doing here?

FATHER Your grandmother died, didn't you know?! Didn't Laure tell you? She called your mother in Cuba, her flight gets in around five.

SISTER Oh man! No way. Where is Laure, anyway?

The DAUGHTER appears, reading.

Is Grandma really dead?

DAUGHTER Yes. They've got her in a fridge at the morgue until Mum gets back. She died yesterday, all alone. Mum'll never forgive herself.

FATHER Merry Christmas, little girl!

DAUGHTER Dad! You came back for Mum's—for Grandma's death? Are you coming to the funeral? Why didn't you come till now?

FATHER I came for the two of you! No, I'm not going to the funeral! I don't want to see either of them. You girls don't know everything, you know. One day I'll tell you all about it, but don't forget, your mother left *me*! I could never make her happy! Then I met someone who loves me—the complete opposite of your mother. I'd love to introduce her to you… she has one hell of a body!

SISTER Of course she does, she's fifteen years younger than you!

DAUGHTER You never loved Mum…

FATHER Everyone has the right to be happy! Here, this is for you, Daddy's big girls!

He offers each of them a large ribboned box. The daughters open them: they contain two large, rather unattractive stuffed dogs. The daughters are uncomfortable.

DAUGHTERS   Oh, thank you, they're very big…

FATHER   I know how much you love dogs.

DAUGHTER   Why are you crying, Mylène?

SISTER   I don't know, I just can't help it somehow.

DAUGHTER   I know what you mean.

The telephone rings.

That's Mum!

Scene 4: The Dream

A little crowd has gathered for a party in a large bourgeois sitting room. The WEALTHY MOTHER, her SON, the MOTHER, the SISTER, as well as the DAUGHTER herself. They are very "classy," but already quite tipsy. The SISTER is lounging on the rug in front of the fireplace with the SON. They are laughing, kissing, knocking back glasses of champagne. Then, with the voice and physicality of a passionate actress, the SISTER starts declaiming Arthur Rimbaud's "Une saison en enfer" to a rapt audience.

SISTER   "Once, if I remember rightly, my life was a feast where all hearts opened, and all wines flowed. One evening I sat Beauty on my knees…. And I found her bitter…. And I reviled her…. I armed myself against Justice. I fled. O sorceresses, O misery, O hatred, it was to you my treasure was entrusted! I managed to erase all human hope from my mind. I made the wild beast's silent leap to strangle every joy. I summoned executioners to bite their gun-butts as I died. I summoned plagues, to stifle myself with sand and blood. Misfortune was my god. I stretched out in the mud. I dried myself in the breezes of crime. And I played some fine tricks on madness. And spring brought me the dreadful laugh of the idiot!"

She laughs like a madwoman.

WEALTHY MOTHER   Rimbaud! "A Season in Hell"! What a poet!

The SISTER approaches the DAUGHTER and plies her charm on her. The latter recoils. Everyone laughs and chuckles.

SISTER   Hey, Big Sis! I'm so happy you and Mum came to my party! Aw, let yourself go for once!

DAUGHTER   I'm here for Mum.

SISTER   Aw! Loosen up!

DAUGHTER   You're drunk. I hate it when you're drunk.

SISTER   You're not jealous by any chance, Big Sis?

The SISTER returns to the party.

DAUGHTER Actress!

WEALTHY MOTHER You're not enjoying the party, dear?

DAUGHTER No, it's not that, you have a very nice place here, it's me, I'm just naturally a bit of a… recluse.

WEALTHY MOTHER Your sister has told us so much about you! We've provided you with a private room where you can be all by yourself. By all means, don't hesitate to go there at any time, if that's your pleasure. Please feel absolutely free.

DAUGHTER Oh, thank you, that's so thoughtful of you. But, no, I'm fine, I like to watch other people… enjoy themselves.

WEALTHY MOTHER Won't you have a glass of champagne, at least?

DAUGHTER No thank you, I had one a little while ago… it was very nice.

WEALTHY MOTHER Something else, perhaps? A glass of wine, a soda, a liqueur?

DAUGHTER No really, thanks, water, I'm fine with water.

WEALTHY MOTHER As you wish! But do enjoy yourself, dear: life is short and we have to make the most of it.

SISTER That's just what I said!

The SISTER goes off toward the SON. They flirt.

MOTHER *(glass in hand, a little tipsy, overwhelmed yet radiant as she pours her heart out to the WEALTHY MOTHER)* Ah, *France*, the *chateaux*.… I must've lived in a palace once, if you believe in past lives.

SISTER A flea palace!

MOTHER Shut up! I love books that are set in the Middle Ages! Like Jeanne Bourin, right? That's my era—and—oh! The South Seas! Tahiti, Martinique. I've been there! Everywhere they speak French, not like the French around here! Creole is such a beautiful language, their rhythms are so lively, the beguine as they say:

(singing/dancing) Ban moé un ti-bo deux ti-bo trois ti-bo doux doux… ban-moé un ti-bo pour soulager gue moé ban-moé un ti-bo *(kiss kiss)* deux ti-bo *(kiss kiss)* trois ti-bo douxdoux! *(the others applaud)* Pardon me… thanks. Oh! And Cuba! The beaches of Cuba are my beaches! I've always been in love with Cuba, way before it was fashionable! People around here are so backwards! "Aren't you afraid of going by yourself, they're all a bunch of commies!" They're just ignorant! Cubans are a lot happier than we are! They don't just think about material things! Cubans are so beautiful, and smart too, take it from me! Well-educated, too! Pedro spoke six languages! Yeah! Thanks to Fidel Castro! Now there's a man for you! Some people try to blacken his name, even my daughters! But I don't believe it! They're jealous! It's the goddamn Americans who started

it, those bastards have to control everything! Now, Fidel Castro would have been just my type! One time I even wrote him a letter to congratulate him for his regime, yes I did! My daughters laughed at me. Anyway, I didn't send it in the end, but still, a little country like that? Standing up to the damn Americans? Fidel stands his ground, he's not an ass-kisser like the rest of them, on their knees for the Americans! Uh—pardon my French, it's not like me, but listen, I get carried away whenever I talk about the Americans, I just don't like them! The Spanish language is so much more romantic, and that music, salsa, tango, flamenco—I love Romanian people too, it's a romance language, Romanian. Italians, Argentinians—I guess I tend to prefer people from somewhere else— Yeah, except for—well—you know—Americans…

And Germans too, I can't stand it, the language is just too ugly. Arabs? Oh no— except when they speak French, some of them can be all right, and their music is very lively. It's called "raï," you know. I discovered it before my daughters did, on TV5. I watch TV5 all the time, it's my channel, I'm not really from here…. I've never felt at home here, except around the time of the FLQ—I thought we had everything it took—everything—to become a northern Cuba. But no, we're way too American! I'd love to have been born… somewhere else. I don't know—preferably in France! People from here don't have—oh dear I'm talking a lot! Must be the wine! But it's different for you people, you have class, obviously, a whole family of artists! Oh! Music! That's another one of my passions!

DAUGHTER Poor Mum.

Scene 5: Hospital Reality

The present. The MOTHER's laboured breathing. The beep-beep of the empty morphine drip. The DAUGHTER awakens abruptly. She runs out of the room. Comes back with the nurse.

DAUGHTER She's in pain…

NURSE Yes, Dr. Dumas asked us to increase the dose—not too much, though, otherwise— When does your sister get here?

DAUGHTER Tomorrow evening.

Refill. Vital signs.

NURSE Okay…

(*to MOTHER*) Mrs. Marjot? It's Alejandro. We want to make you more comfortable. Your oldest daughter is with you.

(*to DAUGHTER*) If you have things to say to her, this is the time. Talk to her. I know what you're going through, I've already lost…

DAUGHTER Your mother?

NURSE Yes. Among others. Do what you need to do with your mother, touch her, put on her favourite music.

A gesture of sympathy between the DAUGHTER and the NURSE before he leaves. The DAUGHTER strokes her MOTHER's feet for a long moment in silence.

DAUGHTER Mum... I—

A long sigh of impotence from the DAUGHTER: the MOTHER is sleeping.

The DAUGHTER presses "play" on the little palliative-care tape recorder: Latin music. The MOTHER unconsciously opens her eyes. The DAUGHTER writes something in her notebook, then goes to lie down on the sofa. The Latin music swells.

Scene 6: Dream

The WEALTHY MOTHER and her SON are at the piano. The SISTER too. Sensual complicity.

DAUGHTER Elegance and affluence go hand in hand.

Suddenly, the SON appears behind the DAUGHTER.

SON So you're the older sister—Laure. I've heard so much about you. You write, don't you?

DAUGHTER Yes, I write—journalism, at the moment—everyone's got to eat. I'm more interested in fiction.

SON What kind of fiction? I can certainly see you writing erotica, with all that volcanic reserve just under that little black dress.... You're private, I love private people, you want to get lost in them. Would you like some of my Scotch? It's very smooth...

DAUGHTER No thank you, I don't drink Scotch, I'm something of an introvert.

SON I love introverts, I have no interest in meeting myself!

DAUGHTER I don't think I'm a very interesting person: I'm forty-eight, a bit uptight, comfortable in black, "the same old widow's weeds" as my sister puts it. I tend to intellectualize everything, that's just how I am.

Silence, unease, he brushes up against her, she becomes agitated.

I'm sorry, it's a little embarrassing, I may be old-fashioned, but mostly I live inside my mind, although I can't seem to earn a living with it!

(small laugh) My living.... *Our* living.... I take care of my mother, she's alone and aging very, very badly. So, fine, for the moment I'm freelancing.... Newspaper assignments, magazines. Pays the rent but my only love is writing,

novels. It's funny, you were just talking about erotica, as a matter of fact the novel I'm working on is—

SON An erotic novel? I knew it. Tell me more! What's it about?

DAUGHTER I'm not very good at talking about my work. Well…

(She launches into it passionately.) Actually, it's the story of a woman with no spinal column who hides herself among columns, pillars, and coils herself around them a bit like a climbing vine, you know? And these pillars are always kind of in everyone's way, but the pillar provides her with a sort of invisibility, a sense of protection, and an opportunity for voyeurism, she loves being a part of the furniture, she observes and everyone forgets about her, it's, well, perfect! She's an invisible exhibitionist. With the pillar between her legs, she brings herself to…. Pardon me!

SON Interesting…

DAUGHTER And it relaxes her! She's part of the human race but she pleasures herself alone while watching everyone else rushing all around her. It's a kind of congenital yet very, very sexual laziness. Her mother keeps wandering around in front of her like a silly old bat but the woman stays invisible yet exposed in the middle of the room, just her and her pillar as one body! Ever changing. Men whom her mother doesn't see cross the sitting room and give her pleasure merely by watching her duelling with the pillar. The more the human ballet swells around her, the more her solitary pleasure rises, and on the point of climax she often cries: "Pillars of the world, I love you!"

The DAUGHTER suddenly becomes aware of her impropriety.

Sorry! That's not… I didn't…

During this crescendo, the SON rubs up against her insidiously, then begins to fondle her with diminishing restraint, while moving her further away from the others.

SON But my dear, that pillar is me! So hot-blooded! That story would make an angel hard!

DAUGHTER *(Uncertain, she likes it, but will not let herself go.)* No, please, let me go, it's the writer in me, I don't have a head for sex.

SON Shh shh shh! "A head for sex"—you're very, very tense, my dear, you suffer from chronic inhibition. Let yourself go a little. Have you ever thought of seeing someone about this? It's the gynecologist in me speaking. It's not good to sublimate your sexuality, it wears the body out. You can already see the damage, too—very pale, dried-out skin, compressed rib cage—it's very bad for your health, you know! Oh! Will you feel these trapezoids! You've got more knots than an olive tree! Tell me if I'm hurting you, all right. Just a nice massage—see, your poor little body is thrilled!

DAUGHTER   I'm not very comfortable with things like this—massages and so on...

SON   Fine, I won't touch you any more if it offends your modesty. I don't want to alarm you, but when was your last complete physical?

DAUGHTER   I don't remember. I don't trust doctors. Oh! I'm sorry.

SON   Don't worry about me, I'm quite used to rejection: but if you only knew how many beautiful, high-strung women like yourself realize too late that they're carrying a cancer in their beautiful breasts. If you let me examine you.... Mother, my kit!

He nods conspiratorially to his mother, who approaches with his medical kit.

DAUGHTER   Excuse me, I have to go and—freshen up.

She tries to get away, but the WEALTHY MOTHER and the SON block her path. A small cry, quickly drowned out by the general noise.

What are you doing? Mum!

The party is going full swing. The WEALTHY MOTHER and the SON have a firm grip on the DAUGHTER, who tries to get away but doesn't want to make a scene. They drag her forcibly into the salon in the midst of the guests, who are enjoying themselves immensely. They lay her solemnly down on a récamier-style sofa: the SON signals for silence. Everything stops so that everyone can solemnly observe the diagnostic spectacle.

SON   Just look at this beautiful woman—so very tense! As a doctor, I can't help but be appalled. Open this collar before it strangles you.

DAUGHTER   No, please, let me go!

SON   So many hooks on this little "Piaf" dress.

SISTER   Well, that's my sister for you! The black widow!

Everyone chuckles, but discreetly so as not to disturb the examination. The DAUGHTER tries to escape.

SON   Stethoscope! Mother, help me hold her!

She does.

I'm going to take some blood samples. I suspect that you suffer from pernicious anemia—blue fingernails—could your mother kindly tell us if there's any diabetes in the family?

MOTHER   *(glass in hand)* Not as far as I can remember—not on my side anyway, maybe her father's. Her grandparents on the Frappier side were first cousins: the whole family's retarded.

DAUGHTER   No, please, no, stop! Mum?! Do something!

MOTHER Been this way ever since she was little—she used to throw such tantrums at the doctor's office!

SON Write this down, Mother: cardiac anomaly. Asthmatic breathing. Palpitations. Oh… just feel this mass under the left armpit!

WEALTHY MOTHER Oh, that's bad.

SON At your age, we should examine the breasts…

They both set to work.

Uh-oh, oh oh oh, my dear young lady—

WEALTHY MOTHER Your left breast is completely disfigured! May her mother come and observe?

SON Of course, Mother, that's the point of the exercise. Come closer, Mrs. Marjot, come closer, everyone.

The two mothers palpate her breasts.

We have here an example of a very advanced tumour.

(He clucks his tongue.) This is a case of negligence. No matter how much we advocate prevention, most breast-cancer victims are still mentally stuck in the Middle Ages.

Little chuckles.

You have let yourself go, my dear—it may be too late—but so be it. This calls for emergency intervention. *(He whispers in his mother's ear, then louder:)* "Abyssectomy"!

WEALTHY MOTHER *(nodding in agreement)* Absolutely! "Abyssectomy"!

MOTHER Abyssectomy?!

DAUGHTER Wait, what does that mean? Mum! Stop them! Someone help me! Mylène?

MOTHER (Sotto voce, *to her DAUGHTER, with all the violence of a knife:*) Not enough talent and too much ambition! You'll learn, darling, that in life, there's a price for everything!

SON Like wildfire! Mother: intravenous!

DAUGHTER No! Mum!

They force her down on the sofa and attach an IV to the needle in her arm. All the guests watch her go under.

SON *(addressing the whole room)* Enjoy yourselves!

The party resumes.

Scene 7: Reality

Several days earlier. The MOTHER, seated on a chair in the hospital room. Very weak, intubated, pathetic. She tries to eat from her tray, can't manage it, spills everything on herself, weeps.

MOTHER   Girls, where are you?

Scene 8: Dream

In the midst of the jubilant crowd, the DAUGHTER is still stretched out on the sofa. The SON leans toward her, turning his back to the group. He takes out his penis.

SON   Touch my penis, you'll see, it'll help you get better.

She tries to cry out, but only a little nightmare sound escapes her lips.

Scene 9: Truncated Reality

About a month earlier. The DAUGHTER is sitting in the sink of the hospital bathroom. Her MOTHER, standing unsteadily, facing away, is emptying her bowel bag into the toilet.

MOTHER   Goddamn this bag! What are you doing sitting in the sink? Are you crazy? Why don't you help me instead!

DAUGHTER   *(to herself)* I'm programming my genes. I'm washing my feet.

MOTHER   That sink isn't clean! It's a hospital and they can't even keep it clean like normal people.

DAUGHTER   *(muttering)* Shut up! YOU'RE DEAD!

We hear a beer commercial coming from the TV in the hospital room.

MOTHER   Goddamn American music! Always the same goddamn beer ads. Would you turn off that goddamn TV!

DAUGHTER   *(to herself)* Please make my mother shut up!

She picks dirt from under her toenails with the point of a pocketknife, chanting to herself: "I'm no one's daughter... I'm made of stainless steel... like this knife." She digs the point under her big toenail.

MOTHER   GREAT! Now it's all over the place!

(the bag) Shit shit shit! Get your head out of your ass and help me! God you're useless! What the hell are you doing in that sink, anyway? What's that you're muttering?

DAUGHTER   *(muttering)* I should have a career working with knives, some nice, red blood. It doesn't hurt a bit.

She turns on the tap and lets the water run over her foot, then gets out of the sink, dripping, the knife still stuck underneath her nail, a red pool forming under her right foot. She limps slightly.

MOTHER You're crazy! What have you done? Go find some rags. No no… not that one! Can't you see that's a towel. Where's your head? Give me that! AH! I'm sick of being weak!

(*She is about to fall.*) Well, come on, hold me up! Sometimes I swear you're not all that bright. Help me with the bag…. Not like that, you're getting it everywhere! Let me do it! I don't want to call the hearses… nurses! I hate them all, goddamn sourpusses. The fag on nightshift won't even look at me, the stuck-up little turd, they always act like you're bothering them, he's in cahoots with the other one, the fat cow. He always sticks up for that fat bitch too: "Yeah, you're just selfish and controlling!" I'll show them controlling! I'd like to see them in my shoes!

(*She weeps.*) I've been in their goddamn hospital for three months, getting treated like a dog. What are you doing? Daydreaming? Well, that's just great! Can't wait to get out of here, can you? What are you making that face for? You're judging me, huh? How about helping me instead! But no, your mother's only dying. "Mum, I gotta go, I've got a meeting—" Shit, you'd think I was asking for the moon, you always blow through here like the wind. If I can't count on my daughters—Forget your goddamn meetings, you'll survive. Right now I need you both! God you're hopeless at this. Bring the wheelchair over, can't you see I can barely stand up? Can't even help your own mother, no, that's too much to ask, you've only got one, one mother, other people can wait! No no no, the wheels aren't locked! Watch it! Ow! My knee! It's almost like you're doing it on purpose, if I can't count on you, who am I supposed to count on? The other one's gone, I'd like to see you in my shoes, you little wimp…. Afraid to look?

(*She aggressively thrusts out her mutilated belly, with the two bags.*) Look—look at me instead of chewing on your toenails. I'm your mother. Are you afraid of your mother?

DAUGHTER (*faintly*) Yes.

MOTHER I'm the one that has to live with it, not you! Wash my slippers and wipe up the floor, but first sit me down properly! My jacket's all bunched up! Butterfingers!

The DAUGHTER chants to herself while she wipes the floor.

DAUGHTER I've found my career: knife-thrower, or maybe even catcher, it really doesn't hurt a bit!

(*Loudly, to her MOTHER, on the verge of fainting, a pool of blood beneath her foot.*) Look, Mum, it's a knife, nothing to it!

The MOTHER turns around, sees her DAUGHTER's blood, and screams.

MOTHER WHAT HAVE YOU DONE?

DAUGHTER Mum, um, I'm sorry if I killed you. *(Then, white as the sink, she faints.)*

MOTHER *(weeping with rage and abandonment)* Goddammit!

Scene 10: Dream

The DAUGHTER wakes up lying on a bed in the room assigned to her by her hosts. The sounds of the party reach her, muffled. She stands up, in a daze.

DAUGHTER Got to get out of this madhouse! Mum? Mylène! This house is huge!

She loses her way. She finds herself in a tiny attic room. Her SISTER and the SON are there, half-dressed, drinking, giggling, petting.

SISTER *(Her voice is distorted.)* Hey, look who's here?! Laure, come sit with us!

SON Oh! Poor sweetheart, what're you doing on your feet? Come let me take care of you!

The DAUGHTER escapes, running full tilt. The SON and the SISTER pursue her. It goes on and on.

WEALTHY MOTHER *(While bringing petits fours, she collides with the DAUGHTER.)* I love to see young people enjoying themselves!

The SON manages to corner the DAUGHTER.

SON Little rosebud, I'm just going to pluck a few sweet, white petals.

Surrender, syringe, sex.

MOTHER What about me?

Scene 11: Reality

Hospital room. Two months earlier. The MOTHER, the DAUGHTER, and the SISTER. The MOTHER is in bed: feeding tube, oxygen. Flowers. The SISTER is taking photos of the three of them. The MOTHER has just had her hair done.

The daughters sing "Happy Birthday" to their MOTHER.

They open a little bottle of champagne. Kisses.

MOTHER You didn't have to do this. You know I can't drink. Drink up, you two.

DAUGHTER Seventy! That's worth celebrating! Look how sunny it is for your birthday.

SISTER   Yeah, it's Indian summer and you look fabulous!

MOTHER   She came to do my hair, it's too poofy.

DAUGHTER   No, it's lovely, it suits you!

SISTER   Yeah, you look like a little girl.

MOTHER   A little girl! Listen to her! Knock it off, you two. I got my hair done for you. When I wake up tomorrow, after the surgery, with bag number two, to hell with my hair!

DAUGHTER   It's for the best, Mum, you know it is. Look, this is for you, open it.

MOTHER   Well help me, I'm all tangled up in my goddamn tubes.

It's a furry little stuffed dog, white with a black spot around its eye.

SISTER   Look, he's so cute!

DAUGHTER   We thought he was pretty cute!

MOTHER   He's all matted, it looks like he's dirty.

The SISTER plays with the dog, puts on a tiny voice.

SISTER   Hi, Mum, I already love you a lot, would you like to adopt me, lady?

MOTHER   He's not even soft.

DAUGHTER   Sure he's soft, he's a little tousle-haired pooch.

MOTHER   You keep him, if you think he's so cute!

SISTER   We bought him for you, Mum, to keep you company.

MOTHER   I don't want your goddamn dog! *(She cries.)*

Scene 12: Dream

The SISTER is in the middle of the dream sitting room, surrounded by people singing "Happy Birthday, Mylène" while bringing her a cake with forty candles. The people retreat progressively and discreetly, but remain in the background.

SISTER   My fortieth! So they organize this big gathering for me. It's like the tropics here. I started the day in a little summer dress. As the hours and the bottles go by, I've been taking things off. And here I am at the end of the day, no panties, my belly on fire, my dog at my heels. In the time it takes to brace myself against the table, my dog relieves himself on me from behind, splashing my dress with a thick, foul-smelling, amber-coloured liquid. His face is so pitiful I think I can see some tears, so I reassure him:

"It's the first time, it's understandable because I reek of sex, but never do it again!"

I take off my dress and look for my missing panties everywhere.

I'm scared that the guests will see me like this.

Sure I'm a grown woman, but one whose femininity has just been amputated: premature menopause. I'm a woman with fragile nerves, who has all this demonic energy and doesn't always know where to put it.

I have a very gentle lover, a monarch butterfly, as glorious and ethereal as that gorgeous insect.

I've always been pencil-thin, but over the last few months, I've been filling out, my breasts swelling, my thighs thickening, my tummy, arms, buttocks rounding. I have fuller lips in a moon face: I think I'm "setting myself free." It's like a whole-body itch: my newly overstretched skin wants to burst under the pressure of a formidable appetite. I devour canapés, wild boar, the punch in the punch bowl. I smile too hard at my guests, I scare them with my over-black eyes, my over-shining flesh, I offer myself like a bunch of overripe grapes, which is off-putting. I'm afraid of creating conflict, anger, envy. I try to scold my breasts, which are very impertinent. And yet I'm on all these medications to help control my voracious nature, this terrible ogress I've been masking with the face of a doe. I live so completely in the moment, what does the past have to do with me, except for that little buzzing in my left ear? Tomorrow, yes, tomorrow excites me: like all bulimics, I'm salivating in advance, I'm fuelled by desire, what sweets will tomorrow spread out before me?

That Italian sculptor with the eyes of a Roman mosaic wants me again after all these years. He eats black olives like gleaming eyeballs from a little bowl, and with every mouthful his moist tongue searches my already oozing intimacies. And my other lover, a bulimic actor starving for sex and food, always shoots up to the point of euphoria in my presence. I loved him hard for one winter of my discontent.

He chases me across the sitting room, forcing the most mouth-watering dishes on me.

"Wonderful pineapple ham, come eat with me," he says, "come eat with me!" We rub up against each other, on separate stools, leaning on our elbows at a little oyster counter, and I get ridiculously wet. When my regular lover, the monarch butterfly, sees us entwined this way, he starts sweeping up underneath me—I do always seem to make a mess—and he's very pleasant to the actor, who finds my lover's attitude very suspicious. The actor said to me:

"I don't believe he doesn't care, this is all going to end badly, you have to choose!" I know, I know! I don't want to hurt anyone!

And suddenly, in the middle of the sitting room, I start to swell, and swell, and swell… like a hot-air balloon! I rise from the floor, I burst through the ceiling, the roof, I pass the treetops, I reach the first layer of clouds, and from up there I hear, far, far away, my sister's voice calling me…

The SISTER may silently, theatrically, mouth the DAUGHTER's words.

DAUGHTER   *(shouting, in the distance)* Stop disappearing on your birthday, you always leave me alone with Mum and everything!

The SISTER seems to fly away.

SISTER   *(flying away)* Leave me in peace!

A dog howls. A plane takes off.

Scene 13: Reality

Hospital room. Before the DAUGHTER has arrived. The nurse enters.

MOTHER   *(in a very weak voice)* When will… my daughter… get here from Québec City?

NURSE   Any moment now, Mrs. Marjot.

The NURSE goes over to the MOTHER's dog Yappy and sits down beside it.

A gift from your daughters?

The MOTHER nods.

He's sweet. Feel how soft he is. Shall we put on some music?

The nurse presses the button on the tape recorder: Caetano Veloso's "Paloma."

Scene 14: Dream

DAUGHTER   Ah…! Where am I this time?! In the attic!? *(She is lying on an old sagging sofa: the SON has his head between her legs.)* Ah!

She screams, struggles wildly, tries to knock him out: he sticks a needle in her.

No, not another injection!

Blackout.

Scene 15: Reality

The present. Hospital room. The DAUGHTER is sleeping on the sofa. The telephone rings. She springs awake.

DAUGHTER   *(quietly, into the telephone)* Yes? Hi Dad… not good… rough… I'm afraid she's not going to make it. What…? Okay, I'll ask her…. Yeah, yeah, sure, but I have a feeling that… yes, too late… I slept a little… had nightmares…

I don't know... thanks, that's nice.... No no, I'll ask her... I'll keep you posted. Bye.

> *The MOTHER coughs, chokes. The DAUGHTER runs anxiously toward her MOTHER.*

Want some water? Here... have a spongy-thing... good... I'll try to lift you up a little...

(The MOTHER cries out in pain.) Should I call someone?

> *The MOTHER shakes her head. The DAUGHTER places a cold cloth on her neck, on her face. The MOTHER calms down.*

Mum, is there someone you'd like to see?

> *The MOTHER shakes her head. Pause.*

How about a dab of your perfume?

> *The MOTHER nods. The DAUGHTER puts it on her, and the MOTHER starts choking again.*

Sorry, sorry.... Here: spongy-thing...

> *The MOTHER finally calms down. The DAUGHTER falls asleep beside her MOTHER.*

Scene 16: Dream

DAUGHTER *(with a start)* Still in the attic!? Oh no!

> *The DAUGHTER is still in her hosts' attic but this time she is standing unsteadily on a chair, a noose around her neck, its end fixed to the ceiling. The SON, blind drunk, is lying prone at her feet. The WEALTHY MOTHER enters and releases the DAUGHTER from the noose with a confidence born of habit.*

WEALTHY MOTHER Oh children! This is all in poor taste, I do want you to enjoy yourselves, but there is more subtle pleasure to be found in restraint. *(She caresses her prostrate SON's hair.)* Oh son, you've got yourself into such a state again, you know how fragile your nerves are, you mustn't overdo it. Rest, love: I'll take care of the young lady.

DAUGHTER She puts her arm around my waist.

> *The WEALTHY MOTHER, supporting the DAUGHTER, gently conducts her to the sitting room and lays her down on the sofa. The SON staggers along behind them.*

WEALTHY MOTHER You're so pale, dear... *(to the MOTHER)* Bring me a cold cloth! Look how this little girl is neglecting herself.

The MOTHER goes out, comes back immediately with a cold cloth, and hands it to the WEALTHY MOTHER, who dabs the DAUGHTER's temples. The crowd files before her with funereal faces.

We'll have to keep her for a while, your daughter is very ill, Mrs. Marjot, we have to trust my son's diagnosis, he is a great gynecologist.

MOTHER You know, I trust you completely, a doctor is a doctor! They know more than we do, after all, particularly a specialist!

(confiding in the WEALTHY MOTHER) She's really mean to me, you know, she's not an easy person to love.

Scene 17: Truncated Reality

In the hospital room. The DAUGHTER is stretched out on her sofa. Then a blinding vision: the MOTHER appears, reduced to a head, a monster screaming with rage as she floats above her deathbed.

MOTHER I know exactly what you think of me: a freak—half dwarf, half giraffe! Up top, her long, mutant neck heaves her head into the clouds! Down below, her tiny torso shrivels away to nothing! And her crowning glory is a truly grotesque array: her three remaining hairs in a brassy red crewcut, and two glassy, far-sighted, grasshopper eyes!

(sardonic laugh) Oh, I'm at the age for "outings," all right: wheelchair, memories of the old days, sepia photos complete with magnifying glass, and of course, my diploma from the circus! Had a few moments of glory, anyway, not bad for a dwarf with the head of a giraffe and a lovely chlorophyll tutu swaying on her cripple hips! "That dwarf has always been sharp, all right," they'd say in my hometown: "sharp as a tack, and on the attack!" Now I live alone, below the poverty line, below a rumbling laundromat on a certain well-known clay plateau. All my life I've sewed for other people, hems and topstitching—always hated sewing—withered uterus, heart hungry for surprise plot twists. I've always dreamed of being rich, with servants in livery, and an occasional young lover whom I reward with my gift: the terrible, cynical clairvoyance of the well-to-do. I dictate my fabulous memoirs to my part-time girl or boy who, each day at dawn, wheels my chair through snow-covered cemeteries up the side of the mountain to the summit, and the black-marble mausoleum of my dear father—the head of our clan—and mythological mother. The clothes are souring in the washing machines upstairs, just above my giraffe head. I should go work in the mines with poor children, my true nation! I take my pleasure with beasts: canaries, lizards, here and there a little brat who comes by to sell me his school chocolate, he pushes my chair and I am easily aroused. Too curious, zap!

(sardonic laugh) The ogress has a taste for children, avenging the childhood she never had. A monster, I'm a monster, I'd love to go for a bike ride with friends my own age. I'm not crazy, just isolated and too young to die and that's what

makes me complain so bitterly, I want Santa's sack full of love and I want it before Christmas. I'm an abortion, here's what an abortion is like: it's a child's bad drawing, but alive, rolled up in a ball at the bottom of the toilet bowl, so for God's sake, stop trying to clean me up, just pull the chain and flush!

Blackout. We slide into reality.

Scene 18: Reality

Hospital room. One week earlier. The DAUGHTER, in a winter coat, is getting ready to leave her MOTHER.

DAUGHTER I really have to go, my bus to Québec City.

MOTHER You've said that three times.

DAUGHTER They're waiting for me, it's my book launch. I'm the author, after all.

MOTHER Author, you're not a real author.

DAUGHTER Thanks. Anyway, I gotta go!

The DAUGHTER leans down to kiss her MOTHER.

MOTHER *(in her DAUGHTER's ear)* Don't go, someone's in the washroom, making love.

DAUGHTER Huh? Who? Where?

MOTHER They're playing a game.

DAUGHTER Game? What game?

MOTHER Yeah, like actors, they're playing a part!

DAUGHTER Who's playing—the nurses?

MOTHER Yes, you don't understand, a game… with tickets… a lottery… they're placing… bets.

DAUGHTER Who—the nurses are placing bets—on what?

MOTHER On me… they buy tickets—it's him.

The NURSE enters.

Don't leave me with him…. He was… with the others yesterday… in X-ray… they were laughing… they tried… to push my coffin… into the elevator… it wouldn't fit…

She cries out.

DAUGHTER It's the drugs, Mum—

She hugs her MOTHER again, the latter, paranoid, doesn't want to let her go, holds on.

MOTHER   NO!

DAUGHTER   Mum—I'm already really late.

> *The NURSE signals conspiratorially to the DAUGHTER, which makes her uneasy.*

NURSE   We'll take good care of you, Mrs. Marjot.

MOTHER   I don't want to see your face! Hippocratic—critic—hypocrite! Dammit! *(shouting at her DAUGHTER)* I told you, stay here with me! Talk to him!

DAUGHTER   Don't yell, Mum, I'm going, I'll call you tonight as soon as I get there.

MOTHER   Don't yell…?! That's it, abandon me like everyone else…. Dammit! *(She weeps with impotence.)*

> *The DAUGHTER rushes out, guilty, shattered.*

Scene 19: Dream

> *The MOTHER, drunk, confides in everyone, in the sitting room, accompanying the little procession that is carrying the DAUGHTER's unconscious body out of the sitting room.*

MOTHER   She doesn't remember this— Poor little girl, she was so scared of the water she'd been going around in her beachwear for a week—just to get used to—the idea—of swimming in the sea— Well, that night—she snuck out of the hotel—I guess—and then she went into the freezing water all by herself—the ocean was damn cold—and—and—

(She giggles.) And it wasn't me—no—it was a dog that saved her! A dog! Well what can I tell you—it was the middle of the night—and, well, I was asleep at the time! Goddammit! I should've hidden her damn bitchwear—beachwear!

> *They go out.*

Scene 20: Reality

> *The telephone rings for a long time in the hospital room. The DAUGHTER is not there. She hasn't arrived yet. The NURSE picks up the receiver.*

NURSE   Yes, she can talk, for a moment, I'll put her on. *(to the MOTHER)* It's your daughter Mylène, she's calling from Mexico.

> *He takes off the MOTHER's oxygen mask and puts the receiver up to her ear.*

MOTHER *(nothing but rasps and whispers)* Where are you? Yes... no... not here yet... what are you doing, why aren't you here... I can't take it anymore.... Why'd you leave? I wouldn't be dead if you hadn't left.... Don't cry.... Come!

The MOTHER has a coughing fit and the receiver is dropped. The NURSE then replaces the phone on the hook and the oxygen mask on the MOTHER.

NURSE There we go, Mrs. Marjot darling, deep breaths, your girls are on their way.

Blackout. The MOTHER's breathing changes.

Scene 21: Dream

DAUGHTER *(She wakes up in the guest room at her hosts'. Her speech is indistinct.)* Where am I?

She is lying on the bed, awakening from a very long sleep. The house is silent. Autumn light through the window. She tries to turn on her side: the room is swimming. She examines herself. In place of her left breast there is a void, completely flat, a fold of flesh, a purple scar, awful but perfectly healed.

They removed my breast? I just want it to be over!

Blackout.

Scene 22: Reality

The present. In the hospital room, the DAUGHTER has fallen asleep beside her MOTHER. The MOTHER murmurs something. The DAUGHTER awakens and abruptly stands up.

DAUGHTER Huh? What? Go on, you're trying to tell me something, aren't you?

MOTHER *(in a barely audible voice)* The mirror... is crooked.

DAUGHTER What? The mirror?!

MOTHER Yes, it's crooked, straighten it!

DAUGHTER Oh... sure. *(She goes and straightens the mirror.)*

MOTHER What time?

DAUGHTER The time? Five o'clock in the morning, Mum.

MOTHER Where is she?

DAUGHTER She's coming tonight—later. I'm here, get some rest.

She moistens her MOTHER's mouth, dabbing it with a cold cloth. Holds her hand. Hums, then lies back down.

Scene 23: Dream

DAUGHTER   (*startled*) Huh? What?

She is still lying in the guest room, but this time she tries to get out of bed. A perilous process.

I'm a wreck.

They must have been drugging her for months: the scar on her breast is too old.

I have the arms of a junkie!

On the verge of passing out, she drags herself over to the window and presses her forehead against the pane.

A black limousine…?

The family are all dressed in black in the distance. One of the silhouettes turns back: her SISTER! The DAUGHTER sees her and screams mutely.

SISTER   It's not my fault!

The whole family turns to her. They are all in mourning!

DAUGHTER   Wait, that's not a limousine! It's a hearse! Wait, who died? My mother? Mylène, what have you done?!

(*She beats against the window, crying, feebly, to her SISTER.*) Please, get me out of here!

SISTER   I didn't do anything!

The family immediately grab the SISTER and hustle her off. Suddenly, the SON appears behind the DAUGHTER and strikes her on the back of the neck.

DAUGHTER   Oh no, not another damn injection!

The SON gathers her up when she collapses. She giggles before losing consciousness altogether.

Great! Falling again…. Oh well, it is fall, after all!

Scene 24: Truncated Reality

Hospital room. The MOTHER plays with the little stuffed dog her daughters gave her.

MOTHER Look what I found this morning at Jean Coutu. A little white dog with a black spot around his eye. I found him, he was rolled up in a ball at the bottom of a shelf, hidden behind the rolls of toilet paper! He looked at me with his little sad eye and I melted. He leaped right into my arms: he's so soft. I held him tight and headed to the cash. The cashier said: "You know you can't bring animals in here?" I told her: "This dog was on special!" Her face fell. That'll teach her! Then I left without paying. I didn't even buy toilet paper! Yappy, that's his name.

She laughs maliciously.

Scene 25: Dream

DAUGHTER *(dressed in black, wearing tinted lenses like the others, as the hearse rolls along)* Where? What? We're driving through the countryside— Sitting on the back seat of the hearse.

She is jammed against the SON. The WEALTHY MOTHER is driving, the SISTER beside her in the front seat.

SISTER *(crying and blowing her nose)* It's not my fault, it's not my fault, it's not my fault.

The DAUGHTER tries to make a move toward her: immediately the SON's iron grip tightens on her arm.

SON Don't even think about it!

Suddenly there's a pounding on the back of the hearse.

DAUGHTER My mother? What have you done with Mum? *(She moves around, turning toward the back.)* What's going on? Where are you taking me?

The SON slaps the DAUGHTER, who giggles as she passes out. Sudden blackout.

It's all gone black, I blend right in, I absolutely blend right in.

Scene 26: Reality

The present. In the hospital room. DR. DUMAS enters. She listens to the MOTHER's chest.

DR. DUMAS *(to the MOTHER)* Mrs. Marjot, it's Dr. Dumas, do you remember me? *(The MOTHER nods.)* Are you in pain? *(The MOTHER nods.)* I'm going to up your dosage a bit. *(The MOTHER nods.)* Your older daughter is here, she's taking good care of you. *(Pause: the MOTHER and the DAUGHTER look at each other.)* You're a brave, beautiful lady. Your other daughter's arriving tonight? I'm going to try to keep you comfortable until then. We'll discontinue the feeding tube… I've come to say goodbye. Dr. Bilanski will be replacing me.

(DR. DUMAS *gives her a kiss on the forehead.*) It's been a pleasure knowing you.

MOTHER   Me you too.

DR. DUMAS   (*to the DAUGHTER*) Your mother and I share the same taste in music.

(*The MOTHER smiles.*) She's very proud of her daughters—two artists. It runs in the family: you're the actress?

DAUGHTER   No, the writer.

DR. DUMAS   (*to the DAUGHTER, softly, taking her aside*) It's a miracle she's still alive: her kidneys aren't functioning anymore, clinically she—she's waiting for your sister. If you have things to say to her, or family to notify, it's time.

(*DR. DUMAS shakes her hand.*) Good luck and take care of yourself. Goodbye.

She leaves. Pause.

DAUGHTER   Mum, is there someone you'd like to see? (*The MOTHER shakes her head.*) Are you thirsty?

> *The MOTHER shakes her head. The DAUGHTER offers her a sponge-stick, which she refuses. The NURSE enters and increases the dosage of morphine. He leaves silently. The MOTHER sleeps while the DAUGHTER sings very softly, to her MOTHER as well as to herself: "Duerme, duerme, negrito... y tu mama esta en el campo, negrito."*

Scene 27: Dream

> *The DAUGHTER is running alone in the middle of a cornfield, but in the distance we hear the ferocious growling of a dog attacking and people screaming—utter carnage. Suddenly the dog materializes in front of her. It orders her to follow it.*

DAUGHTER   (*a yell*) Ah! Dog!

> *She tries to get up. Her legs buckle. The dog offers its body to lean on. She finally manages to get up. She follows it blindly, her body against its body, their gait perfectly synchronized.*

Thank you, dog.

Woods.... Clearing... shack... dog... woman.

> *They walk to the edge of a forest. A few golden leaves flutter on the branches of denuded trees. At last... a clearing. Two giant pines conceal a dilapidated shack. With its muzzle, the dog pushes on a little wooden fence. Two brief yelps. Then a strange woman appears. This WOMAN, a figure from the dawn of time, must exude an unsettling authority. The DAUGHTER falls like an autumn leaf. Blackout.*

Scene 28: Reality

Hospital. A few months earlier. The MOTHER and the DAUGHTER are sitting together. A manuscript between them. The MOTHER is not as sick.

MOTHER I didn't understand it all, it's like there's too many words, the story's confusing… the sex… I don't know… it's pretty dark but it's you all right.

DAUGHTER Thanks.

MOTHER No, that's not what I meant to say.

DAUGHTER I know.

Pause.

MOTHER I don't really know what to say, I don't know about that kind of thing.

DAUGHTER It's fine, don't worry about it.

The DAUGHTER takes back her manuscript.

Scene 29: Dream

In the WOMAN's shack: she has put the DAUGHTER to bed on the ground on a mattress and covered her with a heavy blanket. She tends to her like an animal mother: efficient, tender, and gruff. She intones softly, a chant from the dawn of time. The DAUGHTER is detoxing.

DAUGHTER I feel terrible… total cold turkey. Mum? Grandma? Oh no, I didn't, not in my bed!

She has just soiled herself. The WOMAN cleans her buttocks as one would a child's.

You won't tell, will you? You won't tell Mum?

WOMAN Tut tut tut!

DAUGHTER When I was little, turds were my friends, I had a whole family of them under the porch, big ones, medium ones, small ones, my little family of animals that followed me everywhere: my mother—

WOMAN Tut tut tut!

ASH TLOK HISTASINI WAWA OSHNÉ DJIVINISH! (A prayer, an incantation.)

The MOTHER appears, young. She is crying. She kneels, humbly, before the WOMAN.

MOTHER Mum, how come you never loved me?

WOMAN *MISH KAMA…*

MOTHER   I'm a crybaby, I'm no good at anything, not school or friends or you. I'm not pretty, I'm not smart. Mum, why was I brought into the world?

The WOMAN indicates her DAUGHTER lying on the straw mattress.

WOMAN   *CASH TINÉ.*

MOTHER   Who's she?

WOMAN   *Ta gouch.*

MOTHER   Is that me when I get older?

The WOMAN shakes her head.

WOMAN   *(A prayer, an incantation.)* ACHBAMATOUKLA…. Plaïn Plaïn… KOUBOULECH TAMOK… LA LA.

MOTHER   Do I know her?

The WOMAN nods and gestures "later."

I'm going to know her later.

The WOMAN nods. The MOTHER leans toward the DAUGHTER.

DAUGHTER   Mum?

MOTHER   My daughter? I'm going to have a daughter? What on earth did I do to her? Why does she seem so sick?

DAUGHTER   Why are you younger than me, Mum?

MOTHER   Because I'm a child, I can't have a child.

WOMAN   *Ash fa mek laï pok.*

DAUGHTER   What about me, who's going to bring me into the world?

WOMAN   *Eshtec katimic!*

The MOTHER disappears. Blackout.

Scene 30: Truncated Reality

In the bathroom, the DAUGHTER, at a younger age, is removing her makeup next to her MOTHER, at a younger age. The faucet runs. The MOTHER is washing and washing and washing her hands. The DAUGHTER is crying.

MOTHER   You were so promising…

DAUGHTER   I'm twenty years old, Mum!

MOTHER   Never mind, I always thought you would be somebody—somebody so much better than me.

DAUGHTER   What do you want?

MOTHER Drink some water!

DAUGHTER No.

MOTHER Drink some water!

DAUGHTER No.

MOTHER I said: drink some water!

> *The MOTHER, taking the DAUGHTER by surprise, plunges her head to the bottom of the full sink and holds it there. A dog growls threateningly. The DAUGHTER pulls out a knife and sticks it into her MOTHER's belly.*

MOTHER & DAUGHTER *(doubled over)* I'm sorry if I—

Scene 31: Dream

In the shack. Time has passed, it's winter.

DAUGHTER Winter. Nightmare. Howling wind.

> *The DAUGHTER is still stretched out on the straw mattress, the WOMAN enters, covered in snow, the dog yelps outside, the WOMAN brings in some firewood as well as two dead hares with bloody necks. She deposits them at the DAUGHTER's feet. Then the WOMAN makes her drink a bitter herb tea, as the DAUGHTER grimaces.*

Ugh…

WOMAN Bouch sak… ishkim… plaïn amamish.

> *The WOMAN force-feeds her an orangey vegetable stew, so thick that the wooden spoon stands up by itself in the middle of the rough bowl.*

DAUGHTER No!

WOMAN Mesh… agayoup quésipotolak…. Baou matewotou. *(The WOMAN holds her head in the crook of her arm while she feeds her.)* Méchein douté mi gouf!

> *The WOMAN rocks her and sings her a very, very ancient lullaby.*

Scene 32: Reality

> *The MOTHER, glass in hand, a radiant fifty, her daughters still in their twenties. The MOTHER is playing bolo with the SISTER, who is lying on the sofa, smoking a joint. We hear early Billy Idol at full volume. She passes the joint to her MOTHER, who smokes it, coughing a little. The MOTHER offers the joint to the DAUGHTER, who is seated on the ground, off to one side. She demurs. The MOTHER taunts the SISTER by sending the ball, on its elastic, right into her face.*

MOTHER Why don't you listen to French music!

SISTER   Stop it. That's annoying. You're not funny!

She gives a little push to the MOTHER, who falls on the ground cackling.

Hey hey! You're stoned!

MOTHER   Nah, I don't feel a thing, s'just the wine!

SISTER   Oh yeah?! I don't know if you know this but you're sitting on the grass with your white skirt!

MOTHER   Oh! Dammit!

She jumps up, wiping her skirt, then lies down next to the SISTER, cuddling her.

Oh, sweetie, I'm happy, I'm going to Cuba, I'm going to see Pedro again, I'm in love for the first time in my life!

SISTER   In love— Don't kid yourself, Pedro's a gigolo.

MOTHER   That's not very nice. Why would you say that? He's very nice, he sent me a card.

SISTER   Mum, honestly, you're so naive! One look at your pictures and it's obvious what Pedro does for a living! If you want to screw for the sake of screwing, fine. Just be realistic about it, that's all.

MOTHER   Realistic— Look who's talking! Laure, you tell her to shut up if she doesn't have anything intelligent to say. You're just bloody well jealous! It's a lot more than screwing, as you call it!

(cuddling) Mylène, you're not working, so make an effort! Go see Grandma in hospital while I'm gone, she's really not well, she's slipping. My poor old mum.

SISTER   Oh, no! Not that old bitch! She doesn't even know who we are! Stop fussing over her, she's been slipping for twelve years, she's a vegetable, she depresses me, and anyway, I can't stand death. It'll be hard enough dealing with you.

MOTHER   Boy, you're something else… I don't plan on being dead anytime soon!

SISTER   Anyway, I know what I mean.

MOTHER   Stop talking about your grandmother that way, she's a good person, and your sister goes to see her!

The MOTHER has gone back to sit on the ground with the DAUGHTER, she tries to cuddle her in turn, the DAUGHTER keeps her guard up. They whisper.

SISTER   Fuck you! *(She moves away.)*

MOTHER   You and your fuck yous! And your damn American music!

(cuddling) Come on, Laure, sweetie, you'll go see Grandma while I'm in Cuba, won't you? I'll never forgive myself if the poor old—she's got nobody.

DAUGHTER Mum, why don't you postpone your Cuba trip a bit?

MOTHER Hey! Don't you think I've earned a little break? I go see her every day, she's like my little baby. I tell her all the time: "Hey, Mum, I'm getting back at you now, I can finally touch you as much as I want." She lets me, poor old Mum, you know she was so scared of going crazy. What can you do: life is unfair.

(She cries.) You'll do it for me, sweetie?

DAUGHTER I'll try but I'm not you, Mum.

MOTHER Oh stop!

DAUGHTER No no, go to Cuba, Mum, enjoy yourself.

MOTHER Thank you, my sweet girl.

The MOTHER goes out, dancing. The DAUGHTER faints. A plane takes off.

Scene 33: Reality

The present. The hospital. The telephone rings in the hospital room. It's the SISTER. The daughters weep at either end of the line. We hear only the MOTHER's breathing.

DAUGHTER The same... I know... I'm tired... we're waiting for you.

Scene 34: Reality

A few days earlier. The SISTER is at the MOTHER's bedside, and the MOTHER is less sick. The SISTER is feeding her MOTHER some soup.

MOTHER I liked your ginger soup better.

SISTER Okay!

MOTHER You would've made a good mother, it's a shame you never met anybody.

SISTER Stop it, Mum, I've been with the same man for fifteen years.

MOTHER Oh, him... you be careful, I don't think he's good for you. He's violent.

SISTER That's not the problem, Mum.

MOTHER What is?

SISTER It's you—it's me— Anyway I gotta go...

MOTHER Fine, go ahead, go run around like a chicken with its head cut off. Go back to your American and complain about me! And God forbid you should feel guilty!

SISTER Fuck off!

Scene 35: Dream

Spring. The DAUGHTER is outside the shack in a light dress.

DAUGHTER It's good to be elsewhere.

The DAUGHTER stops and gently caresses her body: she has only one breast. A little shadow of sadness.

Mum... why?

Scene 36: Reality

Night, seaside, crashing surf. The two sisters enthusiastically leading their MOTHER by the hand.

DAUGHTER Look, Mum, this is it— We're here!

MOTHER It's too far. What were you thinking— Dammit, there's holes everywhere, I'm going to twist an ankle. Where are we going? I can't see a thing.

SISTER It's the ocean, Mum—listen—smell!

DAUGHTER Look up there, that's our house.

MOTHER A shack!

Suddenly a dark shape comes from behind and jostles the MOTHER.

(*shouting*) Jesus, what's that?

SISTER What? Oh! It's Yappy, Mum, it's good old Yappy.

DAUGHTER Of course, you love to come to the beach with us, eh Yappy?

MOTHER You two and your goddamn dog! Shedding everywhere, always underfoot, they don't want kids but the dog sleeps in their bed! You care more about your damn dog than about your own mother! You've never had kids, you two, you don't know what it's like!

SISTER Come here, Yappy, leave Mum alone. He loves you.

MOTHER He loves me!

DAUGHTER It's true. He'd love it if you'd love him back.

MOTHER Hey! It's only a dog, you know! Damn it's cold! I hate a cold ocean!

SISTER Look at the house, Mum, look how lovely it is!

MOTHER   It's falling apart!

DAUGHTER   It's old but look—all original stone!

MOTHER   Must be impossible to heat.

SISTER   Jesus Christ, will you shut your trap once and for all! You fucking pleasure-sucking black hole of misery!

MOTHER   Watch your mouth! You better watch your tone! I don't have to take that from you!

DAUGHTER   Okay, let's just calm down.

MOTHER   You know what you can do with your "calm downs"!

DAUGHTER   You watch your tone… fascist!

MOTHER   Fascist…. Would you listen to Little Miss Tight-Ass. Hey! Lucky me! Two daughters to lecture me! Stop trying to tell me what to do, dammit! As if you were so perfect. You're always depressed, and the other one never works. An actress, she says! Don't I deserve a little peace, at my age! Mind your own goddamn business! Keep your goddamn advice for your goddamn dog! Never good enough for you two! So kill me then… once and for all, just finish me off!

She reaches a climax, between anger and tears, and the dog growls.

DAUGHTER   *(softly)* Go on, Yappy, do what you have to do!

The dog attacks the MOTHER, who screams and throws herself into the sea. We hear the plunge.

SISTER   Uh…

In the blackout the soundscape is dominated by a big splash and the roaring of the surf.

Scene 37: Truncated Reality

The present. The hospital. The NURSE enters the room.

NURSE   Can you help me move your mother, I need to change her before I leave.

They try to move her. The MOTHER is in pain.

DAUGHTER   No, leave her, it hurts too much.

NURSE   She'll feel better afterwards.

They turn the MOTHER with ritual slowness. She is in pain.

MOTHER   Find my baptismal certificate, Dad. Why didn't we ever talk to you? I was a bad girl, eh? I deserve it? Why am I bad? Mum, why did you leave me all alone?

DAUGHTER   Mum, I'm here. Want some water?

MOTHER   Bring me my Sunday boots, I want to go travelling. How can I leave you, you're all I have.

DAUGHTER   *(distraught)* I know, Mum.

NURSE   *(to the DAUGHTER)* Don't worry, ma'am, we're taking good care of your mother. *(He adjusts the dosage.)* That feels better already, eh, Mrs. Marjot?

MOTHER   *(to the DAUGHTER)* I'm sorry, dear, if I… *(She slips into unconsciousness.)*

DAUGHTER   Huh? What—Mum?

The NURSE leaves discreetly.

Scene 38: Dream

Near the shack, outdoors, in the vegetable garden. The WOMAN is in the background, digging. The DAUGHTER is turning over the earth in the WOMAN's vegetable garden. Her shovel hits a solid mass. She leans over: tiny bones.

DAUGHTER   Bones?!

She scoops out earth all around: more bones, several skeletons. She tries to reassemble the little skeletons: the bones fit together. She continues turning over the dirt and finds more.

Ha!

Her hands lift a little skull out of the soil, the skull of a child.

A baby?

She digs deeper… another little skull, two little children!

Newborns!

Scene 39: Truncated Reality

Hospital room. The MOTHER is sleeping, the DAUGHTER is lying beside her.

MOTHER   *(interior monologue of a dying woman)* You don't remember, poor little thing, you've always been afraid of the water and I… and I…

(weeps) You *should* love dogs, he's the one who saved you, not me, I was… I was…. Your real mother… is a dog… your mother… dog.

She cries like a pup, waking up her DAUGHTER.

DAUGHTER   Mum? You're crying!

The DAUGHTER rocks her MOTHER and sings the lullaby "Duerme, duerme, negrito," then dozes off.

Scene 40: Dream

The DAUGHTER runs toward the WOMAN, brandishing the two little skulls.

DAUGHTER Look!

The WOMAN slaps the DAUGHTER in the face. Like a gunshot to her cheek.

WOMAN *Mitch tak desh tu gami!*

The dog yelps. Blackout.

Scene 41: Reality

Hospital room. The present. The MOTHER is rasping. She's suffocating, breathing like someone beginning the descent toward death. The DAUGHTER wakes up with a start, very anxious.

MOTHER *(rasping)* What's she doing?

DAUGHTER You can't take any more, eh, Mum?

The MOTHER shakes her head.

MOTHER When will she get here?

DAUGHTER Four or five hours.

MOTHER Do something.

DAUGHTER Should I get someone to help you, Mum?

The MOTHER nods.

Just a sec, I'll be right back!

She runs out of the room, returning immediately with the NURSE.

NURSE Yes, we can give her something to clear her lungs: it might buy her some time.

DAUGHTER The nurse is going to give you something to help you breathe, Mum… poor baby, nobody should suffer like this.

(The NURSE leaves.) Mum, think of Cuba… the beautiful beaches… the turquoise sea… that wonderful ocean breeze. Let's take a deep breath. I love you, Mum.

The DAUGHTER breathes deeply with her MOTHER, a strange, soothing ballet. The latter's breathing stabilizes a little. The DAUGHTER falls asleep beside her MOTHER. The NURSE enters and gives her an injection, then goes out.

Scene 42: Dream

The FATHER finishes digging the earth with a heavy dagger. His DAUGHTER is beside him, feeling trapped. Perhaps the SISTER is in the distance. The MOTHER is in the hole in the ground.

FATHER   Look! Your mother.

DAUGHTER   Leave her alone.

FATHER   I'm trying to understand why I could never make your mother happy.

Pause.

You girls don't know everything, something terrible happened to her when we were courting. She was never the same afterwards. Your mother—wasn't a virgin on our wedding night… by that time I didn't want to marry her, I didn't love her anymore, but she threatened to kill herself. When the two of you were little, she didn't want you, she even tried to—I never loved your mother.

He keeps digging. The DAUGHTER stops him.

DAUGHTER   Stop it, Dad!

She grabs the dagger from him. She bends over the hole and begins tenderly to cover her MOTHER's body with dirt, using the dagger.

Help me bury her again!

FATHER   I stayed for the two of you: children need a family. That was my dream.

DAUGHTER   Shh! I know, Dad. Dig!

The FATHER, sobbing, buries the MOTHER, the DAUGHTER starts singing a very, very beautiful and very, very ancient lament. Healing. Perhaps they cry in each other's arms. The FATHER moves away. The DAUGHTER sets off again.

Then one day, I arrive here.

The MOTHER is lying on the ground, chained, dying, a dog bowl by her side, a horrible mouldy pâté drying inside the bowl. Dream may become indistinguishable from reality. It's the pangs of death.

Mum, what have they done to you?

MOTHER   *(rasping)* Your sister… too long…

DAUGHTER   Where is she? And the others? The family?

MOTHER Gone.

DAUGHTER They mutilated you—abandoned you—like me.

MOTHER *(in her DAUGHTER's ear)* Sorry, I wasn't very nice to you, I tried to kill you once… in the sink… pushed your head down… too long… you were five.

A dog yelps. The DAUGHTER cries with relief.

Your little sister too…

The dog yelps again.

DAUGHTER I know, Mum…

Scene 43: Reality

The present. Hospital room. The SISTER bursts in, pale with worry, her face bathed in tears.

SISTER Mum!

DAUGHTER She waited for you!

SISTER Mum, *no one* could stage a death scene like you.

The two sisters run into each other's arms, and at that moment the dying MOTHER rises from her bed and tries to communicate with her daughters. The daughters lean towards their MOTHER, encircling her, and the latter speaks directly to them, for a very, very long time, rasping and dying. A monologue. Testimony. Testament. No words are comprehensible, but we sense that she is telling them everything that she has never managed to say in her lifetime. We must feel her love. The daughters receive it in all its intensity. It is a birth. A luminous ascent.

A puppy, its tail wagging joyously, cheerfully laps the contents of its water bowl.

DAUGHTERS My mother was beautiful.

The end.

Gisèle's Wedding Dress
(La robe de mariée de Gisèle Schmidt)

by Julie Vincent

translated by Maureen Labonté

For Gisèle Schmidt

Actors are channellers—channellers of dreams.
—Gisèle Schmidt

Even now at sixty, in my dreams, I'm always about twenty years old, quite slim, with lots of hair.
—Federico Fellini

Introduction to
Gisèle's Wedding Dress
(*La robe de mariée de Gisèle Schmidt*)

Gisèle's Wedding Dress is a theatre artist's tribute to one of Québec's most admired actors, Gisèle Schmidt (1921–2005). I stress that it is a tribute from one artist to another and a celebration of theatricality in life and on stage, not a biography. The play vibrates nonetheless with the profound affection and admiration that Julie Vincent felt for her friend and colleague. The career of Gisèle Schmidt spanned most of the twentieth century, since she first appeared on stage at the age of four, and she played a large number of roles from many repertoires until she retired in her eighties.[1] Thus, her life parallels events over the historical period represented in *Gisèle's Wedding Dress*. Vincent has invented a mysterious, shadowy character who represents in the six shifts throughout the play the presence of Schmidt and her conviction that theatre is poetry and the search for love, with all the claims to freedom and knowledge these associations entail. The play's epigraph quotes Schmidt as saying: "Actors are channellers—channellers of dreams."

Gisèle's Wedding Dress is composed of six fictitious scenes—anecdotally, geographically, and historically separate but thematically linked—that could have been played by Schmidt, but were not. While none of the characters find the grand love they seek, the play as a whole is a great, theatrical love story written in homage to an artist whose determination and talent led her to rise above a socio-cultural situation in the first half of the twentieth century that actively discouraged artistry in theatre, particularly when it led to displays of the body's sexual desires and women's longing to speak words that evoked their own experiences.

The subject and thematic composition of *Gisèle's Wedding Dress* are set in the opening Prologue and Shift 1, using a play within a play strategy by staging what Actress #2 calls "that terrible love scene" in Chekhov's *Ivanov*. Chekhov's play is woven thematically throughout Vincent's play and reappears in disturbing substance in the fifth scene, where the characters from the two plays merge into one another. In the opening replay from *Ivanov* the actress is wearing the antique wedding dress, which will wend its way through all the scenes of *Gisèle's Wedding Dress*, in preparation for her wedding the next day. The love scene in Checkhov's play is *terrible* because the audience knows that destructive social forces and, perhaps, unworthy personal motives will have the effect of cancelling the wedding, separating the lovers and producing Ivanov's suicide instead of the fulfilment of their love. All the scenes in *Gisèle's Wedding Dress* dramatize situations in which, like Ivanov and Sacha, the characters dream of a great love, only to have their hopes dashed. Although they remain lonely people with only their dreams or memories of rich and enduring affective and sexual gratification, they are portrayed as daring to give themselves over to moments of intense, although usually tawdry, fulfillment. The fabulous actress Gisèle, who invented the culture of love for herself, is quoted in Shift 1 as having said

"I would have given my entire career to have lived one great love." The fact that she sought such love, without having lived it, resulted in a life lived dynamically, creatively, and empathetically in the unending search to become more and more alive: "Love was, for [Gisèle], a redoubtable and dangerous instrument of learning" (Foreword). Gisèle returns to her dream of a "grand romantic love" in Shift 4, where she states explicitly that such a love is intrinsically erotic. She had a "turbulent youth," had lovers, and feels complicity with prostitutes. She was deemed to be, she says unapologetically, "too profane" to be admitted to Père Legault's Compagnons de Saint-Laurent (1937–1952), the famous company usually credited for the birth of modern Québec theatre in the mid-twentieth century.

The play's central image and prop of the wedding gown that appears in every scene anticipates sexual jouissance along with social integration. In fact, the social integration they hope for never develops for these characters who "had suffered some form of political persecution and had fought to preserve their freedom and individuality" (Production Notes). Nevertheless, they are shown to have enjoyed moments of sexual encounter and intensity. The desire for one great love in one's life echoes through the scenes of *Gisèle's Wedding Dress*, and is repeated for the last time when the man in the sixth scene, "Dorian Grey," places the wedding dress in the coffin of the young man he loved in vain, saying: "I've always said that I would've given my life to have known one great love. For just five minutes."

La robe de mariée de Gisèle Schmidt was published in 2004. Vincent has spoken of Schmidt's delight at knowing that her theatrical career would be preserved this way in celebratory artistic form. However, the play did not have a stage production until early in 2006, just a few months after Schmidt's death. In view of the grief felt by Vincent and the entire cast and their respect for her unique place in theatre, the representation of a fictitious Gisèle on stage right after her death was considered to be inappropriate. No one could replace her so soon after her demise. Therefore, the decision was made when the play was first performed to have the character Gisèle represented by a satin dressing gown, each of the female actors putting it on, sitting in her armchair, and speaking her lines during the shifts. When Vincent directed the play in Montevideo, the role of Gisèle was played by a single actor, who did not otherwise have a role in the play. Because the passage of time produces its own distances, it is Vincent's intent for the English translation for Gisèle to be played in this way with a separate actor or for her presence in the empty chair to be incarnated musically and not corporeally on stage. Whatever the director's decision, the presence of this character remains powerful but shrouded in the mysterious activity of channelling dreams.

The antique wedding dress of the title of the play wanders as costume and prop through each of the six shifts and scenes, losing its freshness and even some of its pieces but never losing its significance. The dress and its long train make their appearance as a metonymy for Gisèle and her career in the theatre when the actors come on stage in Shift 1, pull the dress out of her old chest, and evoke the final scene between Sacha and Ivanov in Chekhov's play, Sacha wearing the dress in preparation for their wedding, which has been planned for the following day. The dress is next worn in 2003 by She, a television actor in the midst of a panic attack who rushes from the set without taking off the dress in her urgent desire to see the river and rethink her career. Ofelia, an immigrant garment worker of Portuguese origin is next represented sewing and wearing the dress in 1970 at the time of the October Crisis in Québec. The third scene depicts seventeen-year-old Simone, a Canadian adventurer, wearing the dress in the port of Piraeus, Athens, Greece in 1975 (a time of brutal political repression in Greece), concealing in the hem the hashish she is selling and the money she has already made. The captain in this scene cuts off the bottom of the dress and burns it. The fourth scene, which takes place in the south of France in 1981, a couple of decades after Algeria's brutal war of independence, depicts Cuisse de mouche, a prostitute from Algeria, wearing the dress found by Pico the Gypsy in Athens. In the fifth scene, "The Carnival at the Ends of the Earth," taking place in the late 1980s, Sacha, a young nuclear physicist with expert knowledge of the catastrophic Chernobyl nuclear accident of 1986, wears the wedding dress under her ski jacket. The man of the final scene carries an embarrassing plastic bag that contains the wedding dress. The dress, having been part of so many violent incidents and reduced to much less than its original self, was found in the classified ads and is now missing the veil and crinoline. Still, its significance as a token of love is undiminished for the man who places it in the coffin of the beautiful young man he loved.

Gisèle's Wedding Dress raises the questions of what love means to each of us and what symbols and myths are associated with a wedding dress. The white wedding dress has traditionally symbolized virginity and the promise of heterosexual coupling within the bonds of Christian marriage. Tellingly, it does not serve this function in any of the play's scenes, although its traditional meaning and the myths surrounding it cannot be set aside as the characters pursue the marginalized course of their difficult lives. Each of them is playing against the hegemonic discourse of dominant power structures and ideologies. In *Gisèle's Wedding Dress*, the dress symbolizes the hunger for love, the erotic longing felt by the characters in their search for a place to be where relationships can be welcoming. Above all, the dress serves in this play as a memento, touch of beauty, costume, and protective shield in a world where all the lonely people are called to play and perform their difficult roles on public and private stages that are never without watchful eyes.

Vincent and her colleagues in her company Singulier-Pluriel created a richly orchestrated and widely varied soundscape to accompany the dress as it wanders from owner to owner and continent to continent. Like the acting of the players, the soundscape serves to channel the characters' dreams through alternative wavelengths. The sound actually picks up the rustle of the dress at times, the breathing or orgasmic ecstasy of characters, footsteps, or telephone rings from others coming and going. It may be musical (jazz, guitar, disco, and classical, Portuguese, Yugoslavian, Greek, and Arabic music) or evocative of surroundings real or imagined (the city with its transportation systems, industrial machines, sirens, and riots, the sea, the river, or the wind).

Vincent has woven together in wonderfully creative ways in *Gisèle's Wedding Dress* a panorama of theatricality, unsentimental perspectives on the urgency of human hunger for love and jouissance, and brief clips of some of the worst socio-political and environmental catastrophes of the twentieth century. With a deft touch that shifts through the spare, frequently harsh dialogue of six "Meetings," she brings into view the dreams and memories of a cast of modest characters caught in the grips of circumstances they barely understand and control in their own lives. The combined leitmotifs of theatre, ceremony, and performance illuminate the fragments that are shown of their experiences and brilliantly brings them together, thereby revealing their profoundly human significance. Running through these meetings and fragments are the theme of love and astounding insights on the historical and political foundations of the culture of love, often the dark sides of love that one always hopes to avoid. The disparate scenes covering many years produce awareness that, despite the danger love always brings, human existence can have little thrill or meaning without the risk of living life with passion. As Julie Vincent says in her Foreword: "every love story true to its historical and political context deserves to be told."

Notes

[1] For information on the career of Gisèle Schmidt, see Diane Godin, "Gisèle Schmidt," in Michel Vaïs, ed., *Dictionnaire des artistes du théâtre québécois* (2008). Montréal: Éditions Québec Amérique: p. 367 and "Gisèle Schmidt, la fabuleuse actrice." *Le Devoir* (February 10, 2005).

About Julie Vincent

Actor, playwright, teacher, and director, Julie Vincent received the Golden Plaque for Best Actress in 1979 at the Chicago International Film Festival for her role as Suzanne in Anne-Claire Poirier's magnificent *Mourir à tue-tête*. Vincent has since starred in many Canadian films and on television. Her approach to acting has always been characterized by a poetic sensitivity that renders her work highly original. Over the past fifteen years she has developed a knowledge of musical and rhythmic structures in theatre, leading her to play roles in musical theatre to enthusiastic critical acclaim with major orchestras on international stages from Montréal to Tokyo to New York. The many performances she has directed have put on stage a range of plays from the international repertoire, several translated by Québec playwrights. Her recent plays have been successfully produced in Montréal by the theatre company Singulier-Pluriel, which she founded. This company develops an important relation with the life stories of immigrants in Canada. Singulier-Pluriel is dedicated to the production of original works. In the process of creation Julie Vincent elaborates a comprehensive research and quest for authenticity with the team of designers from the company: Michel Smith, music composer, Geneviève Lizotte, production designer, and François Régis Fournier, photographer. Day-long workshops precede the work of writing and staging.

Vincent has taught improvisation and acting at the École nationale de théâtre du Canada/National Theatre School of Canada for more than twenty years. She is now Artistic Advisor at the École nationale de cirque. The one-woman show she wrote and in which she played six roles, *Noir de monde* (1988), received the Prix spécial du jury at the Festival du Café-théâtre in Evry and the Mention des critiques for the Festival Off in Avignon, both in France. Following the creation in Montréal in 2006 with the Théâtre PàP of *La robe de mariée de Gisèle Schmidt*, Singulier-Pluriel co-produced the play in Spanish in September 2007 at the Victoria Theatre with InterArte in Montevideo, Uruguay, with Uruguayan and Canadian players.

In 2010, her most recent play, *Le portier de la gare Windsor*, was produced to enthusiastic critical response in the Salle Fred Barry of the Théâtre Denise Pelletier. A revised version of this play will be co-produced in August–September 2010 in the Sala La Carbonera of Buenos Aires for Argentina's bicentenary.

Published Works by Julie Vincent

Noir de monde (1989). Montréal: Éditions de la Pleine Lune.

La Déprime (in collaboration with Denis Bouchard, Rémy Girard, Raymond Legault) (1991). Montréal: VLB Éditeur.

La robe de mariée de Gisèle Schmidt (2004). Montréal: Éditions de la Pleine Lune.

Foreword

Gisèle Schmidt (1921–2005) had a brilliant career as an actor in Québec. The press clippings I found in her files and boxes after her death told me the story of a self-taught artist who made an indelible mark on stage, screen, and television. She was in so many ways a pioneer, a trailblazer, and an inspiration. Her acting was breathtaking, poetic, and true but it hid an immense and often inconsolable loneliness.

I met her when we worked together on a production of *Ivanov* at Théâtre Jean Duceppe. Years later, after she had retired, I visited her a number of times at her home on the shores of the St. Lawrence River in La Malbaie, Québec. She was then eighty-five years old.

I got to know a woman for whom love was a way to travel, to take herself away. Love was, for her, a redoubtable and dangerous instrument of learning.

These six stories for the stage are an homage to Gisèle and to the culture of love she invented for herself. In writing them, I discovered that any and every love story true to its historical and political context deserves to be told.

—Julie Vincent
Montréal
November 2009

Style

Many of the stories in this play are erotic. This is intentional. For example, the story entitled Cuisse de mouche takes place in a whorehouse in Nîmes, France. The two characters are making love throughout the scene. However, my intention is that the physical act of coitus not be shown literally but be transposed. In the production I directed in Montevideo, inspired by German cabaret and Brecht, the scene was staged with the two actors sitting fully dressed on two stools and I choreographed their movements in such a way that there could be no doubt in anyone's mind what they were doing, but there was no nudity and no bed. In the same spirit, we transposed the sexual act in the story Ofelia Rodrigues. On the roof of the factory where she works, Ofelia climbs a tall ladder and, once perched up there, lets down the long skirt of the wedding dress she has been sewing and has put on. It completely covers the ladder and her lover, Zulav, who slips under the skirt and makes love to her. Done this way, the eroticism is provocative (and it should be), but it doesn't overwhelm the political content of each of the stories or the truly poetic nature of these couples and couplings.

J.V.

La robe de mariée de Gisèle Schmidt was first performed on March 21, 2006 by Théâtre PàP and Singulier-Pluriel at Espace Go, with the following company:

Éric Cabana
Jacinthe Laguë
Paul Savoie
Julie Vincent

Directed by Julie Vincent
Set and costume design by Geneviève Lizotte
Lighting design by François Roupinian
Original music by Michel Smith
Artistic direction by Claude Poissant

Characters

The play is written for five actors.
Gisèle is played by an older actress. She is eighty-five years old.
The other parts can be divided as follows:
Actress #1 (between twenty-five and thirty-five): She, Her, Simone, and Sacha
Actress #2 (between forty and fifty-five): Ofelia and Cuisse de Mouche
Actor #1 (between twenty-five and forty): He and Zulav
Actor #2 (between forty-five and sixty): Antonin, the Captain, and Dorian Grey.

In the scenes between the stories, all of Gisèle's lines were actually spoken by Gisèle Schmidt during one of my many visits to her home.

The other characters were, for the most part, inspired by real people I've met. All of them had suffered some form of political persecution and had fought to preserve their freedom and individuality. Of course, I had to mix fact with fiction in order to be able to introduce the wedding dress into each story.

When they're not in a scene, the other actors can remain on stage and watch and listen to the stories.

The play was originally written for only two actors, a man and a woman, and could still be staged that way. In this version, Gisèle's lines would be heard on tape.

Production Notes

The six stories that make up this play unfold in Gisèle's living room.

The wedding dress is found in Gisèle's old pine chest at the beginning of the play and then it travels from one woman to another, from one country to another.

During the scenes between the stories, we see Gisèle daydreaming at her window that overlooks the St. Lawrence River in Charlevoix, Québec. We don't see the window but we do see the dreams.

GISÈLE'S WEDDING DRESS

Prologue

Lights come up on ACTOR #2, dressed in a tailcoat, and on ACTRESS #1, wearing an antique wedding dress. They are performing a scene from Anton Chekhov's Ivanov.

IVANOV It is still possible to stop this stupid, senseless comedy… you're young and pure, you have your whole life ahead of you, while I…

SACHA You've said this over and over again. I've heard it a thousand times and I'm tired of it! Go to the church and don't keep people waiting!

IVANOV I'll go home right now and you, you tell your family that there won't be a wedding. Explain it to them somehow. Enough of all this. I've been pretending to be Hamlet and you the high-minded young woman. It's got to stop.

SACHA Your whining is turning into mockery!

IVANOV Mockery? If only I could mock myself a thousand times more forcefully and make the whole world burst out laughing at me, I'd do it! I look at myself in the mirror and laugh at myself and then I almost go out of my mind from shame! I've never deliberately spoken ill of life, but I've become a chronic whiner and complainer. I complain and everyone who listens to me is infected with a sort of disgust towards life and begins to curse it too… and the tone of voice I use… as though I'm doing nature a favour just by being alive! How could you possibly love me! You should laugh and jeer at my carrying on.

SACHA To love you means I will cure you of your sadness. I will follow you to the ends of the earth…. If you climb to the top of the mountain, I'll climb with you. If you slide down into the depths, I'll slide down there with you too. The more effort love requires the better it is, I mean… do you understand…? The more deeply one feels it.

IVANOV I'm lost!

Shift 1

GISÈLE's living room.

In the middle of the stage an old chest. An armchair faces upstage. At first, we can't see GISÈLE sitting there. Perhaps all we see is a hand resting on the arm of the chair or a hat peeking out over the back of it.

Four actors enter. They walk over and open the chest. They rummage in it and find the long train which is part of the wedding dress. While they do this, they say:

ACTRESS #2 A few years ago, I was acting in a production of Chekhov's *Ivanov*. Gisèle Schmidt was in the cast. Every night, we would stand in the wings together and watch that terrible love scene between Sacha and Ivanov.

We hear GISÈLE's voice:

GISÈLE I would have given my entire career to have lived one great love.

ACTRESS #2 Years later, I went to her home on the shores of the St. Lawrence River. Spending time with her did me a great deal of good…. "Actors are channellers" she used to say…

ACTRESS #1 "Channellers of dreams."

Far
The First Meeting

Montréal. July 2003.

SHE: twenty-five years old. An actress.

HE: forty years old. An actor. Also a boxer.

GISÈLE Schmidt: a presence, an evocation.

The two characters start by speaking in the direction of Gisèle's armchair and then turn out to the audience.

Jazz music can be heard in the distance.

HE I never saw the young woman's face.

SHE I will never forget his body.

HE I was lost. I was nobody.

SHE It was strange. My career was flourishing but I felt very much alone. That day, I had only one thing on my mind: to leave. Leave the television studio. Leave it all. Everything. Tear off the wedding veil I was wearing. Start over. The character I was playing was boring. She was getting married to an Italian. All week long, I'd been wearing this period wedding dress borrowed from the wardrobe department of a theatre in town.

HE My agent had dangled success before my eyes! I was going to get the leading role! The script was *very* challenging! And, I'd be acting with big names. Yeah, well, the part went to a stand-up comic. They offered me a non-speaking role as a cop in a chase scene in the same movie.

SHE At the end of the day, everyone was celebrating in the old studio at Cité du Havre. In the dressing rooms, with my friends, we all drank quite a lot of champagne. I felt myself go limp all of a sudden. I was still wearing the wedding dress. I was very tired and what with the frustrations of the last few days… my head was spinning. I felt dizzy. Instead of going to throw up in the washroom,

I ran for the exit, jumped in my car, and headed for the Bonaventure Expressway, still wearing the wedding dress.

HE I box. I've done a lot of it. It's on my resumé. I'm a good actor. I work very hard on my "instrument," as they say…. It was a big-budget American film…. The stand-up comic was over there, smiling, in his Armani suit, and, right before the take, I jumped him. I grabbed him by the throat in a rage. Assault charges were laid. My agent managed to get me released after putting down a whole lot of money. I left the police station feeling empty and disgusted.

Sounds of the city.

SHE Usually, on my drive back to town, I'd see the bridge, the river, the boats, the word *Five Roses* written in pink on a building, and below *Five Roses* the word *Farine*. Flour. That evening, only three letters were lit on the top of the old flour factory: F-A-R. That's what I read in my rear-view mirror… FAR. That was the word fate had found for me that night.

HE We were in the middle of a Montréal heat wave—torrid, tropical, nauseous-making heat. I walked for a while listening to jazz played live in the streets. It was the festival. On the sidewalk, a guitar player was playing a samba. I dug into my pockets to find my lighter and I realized I was still wearing my costume, the police uniform. I went into a small bar. I drank two, three vodkas.

SHE I parked the car so I could listen to a guitar player near the Berri Métro station. I hid the dress by wrapping myself in a red rain cape that was lying around in the back of the car. And then I dashed into the Métro. I wanted to see the river.

HE I walked a little more. Then, I took the subway to Old Montréal, thinking that I'd like to see the river. I missed the river…

We shift to present time. GISÈLE lights a cigarette. We only see her hands.

There's a huge crowd on the platform of the Orange Line. The sound of drumming somewhere close by.

SHE People are walking in every direction. My heart is beating really fast. I'm hot… wearing the cape… I feel drunk…

They both enter the Métro car.

HE Inside the Métro car, the crowd is packed in like sardines. The car sways as we take a big curve.

SHE Suddenly, the passengers all lean into a curve. The people are like zombies in the heat, jam-packed together. Now, finally… I'm incognito.

Rustle of the dress.

HE In the shuffle, the young woman leans into me. I can't see her face. I don't resist. Common sense abandons me. I go numb. Feel nothing. She's wearing a red, plastic rain cape in the middle of summer. Strips of white material hang from the cape. I can't take my eyes off them.

SHE His body is muscular. Very. Someone shoves me. I collapse against him without even seeing him.

Rustle of the dress.

HE The beauty I *think* I see is so surprising, so terrifying, that I don't move. I don't fight the embrace the train has forced us into.

SHE It's as though we were in the desert. The doors open.... Tam-Tams. Laughter. Lots of noise and sounds.

HE I'm pressed up against her, from behind. Like we were glued together. My breath on her hair makes it flutter.

Sound of the rustle of the dress in the foreground. Murmuring.

SHE His legs fit tightly into the curve of mine. His hands start to gently caress my thighs. He leaves his left hand there. I take it in mine and squeeze it. The doors close.

HE I feel the pressure of her woman's body on mine, her thighs, her ass. Under the red cape, I discover the folds of a slippery, smooth dress. The material, its softness, fascinates me.

SHE No one in the mass of packed bodies pays any attention to us. Grey, bored faces. People waiting. I'm afraid. Of the scandal? Of what will happen to me?

HE I have trouble seeing the young woman's face from the side. She's biting her lower lip. I need her. I need her to be mine. Right now. I press her body hard against my penis. I slip my right hand between her legs.

SHE The hand of an angel on the folds of my vulva. Reaching from behind.

HE The doors open, the music coming from the platforms pours over us. I feel her lips swelling. Suddenly, to get her balance, she spreads her thighs. I feel her lips parting, opening. The doors close.

SHE I'm hot. I shiver. I surrender so totally to his touch that a fine and gentle rain starts to fall between my thighs and seep into my wedding dress. I can hear our sighs. In time with each other now.

She won't speak anymore except through her sighs, her body, her breath. Her eyes are closed.

He sees the old lady. Rustle of the dress. GISÈLE's inner music.

HE My eyes lock with a pair of eyes, which, I know, have been watching us from the beginning. The other passengers are in a stupor from the heat, the music, exhaustion. But I know the woman over there is wide awake. She's looking at us. Her strange smile reminds me of someone. It's a smile full of untold stories. She is far enough away, separated from us by a blind mass of people. From where she's sitting though, she can guess what we're up to. I hold the young woman tighter and I see the face, over there, swaying from side to side with the motion of the train. Like on the ocean. Those eyes never leave my face. I feel an overwhelming need to respond to them. They are immense. Unwavering. They blink a little. A kind of response to me.

Sounds of the sea and of breathing.

Now they shift to the young woman who's starting to tremble. They don't question. They know. My movements become quicker. The girl's pleasure builds. Will her sighs give us away?

Beat. Suspension.

The lady over there has just spotted the first spasm of pleasure on the face of the woman I'm holding. I give in to her old woman's eyes. I want to cry out to her. The doors open, close again. This time a group of musicians takes over the whole subway car. And it's as though a chasm opens under her seat. She starts falling.... There! And, suddenly, the lady hides her eyes in her hands and comes!

Blackout.

The dress rustles... distortion, slower. Beat.

The train is an orchestra of sensations. The lady's head drops. The girl's cape too. Has she fainted?

Beat. Suspension. GISÈLE's hands.

I don't know who I am. My eyes come to rest on the girl's long neck. Superb. The neck of a swan. That's when, at that precise moment, I see two words written in black felt marker. Sewn into the fine invisible lining of the white lace décolleté of her dress: Gisèle Schmidt. An eternity of time. I feel calm inside. A deep unmoving silence. I'm not thinking about anything.

In GISÈLE's living room, the river is more and more present...

The doors opened at my stop and, pushed by a wave of people, I found myself on the platform. I was already asking myself whether it had really happened. I took a few steps... our subway car was already pulling away.... For a fraction of a second, I caught a fleeting glimpse of a young woman in a wedding dress.... Later, I walked all the way down to the river without being able to figure out the truth of the story—a story with no plot but where everything is dramatic like the sad, unsettling slipping away of summer.

Blackout.

All we see is the burning tip of GISÈLE's cigarette as she sits smoking in her armchair.

Shift 2

ACTRESS #2 Gisèle is smoking.

GISÈLE The doctor says that at my age, it's worse if you stop…

ACTRESS #2 She got married at nineteen in a little blue taffeta dress.

GISÈLE Schmidt is a German name. My father worked for Canadian Pacific along with other sons of immigrants.

ACTRESS #2 Sometimes people walk along the train tracks in front of her house. The train stopped running to where she lives a long time ago.

GISÈLE I remember the sound of the trains, a sound that travels, that is a reminder of another time, the heyday of the big factories…. In those days, in Montréal, workers weren't allowed to speak French at work. It was the forbidden language. Many of the workers were immigrants. It must have been confusing for them…

Ofelia Rodrigues
The Second Meeting

Montréal. October 1970.

During the October Crisis.

A textile factory that makes wedding dresses.

A fluid soundscape gives way gradually to sounds that suggest the city and then to the sounds of trains, which in turn transform into the noise of clattering machines. Sewing machines.

OFELIA Rodrigues: a worker of Portuguese origin.

ZULAV: a worker of Yugoslavian origin. He used to earn his living as a clown and acrobat in Eastern Europe. He's an illegal.

A factory in Montréal. OFELIA and ZULAV are working at sewing machines.

ZULAV Ofelia! You cannot sleep, my queen.

OFELIA I don't sleep.

ZULAV Yes, you do. I saw you sleep.

OFELIA No. I think. I dream.

ZULAV You cannot think. You work.

OFELIA I can dream if I work.

ZULAV When you dream, you don't work!

OFELIA I can dream and I can work both!

ZULAV   You're not on a boat, you're in a factory.

OFELIA   You're a stranger here, like me.

ZULAV   Me, I don't dream.

OFELIA   You escaped East Europe on a boat. Maybe your papers are wrong.... Maybe the police outside will take you. The secret police.... You are not my boss.

> We hear the footsteps of the shop foreman.

ZULAV   Did the boss touch you?

OFELIA   Contremestre wants me. He will not get me.

ZULAV   You don't know nothing about this country.

OFELIA   *Toi, tu peux même pas parler français.* You cannot even speak French.

ZULAV   *On peut pas dans l'usine...* speak the French. A politic person is killed this week. Ofelia, we have the army downstairs.

OFELIA   Politic is not me... do not talk me.

ZULAV   Yesterday, you crying and today you dreaming...

OFELIA   I missing my family and I dream my country.

> *He takes out a photograph, which he stole from her.*

ZULAV   Your son?

OFELIA   Give to me.

ZULAV   Your husband was a taxi driver in Lisbon and now he is in Vancouver and he is with another woman.

OFELIA   You don't know.

ZULAV   Everybody knows in this factory. That is why you dream, Ofelia!

OFELIA   I'm so used to that work. I can dream everything when I work. I can dream of God. I can dream of trees, I can dream of stones, and clouds and streets and people walking in the streets, and I dream of my son. My son is in Portugal with my mother. But you're not a part of my dream!

> *He takes off his windbreaker. He's only wearing an undershirt underneath. OFELIA discovers that he is very handsome and she is momentarily distracted.*
>
> *GISÈLE pours herself a cup of tea.*

ZULAV   It is very hot in here. Indian summer!

OFELIA   *Donne-moi la photo.* Give me.

ZULAV You're tired. You sewed all crooked. You are asleep 'cause you work during the night.

OFELIA Of course I work during the night! I work here with you.

ZULAV No. I mean during the night. *La nuit.* You work with me during the evening, but after midnight you work too. I follow you all way to your house with my bicycle. I see the truck pick you up after midnight.

OFELIA Your're crazy! *Donne!* Give me the photo of my son.

ZULAV The truck picks you at midnight on Coloniale Street. With the other Portuguese women.

OFELIA Give me, please!

ZULAV Tell me what you do. Tell me!

> *The sounds of the factory change. We hear a Portuguese fado and breathing that might be GISÈLE's.*

OFELIA Three trucks transport us, me and the other Portuguese women. By the water, in Lachine. We go in the night. We wear lamps on our foreheads. Like the blacks in Africa who collect diamonds. Near the river, the grass is humid. No one speaks. Earthworms are very intelligent. They like the silence. Like the boss in the factory. The boxes of earthworms are sold to rich Americans for fishing. Five dollars for thousand worms. Five hundred dollars for box. I can pick ten thousand in a night.

ZULAV You smell nice, *ma reine!* You smell dirty work!

> *Lights in GISÈLE's area. She picks up the cup of tea very delicately.*

OFELIA On a teacup my grandmother gived to me, there is a landscape of Japan with *uma* geisha. So me, I lean down gently to pick up the earthworms like a geisha is picking up orchids for her beloved.

ZULAV Kiss my hand.

> *Pause.*

OFELIA Give me please the photo of my child.

ZULAV Kiss my hand.

> *She kisses ZULAV's hand. He gives her back the photo. We hear music in the distance, music that is evocative of Yugoslavia.*

When a child, I grow with the animals on a farm not far from Zagreb. I sleep with the chickens, the dogs, the pigs. I begin love to make when I am twelve years. With a very beautiful woman. She is teacher at the school. When a child, I dance. Always. The childrens, they come with rocks. I dance in the pig sty. The children they throw me rocks and they yelling: Look! Look! The little pig who dances! The little pig who dances!

But where the beasts have claws, I grow my talent!

OFELIA And what is it, your talent?

ZULAV Love…. *L'amour*, Ofelia.

OFELIA Ssssht!

ZULAV I make the love every day with the teacher of our district. I learn many things.

OFELIA Be quiet!

ZULAV I have a thirst like the desert! I die of thirst. A thirst for love! For me, to kiss your feet even for three seconds, it is a great occasion of love! I don't count the time that it lasts. Three seconds, it is like fifteen minutes, three hours, thirty days, three years! I make love to the women from all the possible corners of the world because I want to feel the maximum of love! I am pushed to this. Pulled to it by a force from above!

OFELIA I am from a great family of seamstresses in Lisbon. My ancestor sewed the sails for the ship that brought Cabral to Brazil. I am able with a very small needle to make you very very very fast no longer hard. Down there.

They go back to their machines. Beat.

ZULAV Ofelia, I am the best lover of all the countries of the Eastern Block!

OFELIA Don't bullshit, Zulav!

We hear the foreman's bell.

ZULAV Break! Coffee! Ofelia, you take the elevator with me?

OFELIA Hey, my dress!

ZULAV Come with me.

OFELIA No! You steal my dress! Give. *Donne-moi ma robe!*

ZULAV I'll show the boss that the dress is badly sewed if you don't come with me.

They get into the elevator.

Cigarette?

OFELIA *Mon mari ne veut pas.*

ZULAV Forget your husband.

She takes a cigarette.

OFELIA I thought you were a gangster in your country. *Um assassino!* I remember the day you arrived in the factory. We were in snow to our knees and you had not even boots! You hadn't even stockings in your boots! And you haven't none even today.

Sounds of the old freight elevator as it moves up to the roof.

ZULAV   I leaved the pig farm because I was welcomed into a circus. I escaped what was to me a coffin closed with steel bars. I run away and I disappeared into the sky of the circus tent like a red angel!

OFELIA   There are no angels in the communist countries.

> *They leave the elevator. We are now on the roof of the building. We hear the sounds of army helicopters.*

ZULAV   The most beautiful view of Montréal that you can see! The pigeons, they remind me of Europe.

OFELIA   There are boats on the river. The Portuguese, they sail all the way to here a long time ago…

> *She takes off her black sweater and the black scarf on her head.*
>
> *Her skimpy black dress, which is little more than a slip, is worn and old. Her shoulders are bare. He is only wearing his undershirt. Their desire for one another is palpable.*

Indian summer…. Sometimes I dream of a sailor…

ZULAV   You know this sailor? *Tu connais?*

> *She looks at him strangely.*

OFELIA   Maybe…

ZULAV   *Il y a un soldat en bas.*

OFELIA   Better speak English! Give me the dress. *Donne-moi la robe brisée.*

> *She puts on the wedding dress with its long, fancy train.*

Talk to me like sailor talks.

> *With every sentence, he kisses a part of her body now covered by the wedding dress, which is too long for her. We hear the army helicopter.*

ZULAV   *(He kisses her.)* Sometimes I think Yugoslavia doesn't exist anymore. *(He kisses her.)* Maybe I never had a childhood… or maybe the childhood I think I had is only a dream… *(He kisses her.)* The one I created is real. *(He kisses her.)* But now I'm so far from my real past that what exists really is the past of my imagination. *(He kisses her.)* My real wife, I don't remember her face.

> *He gently positions his mouth between her legs under the dress. She takes her pleasure like a queen.*

OFELIA   I try to remember my husband, but the husband I miss is not the one I had… and the husband I miss is more real than the real one.

> *He takes her well under the enormous dress and at last she climaxes joyously.*
>
> *Beat. Portuguese fado and the sounds of the city.*

ZULAV   Let's write to your husband.

OFELIA   I cannot write.

ZULAV   I will write for you. "Dear Ernesto, I am Ofelia. I am free. I am beautiful. Farewell." The pigeon will send to him this letter.

The bell rings. We hear the sound of the old freight elevator again.

Break is over.

OFELIA   *S'il vous plaît.* Help me.

She quickly puts her clothes back on.

ZULAV   *Pourquoi?* Why you let me do?

OFELIA   *Tem saudade!*

ZULAV   What?

OFELIA   *C'est portugais.* My language. It comes from the sailors. *Saudade,* nostalgia! It was beautiful and it was unreal!

They enter the elevator.

Zulav, I like to keep this secret.

ZULAV   I like you secret too.

The sound of the machines. A train in the night…

Music.

Shift 3

Back to GISÈLE's living room. It's windy outside. A high wind. The lace screen moves. We get the sense that there's a full moon shining behind the screen. Doors slam in the wind. She gets up and then sits down again.

GISÈLE   I'm not afraid of being alone or of dying. I have my books. I dream. I watch the boats go by.

ACTOR #2   She remembers that, in 1947, with other actors…

GISÈLE   …we left Montréal on a Dutch cargo ship to go and perform in France.

ACTRESS #2   She remembers that she started to act at the age of four.

ACTOR #2   She watches the news on television for a while and then takes up her book again and reads.

GISÈLE   I'm teaching myself. I'm reading about Greek mythology…. The men are very handsome in Greek mythology. I've never been to Greece. I came close once, but it was during the time of the junta, the generals, and I chose not to go.

And after the dictatorship fell, well, it never worked out. You know how these things happen... I've dreamt of it often though...

Simone and the Captain
The Third Meeting

CIA Agent Robert Welch was assassinated in Athens in November of 1975. Greek left-wing activists and intellectuals were protesting what they called American imperialism in their country and the fact that the US had supported the dictatorship of the generals. Even though the junta had fallen a year earlier, many of the police officers who had been torturers during the reign of the generals still had their jobs and had even been given promotions. This incensed many and caused riots.

The port of Piraeus, Athens. 1975.

The bridge of a boat. Exterior. Night.

We hear the sound of the riots in the distance and of bouzouki music etc...

SIMONE: seventeen years old. A bit of a bum. Damaged. She's asleep with her head resting on a backpack. She has celebrated her wedding with her husband's uncle, the captain of this small boat.

THE CAPTAIN: Vassili Psarandelli. In his fifties. A widower. He wears a black armband. He is the captain of the boat. The bridegroom's uncle.

THE CAPTAIN looks at the girl as she sleeps. A long pause.

GISÈLE is daydreaming. It's nighttime. There's a night light on.

On the boat. Moonlight. THE CAPTAIN lifts the wedding dress's long train and discovers something strange and alarming. He then goes through SIMONE's handbag and finds rolls of bills and a passport.

SIMONE wakes up with a start.

SIMONE   You're going through my bag?

THE CAPTAIN   Where did you get this money?

SIMONE   I work. It's none of your business!

THE CAPTAIN   Who are you working for?

SIMONE   Don't you understand English? What did I just say?!

She takes her bag from him.

THE CAPTAIN   I'm the captain. I ask the questions!

SIMONE   I'm in business for myself!

Pause.

Did I sleep long?

THE CAPTAIN Hours.

SIMONE Do you dream in Greek or in English?

THE CAPTAIN I don't dream anymore.

SIMONE Costa, my husband?! Where is he?

THE CAPTAIN He left with the musicians.

SIMONE The musicians? Why didn't you wake me?

THE CAPTAIN They all left. They're at the Koukaki tavern.

SIMONE Are we going? Let's go. I want to dance some more! Where is it?

THE CAPTAIN It's not for us. It's too far from Piraeus. Not tonight. It's near Kolonaki Square. The Americans go there. The ones that work at the embassy.

SIMONE You said "It's not for us." Us meaning you and me?

Pause.

Something happened when we danced together, the two of us. Something pretty scary has been happening between the two of us since yesterday and you know it!

The wind is rising. Sounds of the ship and the harbour. The wind is playing games with them. The wind will dictate their movements through much of the scene.

THE CAPTAIN I can't hear you anymore. The wind!

SIMONE "You have to pay dearly for immortality."

THE CAPTAIN The wind's rising. I can't hear you!

SIMONE "You have to pay dearly for immortality." When I read that sentence, I stopped believing in God! I've got beautiful legs. Don't you think? What's wrong with you? Don't you like my dress anymore? Costa found it in a second-hand Portuguese clothing store in Montréal.

THE CAPTAIN You're selling hashish! Hashish! The hem of your skirt is full of it!

He lifts up the dress.

The wind is wild now. We can also begin to hear the riots in the distance.

SIMONE Costa swore you wouldn't ask me any questions. You can sleep with me if you want.

Pause.

THE CAPTAIN What else did my charming nephew say to you?

SIMONE He said you held up a bank in Athens. That you and me, we'd understand each other.

THE CAPTAIN Numbskull!

SIMONE What?

THE CAPTAIN My nephew's a numbskull! I'd like to smash his head in! On the rocks!

>   *Pause.*

SIMONE Apparently you're a legend. Apparently, when you were young, you managed to escape from jail by jimmying the locks of your cell with a spoon? And then you made it all the way to the coast of Turkey in a rowboat.

THE CAPTAIN I abandoned the woman I loved to follow my ideals…

>   *An enormous gust of wind blows them into each others arms. The noise of the riots in Athens is becoming more and more present.*
>
>   *GISÈLE is rocking in her rocking chair, making the floor creak.*
>
>   *Soundscape: wind and wood creaking and cracking.*

Raki is too strong. I'm warning you. I can get nasty.

SIMONE Everything is absolutely perfect, Captain. The sky is perfect, the wind is perfect, your hands are perfect… my dress is perfectly white!

THE CAPTAIN The moon does that.

>   *The boat lists. They're having trouble standing. And still, all around them, the noise of the wind and the riots. They look at each other without speaking. They pull apart.*

SIMONE Why did you rob a bank?

THE CAPTAIN To finance the publication of the works of my friend, Pouliopoulos. That was before. Dreams…

SIMONE What are his books about?

THE CAPTAIN The dreams of youth. Socialist dreams.

SIMONE My father, the antique dealer, used to publish the works of revolutionary poets! Fuckin' revolution! He published books in Montréal. For me, the revolution was nothing but a big, bushy moustache that forgot about his children.

THE CAPTAIN Is he… dead?

>   *She takes THE CAPTAIN's black armband and slips it up onto her thigh. Slowly.*
>
>   *Pause.*

SIMONE How come you don't have a moustache like all the other Greek men?

THE CAPTAIN I shaved it off. After my wife died.

SIMONE How long ago?

THE CAPTAIN She disappeared at sea… three years ago. I don't like to talk about it!

SIMONE About what?

THE CAPTAIN About the death of my wife! I try to forget. Memories of her are all around me. Like the sea around the islands. Stop talking about it!

SIMONE I'm glad you don't have a moustache.

>   *Pause.*

THE CAPTAIN You're seventeen. I saw your passport.

SIMONE What's that to you? I'm married.

>   *Pause.*

THE CAPTAIN They killed a man tonight.

SIMONE What?

THE CAPTAIN They killed a man tonight in Athens!

SIMONE Who?

THE CAPTAIN The group.

SIMONE What group?

THE CAPTAIN The group that's become the obsession of the "intelligence" community. Listen. Can't you hear? Riots. There are riots everywhere in Athens.

SIMONE Costa told me the dictatorship was overthrown a year ago. I don't understand… why are there riots?

THE CAPTAIN There are riots because the police who tortured us during the dictatorship still have their jobs. Some of them have even been promoted. That's why.

SIMONE That's why what?

THE CAPTAIN Why they killed a man tonight. They killed the head of the CIA in Athens! To denounce torture!

>   *Pause. They look at each other.*
>
>   *Suddenly, a big spotlight rakes the boat. SIMONE wants to run but he throws her down on the deck. We hear the sound of footsteps receding.*
>
>   *Pause.*

Costa was arrested with the others in the riots tonight.

SIMONE What?

THE CAPTAIN Costa! Your husband! They took him in. He sent someone to warn me while you were sleeping.

SIMONE What! I must be dreaming!

THE CAPTAIN He went off to get drunk with the musicians. He didn't bring you on my boat to celebrate your wedding. You've been tricked! Costa came back to Greece to start his political activities again. This time with new identity papers. With Canadian citizenship. He's a fool to get you mixed up in this!

SIMONE Where is he now?

THE CAPTAIN He's at the Agios Nikolaos clinic. He can't walk.

SIMONE What do you mean?

The sounds of sirens and the sea.

THE CAPTAIN The police made him take off his shoes to do the falanga on him.

SIMONE The falanga?

THE CAPTAIN A torture technique. They hit the underside of the victim's feet with a metal bar and then force him to walk. They let him go because of his Canadian passport. He had to stay at the clinic. He can't walk.

Pause.

SIMONE Fuck! Shit! Let's get out of here! You and me. Let's get out of here!

She goes over and starts to cast off, but he stops her.

THE CAPTAIN And where exactly are we going according to you?

SIMONE The islands! We're going to the Cyclades. You're taking me with you!

The searchlight is all around them again. He puts his hand over her mouth. They're lying body to body on the deck.

THE CAPTAIN Stop yelling! They're going to see us. The port is being watched. We're not going to the Cyclades or any other islands. My nephew is handsome and you love him. And, you're going back to Canada with him tomorrow!

SIMONE I want to stay in Greece! Shit, it's really windy!

THE CAPTAIN I don't want to have anything to do with a girl who sleeps with her head on her backpack and hash in the hem of her wedding dress. I don't want that on my boat! I don't want to have anything to do with you!

We hear music in the distance. A strange Greek melody.

SIMONE Nothing to do with me! Of course! I should've known! You really disappoint me, Captain. You're not a real legend. You're just like my father. *Vive la liberté!* You fight for freedom, especially your own! Isn't that right? Revolutionary heroes who want to make history, but who don't allow anyone into their lives. My father spent his entire life telling me we had a great history. But he could never look me in the eye! "Emotions have no place in history, Simone!" I used to sleep with my great-grandfather's axe hanging over my bed! "The war, my girl, the war in this country, is a war against forgetting!" Then, one night, everything burnt down. My parents too. One night in the dead of winter, everything disappeared in a fire. End of my story. End of my history.

She wants to get up to get her luggage and leave.

THE CAPTAIN Stay here. The policeman is heading back this way. He'll search you if he sees you.

Pause.

SIMONE What are we going to do?

THE CAPTAIN Wait. We wait for Costa to come back. We wait for this to blow over.

The wind picks up again and is so strong, so violent, that it makes them roll over, glued to one another.

SIMONE What's wrong? You're having trouble breathing.

THE CAPTAIN This wind. It's the *meltem*. A very dangerous wind!

SIMONE *(very softly)* It's caught here in my chest. Give me your hand. You'll be able to feel it.... Do you feel it?

THE CAPTAIN Yes! This is a famous wind! Beware! It's trying to distract us. To make us forget we're waiting for Costa...

Pause. We hear their breathing. The strange melody picks up again...

The other day, I was at Cape Sounion, near the temple. That's where I go to think about my wife who disappeared at sea. I pray to the gods to help me find a piece of her. Her dress or a shoe. I was there waiting for something. I don't know what. The oracle? A sign? I'd been silent for quite a long time. A woman came over to me. An American tourist. She wanted me to take a picture of her. She asked as she pointed to the temple: "Parakalo... is it man-made or is it natural?" And I looked around and there, at the foot of the cliff, I spotted a sign. A real one. It said: "No swimming allowed." I looked at the big American tourist lady with her nose dripping suntan lotion. And below, I could see garbage cans, pieces of iron, wrecks washed up, cargo ships breathing their last, finished. I was looking for my wife's shoe in a cemetery of oil-smeared, twisted, steel gorgons. Greece belongs to the tourists and the ship owners. And then, suddenly, on the hill, I saw a woman with a black head scarf. She was watering the bougainvilleas on her balcony. And I said to myself: that's all. That's all that's left of our entire civilization... small gestures like that!

We hear the policemen's footsteps walking off.

Get up! The police are gone. Quick! Quick, I said! Stand up!

SIMONE You're crazy!

THE CAPTAIN Old Greek sailors have a custom. If the wind of death blows in the sails of a boat, you have to sink a knife into the sails in order to counteract the bad omen.

And so, with one deft move of his knife, THE CAPTAIN cuts off the bottom of her wedding dress and then with his lighter he sets fire to the piece of material he's ripped off.

SIMONE Are you insane! That's all the money I have! Now what am I going to live on? My dimes! My dimes of hash!

The searchlight is on them again. SIMONE grabs on to THE CAPTAIN and kisses him, trying to create a diversion.

They're not going to arrest you! They're not. The dictatorship is over!

THE CAPTAIN Don't say anything. Go to Crete. It's safest. Nothing lasts in Greece. Nothing. Not republics. Not dictatorships. Or kings. Everything crumbles—institutions, men, things. Everything is eaten away by the sun and the salt. Look over there. The sun is rising over the Acropolis. It's magnificent. "You have to pay for immortality."

Lights up in GISÈLE's area. A little boat on a side table.

SIMONE It was the fuckin' right thing to do, to dance together, eh?!

THE CAPTAIN It was "fuckin' right," as you say.

VOICE OF A POLICEMAN Vassili Psarandelli! I arrest you in the name of the law!

The police officer leads him off.

SIMONE does a little dance step.

We hear the sound of the sea and, in the distance, the bouzouki playing.

Shift 4

GISÈLE's house. Dawn. GISÈLE is cold. She picks up the red shawl lying on the back of her armchair. Everything turns red.

GISÈLE I've always dreamed of a grand, romantic love. I had a turbulent youth. Lovers. Loves. That's why Père Legault didn't take me into his theatre company, the Compagnons de Saint-Laurent. Père Legault thought I was too… what was the word he used… profane. Too profane! To be a member of his company! Too profane…

In Italy, they had a name for improvisational actresses who gave the poets a run for their money in the public squares. They were called *meriticis honestae*. Honest prostitutes. I met a prostitute once in Nîmes. In France. She was

Algerian and she told me about her mother, who was killed in Oran, during the Algerian war of independence.

Beat.

...it's going to storm.

Cuisse de Mouche
Fourth Meeting

This story takes place in a hotel used by prostitutes in Nîmes in the south of France.

A grey November morning in 1981. It's raining.

CUISSE DE MOUCHE: a prostitute from Algeria.

THE STUMP: plays guitar. He served in the French army during the Algerian War and lost his arm there.

She is wearing a wedding dress pulled up to her waist. He is wearing an undershirt and a kepi. They're making love. All through the scene, we hear the sound of rain falling. It gets louder and louder. There's thunder and lightning. We can also hear other couples in the hotel.

Soundscape: Arab songs and music.

THE STUMP   You're beautiful in that dress. You look like a queen of Egypt.

CUISSE DE MOUCHE   So, where'd you get it? The dress?

THE STUMP   Don't worry. Pico the Gypsy found it in Athens. It's yours! I'm a general in the French army. And I'm your prisoner!

CUISSE DE MOUCHE   And I'm the great-great-granddaughter of an Arab sultan! And I'm going to tie you up! Kiss me!

THE STUMP   You're so beautiful in that dress!

CUISSE DE MOUCHE   It's my fancy dress.

THE STUMP   I want to marry you.

CUISSE DE MOUCHE   Kiss me, slave!

THE STUMP   Don't stop! Harder! Get back at me for your mother and your grandmother!

CUISSE DE MOUCHE   Somebody's gotta pay! Don't stop!

THE STUMP   Yeah, somebody's gotta pay! For all of it! Say yes! Say it!

CUISSE DE MOUCHE   Not now. Not now!

THE STUMP   We're leaving for Canada. Over there, I'll compose music just for you. And you'll sing, like before.

CUISSE DE MOUCHE Look, lightning! The storm's starting.

THE STUMP Who's wailing next door? Sounds like a kid.

CUISSE DE MOUCHE It's that crazy American. He lives down on the coast now. He killed three hundred children in Vietnam. But he cries like a baby over the death of John Lennon. Put my legs up around your neck. Yeah like that! Don't stop!

THE STUMP You smell good. You smell like wild sage. I'm going to eat you with olive oil and rosemary.

CUISSE DE MOUCHE You really like Arab women, don't you! You really, really do!

THE STUMP Yes, Cuisse de Mouche! Oh, yes!

CUISSE DE MOUCHE Say it! Repeat after me: I love Arab women!

THE STUMP I love Arab women! That's what's so good!

CUISSE DE MOUCHE Say it! I love them! I love them madly!

THE STUMP Madly! I love you madly! Now! Right now! Say yes! Yes!

CUISSE DE MOUCHE No! Not now, not yet!

THE STUMP Go easy, not with your teeth!

CUISSE DE MOUCHE Yes! That's good, that's good, Stump! *(singing)* Allonsenfants-de-la-patri-i-e! Oh!

We hear a couple making loud love in another room.

THE STUMP I love you, you know! You feel it, don't you, that I love you. You smell so good!

CUISSE DE MOUCHE Go on! Harder! Don't be afraid! Don't listen to them. I'm telling you, it's just Zara with the American.

THE STUMP Go on, get your revenge! Think of your aunts, your uncles, your cousins, your whole family! Your cat, the dogs! All of them!

CUISSE DE MOUCHE Don't stop, don't stop! Somebody's gotta suffer!

THE STUMP Somebody's gotta suffer for all that!

CUISSE DE MOUCHE My mother, in Oran, during the war in Algeria, she saved her life by screwing some old guy with medals. I was in her belly!

THE STUMP You feel it, don't you? That I love you? Yes! More! Tell me more!

CUISSE DE MOUCHE He forced my whole family into a cave, had them fill it with straw and then set fire to it!

THE STUMP A cave... easy, easy with your feet... not too hard.

CUISSE DE MOUCHE Yes, oh that's good, with your hand, there, yes! I was in my mother's belly, two months old. As the old guy was coming, she could hear their cries! All of them were dying, burning in the cave!

THE STUMP I love you, Cuisse de Mouche! I should've deserted. I can't go on like this anymore. Oh! It's too much! If you want, I'll convert, I'll become a Muslim. I want to marry you. We'll leave this place, get out of here!

CUISSE DE MOUCHE Today's November eleventh and the brothel's full. Louise is on holidays. It hasn't stopped since midnight. They all come here and collapse spent in our arms. Before you, it was the legless one. He's only got one ball left.

THE STUMP Calm down, calm down! You're under the protection of the French army.

CUISSE DE MOUCHE Haarrr!

THE STUMP Don't bite!

CUISSE DE MOUCHE My mother told me that the old guy with the medals, his dick was old and withered. Red, white, and blue like his country's flag.... There were olive and fig trees all around them. And to stop from puking all over his tricoloured whatsit, my mother stared at a small cluster of oleander above her head. She did it out of love for me!

THE STUMP I should've run away, deserted, hidden! I haven't been able to sleep for years now. It's got to stop! Yesterday I wanted to throw myself off the top of the arena, here in Nîmes. What an idiot! The arena!

CUISSE DE MOUCHE Why didn't you jump?

THE STUMP A pigeon shat on my head! Turn over, so I can take you like that!

CUISSE DE MOUCHE Look, another bolt of lighting! The sky... looks like fire!

THE STUMP I want you to sing! I want you to sing! We'll go somewhere else! We'll go far away from here!

CUISSE DE MOUCHE Again! Do that again! Where can we go?

THE STUMP To Holland, to Papua New Guinea, to Canada, to the States!

CUISSE DE MOUCHE Yesterday! A nine-year-old boy at the end of rue de la Fresque. Children selling themselves! Here in Nîmes, just like in Manilla. Oh, it's pouring now! Yes! Don't stop!

THE STUMP At night, I think of your hips! I think of you singing!

CUISSE DE MOUCHE That's too gentle, stroke me.

THE STUMP And that way I forget my guitar. I still dream about the war. I was twenty years old. My invisible arm makes me angry!

CUISSE DE MOUCHE That hurts! Not so hard!

THE STUMP   I was given watch duty. Four hours a night. A grenade in my hand. If you fall asleep, it blows up! Since then, insomnia. Can't sleep. You smell of oranges. Your skin is hotter than the desert sands at noon!

CUISSE DE MOUCHE   Another bolt of lightning! It's going to pour and pour!

THE STUMP   It's the Great Flood, here in Nîmes!

CUISSE DE MOUCHE   Tiny back lanes will turn into raging torrents!

THE STUMP   The La Fontaine Canal overflows!

CUISSE DE MOUCHE   The water rises above the railing of the bridge over the canal near Antonin Square.

THE STUMP   Hasn't happened in years! In a matter of minutes, the puny, little Vistre becomes a raging river!

CUISSE DE MOUCHE   Did you steal the dress, Adrien? Did you steal it?

THE STUMP   I traded my guitar for it. With Pico the Gypsy. He stole it from a tourist in Athens. I'm going to explode! Cuisse de Mouche! Do you want to marry me! I'm a good cook! I can catch trout with only one arm!

CUISSE DE MOUCHE   Take me far away from here! Take me far, far away from here!

THE STUMP AND CUISSE DE MOUCHE   Yes! Yes!

We hear the sounds of orgasm coming from the other rooms in the hotel.

Waves. Ocean.

Shift 5

GISÈLE picks up a photo album. Every now and then, we hear a car in the distance. The car approaches and then accelerates and drives off, fast. Headlights shine into the empty room.

We hear another car, then the sound of a calèche in the distance.

Two rectangles of light appear on the floor.

GISÈLE closes the photo album. She picks up a glass ball and holds it up to the light. She turns it and makes it sparkle. The snow inside it flies about.

GISÈLE   The last role I performed in the theatre was in Chekhov's *Ivanov*. It was a small part. I had very little to say.... At one point, I had to cross a field of corn calling: "The fireworks! The fireworks!" The fireworks.... All I would have to do, really, is not take one of these thirteen pills and everything would be over.

The phone rings, like in a nightmare...

The Carnival at the Ends of the Earth
Fifth Meeting

Chernobyl was a large-scale nuclear accident that occurred at the Lenin Nuclear Power Station in Ukraine, then part of the Soviet Union, on April 26, 1986. It resulted in the meltdown of a nuclear reactor and the release of massive amounts of radioactivity into the environment. Many died, either at the time of the accident or subsequently, due to exposure to radiation. Chernobyl was classified as a seven on the international nuclear accident scale. It is the most serious nuclear incident to be recorded to date.

Winter.

An evening in February.

It is snowing heavily.

Chicoutimi.

SACHA: early thirties. A scientist. Ph.D. in nuclear physics. She is talking to her ex-husband on the telephone. She's wearing a ski jacket over her wedding dress.

ANTONIN: fifty-five years old. A photographer. He's wearing a tuxedo and looks as though he's about to go out.

The music playing in his apartment: Chopin.

The music in her apartment: when the time comes in the scene, something with a disco beat from the late eighties.

SACHA Nicolas, you were supposed to come for the weekend…! I got you a ticket for the theatre…. Chekhov's *Ivanov*…!

ANTONIN *(He's on the phone with Luce.)* Of course, I think we had a beautiful breakup. A successful one, as your therapist would say. I hope you talked to him about it…

SACHA It's Carnival. The Carnival at the Ends of the Earth! It's a lot of fun. Everyone dresses up like in the old days here in Chicoutimi… yes… me too…

ANTONIN You explained everything to me… very… elegantly… oh, and that Chopin prelude you played for me right after telling me: "It's over, I'll never forget you, but it's over." …That's it, hang up. Go on! You old bag…! *(He drops the phone, picks it up.)*

SACHA Of course I've got an old dress…. My wedding dress…. Why not? It's a real period piece. We paid a fortune for it at that antique store…! A dress to celebrate in!

ANTONIN Luce? Luce? I'm sorry! I adore you. My Luce. My light! I adore everything about you. Your skin. It may not be as clear, as translucent as it once was, but it holds its perfume much longer. It has more presence and that's why I love it more than ever...

SACHA   Yes, of course, I wore my wedding dress to class.... It's Carnival! Today they all came to school drunk. They didn't understand a thing... twelve years old, on average.... They'd been drinking.... Caribou... ninety percent alcohol...

The light comes up very briefly on ANTONIN, *who's looking at his rifle. She doesn't see him.*

A light comes up on one of GISÈLE's *feet as it moves slightly away from the armchair.*

ANTONIN's *tone hardens.*

ANTONIN   It's Carnival.... It's snowing.... My self-esteem is at an all-time low and I'm about to sit down to a meal of homemade beans wearing a tuxedo. It's all I have to wear tonight. Other than that? I lost my Nikon.... Yes, at poker...

SACHA   I've spoken only once with the man across the hall. When he's chatting up a woman, he lets on that he's a war photographer, that he's risked his life in war zones around the world, but his real job is taking pictures of electrical towers for Hydro-Québec!

ANTONIN   I have to go to the theatre tonight.... Yes. I really feel like it, I can't tell you how much.... *Ivanov*... Chekhov... I have two tickets.... No, I understand. Perfectly.... Yes, it ended well...

SACHA   I don't know, Nicolas... I love you...

ANTONIN   It's just that, you know, we agreed on a not-too-brutal fade-out.... Yes, I agree. This isn't the right time.... So, are you seeing someone?

SACHA   Are you seeing someone...? No, I'm just asking because...

ANTONIN   Yes, I'm with someone.... No.... I... it's the TV. Yes, I love Suzanne. She's my wife. I can't leave her. I don't want to discuss this again. She's still sick and I'd feel too guilty...! Okay.... You asked me!

SACHA   ...it's as though when I'm not in front of the computer... when I'm not "in the present" I'm wasting my time.... Wasting my time.... So you are seeing someone!

ANTONIN   So you're with him right now...? Who? Young Julien? The one you give piano lessons to...? Oh, he's so sweet...

SACHA   Yes, I can live without you for a little while... but I'm obsessed with time... passing.

ANTONIN   At forty-five, you deserve a little bonus. You've worked hard for it.... No! I'm not being cynical!

He picks up one of his cameras.

SACHA   Before… there was the time when the two of us were together. Time was alive then. We were in love. Now all there is… is dead time…

ANTONIN   …no, I didn't sleep with my neighbour. We chatted on the landing… last April, after the accident in Chernobyl.

SACHA   You and I, we had an ideal. We didn't want to work for the US Defense Department. You didn't want to work for the army. And then there was Chernobyl, and that separated us. They chose you, not me. Even though I was the one who'd studied Russian. Even though I was the first in this country who was able to communicate directly with the Russian scientists…. You slept with her?

ANTONIN   …so you're sleeping with one of your students?

SACHA   Answer me. Did you sleep with her?

ANTONIN   No, I'm not jealous… I have someone I'm interested in… yes, Sacha…

> SACHA *drinks Caribou out of a small flask that* GISÈLE *hands her. She hangs up. The telephone rings. To get back at him, she gets the idea that she'll make him think there are a lot of people at her place. Loud disco music. She dances around.*

SACHA   *(she's crying)* …You're pathetic! No, I'm not crying, I'm laughing, Nicolas…! Excuse me, there are a lot of people here… I'm entertaining…. Oh, there wasn't any noise before because I'd taken the phone outside with me because of the cigarette smoke…. It's insane… there are so many people… talking… having a good time! We're celebrating Chernobyl!

ANTONIN   …I can see her right now…

SACHA   We're dancing!

ANTONIN   She's dancing…

SACHA   Yes, I'm thinking about you…

ANTONIN   …she has an equation tattooed on her left thigh. A mathematical equation!

SACHA   No. Of course I don't hold it against you! A little affair. We're far away from each…. It's bound to happen…. No, it doesn't change a thing. We still love each another… we were taking a "break" anyway…

ANTONIN   …I don't know! She's a woman you have to approach with mathematical precision…!

SACHA   That's great! You're giving a paper in Venice…? I could go with you. It's a dream of mine to…. Yes, that's true. It is very expensive!

> *He picks up the rifle and smiles saying with real sincerity this time:*

ANTONIN ...I'm not being gloomy.... I care for you because you've never refused me, never said no. Not in fifteen years. Of course I can go on living without you, as long as I have a forty ounce bottle of good Scotch... no, I'm joking, I haven't started again.... Okay, all right, darling.... Okay, I won't call you darling anymore.... Yes, yes I'm fine! I'm going to the theatre tonight.... Okay, I'll hang up now.... Have a nice evening with your little find... I mean, your little friend... I mean, enjoy yourself.

He looks at the rifle.

SACHA ...what! A paper on the explosion in India? Hey, wait a minute! You're stealing the topic of my doctoral thesis for your paper in Venice...! What! You're going with her...? You're going with her...! You shit...! Oh, please! Don't think for me! You know how much that infuriates me...! No, I don't think I'm worthless, but I do think you're a total fuckin' jerk...! No, I don't need you.... Of course I can go to the theatre alone.... Yes, I agree. We do talk to each other too often.

She's desperate. At her wit's end, she hangs up and then, like a memory, she says:

"Perhaps it's true that flowers bloom again in the spring, but joy once lived... never lives again!"

Blackout.

Music. Short transition. We hear the distant sound of a theatre audience.

Silence. Light. We're in the theatre. ANTONIN and SACHA perform the excerpt from the Chekhov play.

IVANOV It is still possible to stop this stupid, senseless comedy... you're young and pure, you have your whole life ahead of you, while I...

SACHA You've said this over and over. I've heard it a thousand times and I'm tired of it! Go to the church and don't keep people waiting!

IVANOV I'll go home right now and you, you tell your family that there won't be a wedding. Explain it to them somehow. Enough of all this. I've been pretending to be Hamlet and you the high-minded young woman. It's got to stop.

SACHA Your whining is turning into mockery!

IVANOV Mockery? If only I could mock myself a thousand times more forcefully and make the whole world burst out laughing at me, I'd do it! I look at myself in the mirror and laugh at myself and then I almost go out of my mind from shame! I've never deliberately spoken ill of life, but I've become a chronic whiner and complainer. I complain and everyone who listens to me is infected with a sort of disgust towards life and begins to curse it too... and the tone of voice I use... as though I'm doing nature a favour just by being alive! How could you possibly love me! You should laugh and jeer at my carrying on.

SACHA To love you means I will cure you of your sadness. I will follow you to the ends of the earth…. If you climb to the top of the mountain, I'll climb with you. If you slide down into the depths, I'll slide down there with you too. The more effort love requires the better it is, I mean… do you understand…? The more deeply one feels it.

IVANOV I'm lost!

SACHA What strange, wild logic! How can I give you up? How? You haven't got a mother, or a sister, or a friend…. You're ruined, everything you ever owned has been taken away from you, stolen, there's scandalous gossip about you…

He takes his rifle.

I know what he wants to do! Nikolai, in God's name!

IVANOV I've been going downhill long enough. It's time to stop! Stand back! Thank you, Sacha.

SACHA Nikolai, for God's sake! Stop him!

IVANOV Leave me alone!

He jumps away from her over to one side and then shoots himself.

Blackout.

We come back to the two rectangles of light on the stage floor. GISÈLE's armchair can be seen in the shadows. ANTONIN is stretched out on the floor in a pool of blood. SACHA enters and sees him.

SACHA An ambulance! Quick! He's still alive! Be brave, Antonin, I'll save you. I'll love you and all this will pass. It's Carnival. I don't want to lose you… we just met. It's Carnival. The Carnival at the Ends of the World…. I want to love you! We'll be a couple committed to change. The two of us will go to Chernobyl together. We'll fight to make sure something like that never happens again. You'll take photographs. I'm a woman of science and you'll be my pillar of strength, my support. Our lives will have meaning. Antonin. Antonin! I will love you! I will love you!

She cries. He is motionless in her arms.

We hear the sound of a siren in the distance and the music of the Carnival at the Ends of the Earth.

Blackout.

Shift 6

It's morning. We hear a radio. A news bulletin. A soccer match in Brazil. The rustling of the dress. There's more screen than emptiness this time. GISÈLE takes her medicine.

GISÈLE I left the other day. I was watching the news about the war. It was raining. And I died, I think. I think that was it... I woke up twenty-four hours later. The television was still on. A soccer match was playing. It was a completely different day. From my balcony, I could see the geese in the sun. A ball bounced into my living room. I died and then I came back.

Dorian Grey
Sixth Meeting

A man alone. He carries a white plastic bag in his hand.

He is forty-six years old and is wearing a checkered suit. He works as a financial advisor in a bank, a Caisse Populaire. He wears strange shoes with long, pointed, upturned tips.

The man is standing in front of a coffin, represented by a rectangle of light. He talks to the deceased.

MAN I left the Caisse earlier than usual. It's strange. You see, normally I always leave the office at 5:10. Today I left at exactly five o'clock. On the dot. The cashiers had gone home. The security gate was closed. There hadn't been anyone waiting in line for at least half an hour. It was slow for a Thursday.

I have a terrible migraine because of the air conditioning... and all day long that damn song over and over...

Ten mortgage loans today. I'm not all that pleased, but let's just say I can live with it... at least I didn't get into an argument with Christiane Thibault, even if she did accuse me of being weak because I gave a loan to a student who looked lost and confused. Life does that. I told her that maybe if students had a little more money it would help them figure out what they were doing! That's what I was thinking about when I took a seat in the subway.

It's funny because I was looking at the tips of my shoes. The four hundred dollar shoes I bought myself in Venice when I took that trip alone.... The tips are so long and turned-up that you thought they looked like two gondolas on the ends of my feet. That's what I was thinking about and a lot of other things as I grabbed the transfer to come here. I was playing an old Françoise Hardy tape on my Walkman...

I'd never force you to listen to that kind of music. But, you know something, despite your adolescent tastes, when I talked to you about how much I loved her as a singer, you didn't judge me. I think that's when I really fell.... Is it possible to say at exactly what moment you start to...

I remember how beautiful your face was in the soft light from the candles our first Halloween at Dorian Grey.

Dorian Grey's definitely the chicest gay bar in town and God knows I know all the gay bars in town.... All around us the place was packed with lawyers, judges, and businessmen I knew because they do their banking at the Caisse. All of them were either dressed up as sexy Hollywood starlets or Sean Connery... drinking martinis.... And there you were, looking like a little ruffian right off the boat from São Paulo.... You were dressed as a Russian cavalry officer from the time of the czars! Magnificently out of style! I thought your mother must've made your costume in the hope that some big shot out looking for a young gigolo would notice you!

I've always said that I would've given my life to have known one great love. For just five minutes.... And there, standing in front of me, smiling, was... all of eternity. Fifteen years old with a perfect body that had already been through too much and a smile that had the weariness of an old actor and the joy of a child who has so much talent he can't express it without getting burnt... like the sun at night. I remember when you told me you came from Brazil I immediately said to myself: "That boy in the Russian officer's uniform has sold his body for a soccer ball or a pair of Nikes." That's why I started talking to you about Zidane and Brazil's painful defeat to France in the 1998 World Cup. The Brazilians were too individualistic, I said. They lacked team spirit. That really got you going, but I hit the jackpot because soccer meant everything to you.

Manuel, my angel, we met every Halloween after that and every year you aged so much. I have to confess it secretly delighted me because, with my creams and my discreet and occasional injections, it allowed me to believe I was catching up to you somehow, going backwards in time, acting in a movie that was playing in reverse.

I look like an idiot with this plastic bag. I wish that just once in my life I'd have the courage to see something through...

I'm such a coward. I thought about it all day and all night too, after your mother called me. "Mr. Nadeau, Manuel asked me to.... He wanted me to thank you for paying for his studies.... He won't be going to Dorian Grey's tonight to celebrate Halloween with you the way he has every year.... Manuel is dead."

Of course, all I wanted to do was vomit up my heart.... I took down the information about this place and I hung up.

We'd agreed that I'd pay whatever it would cost for you to get the best education. I promised you that nothing would happen between us until you turned twenty-one. All I asked of you in return, and you agreed, was that we'd speak on the telephone once a week and we'd see each other once a year, on Halloween night at Dorian Grey's.

Your mother called me only one other time. "...you're the one paying for his studies. You should know the truth. You will never be Manuel's father. Manuel's father lives in São Paulo."

Not your father.

Not your lover.

And not really your friend.

In the end what was I to you…? Did we really have any kind of relationship?

Do I really have any kind of meaningful relationship with anyone… anyone at all, on this entire planet?

Have I been spending what amounts to a third of my salary at the Caisse Populaire on someone and, in the end, there's not even an ounce of affection in that person's heart for me?

I'm scared, Manuel.

> GISÈLE *throws the soccer ball. It rolls on stage and bounces.*

I don't believe in signs and things like that…! I don't believe there's anything afterward.

I like watching soccer with a Bloody Caesar in my hand and I hope Brazil will win against Nigeria because, for me, Brazil is you. That's what I believe in!

I think I kidded myself. I think I refused to see that you had it. Of course you had it, that damn sickness. And that's why you were aging so quickly…

It suited me to see you age, every year, at the infamous Halloween party at Dorian Grey's.

It allowed me to think I was getting younger.

It allowed me to think I had the heart of a giant.

The memory of your eyes, ravaged but lucid, made our tête-à-têtes as unforgettable, as memorable, as any love story in the kind of novel you buy in a drugstore or at a train station or whatever…

Your eyes burning with an impossible love gave me the strength to put up with Christiane Thibault, the mortgage queen, with her two beautiful children and her husband who's the picture of health!

Yeah… that was the strength you gave me, Manuel, by agreeing to come to the Dorian Grey Halloween party with me once a year. Without knowing it, you gave me all the wonderful madness of your childhood in São Paulo, all the vitality of your youth spent on the soccer fields of Brazil.

> *He starts to reach for something inside the plastic bag.*

Manuel, I don't have the courage. I'm a coward. I'm an average man. Ordinary. I haven't succeeded in doing anything special in life. I didn't know how to make friends, except…

WHY? Why in such a small body?

Ah! What the hell!

Manuel, I want to put this on you. On your body that's lying there cold, fragile, and no longer… anything.… I want to put a wedding dress on your poor, rotting athlete's body.

Manuel, I love you! You're the man of my life. I found this in the classified ads. The veil is missing and the crinoline. This is insane but I'm telling you now, I love you and I wish I'd…

A man dressed in black enters.

Beat.

—Sir?

The two men look at each other for a brief moment.

—Do you want to leave the dress in the coffin?

Beat.

Yes, I do.

The man walks off. With his long shoes and his checker suit, he looks like a clown. He picks up the ball and bounces it.

Blackout.

Epilogue

GISÈLE's chair is now facing us.

GISÈLE   I'm afraid sometimes. I'm afraid of the unknown. For me, to lose my memory, that's the unknown. Until this cardiovascular incident, I could recite the role of Bérénice by heart without missing a single syllable.… The sun is shining again this morning. It's already autumn…

GISÈLE stands for the first time. She picks up the wedding dress, which was left centre stage after the last story.

"Then it is true Titus abandons me!
And we must part! 'Tis he will have it so!"

Black.

Lights up instantly. The young woman from the subway appears wearing a red cape.

Black.

Sounds of the subway heading off into the distance. Ocean.

The end.

The Sound of Cracking Bones
(Le bruit des os qui craquent)

by Suzanne Lebeau

translated by
Julia Duchesne & John Van Burek

US Congressman Tom Lantos was, as a child, taken to the death camps in Hungary by the Nazis. He said that the thing which haunted him most in his life was not the brutal treatment of the Nazis. What haunted him later in his life were the faces of the passersby, who saw them as children being put on trains and sent to the concentration camps. The mute faces. The silence. Not asking questions.
—Bono, when his band, U2, received the 2006 Ambassador of Conscience Award by Amnesty International

It may be impossible to understand, but it is imperative to know.
—Primo Levi

The sound of boots is frightening, but the silence of slippers is even more so.
—Thierry Van Humbeeck

My tale begins with an extraordinary event: I was almost wiped from the face of the earth and yet, here I am, a survivor; my body is here but how can I tell you, without making you snicker, that a large part of my soul has been driven out of your very social planet.... My story is so unbelievable that you will smile, be troubled, get angry, preach to me, or even worse, find pleasure in the recounting of my sorrows.

But, since I am bound to tell my story if I am to discover who I am, and since you are incapable of hearing it, I will, in the deepest part of my being, endlessly detail the immense ordeal that secretly rules my plan to live, like a myth of genesis, staged for a single spectator, me. I will become the author and actor of my destiny and the only authorized witness of my struggles.
—Boris Cyrulnik, *Les vilains petits canards*

Introduction to
The Sound of Cracking Bones (Le bruit des os qui craquent)

The Sound of Cracking Bones is a work of dramatic fiction. The characters, dialogue, action, narration, and location are all the product of Suzanne Lebeau's imagination and artistry. At the same time, it is a piece of reality theatre addressing an issue of international importance and compelling actuality. This is the issue of child soldiers—girls and boys—who are kidnapped and enslaved to serve in cruel armed conflicts in more than forty countries and on every continent of the planet. Precise numbers of these children are not available, but, since this widespread, opportunistic practice has socio-cultural roots reaching far back into the past and since there seems to be no end to war, a reasonable estimate would be that there are at present 400,000–500,000 of them. After careful, passionately driven research on this subject, extended travels, and a month spent in the Democratic Republic of the Congo, Suzanne Lebeau wrote *Le bruit des os qui craquent*. She has been quoted in several interviews as saying she believes it to be urgent that this situation be known and addressed by those who live in any degree of comfort in countries without war. The reality of the phenomenon of child soldiers is intolerable. Equally intolerable is the complacent will to not know of it in the minds and lives of those whose comfort probably still owes much to a heritage of colonialism or who may even be profiting directly from the exploitation of children through the international trade of people, arms, drugs, diamonds, and other goods.

The quotations chosen as epigraphs for *The Sound of Cracking Bones* highlight the reproach the play addresses to those who will not see, whether individuals, politicians, nations, international corporations, commissions, or agencies. Thierry Van Humbeeck's striking use of metonymy in the third epigraph captures the stark contrast between the lives of those who have no choice but to live with violence and the hypocritical lives of those who care only about their own comfort and security: "The sound of boots is frightening, but the silence of slippers is even more so."

The Sound of Cracking Bones traces the flight of two children from the tropical forest where they were being held and used by a group of rebels—Elikia, thirteen years old, and Joseph, eight years old—and their arrival, after an extremely difficult trek, to relative safety at the children's hospital in Joseph's native village by the sea. Elikia has been held by the rebels for three years; Joseph has recently arrived. The inexhaustible cruelty they have endured and the unimaginable unhappiness of their situation are immediately revealed. The night the terrorized, really small boy arrived in the rebel camp he held a fifty kilo sack of rice, which he was forced to carry for days over long distances; he was kicked, bashed with Kalashnikovs, taunted, humiliated, and starved. Elikia barely managed to save him from having his hands cut off with a machete for the gratuitous, sadistic pleasure of Killer. The audience progressively learns Elikia's story as the play advances. At the time she was kidnapped by the rebels, she had to watch the murder of her brother, the gang rape of her mother, the decapitation of her father, and was forced herself to burn their family home to the ground. She was claimed at the age of ten as the "wife" of Rambo, the rebel leader, and later was forced to become a sex slave in a camp where there were five girls for sixty men. Supplied with a Kalashnikov, she learned to beat and kill (children who did not beat and kill rapidly were themselves killed), to accept the impossible role for herself of both victim and torturer, powerless and guilty. She was constantly drugged, humiliated, and beaten at random. Her women's work, done in addition to the violence she was required to commit and endure, was exhausting. Fear deprived her of her dreams and ability to sleep, leaving no vision for the future and only nightmares for the present: "She was afraid of being swallowed by the dark" (Fifth Hearing). The three years as a slave and soldier with the rebels robbed her entirely of her childhood and her sense of self. She feels only panic and fear when she sees herself for the first time in the hospital and realizes that the little girl she used to be is gone, crushed, replaced by a rebel self she is scared to see: "[...] the little Elikia... who would brush her hair, who would try on all the coloured dresses that her mother made for her, who thought she was beautiful, who had brothers, sisters, friends, who went to school, who'd gaze at the stars.... Where is she, that little Elikia?" (Ninth Hearing). She is afraid of looking at the violent acts she has committed, despite the knowledge that they were done under coercion when she had no choice: "I was so scared [...] of seeing the eyes of the little girls in my eyes, of seeing Rambo's hand on my cheek, of the wounded in the creases of my mouth..." (Scene 10). In the end, it is the rebels who are the cause of Elikia's death two years after her arrival at the hospital, in that their sexual abuse of her is directly responsible for the HIV that kills her.

Despite such suffering, she affirms with pride and strength that her soul is still intact: "The rebels never got my soul [...] When they took my body with their filthy hands, when they threatened me, drugged me, forced me to obey, I thought of my grandmother [...] I kept my soul up high, very high, beyond their reach" (Scene 5). The vitality of her soul and the hope it represents for the resilience of the human spirit are felt, in effect, throughout the play in the tough love she shows to Joseph, who owes to her his survival, return to family, and opportunity to go to school. The same spiritual vitality and resilience are equally evident in the frank record of the experiences Elikia kept in her notebook. Despite her youth, she believed that speaking out and speaking truth was the only way to put an end to the unspeakable violence, horror, and abuse she knew in her short life.

Suzanne Lebeau co-founded in 1975 the theatre company for young audiences, Le Carrousel, with Gervais Gaudreault. As primary playwright for the company, she has been determined to say something to children and not merely entertain them, although the pleasure and engagement of her audiences is always of primary importance. Le Carrousel has earned an enviable national and international reputation for its outstanding artistry, its pioneering work inventing theatre for young audiences, and its thought-provoking productions. As is stated on its website, the unique place it has forged for itself in the world of theatre and culture is one that combines rigorous attention to high artistic quality and the creation of meaningful theatre for children and adolescents, never hesitating to push back horizons and traditionally established narrow boundaries that might conceal unpleasant realities from children:

> Through its view of childhood and art, Le Carrousel has been distinguishing itself on national and international stages for 35 years. Supported by research and creative work that pushes back the limits of the permissible and the possible, the company places at the core of its artistic approach the question "What should we say to children?" and examines the place of children in the world.[1]

Lebeau and Gaudreault have the greatest respect for their young audiences, with whom they engage in frequent communication with regard to reception of their shows, ideas, and subject matter. While they recognize the unique tastes and experiences of the young, they believe children are sensitive to beauty, capable of probing thought, and desirous of understanding the world around them on their own terms, even when that world shows itself to be sordid and disturbing. Therefore, while Lebeau knew that the raw and harsh reality of the lives of the children dramatized in *The Sound of Cracking Bones* was bound to be upsetting, she was determined to speak truth to them. And indeed, her research before and after the play's stage creation has shown that young audiences are appreciative of such thought-provoking fare and eager to explore what it means for them in terms of personal responsibility.

Lebeau, superb artist and specialist in children's theatre, has worked to break down the barriers between theatre for young audiences and mainstream theatre events, believing that it is possible to produce shows that speak simultaneously to young and old, drawing on the knowledge and experience of adults and the clarity of vision and spontaneity of children, thereby evoking a richly complex audience response which will, ideally, nurture conversations and exchanges of ideas across generations. Could the observations and questions of children produce real change in the frequently disturbing ways in which the world turns? As a result of the power of *The Sound of Cracking Bones* to challenge people of all ages to rethink their assumptions, the play has already enjoyed a run and several new productions in many countries and in mainstream theatres, as was the case at the Théâtre d'Aujourd'hui in Montréal and the Comédie-Française in Paris.

The Sound of Cracking Bones draws its compelling power from the reality of the story and socio-political situation it dramatizes and the humanity of the characters who live the story. Its power to speak to a broad age range and people from all walks of life around the world is enhanced by the multiple voices that are heard on several wavelengths in the play. Audience members will tune in on those voices that speak most clearly to their own sensitivities and experiences and will draw their own interpretations from these voices. Lebeau's text throws out a major challenge to directors and actors to work experimentally with the many voices in order to be sure they are all transmitted throughout the entirety of the performance. The first voice that is heard on stage is Elikia's in a narrative mode, as she prepares her flight from the rebels' camp with Joseph. Her narration takes the form of an explanatory monologue, paralleled by Joseph's monologue, thus offering the audience two perspectives on what is happening at this moment, what will be happening in the course of their flight, and what each of the characters is thinking and feeling. Interwoven with these monologues is the quietly desperate dialogue between the two characters as they slip away from the camp and hope against hope they will not be caught, tortured, and killed by the rebels. These monologues and intervening exchanges between the characters are braided around each other throughout the play's ten scenes.

The opening expository scene during which the dramatic action gets underway is followed by the first of ten Hearings, when Angelina, the nurse who welcomed and cared for the children when they reached their destination, testifies to unseen interlocutors, members of a "commission" of enquiry, on behalf of Elikia. Her testimony, drawn from Elikia's notebook, conveys the teen's naive belief that responsible adults will make such abuse stop "once they know" and her wish to say to those that wage war: "if a gun can kill the body of he who is afraid, it also kills the soul of he who shoots." Thus, these Hearings add two more voices to the play's soundscape: Angelina's and Elikia's as written in her notebook after her arrival. The action of the play and its underlying subtext commenting on the harm done by worldwide socio-political and economic norms in the lives of innocent children weave their way through scenes and hearings in a symphony of seeking, suffering, lucid, and compassionate voices speaking from a range of perspectives, places, and moments.

An important voice in the play is the unheard voice of the commission members who are listening to Angelina's testimony and her reading from Elikia's notebook, and who, presumably, would be in a position to make the abuse of children widely known and to take or recommend real remedial action. Angelina urges them to read the notebook for themselves and so discover first-hand what Elikia endured during her three years with the rebels and what impact she hoped for from the record she kept: "Elikia didn't write to denounce, to pursue, to punish. She named no names. On the contrary, she kept them silent to break the chain of violence that calls for violence and which poisons life" (After the Last Hearing).

However, Angelina's pauses and responses to what commission members have said to her while she was speaking suggest that they are impatient with the length and detail of her testimony; they ask her to summarize (Seventh Hearing). In the end, when Angelina recalls the night Elikia died, and she has realized how little the commission members care about these real human beings, the stage directions indicate that she finishes her testimony "frostily" (Tenth Hearing). In her final words addressed directly to the audience, Angelina realizes that the well-fed members of the commission would have no respect for either Elikia's life story or the record she kept so carefully. Their final statement to her: "We don't draft official reports from the writings of children" (After the Last Hearing) is a terrible comment on smugly dead bureaucratic thought, as well as being a dazzling reinforcement of the message that Suzanne Lebeau has conveyed in her theatre right from the beginning of her career: it is essential to rediscover and nurture the ability to see the world through the eyes of children.

The text of *Le bruit des os qui craquent* is dedicated to "all the Elikias of the Earth," whose most powerful weapon is the inextinguishable hope they continue to wear across their chest and to Amisi Mungo Serge and Yaoundé, two young people of the Democratic Republic of the Congo whom Lebeau met in Kinshasa and who recounted their experiences to her. These experiences, distressingly similar to Elikia's, have now been left behind and these men, who are getting on well with their lives, justified the hope that so richly inspires this profoundly moving work of art.

Notes

[1] www.lecarrousel.net/en/the_company.html (accessed 10 February 2010).

About Suzanne Lebeau

Suzanne Lebeau has been drawn to the theatre since 1966. At first, she was headed for a career as an actress: from 1966 to 1973, she played Molière, Ionesco, and Stoppard as she continued her training with Jacques Crête and Gilles Maheu in Montréal, then with Étienne Decroux in Paris. She also spent a year training in Poland, dividing her time between the Pantomime Theatre and the Puppet Theatre in Wroclaw.

After founding Le Carrousel with Gervais Gaudreault in 1975, Lebeau gradually gave up acting to devote herself exclusively to writing. Today, she has more than twenty original plays, three adaptations, and several translations to her credit, is internationally recognized as a leader in playwriting for young audiences, and is among the most-performed Québec playwrights in the world. Most of her works have been published and translated, some into several languages. *Une lune entre deux maisons*, the first Canadian play written specifically for young children, has been translated into six languages; *Salvador*, presented at the New Victory Theatre on Broadway, has been translated five times; and *L'Ogrelet*, produced in French, English, Italian, and Spanish by Le Carrousel, has also been translated into German, Maya, Portuguese, and Russian, and published in Argentina, France, and Mexico. *Le bruit des os qui craquent*, premièred by Le Carrousel, has also been staged by La Comédie-Française. Two essays about her writing were published in France and Spain: *Itinéraire d'auteur*, by La Chartreuse—Centre national des écritures du spectacle (2002), and *Las huellas de la esperanza* by Ensayo ASSITEJ-España (2007).

Since 1993, Suzanne Lebeau has made regular trips to La Chartreuse (Centre national des écritures du spectacle), in France, to give workshops and lectures and to participate in playwright residencies. The Musée de la civilisation in Québec City asked her to act as an artistic consultant for the exhibition *Grandir* (1997) and to write texts for the exhibition *De quel droit?* (1998), produced for the fiftieth anniversary of the Declaration of Human Rights. In 1999, she went to Corsica for a residency at Théâtre Alibi, where she wrote a play with a group of children, and, as a recipient of the Canada/Mexico Scholarship, she did a two-month residency in Mexico, leading workshops with both writers and children; festivals in Africa, Argentina, Spain, Mexico, and the United States have invited her to give lectures and workshops. Since 2007, Théâtre Jean-Vilar de Vitry-sur-Seine and Suzanne Lebeau have been working together through an art exchange agreement with the Conseil régional d'Île-de-France. She was invited by Wajdi Mouawad to be the first artist to direct a workshop for writing for young audiences, which took the form of master classes, for the French Theatre Lab at the National Arts Centre of Canada (2009). She has also taught writing at the National Theatre School of Canada for thirteen years and acts as a consultant for young authors in Canada and other countries, thus contributing to the emergence of new plays for young audiences.

The importance of Suzanne Lebeau's body of work and her exceptional contribution to the rise of the genre of theatre for young audiences, both in Canada and abroad, have earned her many prizes and awards: the Governor General's Literary Award for Drama; the Prix de la critique, young audiences category, awarded by the Association québécoise des critiques de théâtre; the Prix Sony Labou Tansi des lycéens; the Distinction de la Comédie-Française; the Prix des Journées de Lyon des auteurs de théâtre (*Le bruit des os qui craquent* 2009, 2008, 2007); award for best text, FETEN (*Cuentos de niños reales* 2009); the Prix Jack London (*L'Ogrelet* 2007); the Prix littéraire de la citoyenneté de Maine et Loire (*Salvador* 2002); Masque Award for original text (*L'Ogrelet* 2000); the Prix Francophonie Jeunesse RFI (*Salvador* 1995); the Chalmers Children's Play Award (*Les Petits Pouvoirs* [*Little Victories*] 1986); was a finalist for the Molière Awards (*Petit Pierre* 2008 and *L'Ogrelet* 2007); and has been nominated for the Governor General's Literary Award five times. In 1998 the Assemblée internationale des parlementaires de langue française made her a Knight of the Order of the Pleiades for her body of work.

Published Works by Suzanne Lebeau

Une lune entre deux maisons (1980). Montréal: Éditions Québec/Amérique. (Montreuil-sous-Bois, France: Éditions Théâtrales, 2006).

Les petits pouvoirs (1983). Montréal: Leméac Éditeur.

La marelle (1984). Montréal: Leméac Éditeur.

Ti-Jean voudrait ben s'marier mais... (1985). Montréal: Leméac Éditeur.

Comment vivre avec les hommes quand on est un géant (1990). Montréal: Leméac Éditeur.

Conte du jour et de la nuit (1991). Montréal: Leméac Éditeur.

Contes d'enfants réels (1995). Montréal: Leméac Éditeur. (First edition: Montreuil-sous-Bois, France: Éditions Théâtrales, 2009).

Salvador: la montagne, l'enfant et la mangue (1996). Montréal: VLB Éditeur. (First edition: Villeneuve lez Avignon, France: Centre national des écritures du spectacle La Chartreuse/Premières Impressions, 1994; Montreuil-sous-Bois, France: Éditions Théâtrales, 2002).

Contes à rebours (1997). Montréal: Lanctôt Éditeur.

L'Ogrelet (1997). Montréal: Lanctôt Éditeur. (First edition: Montreuil-sous-Bois, France: Éditions Théâtrales, 2003).

Petit Pierre (2002). Montréal: Lanctôt Éditeur. (First edition: Montreuil-sous-Bois, France: Éditions Théâtrales, 2006).

Souliers de sable (2006). Montréal: Leméac Éditeur. (First edition: Montreuil-sous-Bois, France: Éditions Théâtrales, 2007).

Le bruit des os qui craquent (2009). Montréal: Leméac Éditeur. (First edition: Montreuil-sous-Bois, France: Éditions Théâtrales, 2008).

Le bruit des os qui craquent was first performed at the Centre culturel Marcel-Pagnol de Fos-sur-Mer by Le Carrousel and Théâtre d'Aujourd'hui on January 13, 2009, with the following company:

Elikia	Emilie Dionne
Joseph	Sébastien René
Angelina	Lise Roy

Directed by Gervais Gaudreault

Created in residence at Théâtre de la Ville à Longueuil, Québec, in co-production with Théâtre Jean-Vilar de Vitry-sur-Seine and the Fédération d'Associations de Théâtre Populaire with the Aide à la création of the Centre national du Théâtre and support to the author from the Société des Auteurs et Compositeurs Dramatiques of France. It was produced at Théâtre d'Aujourd'hui on March 31, 2009. Gaudreault also directed le Carrousel production of the play in Spanish in Mexico (2009). It was produced at the Comédie-Française in Paris on February 11, 2010 and in French in the Democratic Republic of the Congo.

Characters

Elikia, thirteen years old, a young girl
Joseph, eight years old, a small boy
Angelina, a nurse

Setting

The place of the escape: a forest, tropical and humid, with its darkness and its clearings.

The site of the hearings and the public inquiry: a light that isolates.

Note

To indicate the difference between narrative speech and direct speech, the dialogue between Elikia and Joseph is in italics.

THE SOUND OF CRACKING BONES

Scene 1. Flight

ELIKIA   They were sleeping like swine,
snoring like pigs,
even Rambo was sleeping,
like every night, when they would fill their bellies
and drink like fish.
I had put some hemp in their rice,
hardly any rice in my own bowl and nothing for the boy.
I let him sleep next to me,
after smacking him enough, so they wouldn't get suspicious.

JOSEPH   She took my hand, in the middle of the night…

ELIKIA   *Shhhh!*

JOSEPH   You're breaking my bones.

ELIKIA   *Shhh! Be quiet.*
Get up and don't make a sound.

JOSEPH   *(half asleep)* Let me sleep.

ELIKIA   *Shhh! If you want to make it home in one piece, get up, right now.*

JOSEPH   *To my village?*

ELIKIA   *Hurry!*

JOSEPH   *To my village?*

ELIKIA   *The darkness will keep us safe…*

JOSEPH   I couldn't see who was whispering in my ear
but I guessed it was the girl with boots.
I trusted her… right away.

ELIKIA   *We've got to leave… without cracking a twig.*
Without leaving a trace.
The darkness could also make us trip and fall…
I took him on my back for the first steps, they're the most dangerous.
I took a step…
The boy had an instinct for escape.
He breathed with the wind and I could barely hear him.
I took a second step.
One foot suspended in mid-air, the other barely touching the ground.
Time weighed on my shoulders like an oil drum.
My heart was beating like a tam-tam.

I was afraid its mad pounding would wake up Killer, who'd watch me even in his sleep.
The boy crossed his hands over my heart, which calmed down...
leaving the night to the chorus of snores...
I took a few quick steps, more confident.
We were away.

JOSEPH She put me down in a nest of grass.
Light as a feather, she went back toward the camp to brush away our tracks.
I waited, frozen...
I heard a whisper of ruffled grass.
All at once, she was by my side.
She took me by the hand and started to run,
to run like a maniac.

ELIKIA *Follow me, come on, come on. Run.*

JOSEPH *You're going too fast.*
You're hurting me.

ELIKIA *Run! Faster! Run!*

JOSEPH She was running... running...
I was gasping.

ELIKIA *He didn't have the pace that fear puts in your legs...*

JOSEPH *I can't... I can't...*

ELIKIA *Just look straight ahead.... Run...*

JOSEPH *You're going... too fast...*

ELIKIA He fell down in a heap, his foot caught in a branch.
I went crazy, I hit him.
I was blind with fear.

JOSEPH With her fists. With her feet. With her head, as hard as she could, she hit me.
She hit me so hard...
Leave me here! Leave me alone.

   ELIKIA puts her hand over his mouth to silence him.

ELIKIA *Shut up! You want to get killed?*
Get beaten to death like a mad dog?
When they catch runaways, and they always catch them...
It's twenty blows with a stick, each.
Twenty blows, until you bleed, because anyone who doesn't hit hard enough gets beaten to death, too.
Is that what you want?

JOSEPH   *Just leave me right here.*
I don't want to go with you.
Her rage was burning my shoulders...

ELIKIA   *Your village...*

JOSEPH   *It's too far.*
Why are you taking me?
Why?

ELIKIA   He kept asking: "Why...? Why...? Why?"
As if I had an answer...
To say something, and because it was true,
I said I wanted to go back to school.

JOSEPH   *I've never been to school. I can't help you.*
Why are you taking me with you?

ELIKIA   *On my own, I'm too scared.*
He looked up, to see if I was making fun of him.
My anger dissolved.
He was too little to understand.
You're lucky. I could have hit you with my gun.

JOSEPH   She sat down beside me.

ELIKIA   *Drink.*

JOSEPH   I drank...

ELIKIA   (brutally) *Stop! Don't you know a gourd has to last a whole week...*
You wet your lips...

>   She starts to show him and realizes there isn't a drop left.

That's when I saw what a child he was, and what a burden he'd be.
How old are you?

JOSEPH   *I'm eight...*

ELIKIA   *Eight. Do you know today's date?*

>   JOSEPH takes out a little branch on which he has made notches. He counts.

JOSEPH   *I think it's March tenth...*

ELIKIA   *March...*
I'm already thirteen.
I said "thirteen"... and my heart tightened.
In the forest, they only celebrate the day you're taken.
Where are you from?

JOSEPH   From the coast. From Namba.... We're fishermen.
When the rebels took me, I was selling fish in the market.
My brothers, my father, my grandfather,
my mother, my grandmother,
my whole family lives in Namba.

ELIKIA   Well, if you want to see Namba again, we've got to get moving.

JOSEPH   I don't know the way.
With the rebels,
we wandered around day and night, and the grass was always up to my chin.

ELIKIA   If we follow the river, do you think we can get there?

JOSEPH   She was saying "Village, coast, river, the sea..."
and I completely forgot that my feet hurt.
Namba's not far from a river.
Do you think it's the one you're talking about?

> *In the distance, we hear a vague sound, like movement in the grass.*
>
> *ELIKIA takes JOSEPH in her arms and squeezes him tightly, almost crushing him. She puts her hand over his mouth. He grunts and struggles to make her let go. She shoves her gun in his ribs.*

ELIKIA   Shut up. Shut up. Shut up or I'll kill you.

> *A long silence in the night... we could hear a pin drop.*

I'd said: "I'll kill you" and Joseph had heard me.
He'd rolled away from my gun.
He stayed quiet, so perfectly still,
I couldn't even hear him breathe.

> *She feels around for him in the dark.*

Where are you?
Kid, hey, kid! I didn't bring you along to kill you.
Trust me...

> *Silence.*

Let's find that river.

First Hearing

> *Lights up on the nurse as she testifies. It is not necessary to know where or why she is testifying. All that matters is what she has to say.*
>
> *Her moments of silence can either be her breathing between parts of her testimony or pauses for the questions she is asked and which help her to continue, or comments that bring her back to the heart of the matter.*

ANGELINA I am here to testify on behalf of Elikia Mandoke…
I have the summons that she received.
Elikia did want to come.
She was prepared to tell everything, even the smallest details.
She kept repeating: "It must be known.
They have to know…
Once they know, I'm sure they'll make it stop."

> *A silence during a question.*

They? For her, "they" meant
Those who listen,
those who decide, those who sell the guns.
You, me, the politicians.
The adults, I suppose.
She asked me to give you this notebook.
She wrote in a notebook, to be sure
that she wouldn't forget anything and to be able to say things she didn't dare say out loud.
She said that words from the mouth can't tell everything,
that they're too close to hatred and vengeance.
I would like to read you what she wrote on the first page, if you don't mind.

> *She reads.*

"I want my memories to be useful…
I want to say to those who wage war:
if a gun can kill the body of the one who is afraid,
it also kills the soul of the one who shoots."

> *Blackout on the nurse.*

Scene 2. The Meeting

ELIKIA The boy had arrived in the camp at nightfall,
along with other recruits who carried the loot.
It was a good mission, we got provisions for two weeks.
The boy was carrying the rice. A fifty kilo bag.

JOSEPH The bag fell on her boots, which were covered in mud.

ELIKIA He was really small.
He collapsed on top of the bag, right at my feet.

JOSEPH They laughed at me…
Right out loud.

ELIKIA They bashed him in the ribs with their Kalashnikovs, to push him aside and get the rice for supper.

Rather so I could get the rice for supper,
because it was me who did the cooking.

JOSEPH   They hit me and with every blow they'd have a good laugh.

ELIKIA   That night, I didn't laugh with them.
I was tired. I was hungry.

JOSEPH   By the way she moved her boots away from my feet,
I could tell she wasn't with them.

ELIKIA   My gun hung lifeless, against my thigh.
For the first time in years
I forgot it was part of my arm.
I looked the boy in the eye…

JOSEPH   Something in her look was different from the hostile forest.

ELIKIA   It was like looking in a mirror…
I saw in his eyes the terror I felt when I arrived…
The refusal to believe that this was actually happening to him.
I knew his story.
It was my own story… and that of all the children who arrived at nightfall,
the sack of rice on their back, the barrel of oil, the water supplies, the munitions, the beans,
the slaughtered goat.
They all come from the south and march north, a gun to their back.
He was the smallest one to make it all this way.
There were lots of new arrivals.
Impossible to guess if they knew each other.
They kept their heads down and waited for orders.

JOSEPH   I clung to the sack of rice
to avoid their blows.
I held my breath so as not to attract attention.

ELIKIA   He was barefoot and his feet were covered in sores,
filthy,
infected.
To get him off the sack of rice, Killer gave him a kick
in the crotch.

JOSEPH   I shouldn't have cried out…

ELIKIA   Killer let loose.
He yelled,
"You think somebody's going to help you?
You think you'll escape me?
You belong to me, you're nothing, I'll do what I want with you.

If I want to hit you, I hit you. If I want to kill you, I kill you.
It's me who decides."

JOSEPH He kept saying "You worm, you little shit," and hit me and hit me...

ELIKIA Joseph looked at him meekly... to appease him... to beg him to stop...
Because he didn't know you must never look a killer in the eye.
Killer went berserk.
I saw his eyes change colour; I could tell the smell of blood was rising in his head.
He spoke the fatal words:
"You want to take your fate in your own hands?
I'll show you what we do when someone wants to take his fate in his own hands!
I'll show you!"
I knew what they did to anyone who tried to take his fate in his own hands.
They'd chop off his hand, they'd slap the dead hand on his shoulder and they'd tell him: "There, now try taking your fate in your hands!"
That always made them laugh.

JOSEPH He was raising his machete when the girl with boots stepped between us.

ELIKIA *That's enough! You can't do that!*
Rambo hasn't distributed the recruits.
He's the one who decides; if you touch a hair on his head,
I'll cut you down like a mangy dog.

JOSEPH She was screaming.

ELIKIA *He won't touch you again...*
At least not tonight.
For that one night, I could still protect him.

Second Hearing

ANGELINA Elikia took an enormous risk in fleeing.

Silence.

She'd lived three years with the rebels in the forest
but she didn't have the slightest idea of where she was.
They changed camps constantly.

Silence.

My name is Angelina Karimonjo. I'm a nurse at the children's hospital in Kina and I...
For twelve years.
As you can imagine, in twelve years my work has changed greatly.
In the beginning, I cared for my patients with a smile and clean gauze

and I did it well.
Now, it takes much more than a smile and gauze
to heal the children who arrive at the hospital.
Every day I see them arrive in worse shape.
Every day I see little bodies wrapped in white sheets, carried out the back door,
instead of seeing children walk out the front door to return to school…
This brutal war that's taken over…

Comment by a member of the commission.

To whom should I say these things
if I can't do so here?

Silence.

Very well, I'll answer your questions as briefly as I can.

Scene 3: The River

ELIKIA and JOSEPH are hidden in the grass. Day breaks.

ELIKIA tends to JOSEPH's feet.

They are whispering in the thick silence of the brush.

ELIKIA   The sun's coming up over there… that's the east…
The camp was west of the river,
over there…

JOSEPH   Elikia, I'm thirsty.

ELIKIA   You drank it all on the first day.
You should have saved it…
Now march!
The river can't be far.
I pretended to know where I was going but I had trouble orienting myself.
We'd hide during the day, walk only at night, so I'd lose the way.
It took us five days to reach the river.

JOSEPH   Do you think we're safe now?

ELIKIA   Soak your feet.
Joseph didn't understand that every leaf was a threat,
every tree, every breath of the forest.
He didn't understand that danger comes in the colour of every uniform,
in the face of the most innocent child.
Soak your feet.

JOSEPH   I can walk…

ELIKIA   You want them to cut off your feet in front of your mother, your father,
and every member of your great, big family in Nouma?

JOSEPH   *Namba.*

ELIKIA   *Soak your feet!*

JOSEPH   We spent three days by the river.

ELIKIA   I found a hollow tree where we could sleep at night
and hide during the day.
There's no aloe but these baobab leaves will do the trick.

JOSEPH   The freshness of the leaves did me good
and Elikia's hands were gentle.

ELIKIA   For the first time in three years
I felt my fear subside.
Joseph dove in.
He swam underwater so he wouldn't be seen.
He came back clean, carefree.

JOSEPH   *Come on, Elikia, the water's warm.*

ELIKIA   *I don't know how to swim.*

JOSEPH   *My feet are touching the bottom.
Come on, Elikia, come on.*

ELIKIA   *I don't like water.
Don't go too far… you'll be seen.*

JOSEPH   Sitting by the river, she kept her gun aimed at the forest.
Later, I understood why Elikia wouldn't go near the river.

ELIKIA   At night, he'd fall asleep like a baby.

> *JOSEPH lies down next to ELIKIA.*

JOSEPH   *What did you do, before…?*

ELIKIA   *What…*

JOSEPH   *Before, where did you live…?
Your parents?*

ELIKIA   *It's too far.*

JOSEPH   *Tell me "Joshua's Story."*
She called the story of how the world began "Joshua's Story."

> *ELIKIA tells it.*

ELIKIA   *Amma…*

JOSEPH   *Created the Earth to be his wife.*

ELIKIA   *Amma took some millet,
and gave it to the blacksmith.
Amma gave him beans,*

gave him sesame, and gave him sorrel.
The blacksmith came down from the heavens to Earth,
gave the millet to man,
gave him the beans,
the sesame, the sorrel.
The man took the millet and gave it to the woman...
He gave her the beans, he gave her the sesame...

>*Long silence.*

JOSEPH *After the sesame, Elikia...*
Elikia...
at the sesame... she would stop, every time.

ELIKIA *The day I tell you the story right to the end... that day...*

JOSEPH *She would never finish her sentence.*

>*Night falls.*

ELIKIA *When Joseph's feet looked like feet again,*
we left the hollow tree...

>*ELIKIA takes off her boots and gives them to JOSEPH.*

It's you who'll wear the boots.

JOSEPH *You can keep them, Elikia.*

ELIKIA *Put them on.*

JOSEPH *These boots are too big for me.*

ELIKIA *Wrap your feet in leaves and put on the boots.*
And hurry up, we've lost too much time already.
We can't leave any trace.
It's got to look like it was animals that stopped here.
The path along the river is easier, but it's known.

>*The night is black when they start walking again.*

Third Hearing

ANGELINA *Of course I tried to learn why Elikia didn't run away sooner...*
Why she stayed so long with the rebels...
She explained:
"When you are a child, you do what you're told..."
The rebels are terrifying.
I knew the answer before I asked the question...
I'm sure she'd already thought about it,
and looked for real answers.
I found two passages

that help us understand why children stay with the rebels.
Let me find the first one, where she tells about the night... the night she was taken.

> *She searches for the passage and reads.*

"They said that the rebels were close,
that they'd pillaged the surrounding villages.
That night, my father grabbed the rice, the oil,
everything that was left at the house, and took us into the marshes that surrounded the village.
We hid ourselves in the grass. Each one as best he could.
It was hard to hide, the moon was too bright.
I took Joshua in my arms.
He was excited by the idea of sleeping outside and asked questions about everything.
I held my hand over his mouth and I whispered in his ear the story of how the world was created.
"Amma took some millet,
and gave it to the blacksmith.
Amma gave him beans,
gave him sesame, and gave him sorrel.
The blacksmith came down from the heavens to Earth,
gave the millet to the man,
gave him the beans,
the sesame, the sorrel.
The man took the millet and gave it to the woman...
Everything was silent.
The only sound was my voice in Joshua's ear.
'The man took the millet and gave it to the woman...'
The rhythm of the story..."

> *Silence from the nurse, who is very moved by what she is reading and upset by the comments made to her.*

I am reading it all because Elikia writes very well
and the details help us understand
what goes on in the head of a ten-year-old child
who has never left her village.

> *She takes up her reading again.*

"The rhythm of the story reassured me.
'The man gave the woman the beans,
He gave her the sesame...'
I said the word 'sesame'—I remember because I like the taste of sesame—
when my father hit me on the head.
It was the first time he'd ever struck me and the word sesame caught in my

throat.
Even Joshua went quiet.
The sound of boots drew near...
and the marsh seemed no safer than the village.
Then the shouts...
Shouting like I'd never heard...
Shouting like the world was coming to an end...
When the shouts had surrounded us, my father stood up
and asked the one who seemed like the leader:
'What is it you want?'
The leader replied:
'Because you tried to hide and deprive us of rice,
which we need,
you will give us everything.
Everything.'
They took us back to the village with the provisions, which they put to one side.
On the other side, us, standing...
He said 'everything.' And everything was terrible.
First, Joshua.
He was screaming so loud, one of the rebels took him by the leg,
snapped his neck, and flung him away like a sack of beans.
The silence cut through the night like an axe.
Then, they took my mother... one after the other... right in front of me,
on the ground where I sat at night to count the stars.
They took my father and cut off his head with a machete
when he threw himself forward to defend my mother.
They took everything.
Before leaving they handed me the torch they used for light
and made me set fire to the little that remained.
I burned the first ten years of my life
under my mother's blank gaze
while those who had humiliated her became my brothers."

  A time.

Elikia would never allow us try to find her mother.

  Long silence from ANGELINA.

I will read you another passage, very short, where Elikia talks about the moment Rambo first noticed her.

  She searches for another passage in the notebook. She reads.

"When Rambo said to me: 'It's you that I want, you will be my wife,'
the behaviour of the other men changed.
They no longer had the right to touch me.
I belonged to the leader and I had a gun.

I had a Kalashnikov.
I could silence them,
punish them.
When you have a gun, you're always right.
I understood why the rebels love their guns so much.
Me too... I loved my Kalashnikov.
I always kept it on my shoulder.
At night I'd wake up to feel it against my chest.
Without it, I felt so small, so fragile... a bird...
A tiny bird in the hand of someone who's hungry,
with the sound of cracking bones."

ANGELINA stops reading.

There are other passages that I will quickly sum up for you.
Elikia recounts how children who escape are always afraid of being caught.
In fact, they feel safer in the forest with the rebels
than in their villages with their parents,
and, as soon as they have a bit of power,
they think they can survive.
Also, that power allows them to avoid useless cruelty
like when Elikia stopped Killer from cutting off Joseph's hand.
These little victories ease their conscience,
which doesn't automatically die
when they switch over to the side of the rebels.

Scene 4. This War

JOSEPH *When you were fighting, Elikia... who were you against?*

ELIKIA *I don't know.*

JOSEPH *How could you tell who was the enemy?*

ELIKIA *Our leaders told us...*
At first, I tried to understand... but then...

JOSEPH *Are the soldiers the good guys?*

ELIKIA *There are no good guys, they're all bad.*

JOSEPH *My brother is a soldier...*

ELIKIA shrugs, powerless.

ELIKIA *Like the others.*
They fight for everything and for nothing.
They even kill for diamonds.

JOSEPH *Diamonds?*

ELIKIA   The one who has diamonds gets obeyed.
I figured that out when Rambo called in his second-in-command to ask what he'd
done with the diamonds they'd brought back from a raid.
His friend was called Justice.
More than a friend... a blood brother.
He copied Rambo in everything and Rambo liked that.
Justice had carved into his gun:
"I feed on the enemy's blood..." and it was true.
He killed like he ate, without washing his hands... drugged up to his eyeballs...

JOSEPH   What diamonds?

ELIKIA   I never knew how they got them
or what they wanted to do with them.
But I understood that diamonds were precious
when I saw Rambo...
I saw Rambo torture Justice for hours to find out where he'd hidden the diamonds.
Justice cried, screamed, said he didn't have the diamonds,
that it wasn't him.
No one could find the diamonds anywhere in the camp and Rambo...
sliced open his belly
because he figured Justice had swallowed them
so he wouldn't have to share...

> *After a long silence.*

His belly, they didn't close it back up... Justice was dead.
Me, I was relieved...
Justice scared me...

Fourth Hearing

ANGELINA   Yes, Elikia had a weapon,
a Kalashnikov, of course.
Everyone knows them.
In this country, there are more guns than shoes!
Elikia's gun...
It provoked a lot of discussion among the staff.
When she arrived at the hospital,
the first thing we tried to do was take it away.
The moment we touched it
she rolled herself into a ball and growled like a wild beast.
When we'd leave her alone in her corner,
she'd quiet down, she'd look around, and she'd doze off...
But she'd always keep one hand on her gun, though she never threatened
anyone.
At dawn, I got a little worried when people started to move around in the

hospital...
She would have to give it up.
I insisted...
Impossible, she lay down on top of it.
I realized that to take her weapon away was more dangerous than to let her keep it.
I had to convince the staff; that was the most difficult.
I was afraid of the reaction that the sight of a gun might provoke in the hospital.
These days, everyone is afraid of guns.
Even the smallest children recognize a Kalashnikov.
It was impossible to take it away from her, so I covered the gun with a sheet, to hide it.

Scene 5. Elikia's Nightmares

It is daytime, JOSEPH and ELIKIA sleep, leaning on one another.

ELIKIA *(murmuring) Another one.... No!*
Another girl...

JOSEPH *Elikia... Elikia.... Wake up.*

ELIKIA *No! Stop! Stop!*

JOSEPH *Elikia... you're dreaming.*
Wake up, Elikia... Elikia!

ELIKIA wakes with a start.

ELIKIA *They come into the world, one after another, in a jumble...*
More and more of them,
and every time, they're more brutal.

JOSEPH *Elikia always had the same dream.*
She was afraid of crying out in her sleep and giving us away.
You didn't make any noise, you just whispered.

ELIKIA *The first one had no gun when she came out of my belly.*
She found a Kalashnikov between my legs.
The second was born with a gun in her hands.
The third one didn't even have arms.
Her arms were guns.
She hurt me,
jabbing her guns into my flesh.

JOSEPH *It's a dream, Elikia.*
They're little girls.

ELIKIA   Little girls with guns!
At night when I'm walking,
when I'm trying to find the path,
trying to spot the dangers and the traps,
I'm stronger than those little monsters.
I can make them shut up.
But during the day, when I should feel safe in the light,
they move in, they take over.
They hurt me. They kill me.
I can't get rid of them,
I can't even touch them, but I feel them, under my skin.

JOSEPH   It's a nightmare. Only a nightmare.

ELIKIA   They scare me.
Their eyes are cold, like death.
They have no pity.
Their eyes, Joseph…
It's their eyes that wake me up.
I know what they're looking for, I know what they want…

JOSEPH   Sleep, I'll stay awake.

ELIKIA   They wait till I'm asleep
so they can steal my soul.
The rebels never got my soul.
Not Killer, not Little Soldier, not Rambo,
not even when he gave me my gun…
When they took my body with their filthy hands,
when they threatened me, drugged me, forced me to obey,
I thought of my grandmother…
She always told me to hold my head up high. Always.
Poor Grandma, she didn't know the rebels.
With them, a head held high is death.
I kept mine down
and I told her it was only to stay alive.
But I kept my soul up high, very high, beyond their reach…

JOSEPH   Sleep. Sleep a little.
Look at the sun, it's only noon, you still have time to sleep.
Me, I'll keep watch.
When I kept watch, she slept without nightmares.

Fifth Hearing

ANGELINA   Right to the end, Elikia had trouble sleeping…
Like all children who come back from war.

For these children, sleep is a trap
and the fear that keeps them awake is the only guardian they can trust.
At night, Elikia wouldn't close her eyes.
In three years, not once did I see her sleep through the night.
She'd rock the crying babies,
she'd nurse them with a patience I no longer had.
She'd tell stories to the ones who'd wake up frightened in the night.
She was a guardian angel for the little ones.
They adored her.
In order to sleep, she'd wait for Joseph to come back from school each day.
Do you know what Elikia was most proud of?
Of convincing Joseph's parents to send him to school.
When Joseph would tell her about his day,
do his homework, do his lessons sitting by her side, she could sleep.
But when night fell, she was wide awake.
She was afraid of being swallowed by the dark.
Swallowed.... That's the word she used.

Scene 6. Be Wary Of Everyone

They are searching for a place to sleep when they hear the sound of a helicopter. JOSEPH starts running, waving his arms to attract the helicopter's attention.

JOSEPH   We're saved! Elikia, we're saved! It's the army!
In a helicopter... we'll get to Namba before the boats come back! Elikia!

He shouts at the helicopter, waving wildly to attract attention.

Over here, we're over here.

ELIKIA tackles him, throwing him to the ground to silence him.

ELIKIA   Shut up.
Shut up, you moron! You idiot! You want to get caught?

JOSEPH   (*his voice muffled by ELIKIA's hand*) It's the army, Elikia.
I can see the colours.

ELIKIA   The army! Are you crazy?
The army is worse than the rebels.

JOSEPH   My brother's in the army, he'll protect us.

ELIKIA   The army, the rebels, there's no difference.
I've seen rebels burn villages.
I've seen soldiers burn villages.
I've seen rebels and soldiers getting drunk together...

JOSEPH   That's a lie!

ELIKIA *Stealing, looting, killing, raping… they're the same.*
They're all the same, for them, there's no difference
between a baby and a bag of rice.

JOSEPH *You're lying.*
My brother doesn't kill, he doesn't steal, he doesn't burn villages.

ELIKIA *He obeys orders. Everyone does.*
The rebels obey.
The soldiers obey.
And if your brother refused to obey, believe me, he's dead.

JOSEPH *My brother's not dead. You're lying. I know you are.*

ELIKIA *I bet it's because of your brother that the rebels attacked Namba…*
I bet it's because of him that you are here…

JOSEPH *No, that's not true, it can't be true…*

ELIKIA *Wasn't he proud of having a gun? Eh?*

> *JOSEPH covers his ears.*

Didn't he go and show it to the village?
Didn't he go and show off his new uniform?

JOSEPH *He came to bring money to my mother.*

ELIKIA *And do you know where that money came from?*

JOSEPH *His soldier's pay.*

ELIKIA *And you believed him?*
Do you know where a soldier's pay comes from?
From drugs, from selling guns, from…

JOSEPH *Liar, liar, liar!*
Shut up! I'm not listening…
I'm going to go join the soldiers.
Here, keep your boots!

> *He takes off the boots, throws them in ELIKIA's face, and runs off.*
>
> *He runs after the sound of the helicopter.*

ELIKIA *Go on, go, I'm better off without you!*
Go… I have the heart of a rebel, and the legs.
We'll see who gets there first…

> *ELIKIA watches him go.*

He didn't even hesitate…

> *ELIKIA falls to the ground.*
>
> *We can tell that she's crying by the movement of her shoulders.*

Joseph is gone... he's gone...
That sentence kept turning over in my head.
The helicopter had been hovering
so he had time to catch up with it...

> *We hear the helicopter take off.*

Gone... Joseph is gone.

> *ELIKIA hasn't moved.*

JOSEPH   (*very softly because he's scared it might not be her*) Elikia... Elikia... Elikia...

ELIKIA   *Joseph?*

> *ELIKIA jumps up.*
>
> *They leap into each other's arms.*

JOSEPH   Elikia! I thought I'd never find you again.

ELIKIA   What, the army didn't want you?
He didn't answer, and I didn't ask.
He was crying...
crushed.

JOSEPH   I found papayas.

ELIKIA   We sat down to eat the papayas.
Much, much later, Joseph told me what happened.

JOSEPH   They were right in front of me, the soldiers and the rebels.
The soldiers were shouting to be heard over the helicopter and I hid behind a tree.
I wanted to think I was safe but still, I was terrified...
They made the rebels get down on their knees... kicking them, shoving their guns in the back of their necks.
I counted ten soldiers and three rebels.
One of the rebels was smaller than me.
As he knelt down, he tripped and fell over; his pants were too big.
He didn't have a gun, just a big can of water.
He made a quick move to grab the can...
One of the soldiers shouted not to move.
It was too late...
Another had already fired.
The soldiers just picked up the empty can
and left him lying there, his blood pouring into the dirt.
He was only going to fetch some water...
To fetch some water...

> *ELIKIA stays silent for a long time...*

ELIKIA When the rebels took me, I was ten.
They gave me a uniform that fit me.
I thought of my mother, who was a dressmaker.
Would she have sewn uniforms for children?
Those little legs, little sleeves...
What could those women have been thinking, as they sewed these uniforms?

Sixth Hearing

ANGELINA Did Elikia use her gun?
Is that a serious question?
She never spoke to me about it...
As I've already said, she was reluctant to talk about what she'd done.
But, it seems clear to me.
Elikia spent three years with the rebels...
Three whole years.
How to handle guns is the first thing children learn in the camps.
The second thing... is to kill.
To kill for anything, or nothing,
for rice,
to save their skin, for vengeance, to get respect, to be obeyed...
But most of all, because they're drugged and they have no choice.
During the months she spent at the hospital,
I never saw her threaten anyone...
I never saw her act aggressively.
I was never afraid, not for myself, or for the children around her.
On the contrary, her presence reassured us.

The silence of a question.

Who gave her a gun?
I suppose it was Rambo, because she received a weapon
when he chose her as his wife.
At least that's what I understand from reading her notebook.
I tried not to ask too many questions.
In any case, she never answered them directly.
She only spoke when she was ready...
As if her interior monologue was spilling out...

The silence of a question.

Well, I'd listen to her...
I'd try to calm her fears,
to help her forget what can be forgotten...
and above all to convince her that at ten years of age, she was only a child
and that a child who obeys adults cannot be guilty.
You know, she kept her gun wrapped in the sheet for over a month.

She slept with one hand on her Kalashnikov.
It took a lot of patience,
a lot of care and tenderness,
to convince her to give it up.

> *Silence.*

The day she gave us her gun,
she asked for a notebook.
This notebook here…

> *Silence.*

Scene 7. Joseph's Hunger

> *ELIKIA and JOSEPH walk in silence through the night…*
>
> *We hear only the sound of ruffled grass when, from far off, we hear chanting muffled by the distance.*

ELIKIA Listen!

JOSEPH It's the song of the dead… I recognize it…

> *JOSEPH starts singing.*
>
> *ELIKIA stops and points her gun instinctively.*

Rice, ELIKIA, there'll be rice. There are always big bowls of rice for those who watch over the dead…

ELIKIA Rice! You think you can just show up and ask:
"Can I have some rice?"
"But of course, my child, we'll give you some rice right away…
And how about some chicken?
Would you like some peanut sauce with that?"

> *JOSEPH starts to cry.*

JOSEPH In my village, there was rice for anyone who came by.

ELIKIA Your village is a long way away.
In rebel territory, if you've got rice, you don't share it.
Nobody shares rice with anybody.
Nobody shares chicken.
Anything we can eat, we hide.
We bury it, we don't give it away.
Nobody would give up a single grain of rice.

JOSEPH I'm hungry and I don't want to eat any more sand.
My tummy hurts…
I'm hungry, Elikia. I'm hungry, don't you understand "I'm hungry"?

I have cramps.
I want rice, fish, chicken.
I want some rice...
My head hurts.
I want some rice.

ELIKIA   Shut up! I'm hungry too but I don't whine.
You have no idea...

JOSEPH   Every day you tell me I have no idea.
I obey you.
You want to walk at night, we walk at night.
You want to avoid villages, we avoid villages.
You don't want us to fish so we don't get seen,
we don't fish.
You don't want us to make a fire...
we don't make a fire and we eat raw grass.
When there's no more grass... we eat sand.
We do what you want.
For weeks, we've followed that river...
We hide like animals because we're scared of everything.
I've done nothing wrong.
I don't want to hide anymore.
I want rice.

He yells at the top of his lungs.

I want rice.

ELIKIA   You want rice?
You're sure you want rice?
I'll get you rice.
Wait here. You'll have your rice and your chicken...
I'll get the rice at gunpoint.
Oh, yes, I could kill everyone in that village for a handful of rice.
We did that every day.
Is that what you want?
Is that what I have to do?

JOSEPH   I can get rice without killing anyone.
I've done nothing wrong.
I'm no rebel, they'll give me rice.
I'm not listening to you anymore.

JOSEPH tries to escape. ELIKIA points her gun at him and forces him to sit.

ELIKIA   Shut up. Wait here and don't move. You'll get your rice.

ELIKIA leaves in the darkness.

JOSEPH is left alone in the night.

JOSEPH *I've changed my mind,*
I don't want any rice...
Elikia...
I can eat sand, I'll walk without whining.
Elikia...
I covered my ears
and waited for the gunshots.
I waited...
And waited...
I waited so long, I fell asleep.
When I woke up, Elikia was beside me.

She shows her empty hands.

ELIKIA *I couldn't do it.*

JOSEPH throws his arms around ELIKIA's shoulders and covers her in kisses.

It used to be... so easy...
So easy...

JOSEPH *Even the first time?*

ELIKIA *The first time... no!*
The first time, my hand was paralyzed,
my fingers wouldn't move,
my head—my whole body—was screaming no.
It was my own fear of dying that made me do it.
The second time, I didn't flinch.
From then on, it was routine.
Death comes so fast and the body has so little resistance.
But this time...
It was a real village...
A real feast of the dead... with the smell of hot food,
women weeping.
I... couldn't do it.

Seventh Hearing

ANGELINA If I know what life is for girls in the rebel camps, it's because of Elikia's notebook...
but it's difficult to sum up.
It's the accumulation—of daily humiliations,
of mistreatment,
of unfair punishments—that creates terror.

The random nature of the cruelty… it's unbearable.
The children never know what will bring them punishment.
Elikia was beaten,
thirty lashes in public,
because she had eaten some leftovers that would have gone to waste
while the men were off pillaging…
Elikia's body was covered with scars…
She'd cover herself when we tended to her,
and I won't go into the sexual violence… which you can well imagine.
There were five girls for sixty men.
Elikia wouldn't talk about the violence inflicted on her
nor the violence she'd inflicted on others.
She wrote.
I'll leave you the notebook, you can see for yourselves.
She said that words must look to the future…
even if for her the future was short.

Time for a question.

Yes, she quickly understood that she had little time left
and her notebook became her confidant.
Day after day, she describes her three years with the rebels.
At every page, I thought, surely I've read the worst.
Then I'd turn the page and there was more.
I beg you, please, take the time to read her notebook.
You'll be able to see for yourselves.

Time for a comment or an objection.

I couldn't possibly summarize this.
Elikia lived through hell, and it was every single day.
I don't need to tell you why they take young girls.
The rebels need women
for women's work.
If these young girls make war like men,
they also do the cooking, the cleaning, the washing-up…
but above all, above all they quickly become sexual slaves.
How do you say no when it's a gun giving the orders?
When the arm that holds it is crazed with drugs?
When the man with the gun has all the rights?

Scene 8. The Palm Grove

It's night, but we can see the first light of dawn.

JOSEPH takes out a piece of wood, upon which he carves a notch.

ELIKIA *Joseph, stop it!*
We won't get there any faster...

JOSEPH *Five weeks and three days...*
My mother worries when we're not back by nightfall.
Mama...

ELIKIA We'd been walking for a long time.
Joseph insisted on counting the days.
We must be very close.

JOSEPH *You've been saying that ever since we left.*
You don't know the sea or how to get there.

ELIKIA *I don't know the sea but I can imagine it.*
I don't know how to get there... but I know I will.
March!

JOSEPH *For weeks, the same river's been going by... but the land never changes.*

ELIKIA *Yes it does.*
The forest... is less dense, less humid.
The light's coming through the trees.
Look closely, you can see the sky
and the stars.

> *JOSEPH lets himself fall down.*

Joseph... Joseph.... Come on, make an effort, I can tell we're almost there.
I can smell the salt air.
I feel the air is lighter.
Don't you feel it?
Joseph...

> *JOSEPH doesn't answer. He's asleep, exhausted.*

We'll be there soon and you'll be my brother.
You'll teach me how to swim,
how to fish,
how to tell one fish from another.
I talked to him, I yelled in his ear, I shook him...
Joseph was sound asleep.
I exhausted myself trying to be mad at him
but the feeling of having found a little brother
filled me with a strange sweetness.
I wanted to lie down next to him, to cuddle up to him,
when my foot hit an object that was hard, cold, and round.
The sweetness vanished
and fear came rushing back.
I tapped it with the tip of my foot,

reached out my hand, and found... a coconut.
I split it open and drank.
I crawled around and found another one.
I drank that just as fast.
I found a third coconut,
which I prepared
and placed in Joseph's arms.

JOSEPH   (*groans*) *Let me sleep.... Leave me alone.*

ELIKIA   *Drink, Joseph.*

> *JOSEPH opens his eyes.*

JOSEPH   *A coconut...*

> *He drinks with rage and pleasure while ELIKIA prepares him another coconut.*

> *She runs from one coconut to another.*

ELIKIA   *Coconuts! Hundreds, hundreds of coconuts.*
We must be near the coast.

> *JOSEPH gets up and goes around each tree, giving it a hug.*

> *He starts to dance like a madman.*

JOSEPH   *It's a palm grove...*
It's the one I come to with my uncle to get coconuts.
It's my palm grove, it's mine!
Look! That little coconut tree... I know it, it's mine.
I can climb all the way to the top to pick coconuts.
And at the end of the palm grove is the road to the sea...
To Namba.

ELIKIA   *Are you sure?*

JOSEPH   *There's my uncle's tree... that's my brother's...*
Namba! Namba! Mama!

> *He hugs ELIKIA and dances, repeating:*

Mama, Mama, Mama.

ELIKIA   *You go ahead, Joseph, you go first.*

JOSEPH   *You're not coming with me?*

ELIKIA   *On your own, you can stop a truck.*
A truck that's carrying ordinary things...
Not a rebel truck, not an army truck.
Ordinary things.
If you see soldiers, hide.

> If you see rebels, hide.
> Stop a truck and get a ride to Namba.

JOSEPH   What about you?

ELIKIA   I'll wait for you here...

> She can see the disappointment and doubt in JOSEPH's eyes.

> First you have to ask your mother and father
> if they want another daughter.
> A girl who has stolen, who has killed, who might even have killed their son...

JOSEPH   You're not going to trick me and go back to the rebels?

ELIKIA   Never! I'll never go back to the rebels.
> I'll never go back into that forest.

> JOSEPH hugs ELIKIA tenderly.

JOSEPH   There's a hospital on the other side of the palm grove.
> Come on, they'll feed you and you'll sleep in a bed.
> You'll wait for me there.

Eighth Hearing

ANGELINA   I was on guard duty when Elikia arrived.
> It was two years ago, in April.
> I don't remember the exact date
> but I do remember it was evening, about six o'clock,
> at the time we close the gates.
> It was always difficult to get through the night.
> The hospital had already been pillaged twice.
> But we never stopped providing emergency services, even for a day.
> Twice, we had replenished our stock of rice, beans, linens,
> and medical supplies...
> The rebels knew this.
> So when I heard the sound of cracking branches,
> I got worried.
> I rushed out to double lock the gates
> and I told the watchman to stay close by.
> He's a trustworthy man, very devoted.
> Twice I went out to check, but everything seemed in order.
> I called out, "Is someone there?"

Scene 9. Arrival At The Hospital

ELIKIA   I could just make out the hospital in the darkness
> when Joseph fell.

From exhaustion? Relief?
He was only eight.
I carried him on my back
for the last few metres that stood between us and the gate.
I heard footsteps coming and going from the door to the gate,
from the gate to the door.
I saw a light flickering through the door, which opened and closed.
I guessed at the white shadows that moved inside.
I wanted to cry out but no sound would come out of my mouth.
I wanted to bang on the door but I was paralyzed.
I stared at the nurse's white uniform
and I was ashamed of the one I was wearing,
my uniform of blood and muck.
I was a rebel.
I would always be a rebel.
Everything gave me away.
The grime under my nails, in my skin…
The blows delivered,
the blows received.
The corpses strewn by the wayside,
the burned villages,
the mutilated children,
the little girls with their torn vaginas.
I could picture them, with no hands, lying in white beds,
their backs covered with welts,
their mothers weeping.
The silence of the night was terrifying.
And Joseph slept…
A voice called out:
"Is someone there?"
It wasn't the voice of an adult who gives orders,
but still, I didn't dare answer.
The voice came closer and repeated:
"Is someone there? Who's there?"
By now, the voice was so close I was trembling.
"I'm sure there is someone out there.
Say something, please, just one word…"
repeated the woman's voice.
I sensed that a man was trying to hold her back.
That he was warning her to be careful.
She answered:
"I don't think there's any danger. I'd feel it if there were."
Then the man came nearer.
He had a flashlight; it lit us up from head to toe
And she immediately said:

"They're children, open the gate."
He opened the gate and took Joseph in his arms.
The woman took me by the hand.

Ninth Hearing

ANGELINA   Elikia was so small in her huge uniform, so dirty, so sombre,
but she seemed to be in good health.
On the contrary, Joseph was in a very bad way.
He suffered from fatigue, from dehydration, and his feet were in a dreadful state,
but he wasn't really hurt.
After two weeks of care,
Joseph went home to his family.
Elikia had resisted.
It was she who had marched barefoot but her feet had no injuries.
Her body was used to thirst, hunger, marching, fatigue.
A resistance that I've rarely seen in a child.
She seemed invulnerable.
I locked her in an empty office; it was night,
and I went to find some plain clothes for her.
I didn't want the others to see her in her camouflage fatigues.
Of course, I was afraid of the reaction.
Children are as frightened of uniforms as they are of guns...
Even adults have surprising reactions.
All I could find was one of my own shirts, a blouse with pink flowers.
The shock was enormous.
She recounts it herself with great clarity.
If you'll allow me...

As though she is reacting to signs of impatience.

This won't be long.
Her words express it better than mine.
(between her teeth) If she took the trouble to write it,
the least you can do is take two minutes to listen.

ANGELINA reads.

"The shirt didn't cover my knees...
My legs were bare.
My legs...
I hadn't seen my legs for three years,
not even in the river; I'd never set foot in the water.
Beneath the shirt, you could see the shape of my breasts.
Breasts I had never seen.
I didn't dare to go out, I didn't dare move. I could hardly breathe.

On the wall opposite me, there was a big mirror.
I was drawn to it, as if by a magnet, but I didn't dare approach it.
The mirror reminded me of the little Elikia…
who would brush her hair,
who would try on all the coloured dresses that her mother made for her,
who thought she was beautiful,
who had brothers, sisters, friends,
who went to school,
who'd gaze at the stars…
Where is she, that little Elikia?"

   ANGELINA stops reading.

Elikia hadn't seen herself in a mirror for three years.

Scene 10. The Mirror

  ELIKIA aims at the mirror and shoots.

  The sound of footsteps, a mad rush, JOSEPH runs in and throws himself onto ELIKIA, checking to make sure she is not hurt.

JOSEPH Elikia, Elikia, did you hurt yourself?

  ELIKIA falls to the ground and breaks into sobs.

Was it you who fired?

ELIKIA Yes, it was me.

JOSEPH Why did you shoot? Here, you're safe.
No one's going to hurt you.

  ELIKIA shows him the broken mirror.

ELIKIA I was so scared…

JOSEPH Of the mirror?

ELIKIA Scared of seeing the eyes of the little girls in my eyes,
of seeing Rambo's hand on my cheek,
of the wounded in the creases of my mouth…

  For the first time, JOSEPH looks at her as a boy looks at a girl.

JOSEPH Elikia! You're very beautiful… very, very beautiful.

  He hands her a shard of mirror.

Look…. Look…

  She looks at her reflection.

When I grow up, I want to marry you.

Tenth Hearing

ANGELINA   What could we do with a little girl of thirteen who wasn't ill?
We couldn't keep her.
We had no bed for her.
For the two weeks Joseph spent at the hospital, she slept under his bed.
Joseph shared his water and his food.
She changed his bandages.
It was she who went to notify his family and, once he got better, who took him home.
Then the diarrhea began.
A small bout... that we assumed we could easily treat.
But it wouldn't go away.
The blood tests confirmed that Elikia had contracted the virus, like so many others.
She had her place in the hospital...
She remained there until her death.

> *Silence that gives time for a question.*

At fifteen, what do you think our girls die of?
A bullet, or AIDS...
The night... that she died... I couldn't tear myself away from the hospital.
I could see she was having trouble breathing
and I didn't want to leave her alone.
Joseph stayed, too.
He said he had homework to do...

> *She is interrupted by a comment or a question. She carries on but very frostily.*

Forgive me, I let myself get carried away...
Might Elikia have lived longer with adequate medication?
Might she have led a fairly normal life for a few more years?
If she had lived...
How would she have lived, she who had lost her past, lost her family,
with no profession, no education.
And the others, all the others,
the girls and boys who are seven, ten, fifteen years old, whose guns we take away,
where should we send them?
To school, or to prison for war crimes?
And how should we treat them?
Are they victims, or perpetrators?
These are questions you will have to ask in your report...
and for which you will have to find answers and solutions.

After The Last Hearing

ANGELINA is preparing to leave. Now, she speaks directly to the audience.

ANGELINA The members of the commission arrived on time
for the meal that had been prepared for them
in the little restaurant overlooking the sea.
Although Elikia had asked me to, I didn't leave them the notebook.
"We don't draft official reports from the writings of children."
That's what they told me.
I took it back to the hospital.
I reread it to understand the children who arrive
each day, in ever greater numbers and in worse shape,
and to know how to care for those wounds that do not bleed.
Elikia didn't write to denounce, to pursue, to punish.
She named no names.
On the contrary, she kept them silent
to break the chain of violence that calls for violence
and which poisons life.
She wrote
so that the children of her country wouldn't see what she saw,
wouldn't hear what she heard,
wouldn't suffer what she suffered:
kidnapped at the age of ten,
soldier till the age of thirteen,
and dead by the age of fifteen.
Before she died, she told me:
"You know, Angelina, 'Elikia' means hope.
I only had one life to live, only one, and it's already over.
It was short."

The end.

Bibliography

Barrette, Michèle, Hélène Beauchamp, Joceline Hardy, Francine Noël, eds. "Théâtre-femmes." *Cahiers de théâtre Jeu* (1980). 16.

Bassnett, Susan. "Still Trapped in the Labyrinth: Further Reflections on Translation and Theatre." Susan Bassnett and André Lefevere, eds. *Constructing Cultures: Essays on Literary Translation* (1998). Clevedon, UK: Multilingual Matters. 90–108.

———. "Ways Through the Labyrinth. Strategies and Methods for Translating Theatre Texts." Theo Hermans, ed. *The Manipulation of Literature. Studies in Literary Translation* (1985). London: Croom Holm. 87–102.

Beauchamp, Hélène and Gilbert David, eds. *Théâtres québécois et canadiens-français au XXe siècle. Trajectoires et territoires* (2003). Sainte-Foy: Presses de l'Université du Québec.

Beauchamp, Hélène and Ric Knowles, eds. "Theatre and Translation," "A Servant of Two Masters: an Interview with Linda Gaboriau." *Canadian Theatre Review* 102 (Spring 2002). 41–47.

Bennett, Susan, ed. *Feminist Theatre and Performance* (2006). Toronto: Playwrights Canada Press.

Boyer, Ghislaine. "Théâtre des femmes au Québec, 1975–1985." *Canadian Literature* 118 (1988). 61–80.

Brault, Marie-Andrée. "L'expérimental: entre invention et provocation." *L'Annuaire théâtral. Revue québécoise d'études théâtrales* 35 (2004). 43–54.

Brisset, Annie. *Sociocritique de la traduction: Théâtre et altérité au Québec (1968–1988)* (1990). Longueil: Préambule. Tr. Roger Gannon and Rosalind Gill. *A Sociocritique of Translation: Theatre and Alterity in Quebec, 1968–1988* (1996). Toronto/Buffalo/London: University of Toronto Press.

Burgoyne, Lynda. "Théâtre et homosexualité féminine: un continent invisible." *Cahiers de théâtre Jeu* 54 (1990). 114–18.

Camerlain, Lorraine. "Dans ce numéro." "Un mouvement irréversible." *Cahier de théâtre Jeu* 66 (1993). 5–6, 9–12. No spécial "Théâtre-femmes."

———. "En de multiples scènes." *Canadian Theatre Review* 43 (Summer 1985). 73–89.

Camerlain, Lorraine and Carole Fréchette. "Le théâtre expérimental des femmes: essai en trois mouvements." *Cahiers de théâtre Jeu* 36 (1985). 59–66.

Cliché, Denise, Andrée Mercier, and Isabelle Tremblay. "Passion, parole et libération dans la dramaturgie de Carole Fréchette." Chantal Hébert and Irène Perelli-Contos, eds. *Le théâtre et ses nouvelles dynamiques narratives* (2004). Saint Nicolas: Presses de l'Université Laval. 215–47.

Collectif Clio. *L'histoire des femmes au Québec depuis quatre siècles* (1982). Montréal: Quinze Éditeur. Tr. Roger Gannon and Rosalind Gill. *Quebec Women: A History* (1987). Toronto: Women's Press.

Collective. *Trac Femmes. Cahier de théâtre expérimental* (1978). Montréal: Théâtre Expérimental de Montréal.

Cyr, Catherine. "Du jeu à l'écriture: passages et métamorphoses." *Théâtre. Les Cahiers de la maîtrise* 8 (2003). 63–73.

Davis, Tracy C. and Thomas Postlewait, eds. *Theatricality* (2003). Cambridge: Cambridge UP.

De Lotbinière-Harwood, Susanne. *Re-belle et infidèle. La traduction comme pratique de récriture au féminin. The Body Bilingual. Translation as a Rewriting in the Feminine* (1991). Toronto/Montréal: Women's Press/Éditions du Remue-ménage.

Denis, Jean-Luc, animateur de table ronde. "Le statut du québécois comme langue de traduction." *Cahiers de théâtre Jeu* 56 (1990). 24–37. No. spécial "Traduction théâtrale."

Desjardins, Lorraine. "Deux femmes, deux corps, deux voix: une seule parole." *Cahiers de théâtre Jeu* 66 (1993). 62–64.

Desrochers, Nadine. "Le théâtre des femmes." Dominique Lafon, ed. *Le théâtre québécois (1975–1995)* (2001). Montréal: Fides. 111–32.

Dolan, Jill. *The Feminist Spectator as Critic* (1988). Ann Arbor: University of Michigan Press.

———. *Utopian Performance. Finding Hope at the Theatre* (2005). Ann Arbour: University of Michigan Press.

Duchesne, Michel. *Le théâtre en jeu* (1997). UQAM VHS 13572—Ginette Noiseux, Pol Pelletier.

Dumas, Ève. "Pol redevient Nicole," *La Presse* (November 6, 2004). Cahier Arts et Spectacles: 19.

Du Sablon, Claire. *Chronologie historique des femmes du Québec.* http://pages.infinit.net/histoire/femindex.html (consulted July 14, 2009).

Féral, Josette. "Arrêter le mental. Entretien avec Pol Pelletier." *Cahiers de théâtre Jeu* 65 (1992). 35–45.

———. *Mise en scène et jeu de l'acteur. Entretiens Tome III. Voix de femmes* (2007). Montréal: Québec Amérique.

———. "La place des femmes dans les théories actuelles du jeu théâtral: l'exemple de Pol Pelletier." Betty Bednarski and Irene Oore, eds. *Nouveaux regards sur le théâtre québécois* (1997). Montréal and Halifax: XYZ Éditeur & Dalhousie French Studies. 105–16.

———. "Pol Pelletier: le théâtre est le lieu de rencontre du visible et de l'invisible." *Mise en scène et jeu de l'acteur. Entretiens. Tome II: Le corps en scène* (1998). Montréal/Carnières, Belgium: Éditions Jeu/Éditions Lansman. 229–52.

———. "La Théâtralité. Recherche sur la spécificité du langage théâtral." *Poétique* 75 (September 1998). 347–61.

———. "Theatricality." *SubStance. A Review of Theory and Literary Criticism* 31 (2002). 2–3.

Forsyth, Louise H. "L'acte théâtral au féminin: la transgression de la représentation théâtrale par la répétition et le spectacle." Raija Koski, Kathleen Kells, Louise H. Forsyth, eds. *Les discours féminins dans la littérature postmoderne au Québec* (1993). San Francisco: Edwin Mellen Press. 185–202.

———, ed. *Anthology of Québec Women's Plays in English Translation. Volume I (1966–1986)* (2006). Toronto: Playwrights Canada Press.

———, ed. *Anthology of Québec Women's Plays in English Translation. Volume II (1987–2003)* (2008). Toronto: Playwrights Canada Press.

———. "Feminist Theatre." *The Oxford Companion to Canadian Theatre* (1989). Eugene Benson and L.W. Conolly, eds. Toronto: Oxford University Press. 203–06.

———. "Offrir en anglais un corpus occulté." *Jeu Revue de théâtre* 133 (2009). 89–96. No. spécial *Voies/voix de la traduction théâtrale*.

———. "Passionate Performances: Pol Pelletier and Experimental Feminist Theatre beyond Barriers of Language (1975–1985)." Rosalind Kerr, ed. *Queer Theatre in Canada* (2007). Toronto: Playwrights Canada Press. 197–219.

———. "Self-Portrait of the Artist as Radical Feminist in Experimental Theatre: *Joie* by Pol Pelletier." *Theatre Research in Canada/Recherches théâtrales au Canada* 25.1–2 (2004). 184–201.

———. "A Ship of Fools in the Feminine, Six Characters in Search of Self." Sherrill Grace and Jerry Wasserman, eds. *Theatre and AutoBiography. Writing and Performing Lives in Theory and Practice* (2006). Vancouver: Talonbooks. 167–82.

Fréchette, Carole. "Deux ou trois choses à propos de mon parcours d'auteure." *Théâtre. Les Cahiers de la maîtrise de l'UQAM* 7 (Autumn 2003). 93–95.

Gaboriau, Linda. "The Cultures of Theatre." Sherry Simon, ed. *Cultures in Transit. Translating the Literature of Québec* (1995). Montréal: Véhicule Press. 83–90.

———. "Traduire le génie de l'auteur." *Cahiers de théâtre Jeu* 56 (1990). 43–48.

Gagnon, Lise. "Que sont les féministes devenues?" *Cahiers de théâtre Jeu* 117 (2005). 29–33.

Gilbert, Paula Ruth. *Violence and the Female Imagination. Quebec's Women Writers Re-frame Gender in North American Cultures* (2006). Montréal/Kingston: McGill-Queen's University Press.

Godard, Barbara. "Between Repetition and Rehearsal: Conditions of (Women's) Theatre in Canada in a Space of Reproduction." *Theatre Research in Canada/ Recherches théâtrales au Canada* 13.1/2 (1992). 18–33.

———. "Writing Between Cultures." *The Theatre Review. Études sur le texte et ses transformations* 10 (1997). 53–99.

Godin, Diane. "Femme et universalité. C'est toute l'humanité." *Cahiers de théâtre Jeu* 66 (1993). 27–28.

Koustas, Jane. "From Gélinas to Carrier: Critical Response to Translated Quebec Theatre in Toronto." *Studies in Canadian Literature* 17.2 (1992).

———. "From Homespun to Awesome: Translated Theatre in Toronto." Joseph Donohue, Jr. and Jonathan M. Weiss, eds. *Essays on Modern Quebec Theatre* (1995). East Lansing: Michigan State University Press. 81–109.

———. "Traduire ou ne pas traduire le théâtre? L'approche sémiotique." *Traduction, Terminologie, Rédaction* 1.1 (1988). 127–38.

Ladouceur, Louise. "A Version of Quebec: le théâtre québécois au Canada anglais." *L'Annuaire théâtral* 27 (Spring 2000). 109–19.

———. *Making the Scene: la traduction du théâtre d'une langue officielle à l'autre au Canada* (2005). Québec: Nota Bene.

Lamar, Celita. "Defining Marginal Spaces: Three plays by Anne-Marie Alonso [sic], Abla Farhoud and Pol Pelletier." Michael Bishop, ed. *Thirty Voices in the Feminine* (1996). Amsterdam/Atlanta: Éditions Rodopi B.V. 190–98.

———. "Resetting the Margins: Abla Farhoud's Dramatization of the Female Immigrant Experience in Quebec." Roseanna Lewis Dufault, ed. *Women by Women. The Treatment of Female Characters by Women Writers of Fiction in Quebec since 1980*. Madison Teaneck/London: Fairleigh Dickinson University Press/Associated University Presses. 136–46.

Lansman, Émile. "Éditer des dramaturges de la francophonie: le «cas» du Québec." *L'Annuaire théâtral. Revue québécoise d'études théâtrales* 27 (2000). 82–89.

Lapierre, Karine. "Deux reines, une baronne et une truie." *Théâtre. Les Cahiers de la maîtrise de l'UQAM* 6 (Autumn 2000). 11–18.

Laprade, Louise. "Autour du Théâtre Expérimental des Femmes." *La Nouvelle Barre du Jour* 196 (March 1987). 81–86. No. spécial: *Femmes scandales 1965–1985*.

Lavoie, Pierre. "L'espoir est une poire." *Cahiers de théâtre Jeu* 65 (1992). 24–29.

Leroux, Patrick. "A Nation of Distinct Selves: from Collective Identity to the Individual in Quebec Drama." *Canadian Theatre Review* 125 (Winter 2006). 62–68.

———. "Le Québec en autoreprésentation: le passage d'une dramaturgie de l'identitaire à celle de l'individu" (2009). Thèse de doctorat, Université Sorbonne Nouvelle—Paris 3 (unpublished).

Mac Dougall, Jill. *Performing Identities on the Stages of Québec* (1993). New York: New York University.

Moss, Jane. "The Body as Spectacle: Women's Theater in Québec." *Women and Performance: A Journal of Feminist Theory* 3.1 (1986). 5–16.

———. "Carole Fréchette." *The Canadian Encyclopedia* (2010). www.thecanadianencyclopedia.com (consulted January 16, 2010).

———. "Carole Fréchette et le théâtre au féminin." *French Review* 78.6 (2005).

———. "Creation Reenacted: the Woman Artist as Dramatic Figure." *The American Review of Canadian Studies* XV (1985). 263–72.

———. "Dramatizing the Discourse of Female Desire." Roseanna Lewis Dufault, ed. *Women by Women. The Treatment of Female Characters by Women Writers of Fiction in Quebec since 1980* (1997). Madison Teaneck/London: Fairleigh Dickinson University Press/Associated University Presses. 17–28.

———. "Dramatizing Sexual Difference: Gay and Lesbian Theater in Quebec." *American Review of Canadian Studies* 22.4 (Winter 1992). 489–98.

———. "Family Histories: Marie Laberge and Women's Theater in Quebec." Karen Gould, Mary Jean Green, Micheline Rice-Maximin, Keith Walker, Jack Yeager, eds. *Postcolonial Subjects: Francophone Women Writers* (1996). Minneapolis: University of Minnesota Press. 79–97.

———. "Fillial (Im)pieties: Mothers and Daughters in Quebec Women's Theater." *American Review of Canadian Studies* 19.2 (1989). 177–85.

———. "Francophone Drama." Eva-Marie Kröller and Coral Ann Howells, eds. *Cambridge History of Canadian Literature* (2009). New York: Cambridge University Press. 605–28.

———. "Hysterical Pregnancies and Post-Partum Blues: Staging the Maternal Body in Recent Quebec Plays." Joseph I. Donohue, Jr. and Jonathan M. Weiss, eds. *Essays on Modern Quebec Theater* (1995). East Lansing: Michigan State University Press. 47–59.

———. "In Search of Lost Intimacy: Mothers and Daughters in Women's Theatre." *Modern Language Studies* (1989). 45–52.

———. "Living with Liberation: Quebec Drama in the Feminist Age." *Atlantis* 14.1 (1988). 32–37.

———. "Staging the Act of Writing: Postmodern Theater in Quebec." *The French Review* 71.6 (May 1998). 940–48.

———. "Women, History and Theater in Québec." Paula Ruth Gilbert, ed. *Women Writing in Québec* (2000). Plattsburgh, NY: Plattsburgh State University Press. 97–109.

———. "Women's Theater in Quebec: Choruses, Monologues and Dialogues." *Feminist Voices*. 276.

Nichols, Glen, ed. "Translation/Traduction." *Theatre Research in Canada/Recherches théâtrales au Canada* 24 (2003). 1–2.

Noiseux, Ginette. "De quoi j'me mêle?" *Cahier de théâtre Jeu* 32 (1984). 13–24.

———. "Du Théâtre Expérimental des Femmes à l'Espace GO: une autre manière de dire." *Théâtre. Les Cahiers de la maîtrise de l'UQAM* 7 (Autumn 2002). 44–56.

Nutting, Stéphanie. *Le tragique dans le théâtre québécois et canadien-français, 1950–1989* (2000). Lewiston: Edwin Mellen Press.

———. "Mater/Modernité dans l'écriture dramatique de Carole Fréchette." Hélène Beauchamp and David Gilbert, eds. *Théâtres québécois et canadiens-français au XXe siècle* (2003). Québec: Presses de l'Université du Québec. 237–48.

O'Leary, Véronique. "Le Théâtre des Cuisines et les *Décrocheurs de rêves*." *Cahiers de théâtre Jeu* 113 (2004). 97–103.

Parenteau-Lebeuf, Dominick. "Histoire d'une jeune femme piquée d'héroïnes et de son double qui écrit pour elle." *Cahiers de théâtre Jeu* 66 (1993). 19–22.

Regattin, Fabio. "Théâtre et traduction: un aperçu du débat théorique." *L'Annuaire théâtral. Revue québécoise d'études théâtrales* 36 (2004). 156–71.

Robert, Lucie. "Pour une histoire de la dramaturgie québécoise." *L'Annuaire théâtral. Revue québécoise d'études théâtrales* 5–6 (1988–9). 163–69.

———. "The New Quebec Theater." Robert Lecker, ed. *Canadian Canons. Essays in Literary Value* (1991). Toronto: University of Toronto Press. 112–23.

———. "Changing the Subject: A Reading of Contemporary Feminist Drama." Rita Much, ed. *Women on the Canadian Stage: The Legacy of Hrotsvit* (1992). Winnipeg: Blizzard Publishing. 43–55.

———. "Une carrière impossible: la dramaturgie au féminin." Lucie Joubert, ed. *Trajectoires au féminin dans la littérature québécoise (1960–1990)* (2000). Québec: Éditions Nota Bene. 141–55.

———. "Le grand récit féminin ou de quelques usages de la narrativité dans les textes dramatiques de femmes." Chantal Hébert and Irène Perelli-Contos, eds. *Le théâtre et ses nouvelles dynamiques narratives* (2004). Saint Nicolas, QC: Presses de l'Université Laval. 61–85.

Ronfard, Jean-Pierre. "Vous dites expérimental?" *Cahiers de théâtre Jeu* 52 (1989). 45–50.

Ryngaert, Jean-Pierre. *Lire le théâtre contemporain* (1993). Paris: Dunod.

Saint-Martin, Lori. "La sorcière dans l'écriture des femmes." *Québec Studies* 12 (Spring 1991). 67–82.

———. "Introduction," Collective. *La Nef des sorcières* (1992). Montréal: L'Hexagone. 27–39.

———. "Trois romans métaféministes." *Contrevoix: Essais de critique au feminin* (1997). Montréal: Nuit Blanche. 235–68.

———. *Le Nom de la mère. Mères, filles et écriture dans la littérature québécoise au feminin* (1999). Québec: Éditions Nota Bene.

Simon, Sherry. *Le trafic des langues. Traduction et culture dans la littééerature québécoise* (1994). Montréal: Éditions du Boréal.

———. *Gender in Translation. Cultural Identity and the Politics of Transmission* (1996). London and New York: Routledge.

Vaïs, Michel. "Le théâtre expérimental: de l'hermétique à l'accessible." *Cahiers de théâtre Jeu* 36 (1985). 44–52.

———. "Du Théâtre expérimental des femmes à l'Espace GO. Entretien avec Ginette Noiseux" *Cahiers de théâtre Jeu* 57 (1990). 51–62.

———, ed. *Dictionnaire des artistes du théâtre québécois* (2008). Montréal: Éditions Québec Amérique.

Whitfield, Agnes, ed. *Le métier du double. Portraits de traductrices et traducteurs littéraires* (2005). Montréal: Fides.

———. *Writing Between the Lines. Portraits of Canadian Anglophone Translators* (2006). Waterloo: Wilfrid Laurier University Press.

Wickham, Philip. "Pouvoir lire le théâtre. Dramaturges Éditeurs." *Cahiers de théâtre Jeu* 85 (1997). 171–76.

About the Translators

Crystal Beliveau lives in Montréal where she works as a copywriter. She has translated four plays to date: *Le long de la Principale* (*Down the Main Drag*) by Steve Laplante, *Titanica* by Sébastien Harrisson, *Portrait chinois d'une imposteure* (*Chinese Portrait of an Imposter*) by Dominick Parenteau-Lebeuf and *Jouliks* by Marie-Christine Lê-Huu. She also writes in her spare time, and her creative non-fiction has appeared in *Prairie Fire* and *Liberté*.

Morwyn Brebner's plays include the Chalmers and Dora Award nominated *Music for Contortionist*, *Liquor Guns Karate*, the musical *Little Mercy's First Murder* (winner of seven Dora Mavor Moore Awards, including outstanding new musical), *The Optimists*, which was nominated for the 2006 Governor General's Literary Award, and *The Pessimist*. Her translations include Evelyne de la Chenelière's *Strawberries in January* and *Bashir Lazhar*. She was a finalist for the 2008 Elinore and Lou Siminovitch Prize. She is a graduate of the National Theatre School and a playwright-in-residence at the Tarragon Theatre in Toronto.

Leanna Brodie is an actor, writer, and translator. Her translations include Sébastien Harrisson's *From Alaska*, Philippe Soldevila's *Tales of the Moon*, Larry Tremblay's *Panda Panda*, and Hélène Ducharme's *Baobab*. Her plays (published by Talonbooks) include *For Home and Country*, *The Vic*, and *Schoolhouse*, as well as the CBC radio dramas *Invisible City* and *Seeds of Our Destruction*. Her libretti (for David Ogborn and Craig Galbraith) have been heard in Tapestry New Opera Works's Opera to Go 2008, in Ogborn's acclaimed site-specific piece, *Opera on the Rocks*, and in his song cycle *Emergence*. *The Angle of Reflection*, with New Zealand composer Anthony Young, was recently produced by the Auckland Philharmonia Orchestra. *The Book of Esther*, a love story about urban queers and rural evangelicals, premiered at the Blyth Festival in 2010. *Schoolhouse* has been seen by more than 20,000 Canadians and continues to be produced all over the country.

Nadine Desrochers holds a Ph.D. in French literature from the University of Ottawa, where she studied the role of narration in contemporary French and Québécois theatre. Her acting career led her to the stages of the National Arts Centre, the Great Canadian Theatre Company, Théâtre du Trillium, as well as to different television roles and appearances. She has lectured at the University of Ottawa and at the Université du Québec à Montréal, and has been a journalist for Radio-Canada. From 2001 to 2006, she was a dramaturge at CEAD (Centre des auteurs dramatiques), where she was also responsible for international projects, overseeing translations in French, English, and Spanish for such institutions as the Royal National Theatre (London), the Abbey Theatre (Dublin), Traverse Theatre (Edinburgh), Théâtre de la Manufacture/ La Licorne (Montréal), Playwrights' Workshop Montréal, and the Centro Cultural Helénico (Mexico). She also conducted international translation colonies and seminars. Since leaving CEAD, she has continued to work with playwrights, translators, and directors on a freelance basis. *Rock, Paper, Jackknife…* is her first translation. She is currently working on the English version of *Le Déluge après* by Sarah Berthiaume for Montréal's Talisman Theatre.

Julia Duchesne is a student in the Foundation Year program at the University of King's College in Halifax. *The Sound of Cracking Bones* was her first experience in translating for the theatre. She was especially drawn to this play because of her interest in literature and social justice. She is grateful to her co-translator, John Van Burek, for asking her to join him in this project and for guiding her through it.

Louise H. Forsyth is Full Professor Emerita and Adjunct Professor at the University of Saskatchewan, where she combined teaching, graduate student supervision, and research among the Departments of Women's and Gender Studies, Languages and Linguistics, and Drama, and also served as Dean of Graduate Studies and Research. She worked for many years at the University of Western Ontario, where she was Chair of the Department of French. She has published translations of three early Québec plays in *Canada's Lost Plays*, Vol. IV, Marie Savard's *Bien à moi*, Françoise Loranger's *Double Jeu*, and poems by Québec writer Nicole Brossard. Her translation of Françoise Loranger's *Encore cinq minutes* is currently in print, and she is currently co-editing a special issue of *Québec Studies* on literary translation. She translated into French Margaret Hollingsworth's *War Babies* (unpublished, student production at the University of Western Ontario, 1990).

Maureen Labonté is a dramaturge, translator, and teacher. She has also coordinated a number of play development programs in theatres and play development centres across the country, including Montréal's Centre des auteurs dramatiques (CEAD).

She is Co-Director of the Banff Playwrights' Colony at the Banff Centre for the Arts. She has worked at the colony as resident dramaturge and Program Head since 2003. She is the jury chair for the prestigious Siminovitch Prize in Theatre. She was Literary Manager in charge of play development at the Shaw Festival for three seasons and, previous to that, she worked at the National Theatre School of Canada, first developing and running a pilot directing program and then coordinating the Playwrighting Program and Playwrights' Residency. She still teaches at NTSC.

Labonté has translated more than thirty-five Québec plays into English. Recent translations include: *The Bookshop* by Marie-Josée Bastien, *Everybody's Welles* by Patrice Dubois and Martin Labrecque, *August: An Afternoon in the Country* by Jean Marc Dalpé, and *Holy Cow!* by Montreal's Théâtre de l'Oeil. This past fall, she completed *And Slowly Beauty* by Michel Nadeau at the Playwrights' Workshop Montréal Translation Residency held in Tadoussac, Québec.

She lives in Montréal.

John Murrell is one of the most frequently produced Canadian playwrights, whose works include *Memoir, Waiting For The Parade, Farther West, Democracy*, and *The Faraway Nearby*. He is also an acclaimed translator of Sophocles, Ibsen, Chekhov, and five other plays by Carole Fréchette. Murrell is an Officer of the Order of Canada, a member of the Alberta Order of Excellence, and a recipient of the Walter Carsen Prize for excellence in the performing arts and of the Governor General of Canada's Performing Arts Award for Lifetime Artistic Achievement.

Bobby Theodore is a Montréaler who now lives in exile in Toronto. First obtaining a B.A. in Creative Writing from Concordia University, he then went on to graduate from the National Theatre School's playwriting section and began translating some of Québec's most talented playwrights. His first translation, François Archambault's *15 Seconds* was produced across Canada and was later nominated for a Governor General's Literary Award. Other translations include *Martian Summer* by Nathalie Boisvert, *The Leisure Society* by François Archambault, *Crime Against Humanity* and *The Taster* by Geneviève Billette, *To Men of Good Will* by Jean-François Caron, and *The Sheep and the Whale* by Ahmed Ghazali. Bobby also writes for TV and never turns down an invitation to dinner.

John Van Burek has had a distinguished career in the theatre, nationally and internationally, in both English and French, as a director, teacher, and translator. He has mounted over one hundred productions, ranging from the European classics to opera to new Canadian plays, and his work has taken him to many countries in the world. He is the artistic director of Pleiades Theatre, a company he founded in Toronto in 1997 with a mandate to produce plays that originate in languages and cultures other than English, and to do them in fresh, new Canadian translations. Prior to that, in 1971, he founded Toronto's first French-language theatre, Le Théâtre français de Toronto, which he ran for almost twenty years. Mr. Van Burek has done a great deal of teaching in both English and French, at numerous institutions, including Canada's National Theatre School/École Nationale de Théâtre, Carnegie-Mellon University, the University of Victoria, Ryerson Theatre School, the Nottingham School of the Performing Arts, and York University. He has directed in the UK and in France and in 1996 he led an international theatre exchange project in Bangladesh. In 1999, he completed a series of six television documentaries, broadcast on Bravo, about the development of new plays in Canada.

One of Canada's preeminent translators, most notably the major plays of Michel Tremblay, Mr. Van Burek played a pivotal role in introducing theatre from Québec to English-speaking audiences. Since 1972, he has translated more than forty works for the stage, including works by Marcel Sabourin, Suzanne Lebeau, Marivaux, Molière, and Goldoni.

Mr. Van Burek has been the recipient of many awards and honours, notably the Toronto Drama Bench's award for Distinguished Contribution to Canadian Theatre, a Canada Council "A" Grant, the Prix Alliance for his contribution to French-language arts and culture, and a Queen's Jubilee Medal. He was decorated by l'Ordre de la Pléiade of the Assemblée parlementaire de la Francophonie and most recently he was awarded a Silver Ticket by the Toronto Alliance for the Performing Arts. He has just completed his second term as a member of the Canadian Artists and Producers Professional Relations Tribunal in Ottawa.

About the Editor

Louise H. Forsyth has always loved performance and theatre. As an amateur lover of the stage, she has acted, sung, danced, written, directed, produced, translated, stage managed, served as props manager, and hung out as much as she could as a spectator. Woven into an amateur obsession with theatre has been her professional life, where she wrote two theses on the classic French writer of theatrical comedy, Molière, taught courses and supervised theses in theatre, drama, and dramatic literature, wrote scholarly studies about French and Québec playwrights, and theorized about acting and dramatic writing. Her areas of academic specialization are feminist performance and dramaturgy in Québec. Along with her passion for what the women of Québec have written for theatre, she has been engaged for quite some time with developing theories of dramaturgy and acting *au féminin*, along with revealing the sources of tenacious sexism in the practices and conventions for doing theatre, for studying and evaluating it, and for recounting its history. In short, she has been wondering for quite some time why women's roles have tended to remain stereotypical in works for stage, television, and film, why theatre done by women—when its perspective is explicitly derived from a woman's point of view—is still easily dismissed with a summary shrug as deserving only condescending scorn, why women's theatrical experimentation is so rarely discussed by scholars as serious theoretical work or used by them in their own theoretical reflections, and why the silence of critics on women and their richly creative activities has not yet been overcome when it comes to their accounts of theatre history.